THE WESTERN CRISIS OVER SOUTHERN AFRICA

South Africa
Rhodesia
Namibia

Colin Legum

AFRICANA PUBLISHING COMPANY
New York   London

A division of Holmes & Meier Publishers, Inc.

First published in the United States of America 1979 by
AFRICANA PUBLISHING COMPANY
A division of Holmes & Meier Publishers, Inc.
30 Irving Place
New York, N.Y. 10003

Great Britain
Holmes & Meier Publishers, Ltd.
Hillview House
1, Hallswelle Parade, Finchley Road
London NW11 ODL

Library of Congress Cataloging in Publication Data

Legum, Colin.
  The western crisis over southern Africa.
  Includes bibliographical references.
  1. Africa, Southern—Politics and government—
1975– 2. Africa, Southern—Foreign relations.
I. Title.
DT746.L44 1979   327'.0968   79-9723

ISBN 0-8419-0492-8
ISBN 0-8419-0496-0 pbk.

Manufactured in the United States of America

Contents

Introduction

THE COMING DECADE OF DECISION

Of course one expects to see enormous changes in any country after an absence of eighteen years—especially in one as rich as South Africa, where economic growth has been greater than in almost any other country since World War II. Sadly, the changes that have occurred have increased the risk of a violent racial conflagration in the Republic, and have probably hastened its approach.

When I left South Africa in 1949 to work abroad, the Afrikaner nationalist regime had been in power for only one year. It was still full of optimism that its doctrine of apartheid would provide the answer to the country's racial problems by promoting 'Separate Development' between the 3.5 million (now over 4 million) dominating Whites and the 16 million (now nearer 22 million) Africans, Coloureds and Indians. The Afrikaners had a determined and committed leadership united behind a cause: the achievement of Afrikaner supremacy over English-speaking South Africans and, at the same time, the entrenchment of White rule over five-sixths of the country's land area. They controlled vast economic resources in a country with a rapidly developing industrial and agricultural base, one that was already one of the strongest among the smaller powers. They had a monopoly of military power and powerful allies in the Western world. The Black majority, on the other hand, had no political clout worth speaking of; the Congress movements, though commanding widespread mass support, were easily controlled. They were led mainly from the middle-class elite, which believed in reform and in Gandhi's ideas of non-violent struggle. There was—or appeared to be—nothing that could resist the total power of Afrikanerdom to remake South Africa closer to its dream of a 'commonwealth of states' in which the different races would live alongside each other in a spirit of good neighbourliness—but each in its separate homeland.

The central issue of the 1948 general election had been apartheid: the Afrikaner nationalists had confidently promised to reverse the flood of Blacks into the 'White areas'; to make the cities, towns and farming districts progressively 'Whiter'; and to arrest the process of industry and commerce becoming dependent for its expansion on semi-skilled and skilled Black workers. White South Africa was to be reinforced by a massive immigration programme to attract European (mainly Protestant) immigrants to the country.

These ideals and hopes were still in the ascendancy when I was last in South Africa, at the time of the Sharpeville shootings in 1960. How different it all looked when I returned eighteen years later. The circumstances of my return throw some light on the paradoxical situation that has been created by two decades of apartheid rule. In 1964 my wife and I (both native South Africans now holding British passports) were prohibited from returning home without special visas. The immediate reason for this ban was a book we had written—*South Africa: Crisis for the West*. In it we had argued that the political deadlock in the Republic would be broken only by violence unless the world community intervened. This intervention would consist of a programme of *effective* sanctions aimed at securing the very limited objective of influencing the South African regime to agree to hold a national convention with representative leaders of all the communities to work out a constitution acceptable to all races. Our purpose in writing that book was to show how unnecessary violence could be avoided in the struggle to achieve meaningful political, social and economic change.

When the first of the so-called 'Bantu Homelands', the Transkei, obtained its 'independence' in 1976, we were given the right to *transit* South Africa to visit it. Since the Transkei consists largely of one contiguous territory, the transit could be effected without much difficulty. But the situation was quite different when BophuthaTswana became 'an independent Republic' two years later. This new state is made up of seven different territorial units scattered over three of the four provinces of South Africa. It was impossible to visit them without criss-crossing South Africa itself. How could we, as prohibited people, obtain access to 'independent' BophuthaTswana? The Pretoria regime solved the dilemma by granting us a multiple transit visa entitling us to enter and leave South Africa five times through passport control points. This allowed us to travel widely across the country—which was how we were again able to set foot in the Republic.

THE DILEMMAS OF APARTHEID:
1. THE HOMELANDS

Although there are three recognized passport control points between the Transkei and South Africa, there are a dozen other ways of entering and leaving the Transkei that are not controlled by the police. But there are no such control posts between BophuthaTswana and South Africa. We found it very difficult to know when we were actually leaving one 'country' and entering another. These 'internal borders' are, in fact, only lines drawn on a map. Since one area of BophuthaTswana touches Botswana, and one of the Transkei's borders runs alongside Lesotho's, the task of policing South Africa's borders has become more difficult—and will become even more so if and when other 'independent Black Republics' are created, since several of them abut on Rhodesia, Mozambique and Swaziland. At a time when hundreds of young Black South Africans are leaving the country for military training abroad, and when the first trained guerrillas are already being infiltrated back into South Africa, border-security problems are beginning to assume a new importance.

South Africa's serious concern about security is easy to understand. What is less understandable is the regime's determination to go on setting up more of these 'Black Republics' in spite of the patent failure of Separate Development to achieve its major objective: the creation of friendly African states within and along its borders. After less than two years of 'independence', the Transkei has already severed formal diplomatic links with South Africa. This decision was not, as is often believed, a collusive act between the Pretoria regime and Transkei leader Dr Kaiser Matanzima. It was an act of anger engendered by South Africa's policies over land in a leader like Matanzima, who had been Pretoria's favourite, when he became the first to break ranks with the other Homeland leaders to take the independence offered to the Transkei.

The leader who followed his example, BophuthaTswana President Lucas Mangope, told us in his capital, Mmabatho: 'How can one make the Afrikaners understand that people like ourselves are the last of the moderates who still believe in peaceful co-operation, and who stand between them and the next generation of our young people who believe in violence? If we are to lose control in this country a future government could provide an open corridor for guerrillas to cross the borders into South Africa'.

These two 'Black Republics' face enormous problems. Financial limitations simply make it impossible for them to satisfy the expectations aroused by their claims in favour of independence on the terms offered to them. Strong internal opposition parties point up these inadequacies. More unsettling are the elements within this opposition, which deny the validity of the territories' independence. Serious tensions also exist between the defenders of 'independence' and the million or more Xhosas and Tswanas who qualify to live in the 'White' urban areas, where, against their very strong objections, they are no longer regarded as South

African citizens; they refuse to accept 'citizenship' of an undeveloped and often chronically poor and overcrowded segment of the country, in the process of which they are required to renounce their claims to the wealth of South Africa as a whole.

Another predictable result of the creation of these new ethnic states has been to activate tribal feelings where they did not exist before. These inter-tribal tensions are to be found within the borders of the new Black Republics as well as in the rest of the country. Thus, the Sotho-speaking people of Transkei and BophuthaTswana have already come into conflict with Matanzima's and Mangope's regimes because, if they are compelled to choose, they would prefer to belong to the Sotho ethnic state of QwaQwa and, especially, because Ndebeles and Venda resent what they feel to be the Tswana-oriented policies of Mangope's government. Dr Matanzima himself spoke to us of his deep resentment that the valuable Kokstad-Matatiele area, which divides Transkei in two, was transferred to the Natal province, which he regards as 'Zulu territory'. To our surprise, it was the decision to transfer that territory to Natal—rather than the fact of its not having been incorporated immediately into the Transkei—that triggered his anger against the Pretoria regime and led to his breaking off diplomatic relations.

Since none of the projected 'independent Republics' is free of ethnic minorities, inter-tribal suspicions and conflicts can only increase. Those Afrikaners who see some advantage in inter-tribal hostilities overlook the very real danger of exacerbating South Africa's already intensely difficult racial problems by adding this extremely dangerous element in which they must become embroiled as time passes.

Meanwhile, the majority of Homeland leaders—headed by KwaZulu Chief Gatsha Buthelezi, Gazankulu's Professor Hudson Ntsanwisi, Lebowa's Dr Cedric Pathudi and QwaQwa Chief Kenneth Mopeli—still hold out against 'independence' for their Homelands. Only the small Vendaland—run by Chief Patrick Mphephu, a thoroughly unrepresentative leader—is in line for future 'independence'. This would assuredly produce a highly unstable and unpleasant little pocket-state. The Ciskei is also governed by a leader who clearly enjoys little popular support; even before 'independence', Lennox Sebe had turned the Ciskei into something resembling Papa Doc's Haiti within the South African political system.

One of the problems facing the Pretoria regime is how to complete the 'Grand Design' of Separate Development voluntarily by overcoming the resistance of those who refuse to opt for a kind of independence in which they don't believe. Is it really possible to pass laws in a White Parliament to compel Blacks to accept 'independence' on terms they regard as wholly unacceptable? If not, what is to be the future of those Homelands—including that of the Zulus, who are numerically greater than the whole of the White population?

The policy of creating new 'independent states' within the South African political system has not—as was so confidently expected—alleviated the country's racial problems; it has only exacerbated them. Yet it is hard to see the Transkei and BophuthaTswana surrendering their 'independence', or the Pretoria regime deciding to abandon its policy of creating more 'independent states', which, after all, is the cornerstone of apartheid.

THE DILEMMAS OF APARTHEID:
2. THE IRRESISTIBLE SEEPAGE

The most glaring change since the last time I was in South Africa was the extent to which Blacks have 'taken over' the 'White' towns and cities. Having been politically involved in the 1948 elections that brought the Afrikaner nationalists to power, I have a very clear memory of the impact made on the White electorate by Afrikaner nationalist promises to 'stop White South Africa being flooded by Blacks'. This issue had become sharper during the war years, when the needs of a booming wartime industry attracted large numbers of Africans from the rural areas and began a process, then still quite limited, of opening semi-skilled jobs to Blacks. Dr Malan's party promised to 'turn back this Black flood'. It undertook to make the towns and cities 'Whiter', and to put and end to the integration of Black workers into the White economy: jobs traditionally reserved exclusively for Whites would remain so; and Blacks would not be given the right to organize themselves into trade unions.

However, the towns and cities are now 'Blacker' than they were twenty years ago; the urban Black population has practically doubled since then. Black workers in considerable numbers can be seen everywhere doing what, in earlier times, were taken for granted as being 'White jobs'. In the heart of the 'White' towns, Africans have access to public places where no Black person would have dared to set foot before, except as a menial. Driving through the urban, working-class suburbs, one could see non-Whites—especially Indians and Coloureds —living, albeit illegally, alongside Whites in housing areas where, in Smuts' time, this would have been unthinkable. The local papers were reporting the 'scandal' of Coloured families renting flats even in Hillbrow, the most popular apartment area near the center of Johannesburg.

What had happened to the promise of racial separation in the two decades of Afrikaner rule? The evidence pointed overwhelmingly to a substantial seepage of non-Whites into White society, notwithstanding scores of laws and rigorous police enforcement to prevent this from happening. Far from having been reinforced, the traditional walls of segregation are plainly crumbling. This glaring difference between the intentions of apartheid to separate the races and the reality of an increasingly inter-racial urban society is one of the many contradictions that characterize modern South Africa. Not even a determined Afrikanerdom has been able to prevent it. The natural laws of development have mitigated parlimentary law, and not even the ceaseless police harassment of offenders can entirely halt the process of integrating the different races, at least within the urban society.

In one respect, at least, the rulers are prepared to come to terms with reality: the 'permanence' of Soweto, the great Black city outside Johannesburg, has now been accepted even though the right of individual inhabitants to live there permanently is still being denied. What this means is that any thought of dispersing the many great Black urban centres in 'White South Africa' has been abandoned—in total contradiction to the original intentions of apartheid. Having failed, like Xerxes, to beat the waves into obedient submission, the administrators of apartheid have now turned their minds to producing some workable system that will enable urban Blacks to have some measure of control over their own communities, which exist within areas designated for permanent White control.

THE DILEMMAS OF APARTHEID:
3. THE FAILURE OF IMMIGRATION

Another change for which I was unprepared was the number of Portuguese and Greeks who have been allowed to settle in South Africa. When the Malan government embarked in 1948 on its ambitious scheme to attract European immigrants from war-weary Western Europe to buttress the numbers of the White minority and fill the skilled jobs required by the expanding economy, the aim was to attract principally European Protestants. The 'menace' of Catholicism was another of the dangers against which Calvinist Afrikanerdom was determined to protect itself. Although several hundred thousand immigrants were attracted to settle in South Africa, the numbers did not measure up to the hoped-for accretion of the White community. What is clear, though, is that a considerable number of the new immigrants are Catholic Portuguese and non-Calvinist Greeks—the former coming mainly from neighbouring Mozambique and Angola after the collapse of Portuguese colonialism. One sees in almost every dorp in the platteland shops called Lisbon, Portuguese or Madeira. In Hoopstad, in the Orange Free State, the Boere Saamwerk (Boer Cooperative) is now run by a non–Afrikaans-speaking Greek Cypriot whom I had met briefly when he was a journalist during the Eoka struggle. One became accustomed to hearing complaints about the racial attitudes of Portuguese and Greek shopkeepers, who appear to have learnt nothing from the policies that led to present-day Angola and Mozambique.

The influx of European immigrants over the last two decades has, to some extent, been offset by the exodus of native-born South Africans, especially among younger people and the professional classes. The brain-drain has severely hit the universities and key industries. The University of Witwatersrand has been unable to fill the eighty or so vacancies on its teaching staff for some time—only partly because of the relatively low pay for junior academic appointments.

A Swiss technician I met on the plane flying out of South Africa expressed what, according to other informants, was a fairly typical attitude among the immigrants. 'It's a really good life here; we love it. But will it last? We all keep our original passports, and keep our fingers crossed'. This category of 'new South Africans' is not likely to sweat it out with the Afrikaners once the 'good life' ceases to be as attractive as it is for them at present.

THE GOD THAT FAILED AFRIKANERDOM
When South Africans and visitors to the country insist that great changes have taken place in recent years, they are quite right. Things have been changing—in many ways for the better. There are even glimpses of reality creeping in to soften the harsher outlines of apartheid. Nevertheless, the terrible population removals still continue; and the process of 'migratizing' workers is still accepted as benign: 'The Black man likes it that way', declared the former minister in charge of African affairs, Dr Connie Mulder, before he was forced to resign. This view enjoys wide credence. The habit of no longer referring to 'Blacks' as 'natives'—let alone as 'kaffirs'—seems to have taken hold. But, sadly, almost without exception the Black man still automatically addresses any White as 'boss'— and that, in truth, still defines the prevailing relationship.

So, while it is clear that many things have begun to change, there is one area in which not the slightest change is even contemplated: the sharing of political power. Yet, in the end, this is the only change that can provide any hope for a peaceful future for South Africa—no matter how many concessions (changes) are made to meet African demands.

Far from improving the chances of creating a more harmonious multi-racial society, or of promoting political stability, a policy of concessions can only result in a further sharpening of South Africa's already acute internal contradictions—unless there are simultaneous changes in the basic political system. But while there is an increasing awareness among Afrikaner intellectuals about the need for a new system to allow for a sharing of political power, there is not yet the faintest sign that anything of the kind is being contemplated by the ruling political forces. It is the absence of this sign of change that gives most cause for pessimism.

While many White South Africans now agree that apartheid is the god that has failed Afrikanerdom, and that there is no way out of the country's dilemma apart from changing the political system, they are obsessionally opposed to any idea of 'one-man, one-vote'. Although they currently point to the abuse of this great democratic principle in many parts of Africa—in fact, long before the continent attained independence—any thought of universal franchise was dismissed as the greatest political threat imaginable to their way of life. But if the great majority of Whites (not just Afrikaners, and not just nationalists) are obsessional about the universal francise, so, too, are most Black leaders; they make it the touchstone of any acceptable alternative political system.

Thus, while the real debate in South Africa should be about achieving a political system that will incorporate both the principle of adult franchise and effective ways of safeguarding both individual and minority rights, that debate has hardly yet begun. Both sides are still skirmishing on the edges of the battle-lines drawn by those for and against 'one-man, one-vote'. Yet, only when both sides are ready to face up to the many requirements necessary to produce a democratic, fair and viable system for a society as mixed as South Africa's—and with such a peculiar history—will it become possible to break out of the narrowly confined limits of the present political debate.

In the meantime, South Africa will rely on its superior weapons—military, economic and political—to try and maintain the status quo. It will make concessions without fundamentally changing the political system. However, time has been running against White south Africa since 1960—the beginning of the decade of the African continent's independence and the start of a new kind of militancy among Black South Africans, symbolized by Sharpeville.

Now, at the end of the 1970s, South Africa's situation is vastly different from what it was two decades ago. The Republic already sees itself at war and is arming at a frightful cost. It now finds itself very largely isolated within the African continent, with flames of violence licking all around its northern borders. It has lost its faith in the Western community—a reaction to the growing abandonment by the major Western powers of their former alliances with White South Africa. It is no longer facing a substantially acquiescent Black population, especially not in the urban areas. Above all, doubts have begun to develop within the White laager itself about the wisdom and efficacy of the policies of Afrikanerdom. While their leaders talk as toughly and as resolutely as ever, there is clear evidence of growing divisions within Afrikaner ranks about whether to go further along the path of *verligtheid*, or to retreat back towards *verkramptheid*; this deep internal conflict is personified by two men: the new prime minister, P. W. Botha, and his challenger, Dr Andries Treurnicht.

John Vorster, who suddenly resigned in September 1978, stood in the tradition of the earlier Afrikaner prime ministers: D. F. Malan, J. G. Strijdom, and Hendrik F. Verwoerd. All of them could command the support of the great majority of Afrikaners despite the sniping they had to endure from the more extremist fringe of *verkramptes*. The new prime minister, Piet Botha, lacks the natural authority of his predecessors; from his first days in office, he had to face a substantial number of critics from within the ruling party. Botha seems unlikely to possess the strength necessary to make the big changes required once the failures of apartheid have been acknowledged. His premiership will be dogged, much more than Vorster's ever was, by the fear of splitting the Afrikaner *volk*. He will constantly have to look over his shoulder at the forces ranged behind the right-wing Treurnicht. There appears to be at least an even chance that Treurnicht could be the next prime minister. If this were to happen, Afrikanerdom would be committed to digging in behind its defences to fight it out.

However, irrespective of whether South Africa is ruled by a Botha or a Treurnicht, its present power structure can be maintained only if the country remains economically strong. Its military strength depends both on the state of the economy and on the success of its extensive internal-security system. Judged only by the usual economists' criteria, the Republic's economy is relatively strong; but these criteria take no account of political factors, which, in a country like South Africa (as in Iran), are likely to be critical.

A headline in the London *Financial Times* (25 January 1979) accurately portrayed the actuality: A GIANT ECONOMY WITH FEET OF CLAY. The economy's vulnerability was pointed up by two recent major developments: the sensational decline of South Africa's ability to borrow money on the international money market after the 1976 Soweto troubles; and the desperately serious oil crisis resulting from the overthrow of the Shah of Iran and the threat by his likely successors to stop supplying oil to South Africa. Since 95 per cent of all its oil imports originate from Iran, the upset to its economy if this threat is carried out is obvious. The immediate implications are that South Africa will suffer most of the *penalties* of economic sanctions—hitting at its most vulnerable point—without any move having been made by the world community to implement the long-standing *threat* of sanctions.

Even assuming that South Africa could find alternative sources of oil supplies to make up the deficit of 133 million barrels a year from Iran, it would have to rely on the open market, where, at best, it could hope to buy at a premium of $2 to $3 a barrel. This would add another $300 million a year to its oil import bill of c. $1.2 million. This is on top of an additional $200 million once the full impact is felt of the 15 per cent rise in fuel prices already decided by OPEC. Since oil now accounts for 14 per cent of South Africa's total import bill, these substantial additional costs are bound to seriously impair its balance of trade. (The trade balance had only just managed to crawl back into a small surplus in 1978.)

AFTER RHODESIA AND NAMIBIA

In addition to the steady fall in South Africa's economic performance since the early 1970s, there has been an even more serious decline in its security position, especially after 1976. The example of armed guerrillas successfully using violent methods in the neighbouring territories of Mozambique and Angola has clearly had a strong effect on Black South African thinking. The growing belief in the need for armed violence will undoubtedly be strengthened by developments in Rhodesia as the long struggle there against White minority rule moves to a final resolution, probably within the year. The earlier hopes of a peaceful settlement through the Anglo-American initiative (described in a later chapter) were largely dissipated by early 1979. Even if there were some belated development, it could only favour the stand taken by the Patriotic Front—and this would again be seen as a victory for the methods of armed struggle. At the time of writing, it would appear that the South African regime can hope to gain little from the rise of an independent Zimbabwe.

The issue of Namibia is also likely to be decided before the end of 1979. A successful settlement there would require full recognition of SWAPO—and this, too, would be an acknowledgement of the value of 'armed struggle'. On the other hand, if not settlement should prove possible in Namibia, South Africa would still be left with the problem of SWAPO's armed challenge, as well as having to face greater hostility from the world community and, in particular, from the Western powers.

Therefore, whatever the final outcome in Rhodesia and Namibia, the results cannot improve South Africa's internal situation. The most the Botha regime might hope for is that the South African army can be extricated from its difficult position along the Namibia/Angola border, and that it will not find itself committed to a larger role in Rhodesia. But if the last phase of a violent Rhodesian conflict should threaten to spill over the borders and so heighten a climate of violence in the subcontinent, this could bring the risk of greater international involvement, especially by the Russians and Cubans. If the Soviet bloc were to become the strategic ally of a triumphant Patriotic Front, the entire northern arc of South Africa's frontiers—from Angola through Zaire to Mozambique—would be largely tied to Russian military support. Such a development would crucially affect both White and Black attitudes in South Africa in the critical decade that lies ahead. During that period, it is now fairly safe to predict, the power struggle inside South Africa will be largely decided, if not yet finally completed.

COLIN LEGUM
London
February 1979

PART I:

The Southern African Crisis

The Southern African Crisis

That Southern Africa did not become another area of armed international intervention in 1977, or even in early 1978, was due entirely to a remarkable exercise in diplomacy between Africa and the Western community, which kept open the possibility of negotiated settlements in Rhodesia and Namibia. But while this active diplomacy was effective in preventing foreign intervention on the lines of Angola or the Horn of Africa, there is still no certainty that it will succeed in its major purpose of helping to establish majority rule in the three White-ruled territories. The initiator of this new diplomatic approach in 1976 was the US Secretary of State, Dr Henry Kissinger;[1] but his tentative, ambiguous and highly personal diplomacy was given more shape, clarity and consistency early in 1978 after the advent of the new Carter Administration and the arrival at the British Foreign Office of Dr David Owen. Their new joint initiatives also began to find favour among members of the European Community, changes in the West's attitude to the problems of Southern Africa having been induced by the success of Soviet and Cuban intervention in Angola.[2]

The significant element in this new Western approach was a belated response to the offer of an international accord held out by the Organization of African Unity (OAU) on the basis of the Lusaka Manifesto of 1969.[3] That seminal document opened with the warning that: 'When the purposes and the basis of States' international policies are misunderstood, there is introduced into the world a new and unnecessary disharmony. Disagreements, conflicts of interest or different assessments of human priorities already provoke an excess of tension in the world and disastrously divide mankind at a time when united action is necessary to control modern technology and put it to the service of man.' The Lusaka Manifesto was an invitation to the international community to co-operate in achieving peaceful change in order to avoid more violent conflicts and the introduction of big power rivalries into the area. The appeal was addressed especially to the Western powers because of their direct involvement with the *status quo* regimes; it urged them to come out positively in support of the following two basic African aims:

'Our objectives in Southern Africa stem from our commitment to [the] principle of human equality. We are not hostile to the Administrations of these States because they are manned and controlled by White people. We are hostile to them because they are systems of minority control which exist as a result of, and in the pursuance of, doctrines of human inequality. What we are working for is the right of self-determination for the people of those territories. We are working for a rule in those countries which is based on the will of all the people and an acceptance of the equality of every citizen.

'Our stand towards Southern Africa thus involves a rejection of racialism, not a reversal of the existing racial domination. We believe that all the peoples who have made their homes in the countries of Southern Africa are Africans, regardless of the colour of their skins; and we would oppose a racialist majority government which adopted a philosophy of deliberate and permanent discrimination between its citizens on grounds of racial origin. We are not talking racialism when we reject the colonialism and apartheid policies now operating in those areas; we are demanding an opportunity for all the people of these States, working together as equal individual citizens, to work out for themselves the institutions and the system of government under which they will, by general consent, live together and work together to build a harmonious society.'

The Lusaka signatories affirmed that the form of governments to be established in place of the White-ruled systems 'must be a matter exclusively for the peoples of the country concerned working together. No other nation will have a right to interfere in such affairs. All that the rest of the world has a right to demand is just what we are now asserting—that the arrangements within any State which wishes to be accepted into the community of nations must be based on an acceptance of the principles of human dignity and equality.' They also asserted their preference for peaceful change:

'We would prefer to negotiate rather than destroy, to talk rather than kill. We do not advocate violence; we advocate an end to the violence against human dignity which is now being perpetrated by the oppressors of Africa. If peaceful progress to emancipation were possible, or if changed circumstances were to make it possible in the future, we would urge our brothers in the resistance movements to use peaceful methods of struggle even at the cost of some compromise on the timing of change. But while peaceful progress is blocked by actions of those at present in power in the States of Southern Africa, we have no choice but to give to the peoples of those territories all the support of which we are capable in their struggle against their oppressors.'

Acceptance of these proposals by Dr Kissinger in his own Lusaka Declaration of 25 April 1976[4] opened the way for two major Western diplomatic exercises in 1977: the Anglo-American initiative in Rhodesia, and the mediation effort in Namibia by the five Western powers on the Security Council (US, UK, France, West Germany and Canada). There was also a more purposeful, though less actively pursued, diplomatic approach to South Africa's racial problems.

This new Western approach to the problems of the region contained five major elements. First, every stage of planning and implementing the two initiatives involved close consultation with the African States most directly concerned—the five Front-line States (Tanzania, Zambia, Mozambique, Botswana and Angola), as well as Nigeria. Second, in the case of Rhodesia and Namibia, the leading liberation movements (the Patriotic Front and Swapo, respectively) were brought directly into the negotiating process. Third, the stated objective was to achieve majority rule. Fourth, the agreed aim was to defuse the violence: while not condemning the armed struggle, the premise of the diplomatic approach was that armed violence was not necessarily the only road to majority rule. Fifth, explicit opposition to the introduction of big power politics into the region. (The justification for the Anglo-American role was that both countries were already involved in the area and could use their leverage positively. Meanwhile, no new foreign powers should be brought in as this would complicate the negotiating process and impede the achievement of majority rule.)

These five broad objectives were accepted by both the Anglo-Americans and the African leaders involved in this diplomatic exercise. Thus, for the first time, African and Westernolicies were in harmony in Southern Africa—at least so far as the immediate objectives were concerned; this made diplomatic co-operation possible, although suspicions, misunderstandings and even sharp disagreements were never entirely absent.

Anglo-American/African diplomatic co-operation did not please the Soviet bloc: how could it be otherwise? Yet the Russians and Cubans did not venture to criticize the African leaders openly; their criticisms, though sharp, were implicit and indirect. However, the Africans had no interest in upsetting the Russians and Cubans, which would not only offend their non-aligned aspirations, but also rob them of a vital element of support and leverage against the Western powers. Since the West had begun to change course precisely because of the 'Soviet threat' in the area, the Africans clearly did not wish to lose this source of pressure. Moreover, the Africans could not be sure that the Western powers would consistently and energetically pursue their new Southern African diplomacy or, even if they did, that they would invest sufficient of their resources to ensure final success. The Africans also felt it important to maintain a second string to their bow through the intensification of the armed struggle, both to keep up the pressures against Rhodesia and Namibia and, in the event of the failure of the diplomatic approach, to fight to victory. For this purpose they relied on arms and military training from the Communist world.

This dual strategy of the Africans made it inevitable that if the Western diplomatic effort failed, the Soviet factor would have to be invoked, as in Angola. Thus, while the Western powers held the diplomatic initiative for so long as negotiated settlement seemed possible, the Soviet bloc would be likely to replace them if this failed. The Chinese role in this diplomatic strategy was comparatively minor (see below).

African-Western co-operation was by no means easy. For one thing, many African leaders mistrusted French policy and felt unsure about the future of British policy—especially if there were a change of government. While generally encouraged by the new direction of the Carter Administration, they were uneasy about the possible influence in Washington of Carter's National Security adviser, Zbigniew Brzezinski. They also needed constant reassurance about West Germany's policy. Some of the African leaders (like President Neto of Angola) went along with the Anglo-American initiatives only because they were endorsed by dominant elements within the Front-line States; however, they opposed any major American role on the grounds that it introduced big-power involvement in the region. Somewhat contradictorily, this group favoured a larger Russian/Cuban role.

There were also disagreements among the Front-line Presidents (FLPs) over particularist interests—such as Zambia's favouring Joshua Nkomo's wing of the Patriotic Front.[5] However, President Nyerere's authority as the FLPs' chairman was decisive in maintaining the group's unity, though not without opposition, some of which came at particularly sensitive points in the Rhodesian negotiations. On the other hand, the flow of the Namibian negotiations was not impeded by any serious disagreement between the FLPs and the Western group.

The real difficulties, though, arose from the natural desire of the liberation movements to win the Western powers' unqualified support for their position.

The conflict between the two wings of the Patriotic Front also introduced the Sino-Soviet quarrel into their camp, foreshadowing the possibility of another Angola should the attempts at peaceful negotiations fail. The Russian/Cuban element also came to assume much greater significance in Swapo's strategy, since it relied on the Communists for the training and arming of its guerrillas, as well as a means of applying pressure on the Western powers (and through them on SA) for a settlement on its own terms. While Swapo's annual conference in 1977 went out of its way to praise the Scandinavian countries and Holland for their assistance, it paid special tribute to 'the socialist countries and other progressive forces'.[6]

The links between the African National Congress of SA (ANC) and the Soviet bloc had become so close by early 1977 as to take on the appearance of an open alliance. Although nationalist elements in the ANC-Communist Party front continued to try to assert the movement's non-aligned position, Marxist elements emphasized the 'historic role' which the USSR was playing in the 'liberation struggle in Southern Africa'.

To sum up, the pattern of international involvement in Southern Africa in

1977–78 had the following characteristics:

1. The diplomatic initiative was held by the Western powers in co-operation with the more significant of the African leaders.

2. While these African leaders were willing to support Western initiatives, they remained critical—and always suspicious—of the degree of Western commitment to the need to impose effective pressures before the Rhodesian and South African regimes would make the concessions required to avoid an all-out armed struggle. Meanwhile, they kept the Soviet and Chinese factors in play both to strengthen the liberation movements and as a constant reminder to the West of the presence of possible alternative allies.

3. Although the Soviets, Cubans and Chinese were restricted to the wings, with the West holding the centre of the diplomatic stage, they were significantly increasing their participation in the movements most likely to dominate if Western diplomacy failed.

THE THREE ARENAS OF CONFLICT

1. SOUTH AFRICA

The problems of Rhodesia and Namibia are of course only peripheral to the real crisis area in the region—the Republic of South Africa. Solving the problems of the peripheral areas would actually only clear the decks for what will undoubtedly become the major arena of conflict in the coming decade. However, the way in which Rhodesia and Namibia achieve their independence could decisively determine the shape of the future struggle over SA. There are two likely scenarios. First, that negotiated settlements will be reached in both Rhodesia and Namibia, thus avoiding large-scale violence and the exodus of Whites to the South. Second, that one or other of the two problems will fail to yield to diplomatic pressures and so inevitably result in an all-out armed struggle which will attract greater African, Russian and Cuban military involvement in the region. If attempts to reach a settlement fail in both the peripheral regions, this would further widen the area of territorial involvement.

The first scenario represents the way in which the overwhelming body of African and Western opinion desires to see the future. It would displease only the anti-Western powers and the as yet small revolutionary-minded African movements. The African interest is to see majority rule established under conditions most likely to favour the newly independent regimes in Zimbabwe and Namibia. The Western interest is to offload two of its embarrassments in whatever way is least likely to harm their economic and other interests. If the West had acted much earlier, it would have stood a far better chance of avoiding the second scenario of Namibia and Zimbabwe reaching majority rule as Angola and Mozambique did—through violence, with the new Marxist-type regimes buttressed by the Communist powers and with the exodus of the White communities.

There is the further probability that in Namibia, if not necessarily in Rhodesia, SA will become militarily engaged and that the African liberation movements will in turn be compelled to call on the Soviets and Cubans for massive military intervention. Such a move would be endorsed by many African states for the same reason that they approved of the Communist involvement in Angola *after* SA's military intervention in that country, and would be likely to have at least four major results. First, it would probably weaken the anti-Communist stand of most present-day African governments, since they would have reason to feel (whatever their suspicions or reservations) that the Communist world is a truer ally in a struggle of crucial continental importance. This trend is already noticeable in the changing attitudes of anti-Communist leaders like President Kaunda, who had strongly opposed Russian and Cuban intervention in Angola. Second, it would raise serious problems for the Western powers about their role in a situation of great violence and in all probability of large-scale killing of Whites as well as of Blacks. This could seriously jeopardize detente—in the widest sense of the term—and thus pose a threat to world peace. Third, since there is very little likelihood of any Western military intervention, the outcome of the struggles in Rhodesia and Namibia would be determined by the weight of Soviet military power—thus strengthening Moscow's influence throughout the region. Fourth, Communist involvement would decisively affect the pattern of future political developments in SA.

If, on the other hand, majority rule were to come to Rhodesia and Namibia through negotiation—bringing to power non-Marxist leaders, avoiding economic chaos and offering a future to their White communities—this would in no way reduce the pressures on the SA political system. On the contrary, it would strengthen them. Moreover, a non-disruptive transition in the peripheral states could have a number of positive advantages. It could encourage SA to use the time still available more urgently and more positively to seek new constitutional arrangements acceptable to all South Africans, which would mean involving representative Black leaders in meaningful negotiations. It could also create a less frightened atmosphere in which a purposeful White leadership might hope to convince its electorate of the truth of the warning given by the chairman of the Broederbond, Prof Viljoen, that 'to try and hold on to everything could lead to losing everything'. [7]

But if majority rule were to come to SA's neighbours as a result of a violent struggle backed by the Russians and Cubans, it would be bound to encourage Black South Africans to adopt similar methods and to choose the same allies. The tide of Black violence, the defeat and killing of Whites, and the unwillingness of the Western powers to act decisively would almost certainly strengthen the 'siege mentality' of White South Africans and so toughen their resistance to democratic change. Even if it did not, if the regime did evince a greater readiness for compromise, the possibility of finding representative African leaders willing to negotiate on terms minimally acceptable to the Whites would have been seriously weakened. Black South Africans would undoubtedly be encouraged to believe that power was slipping out of the hands of the White minority and that they could therefore hold out for maximalist terms. One could thus expect a repetition of the familiar historic experience of those with power being prepared to adjust to inevitable change only when it is too late to retain what might be regarded as their proper rights.

For all these reasons, the method of transferring power in Namibia and Rhodesia is likely to be of decisive importance in determining the future course of events in SA. The Vorster regime clearly understands this, which probably explains why it has not been altogether unreasonable in responding to the Western initiative over Namibia. To some extent, too, it has shown a willingness to co-operate with the Anglo-American settlement efforts in Rhodesia, but with one major proviso: a complete refusal to use its power to compel the Smith regime to accept the Anglo-American proposals. In fact, these represent the only hope of ensuring a quick end to the war in Rhodesia and of establishing a representative Black government not beholden to the Communists. It is entirely within the power of Vorster to force the Smith regime—overnight—to give its support to the Anglo-American plan, either by stopping the flow of oil into Rhodesia and/or by halting the supply of arms from SA.

Why, then, did Vorster refuse to act in what would so clearly seem in the interest of White South Africa? There are several possible explanations, including the likelihood that he genuinely misread the chances of the 'internal settlement' working. There is no doubt that he was sceptical about its chances unless Joshua Nkomo could be brought in, and that he tried hard to persuade Smith and others to induce Nkomo to return to Salisbury. More important, perhaps, are the two major constraints on Vorster: his difficulty in getting his White electorate to support a policy of openly pressuring the Smith regime, and his unwillingness to resort to the weapon of sanctions to change the Rhodesian political system since his enemies advocate an economic embargo to end apartheid. The combination of these three factors probably accounts for what could turn out to be a critical mistake in Vorster's calculations of how best to defend his concept of the South African national interest.

The defenders of the *status quo* in SA have three major fears: the growth of urban Black violence in support of a liberation struggle; the advance of Communist powers to positions of influence in countries close to SA's borders; and the abandonment by the West of any support for SA. 1975–76 saw the advance of a Soviet/Cuban military presence up to the border of Namibia—SA's military frontline. 1976 saw the beginning of serious urban Black violence. 1977 brought Soviet President Podgorny and Cuba's Fidel Castro on goodwill visits to SA's bordering states; it also saw the continuation of urban Black violence and, crucially, the beginning of a real threat of Western disengagement from SA.

President Carter's decision to send Vice-President Walter Mondale to Vienna in May 1977 to warn Vorster formally that SA-US relations were 'at a watershed' may in retrospect come to be seen as just such a parting of the ways. Certainly Vorster has interpreted it in that light. The isolation of the West from SA has been traumatic for White South Africans: 'We cannot negotiate on our destruction, either now or tomorrow,' was the biting comment of SA's Foreign Minister after the Vienna meeting.[8] Afraid of the gathering darkness, the Vorster regime has taken to whistling loudly to keep up the courage of White Scuth Africans. A typical reaction was that of the SA Broadcasting Corporation: 'The present campaign against SA being led by President Carter in the US is unifying the people of this country as never before'.[9] Even if this were true of White South Africans, it is almost certainly not true of Blacks. (SA's growing isolation within the world community is discussed in more detail in the chapter on South Africa.)

2. RHODESIA/ZIMBABWE

The US became directly involved in the Rhodesian situation through Kissinger's diplomacy in 1976, although the Secretary of State was careful to limit Washington's role by insisting on Britain's primary responsibility. Thus, although Kissinger's involvement had been decisive in getting Smith to accept the September 1976 Pretoria agreement (which endorsed the objective of majority rule for Rhodesia),[10] the lameduck Ford Administration acted only as an observer at the abortive Geneva conference which was intended to implement the Smith-Kissinger agreement.[11] After the failure of the Geneva talks, the US left the subsequent initiative to Britain through its UN ambassador, Ivor Richard.

Dr David Owen's approach to the problems of Southern Africa was completely different from that of his predecessor, Tony Crosland, who had opposed the idea of the Foreign Secretary taking personal charge of Southern African problems. Owen decided to make the area one of his priorities. Unusual among British politicians, he also strongly favoured an active UK-US partnership in Southern Africa, accepting the need for American 'muscle' to strengthen Britain's negotiating position with both the Smith and Vorster regimes. He made one further crucial policy departure—reversing a position previously strongly defended by Prime Minister Callaghan—by insisting on the need for Britain to assume direct responsibility during the transition period to Zimbabwe's independence. This change in British policy was in part a reflection of Owen's own personal commitment to majority rule in Southern Africa, an element of the belief he shares with Carter in the importance of human rights.

Owen's position would have been untenable had his coming to office not coincided with the arrival of the Carter Administration whose position on Southern Africa was almost identical to his own. This opened the way for a new Anglo-American relationship. When the new US ambassador to the UN, Andrew Young, came to London in February 1977, he responded at once to the opportunity for closer collaboration. 'Our countries,' he said, 'ought to be able to move things forward' from where they were left by the Geneva talks and the Richard's mission.[12] He added: 'I would say that President Carter sees there can be no future for Southern Africa unless there is a rationally-negotiated peaceful and meaningful agreement.' Young later explained that the US government would not have become involved in the joint initiative 'if it had not been for the insistence of African States that we had a role to play in the transformation of the entire Southern African continent and the achievement of majority rule . . . . It is the result of our commitment to majority rule throughout Southern Africa that we became involved in the process of listening to the Front-line Presidents, the liberation movements and all of the parties that have been involved in the struggle.'[13]

Thus the groundwork was laid for what was to become a joint Anglo-American initiative on Rhodesia. Encouraged by Carter's decision to move urgently to impose a ban on Rhodesian chrome imports to the US, Owen went to Washington in March 1977 to explore the possibility of a joint effort with the new US Secretary of State, Cyrus Vance. By early April, Owen was ready to embark on his first African mission which he announced had the support of the US.[14] An element new to British policy since the Unilateral Declaration of Independence (UDI) in 1965 was contained in Owen's announcement that it was wrong 'to think that the only person who can deliver a solution in Rhodesia is Ian Smith. He is only one aspect of White Rhodesian opinion.'[15] After Owen's exploratory talks in Dar es Salaam, Pretoria and Salisbury, his first step was to formalize the Anglo-American initiative by getting agreement for a joint team of officials. John Graham, a senior member of the British Foreign Office, and Stephen Low, the US ambassador in Lusaka, were appointed and began their collaboration in May. The next step was to agree on a set of proposals for a Rhodesian settlement which would carry US-UK endorsement and to plan how the new initiative was to be developed under Owen's chairmanship.[16]

The Patriotic Front—which had been recognized by the OAU Heads of State in June as the only representative body of Black Rhodesian opinion[17]—turned down the Anglo-Americans' draft proposals when these were put to them in Lusaka on 7 July by Graham and Low. They argued that it was wrong to begin by seeking agreement about an independence constitution; the first task was to secure Smith's surrender.[18] Smith's response was to declare the Patriotic Front (PF) as 'public enemy No 1'.

This enmity between the Smith regime and the PF was of course nothing new; on the other hand, the OAU's rejection of the claims to recognition by Bishop Muzorewa's United African National Council (UANC) and the Rev Ndabaningi Sithole's Zanu (renamed ANC-S) did create a new situation which was soon to change the course of events. It was only to be expected that once Africa turned its back on them and they were no longer free to operate externally, their only alternative was to consolidate a power base for themselves inside Rhodesia (in rivalry to the PF and the majority of OAU members) in the belief that they could command majority Black support. The effect of the OAU decision was thus to drive Sithole and Muzorewa into the waiting arms of Smith, who lost no time in exploiting this opportunity.

Owen again visited Washington on 23–24 July to get final agreement for a detailed Anglo-American plan to be presented to all the parties in the Rhodesian conflict as well as to the FLPs. Carter demonstrated his close interest in the initiative by participating in these preparatory talks. A second round of talks followed in London between Owen and Vance, who together had a meeting with the SA Foreign Minister, R. F. Botha. Their aim was to engage SA's support for the Anglo-American plan. At the end of August 1977, David Owen and Andy Young embarked on an African mission to discuss their proposals (in advance of publication) with the FLPs, the PF, Sithole and Muzorewa, Smith and Vorster.

The Anglo-American approach was described by ambassador Young as seeking to establish the following five objectives:

First, the initiation of an irreversible process leading to majority rule in an independent Zimbabwe;

Second, the creation of a neutral political process which would allow all political factions in Zimbabwe to compete fairly for political leadership through elections which truly reflect the will of the majority;

Third, an end to hostilities, followed by the maintenance of stability, law and order during the transition period to ensure the fairness of the process and thus its durability;

Fourth, agreement on an independence constitution that provides for a democratically-elected government, the abolition of discrimination and the protection of individual human rights, including the right of members of the minority as well as the majority;

Fifth, having presented a proposal based on these goals to the Security Council, the US together with the UK [would undertake] a series of discussions and negotiations with all of the principal parties concerned.[19]

It was soon evident that there were differences over how the Rhodesian army should be constituted once a ceasefire was arranged and a British Resident-Commissioner installed in Salisbury. The FLPs were categoric in demanding, in the words of President Nyerere, 'the complete dismantling of Smith's army' and the installation, by stages, of the guerrilla forces in their place. London and Washington accepted the idea of running down the Rhodesian forces and of reconstituting a new army by integrating the guerrillas into it, while introducing a UN Peacekeeping Force to hold the ring during the interim period. But this idea was flatly rejected by Vorster when Owen and Young discussed it with him in Pretoria on 29 August. He saw the plan as a recipe for chaos and dismissed the idea of allowing any role to the 'Marxist-Leninist terrorists' of Mugabe and his associates. He also made it clear that he would not apply any pressures on Smith to accept the Anglo-American proposals, promising only to support whatever was acceptable to the White Rhodesian leader. In effect, Vorster was giving Smith the sole right to veto any proposals put before him. Even before Owen and Young arrived in Salisbury, Smith had made it clear that he would not accept any suggestion which affected the composition of his forces and that he would have his own counter-proposals to make.[20]

When the Anglo-American plan was finally published on 1 September,[21] it left open the future of the Rhodesian forces by proposing only that a new Zimbabwe National Army would be 'formed as soon as possible' after a Transitional Administration was established under a British Resident Commissioner. Field Marshall Lord Carver, who was named for this post, would also be the new Commander-in-Chief. Primary responsibility for security during the transition period would be with the police, supported by a UN Zimbabwe Force. Since a ceasefire was to precede the establishment of the Transition Administration, there would be no immediate call for the services of an army.

The Anglo-American plan was rejected by the Smith regime and heavily criticized by the PF: both found some common ground in viewing it as a 'colonialist' concept. However, Muzorewa and Sithole thought the proposals worth considering and a supportive resolution was adopted by the Security Council. Owen took an optimistic line when he talked to the Young Fabians on 2 October 1977, saying that he believed a settlement could bring independence and majority rule to Rhodesia before the end of 1978—'far more quickly than even the most optimistic supporters of the armed struggle think'.[22] Before the end of October, the Security Council gave even more positive support to the Anglo-American plan by agreeing to designate Maj-Gen Prem Chand as the commander of the putative UN Zimbabwe Force. But when Carver and Chand undertook a reconnaissance in early November to determine the chances of getting a ceasefire, they received little encouragement from either the PF or Smith.

The four months between September 1977, when the Anglo-American plan was published, and January 1978 were crucial in that they gave the Smith regime the opportunity to develop its alternative strategy of an 'internal settlement'. Struggling with its own deep internal divisions,[23] the PF failed to set out its own practical alternative proposals to improve the Anglo-American plan, though still criticizing it in general terms for the 'dictatorial' powers envisaged for Lord Carver. They refused to endorse a UN peacekeeping presence, were ambiguous about their acceptance of elections before independence, and insisted on the PF playing the dominant; though not the exclusive, political and military role during the transition period. They also refused to allow Muzorewa, Sithole and Chirau to have any part in negotiating 'the surrender of the Smith regime'.

The FLPs, too, had their internal difficulties during these months (see below), mainly over the question of whether elections should be held before or after Zimbabwe's independence. Both the PF and the FLPs argued that the Western powers had the strength to force Smith's 'abdication' by exerting direct pressures on Vorster to stop the flow of oil and the supply of arms to Rhodesia, which alone made it possible for the regime to hold out. The African argument was that if the Western powers were as committed to achieving the removal of Smith as they claimed to be, they should be ready to use their leverage against SA to force Smith to step down. The Anglo-American reply was that its task of removing Smith would be considerably facilitated if there were agreement with the PF, underwritten by the FLPs, about the way in which the new Zimbabwe was to be created. The US and UK were clearly not willing to implement tougher economic sanctions against SA in an effort to compel it to observe the embargo against Rhodesia. Although disputes over these issues troubled relations between the FLPs and the Anglo-Americans, there was no sign that the African leaders intended to break off or abandon the negotiations. However, the FLPs did support the move to increase the fighting effectiveness of the Zimbabwe guerrilla forces, insisting that this could be achieved only if the two wings of the PF agreed to integrate their 'armies'. But although the FLPs gave high priority to achieving this military unity, their efforts were unsuccessful.

A new situation arose in January 1978 when Smith announced that he was willing to accept majority rule and independence by the end of 1978, having persuaded first Sithole and Chirau, and later Muzorewa, to begin serious negotiations about an 'internal settlement'. This prospect produced a greater sense of urgency in the ranks of the FLPs and the PF to intensify the Anglo-American initiative. In February 1978, the PF leadership travelled to Malta for talks with the US and UK and for the first time produced detailed counter-proposals to the Anglo-American plan. [24] These included a number of important concessions such as acceptance of elections before independence with the right of all White and Black Rhodesians to participate freely in them; a readiness to consider a possible UN role during the transition; and an indication that if a negotiated settlement were possible, they would not insist that the 'armed struggle' offered the only path to independence.

There were concessions, too, from the Anglo-American side. In order to meet the objection to Lord Carver's 'dictatorial powers', it proposed that he be assisted by an advisory Governing Council which would comprise himself, a UN representative, and two members each from the Smith regime, Muzorewa's UANC, Nkomo's Zapu, Mugabe's Zanu and Sithole's ANC-S. The PF objected that the new proposals would leave it in a minority of four against eight—and of four to six against those participating in the 'internal settlement'. They objected even more strongly to the Anglo-American proposals for an interim Security Council (which would exercise control over all the security forces including the guerrillas) since it would be composed in the same way as the Governing Council. The PF argued that the only reason why Smith had reversed his position on the issue of majority rule was because of the pressures of the armed struggle which the PF alone was waging; now claiming the upper hand militarily, it insisted that its dominant position be recognized in the transition institutions. While the Malta talks thus made some gains, the gap between the PF and the Anglo-American positions still remained very wide.

The announcement on 15 February 1978 of the successful conclusion of the 'internal settlement' negotiations in Salisbury marked the opening of a new chapter in the Rhodesian crisis. The PF saw it as an act of betrayal by 'Smith's Black collaborators'; it refused to take seriously Smith's promise to hand over power to the majority and regarded the agreement as simply another of his ploys to 'divide and rule'.

These attitudes were fully endorsed by the FLPs. What the African Presidents expected was unequivocal condemnation of the 'internal settlement', but this was not forthcoming, either from London or Washington. The British Foreign Secretary said in the House of Commons on 16 February 1978: 'It seems there are crucial issues yet to be resolved including the composition of the transitional government and its powers; the composition of the security forces and the extent to which other nationalist parties will be involved in the transition and in fair and free elections on the basis of universal suffrage. We will continue, as we have done from the start of the Anglo-American initiative, to work with all parties, inside and outside the country, to promote an overall settlement compatible with the principles endorsed by this House and to work for the cessation of all violence.'

Although Andy Young was known at first to have favoured outright condemnation of the 'internal settlement', he came round to accepting an agreed position developed within the Administration after consultations with the British. President Carter described the 'settlement' as inadequate. A fuller amplification of the American position was offered by Andy Young in a statement to the Security Council on 15 March:

'I am the first to recognize that anything which Mr Smith has negotiated merits the most careful scrutiny. But I am also willing to credit good faith to the participating Nationalist leaders. They, as much as the other Nationalist leaders of Zimbabwe, want freedom and independence for their country and full political equality for all the people of the country. It is fair, then, to ask what they have achieved in Salisbury. Compared with the kinds of settlement proposals which Smith has entertained in the past, the Salisbury Agreement marks some progress. (1) The nationalist leaders have gotten Mr Smith to agree to the principle of universal adult suffrage. (2) Smith's signature has been obtained on a commitment eventually to step down. There is still no ironclad assurance, however, that he will do so. (3) Finally, there is recognition that during the transition period, some sharing of power must take place among the participating groups. . . . We must consider whether the agreement announced in Salisbury takes sufficiently into account the enormous difficulty of managing the transition period. This crucial watershed must be handled in such a way that the violence of the present struggle for liberation can be transformed into an irreversible political process which will result in the approval by all the people of Rhodesia of their own form of government and the selection of their own leaders.'

The Security Council adopted a resolution on 15 March 1978 which described the 'internal settlement' as 'illegal and unacceptable', and condemned 'attempts and manoeuvres' by the White minority to retain power. The five Western members of the Security Council abstained from voting on the resolution. This was after the African group had softened their original proposals, which included the threat of sanctions against SA, because of threats by the US and UK to exercise their veto. Nigeria's ambassador to the UN, Leslie Harriman, had in turn warned that his country would leave the Commonwealth if Britain were to use its veto against the resolution.

The PF was deeply suspicious that Britain in particular might be tempted to move towards endorsement of the internal settlement, to abandon the Anglo-American plan and turn against the Front. Although these suspicions are understandable, there was in fact never any question of either the US or UK governments moving in this direction for reasons of polity as well as principle. The point of principle, repeatedly stated by Dr Owen, was that 'any settlement must be acceptable to the people of Rhodesia as a whole'. The major political reason, he told the Commons, was that 'an internal settlement which excludes one of the leading nationalist groups cannot bring about a ceasefire during the elections or give peace and stability to a newly independent Zimbabwe. Nor would it eliminate the threat to international peace and stability and therefore would be most unlikely to be recognized by the Security Council. . . . It is necessary for the UN to have a crucial role in this settlement, either in a military, peacekeeping or supervisory role in order to ensure fair elections and for any administration by a British Resident-Commissioner to be seen to be fair. . . . We cannot ignore the weight of international opinion, the Security Council, the Commonwealth and the OAU. . . . How can it be seriously argued that Britain, in the midst of a major conflict which clearly demonstrates a divided nation, unilaterally and in direct contravention of the fifth principle, recognize the internal settlement and lift sanctions? It would be utterly wrong to do so. It would leave Britain with barely a friend in the world, discredited and despised, and even more important, it would be a betrayal of the people of Rhodesia as a whole. We owe them a debt of honour, and it is a debt I intend to discharge. Britain had no debts or obligations to individuals or parties in Rhodesia. They had no interest in choosing between the differing Black nationalist leaderships. This was for the people of Rhodesia as a whole'. The plan always envisaged that sanctions would be lifted at the start of the transitional period and in order to achieve international support for lifting sanctions, they had to ensure the irreversibility of the process towards independence. This irreversibility was fundamental if they were to satisfy others that sanctions should be lifted and recognition should be given to any government. Under the internal settlement, there was no such guarantee, no transfer of power and no ceasefire. . . . As to saying that progress can be made only when the PF agrees, it is a fact that while two armies fight each other, we need both sides to agree to a ceasefire. A ceasefire between two armies, neither of which has won or lost, is extremely difficult to achieve. History shows that. One should strive to do this, however.'[25]

Both before and after the 'internal settlement', the aim of Anglo-American policy was to try and secure agreement among all the major Zimbabwe leaders—first because of the need to fulfil the principle of 'acceptability' by the majority of the country's inhabitants; and second, in order to avoid the real risk of a civil war developing among rival Black movements after independence, as occurred in Angola. This latter threat was a major concern of the FLPs. In retrospect, it will be seen that the OAU's exclusive recognition of the PF was a major precipitating factor in deepening divisions among Zimbabweans—a danger fully recognized just before the 'internal settlement' was signed when Nyerere and Machel sent urgent messages to Muzorewa urging him not to enter into any deals with Smith, as this would finally put him 'beyond the pale'. But by then, Muzorewa had come to feel so bitterly towards the FLPs he did not even deign to reply to Nyerere, and responded with an extremely provocative letter to Machel telling him not to interfere in the internal affairs of Zimbabwe.

The thrust of the Anglo-American initiative after February 1978 was to try and bring all the major leaders in both the external movement and the 'internal settlement' to an all-party conference to try to find common ground. In mid-April 1978, the British Foreign Secretary and the US Secretary of State embarked on another trip to Dar es Salaam, Salisbury and Pretoria in an attempt to persuade the PF and the new Rhodesian Transition Administration to agree to all-party talks. Although Nkomo and Mugabe accepted the idea and made further concessions on the Anglo-American plan (such as over the role of a UN force after the achievement of a ceasefire, and for an Executive Council to meet under Carver's chairmanship), the 'internal settlement' signatories replied that they could see no value in trying to hold talks with the PF.

While the Anglo-American initiative remained alive up to July 1978 and still had the support of the FLPs and even of the PF, it appeared to offer little hope of progress. Nothing would be achieved until it became clear that the 'internal settlement' could not meet the three basic requirements to establishing peace and an orderly transfer of power to a majority-ruled Zimbabwe: a ceasefire leading to an end of hostilities; the lifting of sanctions, which requires the approval of the Security Council; and free elections to test the opinion of all Zimbabweans—a prerequisite for the introduction of legislation by the British parliament to grant legal independence to the new State.

3. NAMIBIA

'Namibia is a challenge without parallel to the authority of the United Nations.'
—Dr Kurt Waldheim, UN Secretary-General,
20 May 1977

In 1947 a relatively little-known Anglican cleric, the Rev Michael Scott, first appeared in the lobbies of the UN carrying a petition from the then Herero chief, the venerable old Hosea Kutako. It was Scott's intervention which blocked an attempt by the then South African Prime Minister, Gen J. C. Smuts, to have the old League of Nations mandate set aside and incorporate the territory (known as South West Africa) into the Republic. [26] Over the next 30 years the world body tried, though not very hard and without any success, to bring Namibia to independence under conditions that would free it from SA's hegemony. [27] By early 1977, SA stood poised to confer its own approved style of independence on the territory through a constitution prepared by the Turnhalle conference. [28] At this point the Western nations for the first time asserted their authority and influence to stop SA in its tracks.

The nine members of the European Community warned Pretoria on 7 February 1977 that the Turnhalle proposals did not meet with their approval and would certainly not be accepted by the UN, which had international responsibility for the future of the former trust territory. This collective European confrontation with the Vorster regime reflected two major Western concerns. First, by going ahead with its own plan for Namibia's independence, SA would inevitably invite a tough UN reaction along the lines developed by the OAU, including the application of extensive sanctions against SA. While this course of action was not favoured by the Western nations, they felt they would have no choice but to support it because of the need to uphold the authority of the UN and to avert a dangerous rift with the African nations. Second, the West could foresee that the result of unilateral action by SA in Namibia would be international military intervention. The challenging Swapo liberation movement, based largely in neighbouring Angola, would intensify its armed struggle with the full support, not only of the OAU, but also of the Russians and Cubans who were already engaged in training and arming Swapo's People's Liberation Army of Namibia (PLAN).

The Western nations agreed that no acceptable settlement could be achieved for Namibia which did not involve both SA and Swapo. Dr Kissinger's efforts to get Vorster to involve Swapo in the negotiations for Namibia's independence in 1976 had been fruitless. Vorster adamantly insisted that under no circumstances would SA agree to meet with 'a bunch of communist terrorists'. [29]

In February 1977, faced with the imminent prospect of the UN being called upon to react to an 'internal settlement' in Namibia, the five Western members of the Security Council (US, UK, France, West Germany and Canada) met to discuss how to avert this threatening crisis and agreed that Security Council Resolution 385 of 1976 must be upheld. This demanded that SA accept elections under UN supervision and control before independence; release all political prisoners; abolish racial discrimination; permit all exiles to return without fear of arrest or intimidation; and withdraw its illegal administration in favour of a temporary UN presence. The five were also agreed that Swapo must be fully involved in the negotiating process. They then consulted with the Africa Group at the UN, as well as with the UN Secretary-General, both of which accepted the proposed Western initiative to mediate between SA and Swapo.

That was the beginning of what came to be known as the 'Contact Group'—or more derisorily the 'Gang of Five'—under the chairmanship of ambassador Don McHenry, deputy to Andy Young at the UN. McHenry was formerly involved in South African affairs in two ways: as a State Department official, he had strenuously opposed the implementation of the National Security Council Memorandum 39 (NSM 39) endorsed by President Nixon on Kissinger's recommendation; [30] having lost that fight, he resigned and later visited SA to complete a study on the role of US firms in the Republic. [31] At the first meeting of the Contact Group and Vorster in April 1977, the South African Prime Minister—faced with a collective Western stand—adopted a much more compromising position than at any time previously. The explanation Vorster gave for his turnabout was that whereas 'in the past, SA had been ignored, Western countries had now realized that this could no longer be done, and that it was in their interests and in those of SA to sit around a table and discuss problems'[32] (a statement quite at odds with the long efforts made by Western nations to involve SA in negotiations with the UN and Swapo). The Contact Group and SA together established the following basic principles for negotiations: SA recognized the need for an internationally acceptable solution in Namibia; SA recognized the need for elections in Namibia held under universal suffrage without literacy qualifications; SA said that the electorate would initially choose the members of a constituent assembly whose immediate and principal responsibility would be to draft a constitution for an independent Namibia; SA accepted the principle of UN involvement in the elections; all people and parties would be free to participate in the elections; freedom of speech and assembly would be guaranteed; political prisoners and detainees would be released; SA would withdraw from Namibia in stages, 'in consultation with those mainly involved'. In addition, SA planned to establish a central administrative authority to govern the country before independence; it agreed to refrain from seeking parliamentary approval for the Turnhalle constitutional proposals, as part of its general understanding that it will avoid taking steps which might foreclose an internally acceptable solution.

In pursuing its initiative throughout 1977, the Contact Group was faced with two major problems (more fully discussed in the chapter on Namibia). The first was to decide whether the Vorster regime seriously meant the negotiations to succeed. Was it going through the motions simply to give the West an appearance of reasonableness while believing, or hoping, that Swapo's obduracy would cause the negotiations to break down? Or was it genuinely interested in reaching an internationally acceptable agreement? Don McHenry confessed that he could never quite make up his mind about what he described as Vorster's 'two-track strategy': 'SA would prefer an internationally acceptable solution if the price is right. At some point, if they conclude that the price is too costly, they would go off on their own internal settlement. They are probably trying to do as many of those things that are internationally acceptable as they possibly can as a way of rationalizing the internal settlement. Up to this point, track one and track two have been down the same road. The real question comes what happens when you get to the fork; whether you must turn left to get to track one which is the international settlement, or you must turn right to track two. It . . . is something which we and the South Africans have always taken in account from the very beginning.'[33]

The second problem was the extreme suspiciousness of Swapo and especially of its leader, Sam Nujomo, about the Contact Group's dependability. Nujomo's view was that the West's 'declaration of principles' on Namibia was worthless unless backed up by a Security Council economic and arms embargo against SA. Short of such a Western policy, he remained convinced that Namibia would finally be liberated only through 'a protracted armed struggle'.[34] This led him to concentrate on building up PLAN's military power in co-operation with Cuba and Russia. In March 1977, for instance, he asked President Podgorny during his visit to Zambia for increased arms supplies. McHenry's view was that Swapo, like SA, was also engaged in a two-track strategy: 'they co-operate and engage in negotiation but fear all the time that they may be walking into a trap' and so remain ready to go on fighting if they cannot achieve their goals through negotiations.

By the end of 1977, the Contact Group had established its terms for a negotiated settlement.[35] While the proposals, based on the requirements of Resolution 385 and the maximum concessions it believed could be extracted from both sides, won the broad approval of the FLPs, neither SA nor Swapo was ready to endorse the plan when it was finally presented to them in February 1978. SA's Foreign Minister, R. F. Botha, broke off his talks with the Contact Group in New York, declaring: 'There are aspects of these proposals that would be so totally unacceptable and so dangerous that there is a serious and real danger of the people in the territory being overrun and being governed by a Marxist terrorist organization. I have not said that there is no hope left, but it is a very serious situation.'[36]

Swapo was equally antagonistic to the proposals, mainly over the location of the remaining 1,500 South African troops during the transition; the failure to include Walvis Bay in an independent Namibia; the role of the South African police during the elections; and the failure to provide for the dismantling of the Bantu tribal authorities.

Although these tough reactions seemed to doom the Western mediation effort to failure, a renewed initiative in March and April 1978 in favour of a slightly modified set of proposals brought new hope. The role of the FLPs was decisive in sustaining the talks, which seemed almost certain to collapse after the South African army's massive attack against Swapo civilian and guerrilla camps at Cassinga, deep inside Angola, early in May 1978.[37] This coincided with the last and most critical phase of negotiations. Yet within a few weeks, on 25 May, Vorster announced SA's acceptance of the Western proposals. If he was gambling on Swapo rejecting them and so giving SA a strong diplomatic advantage, he had reckoned without the FLPs (including Neto). They again proved their inestimable value in helping to promote a peaceful settlement by persuading Swapo not to break off negotiations, despite SA's singularly provocative attack.

In mid-1978, the FLPs arranged a meeting in Luanda between the Contact Group and Swapo's leadership; this time a major breakthrough was achieved when Sam Nujomo accepted the Western proposals on 13 July. With both SA and Swapo giving their broad support to the terms for achieving Namibia's independence, the West's new African diplomacy brought hope that, barring accidents, one of the three crisis areas might be rescued from the violence and disruption of an all-out armed struggle.

THE AFRICAN ROLE IN THE DIPLOMATIC PROCESS
THE FRONT-LINE PRESIDENTS

The FLPs' basic approach to the Rhodesian problem has remained unchanged since late 1976. Despite temporary divergences by both Kaunda and Neto, the group maintained its internal unity by accepting majority decisions. The role of Julius Nyerere as chairman was also of decisive importance.[38] The starting point of the FLPs' approach was that Smith was the only obstacle to progress and that he should therefore be 'removed, voluntarily or otherwise'. (No clear indication was ever put forward as to how this should be done if he refused to step down of his own accord: that, they felt, was up to the British and Americans. As Kaunda put it on one occasion: 'If the Western powers could get rid of Hitler, what is so difficult about removing a pigmy like Smith?') The FLPs supported the idea of a two-year transition period leading to independence, during which time a Black majority caretaker government should be formed, but only after a conference, under British auspices, had drawn up an independence constitution. They were insistent that there should be elections before independence—a point on which Kaunda was in a minority (see below).

The explicit assumptions underlying these proposals was that responsibility should rest with Britain until independence; that there should be a carefully planned transition to final independence; that Black unity, especially between the rival guerrilla armies, was essential; and that the principle of NIBMAR (no independence before majority rule) should be upheld.

Despite the failure of the Geneva talks and of the subsequent Richard's mission, Nyerere urged in January and again in February 1977 that 'it would not be wise' for Britain to give up the search for an agreement simply because Smith had rejected the British proposals: the aim should be to get agreement between Britain and the nationalists.[39] However, at the same time, the FLPs were agreed on the importance of maintaining and if possible of increasing their pressures on both Smith and the British through the armed struggle. In April 1977—immediately after President Podgorny's visit to the region (see below)—the FLPs met in Quelimane (Mozambique) to review his offer of military and other support. They also discussed how to strengthen the PF's forces and how to defend Mozambique, Zambia and Botswana against incursions by the Rhodesian army. Although Mozambique signed a 20-year Friendship Treaty with the USSR during Podgorny's visit—which allowed the Frelimo regime to call on Moscow for assistance in situations threatening its peace—President Machel at no time objected to American involvement in the Rhodesian negotiations as Neto originally had done.[40] The Soviets naturally strongly opposed American involvement from the beginning. Even when the Anglo-American's initiative in Rhodesia and the Contact Group's mediation in Namibia were attacked by Robert Mugabe and Sam Nujomo at the UN Conference in Support of the People of Zimbabwe and Namibia, held in Maputo in May 1977,[41] Machel insisted that Britain's new initiative could constitute 'a positive factor'. He stated that the Western negotiations over Namibia 'could contribute to the acceleration of the resolution of the conflict'—so long as the aim was to achieve genuine independence.[42] On the other hand, the Angolan President objected to American involvement, but not so strongly as to dissociate himself from the FLPs' decision to engage in both Western initiatives. Tanzania's Prime Minister, Edward Sokoine, told his National Assembly on 22 June 1977 that 'Africa respects the efforts currently being shown by Western powers in ending racism and bringing about majority rule in Southern Africa'.

At their July 1977 meeting, the FLPs devoted most of their time to discussing the problem of disunity within the PF. Nyerere said after the meeting that it was not the FLPs' intention to 'impose leaders on the people of Zimbabwe—they must elect their own leaders'; but they felt it was necessary to have a single liberation army because of the dangers of several armies and the necessity to sharpen the armed struggle.[43]

During his visit to the US, Canada and Britain in August 1977, Nyerere placed great emphasis on the importance of adhering strictly to the agreement reached at the June Commonwealth Prime Ministers' meeting.[44] This stated that any negotiated settlement for Rhodesia 'must entail not only the removal of the illegal Smith regime, but also the dismantling of its apparatus of repression in order to pave the way for the creation of police and armed forces which would be responsive to the needs of the people of Zimbabwe and assure the orderly and effective transfer of power'. After his London visit, Nyerere said he had come away feeling 'confused' about the British position towards dismantling the Rhodesian forces. He felt that the British 'should show the same sense of urgency' about getting rid of the 'racist regimes' in Southern Africa as he had found in the US where President Carter was 'speaking the same language' as himself. He was not asking the West for arms. 'The Russians are giving us arms. The US should provide us with the rest of the pressures needed against the racist regimes.'[45]

The question of dismantling the Rhodesian army became the central point of disagreement at the summit meeting between the FLPs, the PF, Dr Owen and Andy Young held at Lusaka on 26–27 August 1977. The purpose of that meeting was to convey details of the Anglo-American plan before it was published. Speaking as chairman of the FLPs, Nyerere made it clear that unless the proposals were changed to meet the African demand for dismantling the Rhodesian forces, they would be unacceptable. [46] When the plan was published on 1 September, it did reveal some important changes in this respect (see above), but nevertheless received only a cautious welcome from most African governments and a rather critical reaction from the Angolans. [47] However, when the FLPs met to discuss their reply in Maputo on 23–24 September, they agreed that the proposals 'form a sufficient basis for further negotiations between the parties concerned'. Nyerere qualified his support by saying: 'We find that these proposals still have many negative elements and leave many questions unanswered'. [48]

The FLPs' cautious support for the Anglo-American plan was considerably strengthened over the next three months—partly due to greater clarification of some of the proposals, but principally to changes in Salisbury where negotiations for an 'internal settlement' had begun to prosper. Alarmed by this development, the African leaders began to find the Anglo-American alternative increasingly attractive.

By early 1978, after the signing of the 'internal settlement' agreement, the FLPs' immediate concern was whether the Western powers would allow the Anglo-American plan to wither through inactivity, and whether the US and UK would move towards accepting the Salisbury alternative. From February, they began to insist on the rapid implementation of the Anglo-American plan, and to persuade the PF to modify its objections to facilitate this process. Praise for the plan from individual Presidents was heard rather more often than criticism. For example, on 23 February, the Mozambique Foreign Ministry issued a statement affirming the 'positive points' in the plan which made serious negotiations possible. The statement called for the rapid and positive conclusion of the talks between the PF, the US and UK. Under this kind of pressure from the FLPs, Mugabe and Nkomo agreed to attend the Malta talks in February and to adopt a more constructive attitude to the proposals, though they themselves were by no means yet satisfied with them.

At their meeting in Dar es Salaam on 25–26 March 1978, the FLPs addressed the following statement to Washington and London: 'If they still support these proposals, they should move ahead and convene in the shortest time possible a meeting to follow up what was agreed in Malta. If, on the other hand, they have decided to abandon their commitment to their own proposals for which they had requested and obtained the support of the PF, the Front-line States and the international community, they should so declare unequivocally without any further delay.' A few days before this summit meeting, Nyerere had declared that the Front-line States 'would continue to regard the Anglo-American proposals as the basis for genuine independence for Zimbabwe'. His forthright endorsement was not reflected in the attitudes of the PF, however. Although it began to move forward from the positions adopted in Dar es Salaam on 13 April in their meetings with Cyrus Vance and Dr Owen, the differences between the two sides were still too great to allow new momentum to be built up in favour of the Anglo-American initiative. This had been considerably slowed down both by the prolonged negotiations to win PF acceptance and by the new situation created by the 'internal settlement'. In a communique after their next meeting in Beira on 17–18 April 1978, the FLPs 'reaffirmed their commitment to the principle of negotiating with the colonial power the modalities of the transfer of power to the people of Zimbabwe, underlining the positive aspects of the Anglo-American proposals'. The Presidents also renewed their commitment to the armed struggle and to 'a single leadership structure' for the PF.

While Nyerere was successful in June 1978 in getting Nkomo and Mugabe to agree to attend all-party talks (proposed by the Anglo-Americans in an effort to bring together all the external and internal elements), this further attempt to seize back the initiative from Salisbury failed to materialize.

THE ROLE OF ZAMBIA

Although President Kenneth Kaunda supported the FLPs' overall strategy, he nevertheless embarked on a number of unilateral initiatives which at times separated him from his two closest colleagues, Nyerere and Machel. Mounting internal economic, security and political problems made it less easy for Kaunda than for the other FLPs to wait patiently while the Anglo-American initiative unfolded. He was also more anxious over the PF's failure to establish a truly united movement. Kaunda's policies differed from those of his colleagues—and especially from Nyerere's—over three major issues: his championing of Joshua Nkomo as the major leader within the PF; his doubts about the wisdom of insisting on elections before independence; and his greater readiness to involve the Cubans and Russians in the struggle against Rhodesia.

In February 1977, Kaunda and Nyerere took different positions over Britain's central role in the Rhodesian negotiations. The Tanzanian leader insisted that he did not think it wise for the US to take over Britain's responsibility for Rhodesia; the Zambian leader, on the other hand, told Andy Young that he believed the British lacked 'the will and ability' to fulfil their proper role in Rhodesia and suggested that 'it is now up to the US to decide how to do it'.[49]

During the Angolan civil war in 1975–76, Kaunda and Nyerere had strongly disagreed over the Russian/Cuban intervention: while Nyerere had approved, Kaunda had not only condemned their action but had warned Africa of the threat of 'a tiger and its cubs' to the continent.[50] But in March 1977, on the eve of President Podgorny's visit to Lusaka, Kaunda contrasted the failure of the West to provide a single weapon for the liberation movements with what the Russians and other Communist countries had done. 'We and the Soviet Union are colleagues and comrades in the struggle, and this is going to be the case until the wars of liberation accomplish their objectives.'[51] On 31 March, he declared: 'If the West is afraid that the visits of President Podgorny and Dr Castro are going to end up in Southern Africa being communist-influenced, it is the West that is to be blamed'.[52] He was especially bitter over the failure of the Western nations to ensure that their oil companies did not break the Rhodesian embargo, and began legal action against four oil multinationals whom he accused of keeping Smith's 'war machine' operating.[53] He stated: 'We are at a turning point in the Southern African revolutionary struggle. The pace is intensifying and the Soviet Union is one of the major representatives of the progressive forces in the world fighting for liberation. . . . Anyone who assists the liberation struggle is welcome.'[54] He also indicated that the time might come when, if Rhodesian attacks continued against Zambia, he might find it necessary to invite 'a foreign power' to come to his country's assistance; he did not specify any particular country. In May 1978—on the eve of an important mission to Britain and America—he said that he could foresee the possibility of the PF wishing to invite the Cubans to assist them actively in their struggle against the Smith regime. He indicated that if this were to happen, he would be willing to allow them to use Zambia as a base country.[55]

Kaunda was mainly responsible for persuading the OAU summit in Libreville in June 1977 to give exclusive recognition to the PF. Yet despite his general support for the Front, there was no doubt about his personal commitment to Joshua Nkomo and his Zapu forces who were established on Zambian soil. On 25 September 1977, Kaunda met Ian Smith in Lusaka, where he listened to the Rhodesian leader's proposal that Nkomo be persuaded to join in the move towards an 'internal settlement'. This meeting greatly incensed Mugabe, who accused Kaunda of acting behind his back and of spreading disunity in the ranks of the PF.[56] The Zambian Press in turn ferociously attacked Mugabe, calling him an 'imitation freedom fighter' and even proposing that he be banned from Zambia.[57] Although nothing came from the meeting with Smith, Kaunda defiantly declared that if he thought anything could be achieved, he would be willing to talk to him again. Soon afterwards, however, he finally became convinced that nothing could be hoped for from the Rhodesian leader.[58]

One crucial difference between Kaunda and Nyerere was over the FLPs' stand on elections in Rhodesia before independence. Nyerere remained firmly committed to his longstanding demand of 'no independence before majority rule'—a formula he had been the first to put forward. In late September, Kaunda began to argue that to hold elections in Rhodesia during a six-month transition preceding independence would only exacerbate deep racial, tribal and clan tensions. Instead, he believed Zimbabwe should become independent with a 'Government of National Unity' based on the PF, whose guerrillas would also form the core of the new national army. This serious difference of view between Kaunda (supported only by Neto) and his colleagues persisted until late November 1977 when, at a meeting between Kaunda and Nyerere at Mbale, the Zambian gave way, although still remaining unconvinced about the wisdom of NIBMAR.

In December 1977, Kaunda angrily announced that he was pulling out of the Anglo-American negotiations because of the response of Dr Owen to a Rhodesian attack on camps in Mozambique in which 1,200 Zimbabweans were reported to have been massacred. He said: 'We withdraw from the debate. We will no longer sit around a conference table to discuss the proposals.' Dr Owen at once said he regretted that his remarks had given offence to the Zambian leader whom he greatly admired. Anglo-Zambian accord was finally restored when Kaunda visited London in May 1978.

THE ROLE OF OTHER AFRICAN STATES

Although the OAU endorsed the role of the FLPs in masterminding African strategy in Southern Africa on a number of occasions, this endorsement was not without its critics. For example, there was strong opposition to the FLPs' recommendation to the OAU summit in June 1977 that African Heads of State give exclusive recognition to the PF.[59] Several OAU members maintain close relations with Muzorewa's UANC or Sithole's ANC: Libya has trained guerrillas for both groups, and both Presidents Amin and Banda continue to support Sithole. A number of Francophone African states, notably Ivory Coast and Senegal, also look with favour on Muzorewa and Sithole but have not come out in support of the 'internal settlement'.

President Mobutu was an especially sharp critic of the FLPs, for his own particularist reasons. In March 1977, he attacked them for seeking 'to divide Africa. . . . In fact, we are now watching the birth of a restricted club, a club where hypocrisy is the only slogan.'[60] He accused members of trading with Pretoria (meaning Zambia, Mozambique and Botswana) 'and even of receiving loans from SA's economy and therefore [benefiting] from its apartheid policy'. While it is true that the three FLPs do trade with SA, their policy is openly declared and has been accepted by the OAU as necessary to their survival. None of them receives 'loans from SA', whereas Zaire both trades with the apartheid Republic and receives loans from it.[61]

By far the most important supporter of the FLPs is Nigeria, which threw its weight fully behind their efforts in Southern Africa in 1977, having begun to move in that direction in 1976. Nigeria is not only a major force in the OAU system, but has also come to be regarded by both Western and Communist nations as the most important country in Black Africa—a view endorsed by Andy Young when he went to Lagos for talks in February 1977. After his meeting with Gen Obasanjo, the Nigerian leader said: 'Generally, we agreed on what should be done, our courses of action, methods of approach and our tactics'. The US ambassador in Lagos, Don Easum, characterized the meeting as 'the most interesting and perhaps the most important conversation of this nature I've had in 23 years in the Foreign Service'.[62] One result was that Nigeria endorsed an American role in Southern Africa. Obasanjo visited Lusaka in September 1977 where he discussed how his country could participate more effectively in the FLPs' strategy. Despite a willingness to cooperate with the Western initiatives in Rhodesia and Namibia, Nigeria's leaders continued to maintain a suspiciously critical attitude to Western policies. Thus, the Commissioner for External Affairs, Brig Garba, insisted that 'Africa will never trust any foreign powers as mediators in the situation in Zimbabwe until the territory achieves independence'.[63]

The Nigerians have been especially concerned about the failure of the African countries to organize their own defence system to deal with threats to security in the continent. On a number of occasions, their spokesmen referred to the 'shame' of African countries having to rely on foreign forces of intervention. In one such typical comment, radio Lagos said on 28 March 1978: 'One would have thought that by now the OAU would have found an answer to Smith's naked aggression of the Front-line countries'. Referring to a reported decision of Mozambique and Zambia to organize a joint force to defend their borders, radio Lagos called on the OAU to help bring this proposal to reality. 'Apart from serving as a deterrent to Ian Smith, its value is that it can be the beginning of a much-desired African High Command.' There were numerous reports in 1977 that Nigeria was prepared to use its large army to assist the Front-line States or to take over from the Cuban forces in Angola, but this kind of speculation was repeatedly denied by Lagos.

THE ROLE OF THE PATRIOTIC FRONT

The PF's role in Anglo-American-African diplomacy was typical of any liberation movement which believes that victory is within sight—though not yet within immediate grasp. While accepting their need for African and foreign support, both Joshua Nkomo and Robert Mugabe fiercely defended their independence and resisted any attempt to shape their tactics or to make them submit to 'unacceptable' conditions. They strongly resented anything that smacked of 'interference', irrespective of whether it came from African Presidents or from Westerners. Both wings of the PF were particularly suspicious of any move which appeared to favour one side over the other—hence the tensions between Zanu and Zambia and to a lesser extent with Tanzania. Mugabe was also resentful of the Western capitals' clear preference for Nkomo.

The principal source of trouble between the PF and the FLPs was over the latter's repeated attempts to unify the two guerrilla armies—Zanla and Zipra. Although both Nkomo and Mugabe recognized the military importance of a single integrated army and of a Joint Command, neither for a moment lost sight of the power struggle between their rival movements which proceeded simultaneously with their liberation war.[64]

The PF leaders felt ambivalent toward the Anglo-American initiative throughout

1977–78, welcoming it only insofar as they believed that London and Washington were committed to 'removing Smith' and preparing the way for a PF victory—not just for majority rule. But for the most part they remained unconvinced of the genuineness of Anglo-American intentions; at no time did they feel that the Western powers would act decisively to topple the Smith regime, for example, by exerting direct pressures on SA to halt the flow of arms and oil into Rhodesia. Nevertheless, under the persuasions of the FLPs, they engaged as reluctant partners in the Anglo-American negotiations, becoming rather less reluctant after the signing of the 'internal settlement' (see above).

This uneasy involvement in Anglo-American diplomacy was only one option in their strategy, however. The second was to pursue the armed struggle with un-diminished vigour, in which course they were forced to rely on the anti-Western powers for arms and military training. For this reason the Communist factor gained strength as the Anglo-American negotiations became more prolonged—a prolongation due partly, but only partly, to the PF's insistence that any plan for independence should essentially reflect their own ideas about what was acceptable. This duality in the PF's role—co-operating with the West politically while relying increasingly on the East militarily—guaranteed that if Western diplomacy failed, Communist intervention would almost inevitably follow. Another dimension to the progressive internationalization of the Rhodesian problem was Sino-Soviet rivalry. From the beginning of Zanu's armed struggle in the late 1960s, the movement (then still based almost entirely on Tanzania) relied on the Chinese for military support. This prompted the Russians to back the rival Zapu, despite the fact that Nkomo hardly cuts the figure of a revolutionary Marxist. Pragmatist that he is, Nkomo willingly accepted offers of Russian and Cuban assistance, particularly after he began to build up Zipra's numbers to rival those of Zanla. As Kaunda was unwilling to have Russian and Cuban instructors in Zapu camps in Zambia, Nkomo was obliged to transfer his guerrillas to Angola for training—where the Russians and Cubans were *in situ*.

Typical of situations in which rival liberation movements find themselves sup-ported by Moscow and Peking, Nkomo began to make the kind of speeches which would please Moscow and Havana, while Mugabe came increasingly to move in a Maoist direction, the difference between the two being that, by September 1977, Mugabe was genuine in his commitment, describing himself as a Marxist-Leninist of 'Maoist Thought'.[65] Zanu and Zanla cadres were being schooled, not just in guerrilla tactics, but in Maoism as well. During a visit to Peking in May 1977, Mugabe criticized the Russians in familiar Chinese parlance as 'social im-perialists'.[66]

By March 1978, Nkomo no longer denied the support his forces were receiving from the USSR and Cuba. In reply to interviewers who asked whether he thought the Russians and Cubans could become more involved as the fighting increased in Rhodesia, Nkomo said they were already giving him 'all necessary help'.[67] He added that the fighting would be intensified with 'more men, more arms, more war. . . . Things are taking a very dangerous turn. . . . We are reluctant, but we have no alternative.'

THE INTERNATIONAL DIMENSION OF THE SOUTHERN AFRICA CRISIS
AMERICAN POLICY[68]

Testifying before the Africa subcommittee of the House of Representatives' Committee on International Relations, Philip C. Habib, Under-Secretary for Political Affairs, said on 3 March 1977 that 'the whole question of US policy towards Southern Africa is under urgent and comprehensive review within the

Department of State and other concerned executive agencies. I can tell you that the general thrust of our policy review has been to find ways of strengthening the commitment of the US to social justice and racial equality in Southern Africa.' He described US principles and goals in the region as follows: (1) A firm and clear commitment of opposition to racial and social injustice wherever it exists, with a reminder of Carter's personal commitment to human rights. (2) A belief that the people of Africa hold the key to the solution of African problems. While the US would use its political and economic influence and its diplomatic offices to support racial and social progress on the African continent, 'it is not for us, or for any other external power, to attempt to impose its own ideas and solutions'. Another important reason for preferring African solutions is 'to avoid situations which make Africa an arena for great power rivalry, as in Angola'. (3) Prolonged violence in Southern Africa 'could create opportunities for foreign intervention and confrontation'. (4) Recognition that other developed nations also have important interests in Southern Africa, especially Europe and Japan. (5) The US has nothing to fear for its economic and strategic interests from 'the necessary and inevitable achievement of racial equality and social justice in Southern Africa'. (6) The US has a stake in what happens in the region 'because of our belief that political harmony can and must be achieved in diverse societies like our own. . . . Success in achieving orderly transitions to democratic rule in Southern Africa, with protection of human rights for all, will help those everywhere who seek peaceful resolutions to conflict arising from ethnic, racial or religious differences.'

Jimmy Carter's own approach to the problem of Southern Africa was unusual in that he was the first US President who, from his first weeks in office, personally supervised the development of an American policy for Southern Africa—a region that, except for a very brief period in Kennedy's Administration, has hardly figured on the White House agenda. One of Carter's earliest actions was to send his Vice-President, Walter Mondale, to meet with Vorster in Vienna in May 1977 with a clear message that future relations between the two countries would depend on SA moving positively towards democratic rule. [69] Carter's visit to Nigeria and Liberia in 1978 was undertaken primarily to underline US commitment to its African, and especially its Southern African, policy. In Lagos, Carter summed up the aims of this policy as freedom from racism and the denial of human rights, freedom from want and suffering, and freedom from the destruction of war and foreign intervention.

As Vice-President Mondale pointed out in a NBC television programme on 8 November 1977, the key figure in the making of America's African policy was ambassador Andy Young. His approach to the problems of Southern Africa was blurred and often distorted by the American and British Press which focused on his lack of 'diplomacy'. Young's approach to Africa included the following five essentials: (1) By marshalling political and economic forces, it is possible to bring about change without resorting to armed struggle. A combination of pressure and incentive can prove more effective than violence. [70] (2) A peaceful settlement of the problems of Southern Africa is the best way of ensuring that Americans 'who are dependent on the region for 13 natural resources and minerals' will continue to get reasonable access to them. (3) Sanctions are not necessarily the surest way of achieving desired goals, especially if they are not directed at specific targets. (4) The US ought not to have any pre-determined formula for solving SA's problems, but should challenge 'the blanket denials of the rights of the Black majority to participate in the shaping of their destiny'. [71] (5) The US should not seek to force SA into isolation in the world community; the extent to which this was happening was the result of SA's own policies. [72]

Although from early 1978, Young and Brzezinski disagreed about the right way to respond to Soviet and Cuban policies in Africa, the President's National Security Adviser did not challenge the Administration's policies for Southern Africa. Unlike some in the Administration, however, he did not perceive the problems in the region as likely to explode 'in the near future' in a way that would pose a major threat to US policy—an assumption he put forward in a little-criticized 12-page memorandum written to the Black Caucas on 27 December 1977 in response to their 12 recommendations for US policy towards SA. The Brzezinski memorandum begins: 'The discussion which follows must be seen in light of the Administration's general approach to SA. We do not believe that the problem of apartheid and hence the problems in US-SA relations will submit to either an easy or a quick solution. Cataclysmic changes, events or reversals are unlikely. Therefore we see this situation as one whose progress will only be made by determined effort over the long haul. This is the intent behind our actions towards SA. It is also clear that our influence and leverage within SA are limited. We do not have the capacity to greatly influence events from afar according to our will, and therefore our policy must proceed on this basis. As we are operating with limited resources, and as we see this to be a struggle over the long haul, we believe it quite important to husband our limited resources and use them when they promise to do most good.' The 'long haul' view was of course the basic premise of British policy in the 1960s until the changing of the guard in the Foreign Office in late 1976. Like Brzezinski, British policy-makers also argued, and still do, that the UK's leverage and resources are limited.

The Secretary of State, Cyrus Vance, took a position rather closer to Young's than to Brzezinski's. In a number of major speeches, he warned of the need to make quick progress because of the dangers existing in Southern Africa: 'The risk of growing conflict and of increased foreign involvement in the racial disputes in the region 'was real, and violence was growing in SA. . . . A policy of leaving apartheid alone for the moment would be wrong and would not work. . . . The beginning of progress must be made soon in SA if there is to be a possibility of peaceful solutions in the longer run.'

The Administration's African policy was not seriously challenged in Congress—but neither was it significantly supported except by stalwarts on Senator Dick Clark's and Congressman Charles Diggs' sub-committees on Africa. The most professional of the snipers at the Administration's policies was George W. Ball, a former Under-Secretary of State under Kennedy and Johnson, who had won great credit for his steadfast opposition to US policies on Vietnam. On the issues of Southern Africa, he spoke for the great conservative majority of American—and European—public opinion. Only his formidable intellectual approach and polished diplomatic style disguised the placebos he was offering in place of realistic policies. There can be no doubt about Ball's deep loathing of apartheid, but he has chosen to follow other Brahmin diplomats, like the late Dean Acheson and George Kennan, in proposing that neutrality and inactivity are the best ways for the US to influence events in SA: 'No matter how much we abominate the excesses of apartheid, we are not—nor should we become—the ally of any particular South African race, group or faction. . . . Our best chance to discourage any adventures by the Soviets, the Chinese or their surrogates is for us to hold firm to the thesis that this is a South African problem which the people of SA must settle in their own way. . . . No one this side of the Iron Curtain wants a military crisis in SA; that is the last thing we need.'[73] This argument for doing as little as possible, as decently and quietly as possible, while hoping for the maximum benefits, has obvious attractions for those who think that the West should not 'interfere' in SA for fear of upsetting the apple-cart. If Carter's politics fail to yield successes, the Ball thesis is likely to attract influential support, and not just in the US.

BRITISH POLICY[74]

Except for the factor of geographic proximity, Britain is in every sense a Front-line State in Southern Africa: it is internationally responsible for Rhodesia; hundreds of thousands of British subjects or close kinsfolk live in Rhodesia and SA; and its economy is closely interwoven with those of the whole region. In the past these interests have had a severe inhibiting effect on British policy in the region, but concern about them began to take the country in a different direction in 1977. 'We stand to lose more than most if things go wrong', the Foreign Secretary told a Labour Party meeting in Cumbria on 17 March 1978. 'Prudent businessmen and prudent investors, no less than the British Government, should be taking a hard look at their South African connections.' For over 20 years, critics of British policy had been saying just that; it took Angola in 1975 and Soweto in 1976 to make British policy-makers and investors aware that the old order in Southern Africa was in the process of collapsing. Another major new factor contributed to Britain's rethink of its Southern African policy: the changing pattern of British trade between SA and Black Africa, and Nigeria's decision to begin to force Western multinationals to choose between doing business with Nigerians or with the apartheid republic.[75]

Dr Owen signalled a change of course in a major speech he made to Young Fabians in Brighton in October 1977,[76] which received only scant attention in the British Press. Even less notice was taken of a second major statement on the need for policy change (made in a speech in Cumbria in March 1978):

'The very closeness of our economic relationship with SA makes us dangerously vulnerable. Our huge economic involvement in a Republic whose future is uncertain and where the risk of social disruption is high is not only bad politics: it has now become economically risky too. As regards investment, figures are not easily obtainable, but it is generally understood that the total stock of UK investment, including portfolio investment, in SA measured in market values is of the order of £5,000m. This is probably double that of the US or of Germany and greatly exceeds that of France or any other Western country. As far as trade is concerned, our relationship is also closer than that of our partners. British exports to SA in 1976 were worth £653m, somewhat lower than those of the US and Germany, while our imports from SA, at £612m in 1976, were in round figures about double those of Japan, the US and Germany. But another very important consideration is that our exports to Black Africa (£1,329m in 1976) and our imports from Black Africa (£1,058m in 1976) are now almost double the exports to and imports from SA. At the moment we are in the position of depending on SA far more than is healthy if we are to pursue consistent and viable foreign and economic policies. But since we already have economic links with SA, we should use them positively to bring about change. . . . In investment and in trade, this country faces a painful dilemma in its relationship with SA. We must reduce our overdependence on that country economically. We stand to lose more than most if things go wrong.'

Other government spokesmen supported the new line taken by the Foreign Secretary, including the Chancellor of the Exchequer, Denis Healey (see chapter on SA: Relations with Britain).

British policy in Rhodesia and Namibia (as described above) took full account of the risk of the region becoming an outright war zone. Speaking in Dar es Salaam in April 1978, Dr Owen lamented that African leaders appeared to understand far better than some people in Britain the threat of Communist military intervention in Rhodesia and elsewhere if the Western initiatives faltered or made a false step.[77]

EUROPEAN POLICIES

The former West German Chancellor, Willy Brandt, warned in Lusaka early in 1978 of a 'real danger that racial conflict and armed struggle in Southern Africa could plunge the world into a bloody conflict'.[78] A few months later, when Schmidt paid his first visit to Angola and Zambia, he too spoke gloomily about developments in the sub-continent.

The former Swedish Prime Minister, Olof Palme, led a delegation of distinguished social democratic leaders on a fact-finding mission to Southern Africa in June 1977 on behalf of the Socialist International. They subsequently produced a programme of action calling for wide-ranging policy changes by European and other governments.[79] Palme also strongly endorsed the findings of the Stockholm International Peace Research Institute (SIPRI) that Southern Africa may become the next major international battlefield. 'The SIPRI study,' he said, 'also points to the risk of the extensive international investments in SA helping to internationalize the conflict. The country's raw material resources and its strategic position may furnish a pretext for further involvement on behalf of the White dictatorship. At the same time, however, such involvement would encourage the other super-power to become more active in the area. Thus there is a serious risk of Africa becoming a new battlefield between East and West. This is something which is least of all desired by the Africans themselves. In this situation, European social democracy should have the important task of working for peace, liberty and social justice, exactly as we did in Greece and Portugal.'[80]

As discussed above, the European Community began to act in concert on issues affecting Southern Africa in 1977–78, making two démarches to Pretoria over Namibia; endorsing the Anglo-American initiative in Rhodesia; adopting a Code of Conduct for European firms in SA; and sending a collective Note to Pretoria, not just protesting against South African policy, but calling for the revocation of the bannings and the release of prisoners taken during the massive operation to crush the Black Consciousness movement in October 1977.[81] The Note also expressed strong concern about the direction that events were taking in SA and emphasized the need for a peaceful evolution towards the granting of full rights to all of SA's inhabitants.[82] (For further details about the policies of the EEC, see chapter on SA: West European Relations.)

SOVIET UNION'S POLICY

While Moscow's principal African preoccupation during 1977–78 was with the Horn of Africa and in buttressing the MPLA regime in Angola, the Russians were extremely active in Southern Africa. The new emphasis being given to the region was shown by the decision to send President Podgorny on a visit to Mozambique, Zambia, Tanzania, as well as Somalia (before the break with that country).[83] The USSR now has two Treaties of Friendship in the region—with Mozambique and Angola—both of which include Russian commitments to come to the aid of these two Front-line States in case of any military threat to their borders.[84] Moscow's two declared aims in the region are to strengthen the liberation movements and to improve its ties with the Front-line States. Aleksey Nikolayev explained the Soviet's policy of giving 'multilateral aid to freedom fighters' (i.e. through the OAU or African governments): 'A basic characteristic of Soviet help should be underlined. By giving disinterested support to all those fighting against national and social oppression and against capitalist exploitation, the USSR has, contrary to what Rhodesian and South African ministers say, never helped any nationalist movements, that is, any splittist groups. Using the pretext of struggle for national independence, the leaders of those movements are in fact seeking to obtain advantages for themselves and for the imperialist monopolies which are behind them.' He identified the 'splittists' in Angola as Unita, FNLA and FLEC, and added: 'The MPLA alone embodied the interests of the whole nation, and it was this movement which was given the wide support of the socialist countries, above all the Soviet Union and Cuba. In Southern Africa, the USSR supports Swapo in Namibia. In SA, the USSR supports the ANC which operates in alliance with the South African Communist Party. In Zimbabwe, the USSR supports those forces which would not let themselves be influenced by national differences existing between the Shona and the Matebele peoples, and which are now fighting for the liberation of the country from the racist and imperialist rule. This is the core of the Soviet policy towards the national liberation movements. It is totally different from the policy pursued by the imperialist forces which, as Nikolai Podgorny said at a dinner given in honour of the Ethiopian delegation, use a whole series of manoeuvres which are as old as imperialism itself, namely exacerbation of national antagonisms, provocation, blackmail and pitting peoples and countries against one another.'[85]

Nikolayev's explanation raises several interesting issues. The first is the definition of 'splittists' as being all the groups not supported (and therefore mentioned) by the Russians—e.g. Mugabe's Zanu and the PAC of SA, apart from Unita, FNLA, etc. It is also interesting to note that Nikolayev does not identify Nkomo's Zapu as the recipient of Moscow's favours. Did he perhaps forget its name or is there another explanation, perhaps that Moscow supports some elements in Zapu but not the movement as a whole? The emphasis on the alliance between ANC and the South African Communist Party is now standard practice in all Russian broadcasts and is particularly significant in that it is the only case in the history of Moscow's support for liberation movements that a local communist party has been recognized alongside a nationalist movement. This raises important questions about the exact relationship between the ANC and SACP.

As might be expected, Russian commentaries on the Western initiatives over Rhodesia and Namibia all followed the same strongly hostile line: the Anglo-American moves were designed 'to achieve a neo-colonialist settlement',[86] and the Western powers were continuing their 'efforts to impose on the Front-line States their version of a Rhodesian settlement'.[87] The issue never discussed by Russian commentators was why, if Moscow could read Western designs so clearly, the liberation movements like Zapu and Swapo (which have its support) were also not clever enough to see through these 'imperialist' manoeuvres and refuse to join in them? Even more slighting was the suggestion that the Front-line Presidents (who, after all, include some good Soviet friends like Machel and Neto) might somehow be pressured to accept Western settlement conditions. The fact that Machel not only warmly advocated the Anglo-American initiative in Rhodesia, but also commended its plan as offering 'positive elements', might suggest (in Russian eyes) that he had in fact allowed himself to be 'imposed' upon by the 'imperialists'. It is of course possible that the Russians fail to appreciate the insulting nature of this line of propaganda; yet what other line can they take when Marxist and other African Presidents, as well as approved-in-Moscow liberation movements, choose to co-operate with the Western powers in their search for peaceful solutions?

Although the Western initiatives were treated with hostility by the Russians, they might well draw encouragement from the obvious fact that, as yet, the Western powers have no coherent policy to offer for SA, even though they can put together credible solutions for Rhodesia and Namibia.

THE CUBAN POLICY

Fidel Castro's personal entry into the Southern African zone early in 1977 was undoubtedly a great personal triumph—much more so than that of the elderly and rather less glamorous Russian President whose itinerary was overlapped by Castro's.[88] Soviet-Cuban policies in Southern Africa appear to coincide—as they did in Angola and in the Ogaden campaign, if not in Eritrea. In a joint communiqué issued in Moscow on 23 April after a visit by Cuba's Foreign Minister, Isidoro Malmierca Peoli, the two countries pledged support for Swapo, ANC and the PF. The fact that they did not single out Nkomo's wing of the PF for approval and reject Mugabe's was possibly just a tactical decision. Despite this close co-operation between the Cubans and the Russians, African leaders like Kaunda and Nyerere make a clear distinction between the two. They see Cuba as an independent revolutionary country within the Third World, and Russia as one of the super-powers. The question is whether 'the cub' will ever operate in a crisis area without 'the tiger'.

The Cubans acquired a key role in 1977 in the training of Swapo and Zapu guerrillas in Angola. While there are some Cubans in Mozambique, there is no hard evidence to show that they are involved in training the Zanla forces of Mugabe, whose main instruction is provided by the Chinese.

There was considerable speculation in 1978 about whether the Cubans would be willing to become actively involved as combatants in Rhodesia (as they did in Angola and Ogaden) if invited to do so by the PF. According to one reliable source,[89] Cuban diplomats gave firm assurances to Washington that Cubans would not fight inside Rhodesia, although they would continue training Zimbabwe guerrillas. However, since the PF leaders still insist that they must fight their own war, the question may never arise, at least not unless Zimbabwe's independence were followed by a civil war between rival guerrilla forces.

CHINA'S POLICY

Peking's only direct involvement in Southern Africa was through its close political ties with Mugabe's Zanu and its military training programme for the Zanla forces in Tanzania and Mozambique (see above).

China sees Southern Africa 'as one of the explosive spots' in the continent partly because of the rivalries of the two super-powers, but mainly because of the aims of the 'arrogant new tsars'. The official Peking view of the situation is as follows:

'The Soviet Union covets the rich resources there and has for years attempted to seize control of the supply line to Europe from the Indian Ocean round the Cape of Good Hope. Especially since its setback in Egypt, Moscow has stepped up its drive to dominate Southern Africa as part and parcel of its major strategic plan. This constitutes a grave threat to the Southern African people in their struggle against colonial and racist domination and for national liberation. Since the beginning of 1976, the Soviet Press has time and again stressed that the outcome of the Southern African liberation struggle "depends on external factors," in other words, on Soviet interference. . . . To win victory in their liberation struggle, the people of Southern Africa, while intensifying their armed struggle, have engaged the enemy sharply at the negotiating table. However, Moscow resorted to different tricks of deception out of its need to contend with Washington and control this part of Africa. At one time it prattled about "reconciliation" being the "correct line", and at another, it pledged "support" for the armed struggle there.

'What deserves attention is the Soviet stock trick of division and disintegration, a trick it played in Angola and is playing in Southern Africa. It is sowing dissension among the Front-line countries, infiltrating into the liberation movement to split it by supporting one faction and attacking another, and waiting for an opportunity to stir up another fratricidal war among the Africans. Thanks to the lesson of Angola, the people in Southern Africa are fully aware of the consequences of Soviet interference in their liberation struggle. Therefore, they have time and again reaffirmed that the destiny of Southern Africa must be placed in the hands of the people there. Robert Mugabe, a leader of the Zimbabwe Patriotic Front, said: "We will not call in anyone; we flatly refuse refuse to let those who give us help make themselves our masters." A leader of the Pan-Africanist Congress of Azania said: "The Soviet Union pays lip service to supporting the national liberation movements in Africa. Its real aim is to split them. We will never allow the Angola incident to be repeated in Azania," he declared. In the past year, the Southern African people have closely combined the struggle against racism with that against hegemonism, refusing to be taken in by the Soviet Union in its southward offensive and severely punishing the racist regimes. This is bringing about a new situation both in the armed struggle and in the mass movement.

'Playing with fire in the heartland of Africa, the Soviet Union has wilder ambitions than the old-line colonialists. Its strategic goal is to grab the whole of Africa and threaten Western Europe by cutting the African continent right in the middle to facilitate its southward invasion and to isolate and encircle the independent African countries. . . . The new tsars are more crafty than their old colonialist predecessors. They drove mercenaries to the front as cannon-fodder while they themselves remained behind the scenes. Soviet armed invasion of Zaire through mercenaries aroused the African people to action against their common enemy. To fight against aggression, they formed a joint armed force which, in 80 days of bloody fighting, badly battered the Soviet-armed mercenaries and sent them fleeing helter-skelter. Experience of this war against Soviet mercenary invasion opened a new way for the African people to fight future Soviet aggression. The Soviet-paid mercenaries looked powerful when they temporarily succeeded in their armed intervention in Angola in 1976. But their repression and persecution of the masses incurred bitter hatred, and the Angolan people rose in opposition. Guerrilla activity all over Angola has set the mercenaries on tenterhooks.'[90]

NOTES

References are to chapters or essays in *Africa Contemporary Record (ACR)* Vol 10, 1977–78. Unless otherwise mentioned, all the sources quoted are South African newspapers or journals.

1. See *ACR* 1976–77, pp. A3ff.
2. See *ACR* 1975–76, pp. A3ff.
3. See *ACR* 1969–70, pp. C41–45.
4. For text, see *ACR* 1976–77, pp. C159ff.
5. For a discussion of their role, see *ACR* 1976–77, pp. A10–12.
6. See chapter on Namibia.
7. *Sunday Times*, 6 March 1977.
8. *The Observer*, London; 22 May 1977.
9. Radio Johannesburg, 31 October 1977.
10. See *ACR* 1976–77, pp. C157ff.
11. *Ibid*, pp. A41ff.
12. *Rand Daily Mail (RDM)*, 3 February 1977.
13. Statement by Ambassador Young to Security Council on 28 September 1977.
14. For details of Anglo-American initiative, see chapter on Rhodesia.
15. *The Guardian*, Manchester; 4 April 1977.
16. *The Times*, London; 6 June 1977.
17. See essay, 'The Disunited OAU', and Documents section, p. C3.
18. *International Herald Tribune (IHT)*, Paris; 8 July 1977.

19. Speech by Ambassador Young to Security Council on 15 March 1978.
20. *Daily Telegraph*, London; 31 August 1977.
21. For details, see Documents section, pp. C59–72. Also see chapter on Rhodesia.
22. *The Times*, 3 October 1977.
23. See chapter on Rhodesia.
24. *Ibid.*
25. Statements to the House of Commons, 26 January, 3 February and 5 May 1978.
26. Michael Scott, *A Time to Speak* (London: Faber, 1958).
27. For brief background see ISIO monograph by Colin Legum, *The UN and South Africa* (University of Sussex, 1970).
28. See *ACR* 1976–77, pp. B769–70; and chapter on Namibia in this volume.
29. See *ACR* 1976–77, pp. A26–27.
30. See *ACR* 1974–75, pp. A93ff; 1975–76, pp. C93ff.
31. Don McHenry, *US Firms in South Africa* (London: Africa Publications Trust, 1976).
32. Radio Johannesburg, 1 May 1977.
33. Interview on Voice of America, 18 November 1977.
34. Agence France Presse (AFP), 11 April 1977.
35. For details see Documents section, pp. C211–15.
36. *The Times*, 13 February 1978.
37. See chapter on Namibia.
38. *The Observer*, 19 September 1976.
39. *The Star*, 12 February 1977.
40. For text of treaty see Documents section, pp. C17–19. For statement by Machel during a visit to Finland, see *Financial Times (FT)*, London; 5 May 1977.
41. For text of conference resolutions see Documents section, C31–38.
42. *The Times*, 17 May 1977.
43. Radio Lusaka, 25 July 1977.
44. For Commonwealth decisions see Documents section, pp. C44–49.
45. *The Guardian*, 16 August 1977.
46. *The Observer*, 28 August 1977.
47. Radio Lusaka, 7 September 1977.
48. *FT*, 24 September 1977.
49. *IHT*, 7 February 1977.
50. See *ACR* 1975–76, pp. A27–29.
51. *Daily Telegraph*, 26 March 1977.
52. *The Times*, 1 April 1977.
53. For details, see chapter on Zambia.
54. *To the Point*, Brussels; 4 April 1977.
55. *The Observer*, 7 May 1978.
56. See chapter on Rhodesia.
57. *The Guardian*, 22 October 1977.
58. For details of the Smith-Kaunda meeting, see *FT*, 26 October 1977.
59. See essay, 'The Disunited OAU'.
60. Radio Kinshasa, 14 March 1977.
61. For details, see chapters on Zaire and South Africa.
62. *IHT*, 11 February 1977.
63. Radio Lagos, 21 January 1978.
64. See chapter on Rhodesia under Patriotic Front.
65. *Ibid*; also see *Zimbabwe News*, Maputo; Vol 9, No 3, 5 June 1977.
66. *Peking Review*, 1 July 1977.
67. Interview with James Pringle in *Newsweek*, Washington; 6 March 1978.
68. See essay on 'The US Year in Africa'.
69. For text of Mondale statement, see Documents section, pp. C27–31.
70. *The Times*, 20 May 1977.
71. Speech to Security Council, 1 November 1977.
72. *Ibid.*
73. *The Atlantic*, New York; June 1977.
74. See essay, 'Britain's Year in Africa'.
75. This is discussed in the chapters on South Africa and Nigeria.
76. For a summary of Dr Owen's speech, see Documents section, pp. C19–21.
77. *Daily Telegraph*, 17 April 1978.
78. *The Star*, 7 January 1977.
79. See *X-Ray on Southern Africa*, January/February 1978 (London: Africa Bureau).
80. *Socialist Affairs*, London; July–October 1977.
81. See chapter on SA: Black Consciousness.

82. *The Times*, 28 October 1977.
83. See essay, 'Soviet and Chinese Policies in Africa'.
84. See chapter on Mozambique.
85. Radio Moscow, 13 May 1977.
86. Tass, 11 July 1977.
87. Radio Moscow, 5 April 1977.
88. See essay, 'Cuba: The New Communist Power in Africa'.
89. Jonathan Steele in *The Guardian*, 15 April 1978.
90. *Peking Review*, 6 January 1978.

PART II:

South Africa

South Africa

Political, economic and international trends in 1977 and early 1978 all served to underscore the fact that 1976 marked a watershed in the modern history of the Republic of South Africa (SA).[1] 1977 was the year in which the Republic's facade of internal stability was finally shattered; it marked the beginning of a new and sharper confrontation between entrenched White power and its Black challengers; and it shook Western political and economic confidence in the Republic's ability to maintain its existing system. In the words of the SA banker, Dr Frans Cronje, the events of 1977 emphasized that 'past political and social stability is at an end, or ending'.[2] The eruption of Black anger in the urban areas, triggered by the protest movement of Soweto's schoolchildren on 16 June 1976, continued to mount and find political expression through Black Consciousness. This in turn inevitably led to the draconian banning in October 1977 of all organizations, leaders and newspapers most closely concerned with the Black Consciousness movement. The severity of this repression was symbolized by the violent death of the charismatic leader of the movement, Steve Biko, at the hands of the security forces. His close friend, Donald Woods, former editor of the East London *Daily Dispatch*—who was himself banned in October and then escaped from the Republic—put the circumstances of Biko's death into historic focus: '. . . Things have never been worse in this country, from every important point of view, than right now. Apartheid is on direct collision course with Black anger as never before, and the Afrikaner Nationalists who rule us are seriously underestimating the depth and scope of this anger. They underestimate it because they are ill-informed about the realities of their own country; and they are ill-informed about it because they have so cocooned themselves and cut themselves off from it in almost total separation that today they are living in a world of unrealistic whiteness, socially, economically and politically. It is a world of parades, medal presentations, civic ceremonial and linguistic exclusivity. Rousing in-group songs are sung, and party rallies are occasions for mutual reassurance—and dangerous complacency.'[3]

The extensive bannings, arrests and other forms of repression predictably served only to widen the racial cleavage, which is the rotting core of SA society. The powerful White minority of 4m—while willing to undertake extensive modifications within the existing political system—refused to contemplate *meaningful* change, which essentially would involve a readiness to share political power with the Black majority of 21m. That percipient SA political writer, Stanley Uys, summed up the situation in this way: 'Wherever one goes in SA today, one has to listen to this unreal debate about whether "we will pull through" or whether "things will be all right". Of course they will not be all right. Blacks have started now in earnest to fight for their rights, and Whites are resisting them. The result can only be conflict, and increasing conflict; and because Blacks outnumber Whites five to one they have the capacity eventually to plunge the country into one crisis after the next. . . . The power struggle in SA today is between Blacks on one side and Afrikaner nationalists on the other, and the only imponderable factor in the situation is—how much destruction will the Afrikaner nationalists inflict on the country before they are forced to come to their senses? My own guess is that the destruction will be considerable. Afrikaner nationalists are more than a political party: they are a living organism. For the past 50 years or longer, they have painstakingly woven the threads of Afrikaner nationalism into the very fabric of SA life, through a multiplicity of organizations and laws, control of key jobs and institutions, and an all-pervasive influence.'[4]

These internal developments would be serious enough without the immensely complicating fact of SA being seen more and more as a world problem. This is because the struggle of a Black African majority for its rights gives the conflict a continental dimension; because human rights have become a major international concern, especially since President Carter's assumption of office; and because of the longstanding Western connection with the Republic (which depends heavily on continued support from Europe and North America). It was thus inevitable that one day the West would be compelled to take stock of and assume responsibility for its role in SA.

More than 20 years ago, a group of SA intellectuals forecast that the Republic's political destiny would be determined by the interplay of 'increasing internal explosions and growing external pressures'. The accuracy of this analysis has been shown by the increasing pressures mounted by the world community after each new internal explosion—Sharpevill in 1960, Swoeto in 1976, and the October 1977 clampdown on Black Consciousness.

More than 20 years ago, a group of SA intellectuals forecast that the Republic's political destiny would be determined by theinterpaly of 'increasing internal explosions and growing external pressures'. The accuracy of this analysis has been shown by the increasing pressures mounted by the world community after each new internal explosion—Sharpeville in 1960, Soweto in 1976, and the October 1977 clampdown on Black Consciousness. While increasing pressures on the one hand, the West has steadily distanced itself from SA on the other, leaving the White minority feeling abandoned by its traditional friends and isolated at the most difficult hour in its history. This threat of isolation was acutely felt in 1977 when the possibility of economic sanctions came to be accepted as very real, especially after the Security Council's decision in November 1977 to make the arms embargo mandatory.

Until 1976, the West still believed that compared with the rest of the continent and despite its internal crisis, SA was essentially stable and a safe place for foreign investment. That misconception was dispelled by the evidence of urban Black discontent and by the failure of the 'independent' Homelands' policy to produce an acceptable basis for 'power-sharing'. The last lingering hope that these Bantustans would promote better race relations was extinguished by the rash but predictable action of the Transkei in breaking off diplomatic relations with Pretoria in April 1978. Foreign investors began to have second thoughts about their stake in the Republic; some actually started to disengage; many more decided not to increase their capital investment. The international money market began to cold-shoulder SA requests for short-term loans. Nigeria played a major role in accelerating Western economic disengagement through its policy of compelling Western multinationals to make a choice between doing business with Nigeria or with the Apartheid Republic. (Since Nigeria has become a more important market for most Western countries than SA, there was considerable clout behind the Nigerian challenge.)

These accumulating pressures have forced White South Africans to accept the necessity of change, but while intensifying debate about possible constitutional reform, they did not yet feel compelled to surrender any political power, nor begin genuine consultations with representative Black leaders. Instead, the Government chose to work out a constitutional alternative of its own. This the Prime Minister submitted to his exclusively White electorate, at the same time asking it to close ranks behind the Afrikaner nationalist leadership in a display of unity to the outside world. Yet in spite of achieving the most resounding electoral victory ever gained by a SA Prime Minister, Vorster was still not able to implement his constitutional proposals, both because of opposition from the Indian and Coloured leadership (who stood to gain something from the proposed changes), and because of continued divisions within his own ranks. Meanwhile, a new approach to constitution-making began to emerge, with proposals for institutions which would reflect the pluralist nature of SA's society—an adaptation of Swiss confederalism. But these, too, would exclude the African majority from sharing in a single parliamentary system.

Another increasingly evident political current was the growing influence of the military on a society girding itself for what the generals described as 'total war', though a 'war of low intensity'.[5] What these generals seemed to be advocating was some form of military regime (see below). Maj-Gen N. Webster contended that a strong defence force would underwrite political stability and economic potential and would 'allow necessary changes (that must develop in the socio-political order of the country) to come about in an orderly and secure manner'. The army chief, Gen Magnus Malan, was only a little less vague when he talked of the 'conflicting requirements of a total strategy and a democratic system of government'. Since the generals were advocating preparations for 'a total war', the natural assumption was that where this conflicted with 'a democratic system', the former must prevail.

This recommendation that the Republic commit itself to a 'total strategy' for survival (the phrase is Gen Malan's), inevitably raised the question, both inside and outside the country, what SA's chances of 'survival' were anyway—meaning the survival of a White-dominated State. Lord Goodman, the noted British lawyer and political trouble-shooter, visited SA in mid-1977 and found it 'a world of tragic disillusion'.[6] He wrote: 'SA today presents a problem of historic difficulty with a system which excludes the vast majority of the population from participation in human rights. Will it survive or will it go down in flames and carnage? Is it a remote possibility that the world will enjoy the boundless felicity of seeing good emerge from evil and men of all colours, irrespective of numerical preponderance, living in peace and harmony? It is probably the greatest challenge presented to any community. Only a very worthy community could hope to achieve it.'

Judged purely in terms of its economic and military strength and the undoubted commitment of White South Africans to using this power to ensure their survival, the Republic's position would seem, if not impregnable, at least fairly secure. But such an evaluation fails to take into account two critical factors: SA's long-term dependence on powerful Western economic and diplomatic backing, and the system's devastating internal contradictions. Both these factors are likely to be crucial in deciding the Republic's future, the latter in particular. In spite of 30 years' commitment to 'separating the races'—quite regardless of the cost in terms of money or human suffering[7]—the races are actually more closely integrated within a single society today than ever before. Not only are there about twice as many Africans in what is still regarded as 'White SA' than when apartheid policies were introduced in 1948, but the Government was finally forced in 1977 to backtrack on the crucial point of treating urban Blacks as part of a permanently settled community within 'White' towns and cities. For the first time in 1978 they were given the right to buy their own homes on 99-year leases, which virtually means permanent tenure. Strict segregation in private schools and churches was modified. Many more Black workers now do semi-skilled and even skilled work; Job Reservation, intended to protect White jobs, has to all intents and purposes become a dead letter; and Blacks in larger numbers are now recruited into the army. The original apartheid policy of repatriating Indians has been replaced by a proposal to give them a place, along with the Coloureds, in a three-tier multiracial Cabinet system.

In social terms, the most remarkable change has been the degree to which the authorities have closed their eyes to social mixing in public places—something regarded as the deadliest of all sins in Afrikaner traditional mores. Nightclubs like 'Club New York City' and 'Las Vegas' are allowed to operate openly in Johannesburg, where Whites and Blacks drink and dance *together* and no doubt mix sexually as well—in violation of the Immorality Act. Once a cornerstone of apartheid policy, the repeal of this Act was publicly advocated by two senior ministers in the Government.[8] The walls of White society—far from having been reinforced by the rigorous separation laws—have in fact crumbled in ways that would have seemed impossible only a decade ago.

Another crucial factor has been the effect of SA's domestic policies on its international economic creditworthiness. The Minister of Economic Development, Chris Heunis, admitted in April 1978 that the shortage of new capital for development remained 'one of the country's biggest problems. He suggested that there would be no point in South African soldiers fighting on the border if there were political and economic instability at home.[9] The Natal Chamber of Industry reported that 'international hostility' was having a serious effect on the domestic economy.[10] For the first time ever, the first quarter of 1977 saw a net *outflow* of long-term capital. The estimated outflow for the whole of 1977 was R1,000m (cf a net inflow of R1,900m in 1975)—a staggering turnabout of almost R3,000m.[11]

The nervousness of foreign capital, compounded by balance of trade problems, had the effect of increasing unemployment among Africans—a sensitive factor at a time of growing Black discontent. The executive director of the Associated Chambers of Commerce, Raymond Parsons, predicted that more than 1m Black workers would be unemployed by 1981. The chairman of Nedbank, Dr Frans Cronje, warned that if present employment rates were to be maintained and more jobs created for those already out of work, the economy would have to grow by 7-8% per year, far above present rates which depend in part on the continued inflow of foreign capital.[12]

The restoration of international economic confidence depends essentially on two requirements: evidence of an improved security situation and of meaningful change to defuse the risk of a racial conflagration. To judge by events in 1977 and the first half of 1978, the evidence was all in the opposite direction. Conflict along the border with Angola increased significantly during this period, while the number of acts of political violence inside the country also rose sharply: the threat of urban and external guerrilla action had to be taken much more seriously. In June 1978, Brig C. F. Zietsman, Chief of Security, disclosed that 2,000 SA guerrillas were being trained in neighbouring countries;[13] sophisticated weapons were also discovered smuggled into Soweto and other places. Armed violence in SA was clearly on an escalator—and no longer just from the government side.

Another significant indicator was the drying up of new White immigrants. In 1977, for the first time, there were more people leaving the country than entering it (see below).[14]

Part of official SA mythology, that Whites in the country are entitled to their place because they moved into present-day SA at about the same time as 'the Bantu' were coming in from the north, was again disproved in 1977. Using finds from the St Lucia Lake area, an ethno-archaeologist at Natal University, Martin Hall, proved by carbon testing that Black people were living there from 300 AD.[15] Whites arrived in Natal in the 1830s and in the Cape Province in 1652.

Yielding to sustained African objections to being officially classified as 'Bantu' (a linguistic generic), the Government finally agreed in 1978 to use the term 'Blacks'.

At the same time, the Bantu Affairs Department was renamed the Department of Plural Relations and Development.

FOUR AREAS OF CONFRONTATION
1. WHITE NATIONALISM VERSUS BLACK CONSCIOUSNESS
The conventional triptych of South African history depicts a struggle among 'Boer, Briton and Bantu'. While this adequately represents a facet of the political evolution of the modern Republic, it fails to illuminate the three basically different political ideas which, over the last three centuries, have contested for supremacy: White nationalism, Black nationalism and a shared society based on democratic pluralism. Until 1948, the two leading contenders were the first and the third. The 1948 triumph of apartheid—the political philosophy of Afrikaner nationalism—had two results: it greatly weakened the political forces favouring the idea of a shared society (now represented in Parliament by only 17 Progressive Federal Party MPs); and it stimulated the growth of Black Consciousness.

The murder of Steve Biko by security police on 12 September 1977 and the total repression of the Black Consciousness movement and its White allies a month later underline two realities about the present situation: the overwhelming physical power still held by the defenders of White supremacy, and the fear felt by these powerful forces of the putative strength of a Black Consciousness movement.

The originator of Black Consciousness, Robert Mangaliso Sobukwe, who founded the Pan-Africanist Congress (PAC), died of cancer in March 1978.[16] During the 18 years he had spent as a prisoner and a banned person, his ideas were further developed and popularized by the SA Students' Organization (SASO) under the leadership of Steve Biko. Biko outlined his two central ideas in a message to the conference of African and American leaders held in Maseru in December 1976: '. . . Since the thesis is a White racism, there can only be one valid antithesis, i.e. a solid Black unity to counter-balance the scale. If SA is to be a land where Black and White live in harmony without fear of group exploitation, it will only be when these two opposites have interplayed and produced a viable synthesis of ideas and *modus vivendi*. We can never wage any struggle without offering a strong counterpoint to the White racism that permeates our society so effectively. One must immediately dispel the thought that Black Consciousness is merely a methodology or a means towards an end. What Black Consciousness seeks to do is to produce at the output end of the process real Black people who do not regard themselves as appendages to White society.'[17]

The initial reaction of the Afrikaner Establishment to the development of Black Consciousness was on the whole strongly favourable, since it expected the movement to encourage Africans to shape a separate political future for themselves rather than to continue demanding participation within the central institutions of 'White South Africa'. This complete misreading of the thrust of Black Consciousness was made evident by the traumatic urban revolt by Black youth which began in Soweto on 16 June 1976 and spread to most urban centres throughout the Republic. Although it was possible to contain the violent nature of the protest, it was clear by October 1977 that the Black Consciousness movement was becoming a serious threat to the apartheid regime.

THE EVENTS OF OCTOBER 1977
A little over a month after Biko's death and shortly before the inquest findings were due to be announced, the regime cracked down on the Black Consciousness movement and its White allies with the same comprehensive repression as was shown in outlawing the Congress movements after the Sharpeville shootings in

1960. It declared 18 African organizations and the Christian Institute illegal, arrested 40 prominent Black leaders, closed down the two leading newspapers for Africans, and banned seven prominent Whites. The banned organizations were:

The Black People's Convention (BPC) founded in December 1971. In February 1977, Steve Biko was made honorary president. The convener of the BPC's first national convention was Drake Koka, former Transvaal vice-chairman of the Liberal Party. Its president at the time of the banning was Hlaku Rachidi.

The Black Parents' Association, founded after the 1976 Soweto unrest. Its chairman was Dr Manas Buthelezi, a respected churchman. Executive members included Dr Aaron Matlhare, Mrs Winnie Mandela, the wife of Nelson Mandela, and Father Smangaliso Mkhatshwa, a Roman Catholic priest.

The SA Students' Organization (SASO), founded in the late 1960s by Black university students, led by medical students at the University of Natal. Its entire executive was banned in 1974, and in 1977 nine former members were sentenced to between five and six years' imprisonment after the longest Terrorism Act trial in SA. Its members included Steve Biko.

The Soweto Students' Representative Council (SSRC), which came to prominence shortly before the June 1976 unrest. It was made up of high school pupils.

The South African Students' Movement (SASM), a nationwide organization for high school pupils, founded in 1970. It established a cultural wing, the National Youth Organization, with branches in all provinces.

The National Youth Organization (NAYO), an educational and cultural youth organization, formed in 1973. Many of its members belonged to SASM. Affiliates of NAYO also banned included the Border Youth Organization, the Eastern Province Youth Organization, the Natal Youth Organization, the Transvaal Youth Organization and the Western Cape Youth Organization.

The Association for the Educational and Cultural Advancement of Africans (ASSECA), formed in 1969 by the late Soweto civic leader, P. Q. Vundla. Launched the R1m fund for African education.

The Black Women's Federation, formed in Durban in 1975. Within a year, no less than seven of its members were detained. Mrs Winnie Mandela was the first BWF executive member to be banned. The Federation's first president, Natal sociologist Mrs Fatima Meer, was banned during the same month.

Black Community Programmes, which broke away from Spro-cas (see below) to become autonomous in March 1973. A Black self-help body which organized welfare projects in King William's Town, Durban and Soweto. Within its first few months, four of its leading members, including Steve Biko, had been banned.

The Zimele Trust Fund, a charitable organization started in King William's Town to aid political prisoners and their families. It established the Zanempilo Clinic in King William's Town, whose director, Dr Mamphela Ramphele, was banned and restricted to the Northern Transvaal.

The Medupe Black Writers' Union—popularly known as Medupe, a word meaning 'rain which falls incessantly'. Formed at the beginning of 1976 and originally called the Azanian People's Poetry and Writers' Association, it had more than 200 members.

The Union of Black Journalists, formed in 1973. With a nationwide membership of more than 100 Black, Asian and Coloured journalists, it consistently refused to have dealings with the former predominantly White SA Society of Journalists, to which Africans could not belong.

The Christian Institute, formed in 1963, had a membership of 2,000 when banned. In conjunction with the SA Council of Churches, the CI sponsored the 'Study Project on Christianity in Apartheid Society' (Spro-cas), which produced ten reports on various aspects of SA society. It consistently rejected violence as a means for fundamental change. Two of its office-bearers fled the country without passports, Horst Kleinschmidt and Mrs Oshadi Phakathi. The CI was the only multiracial organization banned and one of the few multiracial organizations which had credibility among Blacks.

The two banned newspapers were *The World*, the second largest daily paper in the country, with a circulation of 147,193 and an estimated readership of 891,000; and its sister paper, the *Weekend World*, which had a circulation of 204,207 and an estimated readership of 1.788m. In the seven years of his editorship, Percy Qoboza (who was among those banned) had turned 'a rather grey fence-sitting paper into a voice reflecting hard-hitting Black opinion'.[18] Although owned by the Argus newspaper group, *The World* had come to be regarded by Black South Africans as their own newspaper. In 1975, Qoboza spent ten months at Harvard University on a Nieman fellowship. A devout Roman Catholic, his first incursion into politics was as a supporter of the Progressive Party with which he shared a vision of a truly multiracial SA. He was shot in the stomach in 1973 by an unknown assailant and has since suffered from serious stomach ulcers.

Qoboza was the fifth *World* journalist to be detained. Three others—Joe Thloloe, Willia Bokala and Moffat Zungu—were held for their reporting of events in Soweto. The fifth, Aggrey Klaaste, *Weekend World*'s news editor, was detained with Qoboza.

Among the 40 leaders of the banned organizations—known collectively as 'The Soweto Committee of Ten'—who were themselves banned or arrested were Dr Ntatho Motlana, chairman of 'The Soweto Committee of Ten', and Kenneth Rachidi, president of BPC. Many others were students and leaders of women's groups.

The following seven Whites were banned: (1) The Rev C.F. Beyers Naude (62), who left the Dutch Reformed Church and resigned from the Broederbond (see below) in 1960 after the Sharpeville shootings which he said had opened his eyes to the true dimensions of the racial conflict in SA. He founded the Christian Institute as a multiracial ecumenical movement. (2) Cedric Radcliffe Mayson (50), the British-born editor of the Christian Institute's *Pro Veritate*, who came to SA from Britain in 1953 and became a SA citizen. He was a Methodist minister for 20 years. (3) The Rev Theo Kotze, an Afrikaner and the Cape Director of the Christian Institute. (4) The Rev Brian Brown, a member of the Johannesburg staff of the CI. (5) The Rev David Russell, an Anglican priest who won recognition for his work in the resettlement village of Dimbaza and subsequently for opposing population removals. (6) Peter Randall, a former president of the Liberal Party and director of *Spro-cas*. (7) Donald Woods (44), editor of the East London *Daily Dispatch* and correspondent of the London *Observer*. He had made the *Dispatch* one of the leading campaigning newspapers against apartheid. An intimate friend of Steve Biko, about whom he wrote a book while under detention,[19] he escaped from SA to Britain in January 1978.

The official reasons given for the clampdown by the Minister of Justice, J. T. Kruger, reflected the alarm felt about the danger of 'a revolutionary climate' being created.[20] He said: 'People who think that the Government will allow itself to be intimidated or dictated to are making a big mistake. The Government is determined to ensure that the peaceful coexistence of peoples in SA is not disturbed by a small group of anarchists. The situation will thus be watched closely, and if necessary new measures will be considered. Grievances initially presented as the causes have long since disappeared into the background. New grievances, new objectives and new processes are being brought into focus practically day by day to ensure that the unrest continues and in an attempt to achieve the desired confrontation between White and Black. A relatively small group is taking the lead in this, but use is made of a whole number of organizations, and of many human vehicles. Much damage has already been done in the process and much suffering caused. . . . Police action was largely successful. The big organizers, however, keep themselves in the background and continue to use . . . almost exclusively young people for the creation of a revolutionary climate and for the organization of unrest. As has already been said many times, all grievances will be investigated and, where justified, eliminated.'

The lines of confrontation drawn by the regime were explicitly stated by the pro-Government paper, *Die Beeld*: 'There can be freedom of speech if media across the colour lines accept that the Government is not opposed to change, but that the process must be controlled; otherwise there will be anarchy. With this must come acceptance of the philosophy of group politics; those whose ideologies are opposed to it will get confrontation.'[21] 'There you have it,' wrote Allister Sparks, editor of the *Rand Daily Mail*.[22] 'Group politics, i.e. Separate Development, must be accepted. Those who have different ideologies will get confrontation (and you know what that means!) Their freedom of speech will not be tolerated, because it will be said that it runs the risk of causing anarchy. You can plead for change—but only if you accept the Nationalist Government's willingness to introduce it, and that it can only be introduced through the system of Separate Development. Which is not very different from Russia, where people can plead for anything they like so long as it is communism. And even have elections, so long as the only candidates are communists.'

White and Black opposition in the Republic reacted with deep dismay. Stan Uys wrote: 'SA crossed some kind of Rubicon last week. In the words of its Minister of the Interior and Information, Dr Mulder, it had to decide which came first—its international reputation or internal security. It has chosen the latter. SA's course has been set for the next grim stage of the apartheid saga.'[23] He added that the bannings would have two results: 'To eliminate the last tenuous vestiges of contact, or channels of communications, between the Government and protesting Blacks; and to drive the Black struggle even further underground, so that it will only be able to manifest itself in future in unpredictable mass demonstrations or in fresh waves of recruits for the Black guerrilla organizations scattered around southern Africa. The authorities justified last week's security clampdown by saying that the time had come to clean up the Black unrest. They have been saying this for the past 30 years of National Party rule, and with each successive action the problem has become more stubborn and the solution more elusive.'

The *Financial Mail* (21 October 1977) published an editorial headed 'Into the Darkness': '. . . One thing is certain. Kruger's action has taken SA another step away from the possibility of peaceful racial reconciliation and further down the road that leads to violence. For in the longer run what is much more important than Kruger's motives is the answer to the question: what is going through the mind of SA's Black world at this very moment? It has been robbed not only of a courageous newspaper and many of its most clear-sighted and articulate leaders, but probably also of much of whatever faith it might still have had that SA's problems could be solved in a peaceful way. Kruger appears to have learned only half the lesson of the history of SA in the sixties. Bannings and mass detentions in the wake of Sharpeville and the passive resistance campaign did indeed eventually restore a semblance of calm to the country and prevent organizations like the ANC and PAC from initiating further defiance campaigns. But the other half of the lesson is that these organizations then went underground, and some of their members began plotting sabotage in secret. Still others went into exile, where some of them were trained as guerrillas with a view to fighting apartheid and unjust laws by military action. There can be little doubt that their ranks are now going to be joined by township Africans who no longer have a Committee of Ten, a Black People's Convention, or a Soweto SRC to speak for them.' The accuracy of this prediction was shown by the statement just six months later by Brig C. F. Zietsman, Chief of Security, who said that many of the youngsters who had fled Soweto had joined the ranks of the guerrillas (see Security, below).

The *Star* (20 October 1977) wrote: 'Repression in a land that has already experienced democracy and freedom is a bitter admission of failure'. The editor of the pro-Government *Die Vaderland*, Dirk Richard, admitted that the action represented a 'very drastic step that would have worldwide repercussions'. [24]

Reactions in the Western world were sharper than anything known hitherto. The US recalled its ambassador for urgent consultations. The White House spokesman, Hodding Carter, said: 'It has been our hope that the South African Government would recognize dialogue with all segments of the society as the prerequisite to peaceful progress and lasting social tranquillity. However we have now witnessed unfortunate actions that seem to represent a very serious step backwards.' The US ambassador to the UN, Andrew Young, said that America would not use its veto to stop a Security Council decision against SA. 'If we use our veto, it would undermine America's entire African policy.' He added that Western attempts to persuade African countries to be reasonable were being thwarted by South Africa's unreasonableness. [25] Britain and West Germany also recalled their ambassadors for consultation. The British Foreign Secretary, Dr David Owen, said the SA Government's actions 'run counter to our most cherished ideals of personal liberty and free speech'. [26] The Conservative spokesman for foreign affairs, John Davies, said he would be taken if the disorders in the Black townships did not end.
Pretoria's actions had made the immediate situation more tense, as well as inflicting a setback on the long-range reconciliation between SA and the West. [27]

However, Vorster dismissed this Western criticism as 'irrelevant'. For ten months, he said, the Carter Administration had been trying to make policy for SA. 'It would be nice for a change if they make their own policy.' His Government was not prepared to allow itself to be prescribed to on how it ran its own affairs, 'neither today nor tomorrow'. [28]

The bannings produced widespread new disorder. At Queenstown, an African was wounded and 12 others arrested when they attacked a house in which a policeman had taken refuge. At Peddie, near East London, 14 youngsters were arrested for stoning a school; at Stinkwater, near Pretoria, 300 youths attacked buses. In the Venda Homeland, 18 vehicles were set on fire. In the Lebowa Homeland, an attempt was made to burn down the administrative building. At Sharpeville, 54 arrests were made, with 30 in King William's Town. The head of BOSS (see below), Gen Hendrik van den Bergh, warned that 'even sterner action' would be taken if the disorders in the Black townships did not end.

At the UN, the Africa Group demanded total mandatory sanctions against SA over the bannings. When the Western nations refused to go so far, the Security Council adopted a motion making the arms embargo against SA mandatory. This received unanimous support (see below).

2. THE VORSTER REGIME VERSUS THE WHITE ELECTORATE

Notwithstanding the Prime Minister's granite-like rejection of any suggestion that apartheid should be scrapped, he is by no means unpersuaded of the need to make fundamental changes (see Prime Minister's role, below). Thus, in a speech at Stellenbosch in March 1978, he said he believed there must be reform and that changes would come, but that these should be introduced 'practically and in a planned way'.[29] Vorster spelled out the limits of his reformist policies in a major statement to the Association of Chambers of Commerce in April 1977.[30] While he pledged the government to provide all race groups with an increased stake in the economic system and to do away as quickly as possible with 'petty racial discrimination', he insisted that on some fundamental points there would be no yielding: 'These include the right of our White people to retain control of their own destiny, the maintenance of law and order and the determination of the kind of economic system under which we are to live and work.'

Vorster's essential problem, however, lies in persuading his White electorate—which holds all effective power in parliament—to support even such a limited reform programme as he envisages. The dilemma of all South African Prime Ministers has been how to move in new directions without getting too far ahead of their White electorate who have traditionally either rejected their initiatives or dumped them altogether. In this sense, even the strongest Prime Minister remains a prisoner. An additional complication of this exclusive entrenchment of political power is that the electoral system gives preponderance to the mainly Afrikaner voters in rural areas—the most conservative element in the country. *Platteland* (rural) MPs in the ruling party's parliamentary caucas form a fairly solid reactionary bloc which exercises a veto over the policies of the Government. In the past, the caucas has blocked Vorster's most modest attempts to implement a less rigid colour bar in sports. If the Prime Minister has trouble in getting even his sports policy through parliament, it hardly needs saying that, even if he wished, he could not win his caucas' support to introduce meaningful political rights for Blacks.

Vorster tried to face up to this problem in 1977—not by satisfying African political aspirations, but by bringing Coloureds and Indians into the political system. He hoped that his proposed constitutional changes (see below) would achieve three results. First, by incorporating the Coloureds and Indians into the political system, the 1:5 numerical disproportion between Whites and non-Whites would be diminished. With the Coloureds, Indians and Whites together, the proportion would become 1:3. Second, by making the Prime Minister responsible to three Cabinets instead of one, his policies would no longer be subjected to the exclusive control of his own caucas, thus giving him more room for manoeuvre and increasing his personal power to take decisions. Third, he could hope to persuade the Western powers that SA was moving in the direction of meaningful change.

However, two essential conditions had to be met by Vorster to ensure the success of his new constitutional proposals. First, he had to persuade the representative Coloured and Indian leaders that the new deal and the new alignment would compensate for breaking off their political ties with the Africans. Second, he had to be assured of the support of his own parliamentary caucas. That was a major reason for his decision to hold an early election: he hoped that all ruling party MPs who agreed to stand and campaign for the new constitutional proposals would continue to support them in parliament. Yet, even though the ruling party won a resounding electoral victory (see below), his tactics nevertheless failed. The Coloured leaders, in particular, refused to swallow the bait, and the new parliamentary caucas was more critical of the constitutional proposals than was consistent with its support for them during the election campaign. Thus, although Vorster had led everybody to expect that parliament would be asked to adopt the new constitution, in January 1978 he was forced to announce that no legislation would be passed—'probably' before 1979.[31] He explained that legal advisers required 'some time' to prepare the necessary legislation.

3. SOUTH AFRICA VERSUS THE WEST

SA's oldest haunting fear has been that it might one day find itself 'abandoned' by the West—to which its White leadership feels it belongs—and so end up totally isolated within the world community. Never has it come so close to seeing this fear realized than in 1977. But although its only hope of averting this disaster lay in adopting policies that could be more easily defended by Western governments, it chose instead to move in precisely the opposite direction—as exemplified by its further repression of Black opposition in October 1977. The Vorster regime therefore landed itself in a double crisis: the one external, the other internal. A resolution of the former depended on overcoming or at least diminishing the latter, whereas the deepening internal crisis could only widen the gulf between the Republic and the West.

The hostility of the Communist world and of much of the Third World has never seriously troubled the Pretoria regime; what mattered was its ability to keep communications open with a sizable part of Black Africa and with the major Western powers. However, SA's disastrous intervention in Angola in 1976[32] virtually paralysed its strenuous efforts to sustain a dialogue with the rest of the continent.[33] The only significant Black states still willing to talk to Pretoria in 1977 were the Ivory Coast, Zaire and Malawi; even Senegal refused to have any further talks. This meant that it was no longer possible for the Vorster regime to take any independent diplomatic initiative in Africa. Yet, as Vorster himself was to acknowledge in 1977, SA's only way of winning back the West lay in winning over Africa (see Prime Minister's role, below). Although he no longer expected friendship from the Western nations, he still continued to hope for Western 'understanding' of the Republic's difficulties and, above all, for continuing economic, military and diplomatic links which, he argued, were necessary to defend mutual interests. He repeatedly said that he could not understand how the West failed to see that its best interests lay in a strong SA. On the other hand, the Western leadership could not understand why Vorster failed to appreciate that an alliance with the apartheid Republic would marvellously suit Russian interests.

In the hope of reaching some *modus vivendi* with the new Carter Administration, Vorster went to Vienna in May 1977 for talks with Vice-President Walter Mondale. But far from getting onto a better footing with Washington, Vorster found himself faced with what could rightly be regarded as an ultimatum. Carter's message was that White SA could expect no support from the US unless there was progress on 'majority rule for Rhodesia and Namibia, and a progressive transformation of SA society to the same end'. (For the full transcript of Mondale's Vienna Press statement, see Documents section, pp. C27–31.) Mondale made it clear that the US did not expect changes to come overnight, but that steps should be taken towards the ultimate goal of a democratic society. The decisive change in Washington's position was marked by Mondale's carefully-worded warning: 'We hope that SA will carefully review the implications of our policy and the changed circumstances which it creates. We hope that South Africans will not rely on any illusions that the US will in the end intervene to save SA from the policies it is pursuing, for we will not do so.' In other words, if SA found itself in a military conflict with Africans— even if they had Communist support—the US would not intervene militarily to defend apartheid.

On his return home, Vorster announced that the US had demanded that he give one-man one-vote to everybody in the Republic. This he vowed he would never agree to. In fact, however, Mondale did not himself mention universal franchise: that question was raised in the meeting by Vorster when he asked Mondale whether his idea of democracy included the principle of one-man, one-vote. To this question, Mondale could give only one possible reply: the equal right of every person to vote was certainly the way Americans interpreted democracy. But it was not one of the US demands; Mondale had deliberately not put forward any specific proposals.

Despite the shock of Vienna, Vorster agreed to co-operate both in the Anglo-American plan to achieve majority rule in Rhodesia, and in negotiating with the five Western members of the Security Council, the so-called Contact Group (comprising the US, UK, France, West Germany and Canada). This was in an attempt to find an agreement for Namibia's independence acceptable to both SA and to Swapo, which also admitted the element of one-man, one-vote. However, he broke ranks with the West in giving his strong backing to the 'internal settlement' in Rhodesia. He also seriously prejudiced the Western initiative on Namibia by sending South African troops deep into Angola to attack Swapo camps in the last crucial days of negotiations at the UN in May 1978.

However, two more critical issues which changed SA-Western relations were the October 1977 action against the Black Consciousness movement and the plans to test a nuclear device in the Kalahari. While the permanent Western members of the Security Council (US, UK and France) used their veto to block comprehensive mandatory sanctions against SA in October, they readily voted for action under Chapter Seven of the UN Charter to make the arms embargo both compulsory and all-inclusive. The previous embargo was not mandatory, which allowed France, in particular, to contribute to SA's 'external defence'. The French change of policy was a particularly severe blow for SA, cutting off its only major source of Western arms. The French also shocked SA by the severity of their response to the air satellite pictures showing that a nuclear device test was imminent. Although the US, UK and other European countries all warned SA not to engage in nuclear testing, only the French threatened diplomatic and economic sanctions if the warnings were ignored (see Nuclear Power and Foreign Affairs, below).

A question frequently posed by the SA Government was what exactly the Western powers were asking of it. The answer was given in October 1977 in a 'Declaration on Southern Africa', drafted by the US and accepted by the UK, France, West Germany and Canada. However, an attempt to have it adopted by the Security Council was blocked by the Africa Group which opposed paragraph 15; this would have committed the Security Council to work with the South African Government for a peaceful solution. The Group also had some minor objections to paragraph 13, seeking to obtain South African recognition of Namibia's international status. The full text of the Declaration is as follows.

1. Freedom, justice and peace in the world are founded on the recognition of the inherent dignity and of the equal and inalienable rights of all members of the human family.

2. Conditions in southern Africa require a particular reaffirmation of these basic rights.

3. Every person in southern Africa, as elsewhere, is entitled without distinction of any kind as to race, sex, language or religion, to the full and equal enjoyment of political, civil, economic, social and cultural rights within his country.

4. The fundamental problems in the area are: in SA, the denial of basic human rights through the existence of institutionalized racism, apartheid; in Namibia, illegal occupation of international territory; in southern Rhodesia, the existence of an illegal repressive minority regime.

5. The fundamental responsibilities of the UN are the maintenance of international peace and security and the promotion of social progress and better standards of life in larger freedom.

6. The Security Council rejects all aspects of the apartheid system and all related systems which impose separation based on racial discrimination, including the imposition of 'Bantustans', which seek

to divide the population and deprive the people of a just and equitable sharing of their national production and resources.

7. The Security Council regards these inhumane systems as fundamental violations of human rights and of the purposes of the Charter of the UN. It considers these systems to be economically and socially unworkable attempts to arrest change and divide the society at a time when economic and social forces within the society and the world are pressing toward integration and interdependence.

8. The Security Council recognizes that apartheid and related systems threaten to lead to an ever-widening deprivation of human rights whether by support of other minority regimes, no matter how illegal, the torture of political prisoners and the death of detainees, and the growing elimination of freedom of thought and expression by such ominous acts as restraints on the Press.

9. Governments deriving their authority from consent of the governed must replace these repressive steps. Full and equal partnership of all individuals must find its expression through majority rule which means that all, regardless of race, are entitled to participate in all phases of national life and to join in freely determining the political, economic and social character of their society with full regard for the rights of minorities.

10. Failure to end the institutions of apartheid and related systems as well as the oppression required to attempt to maintain them have produced violence and will inevitably encourage even greater violence.

11. The Security Council expresses its support for and solidarity with all those rightly striving for the elimination of apartheid and racial discrimination and all victims of violence and repression in the area.

12. The Council and its members affirm their intention to use their collective efforts to bring about the elimination of apartheid and all forms of racial discrimination and recognize the need for international assistance for the victims of such oppression.

13. The Security Council recognizes the complexity of the issues and the difficulty of resolving them. While some changes have been made and there has been some recognition by SA of the international status of Namibia, nevertheless no steps have been taken to dismantle apartheid.

14. SA must:

   (a) Take timely steps to eliminate the policy and practice of apartheid and grant to all elements of the population equal rights including a full and free voice in their destiny.

   (b) Terminate all systems and plans under whatever name which forcibly separate elements of the population on the basis of race whether within a unitary state or in the form of separate political units.

   (c) Bring its illegal occupation of Namibia to a speedy conclusion.

   (d) Facilitate the holding in Namibia on a territory-wide basis of free elections under the aegis of the UN and refrain from any steps inconsistent therewith.

   (e) Comply with the relevant Security Council resolutions on the questions of Namibia and Rhodesia.

15. The Security Council will seek to work constructively with other principal organs and with the Government and people of SA for a just and peaceful solution to the problems of the area.

16. Through peaceful co-operation and widening recognition of the need to find solutions to these problems, a new era in the history of man can be brought into being and a major step taken to realize the goals for which the UN was established.

17. Only in such circumstances can the independent governments of Africa fully devote their time and attention to pressing developmental problems and can SA make its full contribution to the continent.

18. The Security Council and its members declare their intention to support actions and initiatives designed to promote the resolution, in accordance with the above principles, of the pressing problems of southern Africa, to assist in the development of practical progress so that all men may practise tolerance and live together in peace.

Predictably, White South Africans' feelings towards the West became more ambivalent as a result of all the evidence interpreted by them as 'the West ganging up against SA'. The positive side of these feelings showed itself in the serious lobbying of the Western community, urging it not to abandon its 'best and most reliable friend in the continent' and stressing mutual interests; the negative side came out in angry and bitter condemnations of 'Western betrayal' and complaints about the West's 'double standards' in its dealings with SA and other nations whose policies it deplores. Even though SA Government leaders know very well that they cannot find alternative allies to the West, in desperation they actually contemplated invoking anti-Western support. Thus, reacting to the strong French warning against SA carrying out its own nuclear weapons' tests, the Defence Minister, Piet Botha, told parliament that the West should not count on SA's 'automatic support' and recommended that it consider following a policy of strict neutrality. One government MP, Dr Paul Viljoen, advocated that SA no longer look 'slavishly' to the West, but instead 'look to the East'. The Minister of Information and Plural Affairs, Dr Connie Mulder, quoted Confucius: 'My enemy's enemy is my friend'.

Much more credible, though, was Vorster's threat after his Vienna meeting with Mondale that if the West took any action which was tantamount to 'putting out our eyes', it should remember the Biblical story and be aware that 'SA will pull down the pillars with us'. In an interview with the American Broadcasting Corporation, Vorster said that the US had started to turn against SA when Carter took office.[74] 'Whereas it appears to us at the moment that the Soviets want to kill us off by force, the US wants to strangle us with finesse.'

4. SA VERSUS THE INTERNATIONAL COMMUNITY: THREAT OF SANCTIONS

The threat of economic and military sanctions, first mooted after Sharpeville in 1960, has never been treated lightly by the SA Government: since the mid-sixties it has pushed ahead with the high-cost development of the oil-from-coal complex, Sasol, which by the early 1980s could provide 40% of domestic needs; has built up considerable reserves of oil in converted mine shafts and other storage places; has spent large sums on oil exploration; has stockpiled other strategic materials, and has established its own arms industry through Armscor. However, the threat came to be taken much more seriously in 1977 because of a number of changes: Carter's new policy; a greater willingness by Britain and the rest of the EEC to contemplate the use of selective sanctions; the Nigerian policy of forcing a choice on Western firms between operating in their country or in SA; and, perhaps most important of all, the growing tendency of Western governments to disengage themselves from SA more effectively to counteract Soviet policies in the continent.

The Security Council's mandatory arms embargo in November 1977 (which finally broke SA's arms connection with Paris and probably also with Israel) was seen in Pretoria as proof that the 'unthinkable'—Western support for an international programme of sanctions—could no longer be ruled out. The Vorster regime also looked with alarm at the role played by Western spokesmen in the two major international conferences sponsored by the UN in Maputo in May 1977 and in Lagos in August 1977.[35] Both conferences were primarily aimed at increasing international support for sanctions against SA. Other action taken during the year included the adoption of an arms embargo against SA; the call by the General Assembly's Fourth Committee on all oil-producing states to cut off petroleum supplies; and approval of a resolution on Namibia in the General Assembly (4 November) which included a proposal for an oil embargo against SA. Significantly, all the OPEC countries, including Iran, voted for the resolution. (Iran supplies 90% of all crude oil imported by SA). In addition, the Commonwealth Committee on Sanctions agreed in October 1977 to back a mandatory UN oil embargo against SA unless it gave effective guarantees not to allow oil to find its way to Rhodesia.

The Government repeatedly admitted its anxiety over this trend. After visiting the US, the Minister of Economic Affairs said that SA 'should not underestimate the threat of economic sanctions'.[36] The army chief, Gen Magnus Malan, said that SA would have to prepare for 'an economic war of survival'.[37] The Minister of Defence admitted that SA was 'finally cut off from the great arms-producing nations. All countries which in the past provided SA with weapons have finally joined the arms boycott.'[38] The Prime Minister said that while SA 'could go it alone indefinitely', sanctions could kill states like Lesotho and Botswana.[39] The Foreign Minister was reported to have told the Ivory Coast President that if SA were faced with sanctions, it 'would fight like a cornered animal' to survive world pressure.[40]

PREPARATIONS FOR SANCTIONS

SA moved purposefully to prepare for sanctions and (in the words of the Minister of Economic Affairs) reduce 'the strategic vulnerability of the economy'. After the

UN arms embargo,[41] he made the National Supplies Procurement Act of 1970 operative. This enabled him to manufacture or produce any goods for the State should he 'deem it necessary' for security; to direct owners or suppliers of goods and services to supply, deliver or sell them to him or to any 'specified person'; and to direct any manufacturer to 'produce, process or treat a specified quantity of goods and supply them to him'.

The SA Auditor-General revealed in his 1977 report that the government had spent R557.2m in stockpiling oil during the year.[42] The true figure was no doubt higher. According to one report, SA spent over R800m on oil and arms imports during the first half of 1977 alone. This was arrived at by comparing the import figures given by the Reserve Bank for the period (R3,381m) with those disclosed by the Department of Customs and Excise (R2,550m) which left a shortfall of R831m unaccounted for.[43] Oil and defence imports for 1973 were estimated at R250m; for 1974 at R840m, and for 1975 c. R1,170m. Another informed estimate put the total cost of oil and military imports in 1976 at R1,500m, R300m more than in 1975.[44]

OIL AND THE SA ECONOMY

The importance of oil to the SA economy was examined at some length by the SA *Financial Mail* (30 September 1977). Only a quarter of the country's total energy needs depends on oil, the rest being supplied by abundant coal resources. 'This doesn't mean we don't need oil. We do—at an estimated rate of some 320,000 barrels a day (b/d) or 15.4 million tons (Mt) a year. At c. R80/t this means a foreign exchange drain of almost R1,300m a year. Oil production from Sasol I, the oil-from-coal plant, amounts to only c. 5% of petrol demand: so an oil boycott . . . would have grave consequences for the economy. But would it bring SA to its knees? SA's four major refineries produce almost 60% of oil in the form of light and middle distillates—petrol, paraffin, diesel fuel, etc. Almost 25% is in the form of heavy ends, industrial furnace oil, bunkers, etc (of which SA has too much). But the refineries have embarked on plant upgrading programmes (at an estimated total cost of R160m) which will change the ratios by 1980. By then, they'll be producing c. 69% in light and middle distillates, and only some 16% of the heavy stuff. [But this still depends on] crude pouring in to be refined . . . until 1980–81 when Sasol II comes on stream.

'SA has some time because of the stockpiling of oil reserves. . . . Current estimates (although nobody *really* knows) are that the Republic has crude oil reserves of c. 42 Mt, or just over two-and-a-half years' supply at present consumption. In the face of sanctions, however, this supply would be stretched in a number of ways. There would have to be very strict energy-saving measures, cutting back on domestic transportation. While petrol is a problem, diesel fuel would be a greater one. Trains and planes would only run when full, and services would be reduced. Private motoring would be drastically cut. Out of today's domestic petrol market of 4.3 Mt, SA could probably save 1 Mt or so without serious disruptions. SA would no longer supply bunkers to passing ships, and the heavy fractions— perhaps 2 Mt a year—could be converted by the Natref refinery at Sasolburg (which is of special design) into lighter, more useful distillates. By such measures—and no doubt many others—the country could cut demand to c. 10 Mt/year. This would have the effect of stretching hidden reserves from two-and-a-half years' supply to nearer four years, i.e. until Sasol II is on stream. Not that the R2,500m synthesis project is the whole answer. Stated production will still fall short of SA's needs.

'When Sasol II comes on stream, it will produce 1.5 Mt of petrol, diesel and light fuel oil, equivalent to between 25–28% of domestic demand in 1981–82 at today's levels. It will also produce petrochemicals: ethylene (for plastics) 165,000 t/year, ammonia 110,000 t/year; pitch 60,000 t/year; creosote 90,000 t/year, and alcohols and acetones 155,000 t/year. Sasol I currently produces 235,000 t/year of petrol, diesel and other oil products. It also produces large quantities of methane gas which is piped to industries around the Reef. This could be piped to Sasol II where it could be processed into liquids. [With new technology, it could possibly get as much as] 20% more out of its giant oxygen plant. Its gasifiers are also conservatively rated and it might be possible to get an extra 30%. . . . Another emergency measure could be to build greater plant capacity by, say, 50%. If there's an oil boycott, savings on crude imports will be immense and the cash could be put to this use. . . . [However, SA's final assessment is that] it seems unlikely that an oil embargo could work. For one thing, Iran, which has 17% equity share in the Natref refinery at Sasolburg and which supplies [90% of SA's] crude oil [is thought unlikely to use the oil weapon against SA]. Secondly, the world is awash with oil.'

However, the foregoing is the most optimistic SA view. It leaves out of account two possibilities: that Iran might reverse its pro-SA policy because of its other major interests; or that an oil embargo might be enforced by a naval embargo.

THE LIKELY EFFECTS OF SANCTIONS
Although most SA economic analysts agreed that the Republic could 'survive' sanctions, there were disagreements about their likely impact. The President of the Afrikaanse Handelsinstituut, A. P. J. Burger, said SA could live with sanctions, but that they would probably lead to a drop in living standards. Arnt Spandau, Professor of Business Economics at Witwatersrand University, examined the effects of both a 20% and a 50% drop in foreign investment on 1976 figures. [45] The former would cause total disposable income to fall by R101m; the latter by R247m. Applying Spandau's figures to Reserve Bank income data, the *Financial Mail* calculated that a 20% investment boycott would reduce disposable income by only 0.5%. A 50% boycott would reduce it by 1.3%. Spandau estimated that a 20% boycott would result in an increase in unemployment of c. 37,000 (11,368 of those affected being Whites). With a 50% investment boycott, joblessness would rise by c. 90,000 (27,344 Whites). Spandau maintained that, in all likelihood, a total investment boycott in 1976 would not have decreased SA's GDP by more than 5%, and that the additional unemployment would not have exceeded 40,000 in the case of Whites and 80,000 in the case of Blacks.

'In contrast,' he argued, 'a trade boycott would be considerably more expensive. In 1976, a 50% trade boycott would have reduced SA's exports by R4,280m, and this would have meant a deterioration in the balance of payments of R3,746m. More than 1.1m people would have become unemployed.' He also estimated that personal incomes would have dropped by as much as 14%. Spandau reckoned that if sanctions could be effectively enforced, things would tighten up after an initial easy stage of import displacement and import substitution. The lack of foreign know-how and competition would tend to decrease efficiency, resulting in 'high cost industrial establishments'.

However like others, Spandau acknowledged that apart from its economic effects, sanctions would have psychological and strategic consequences. Among these would be a further drop in immigration, an acceleration of the rate of emigration, and a sharp rise in Black unemployment (see Immigration and Employment, below).

EFFECTS OF LOWER WESTERN INVESTMENT
Meanwhile, leading industrialists, bankers and economists commented gloomily on how the SA economy was already suffering—even prior to concerted sanctions—

because of difficulties in obtaining capital loans abroad on reasonable terms, because of the rate of capital exports, the slowing up of new investments and the balance of trade difficulties (see Economy, below). The South African Reserve Bank's 1976–77 report revealed that the country was losing R1,200m a year in the export of foreign capital. Real GDP rose only 1% in the year, half that of 1975–76. The *Financial Mail* (26 August 1977) drew attention to the result of the clotting up of foreign capital inflows, 'the lifeblood of SA's economic development'. The capital account swung from a R528m inflow in the second half of 1976 to a R649m outflow in the first half of 1977. After the Soweto troubles in June 1976, foreign capital began to leave the country at the rate of R100m a month—an indication of what is likely to happen if political and economic conditions.deteriorate further.

This point was driven home by Dr Frans Cronje, chairman of Nedbank, who said that if, for political reasons, foreign capital were to cease, the economy could continue to grow more or less at past rates (i.e. average 4.5%), but that a growth rate of 7–8% was required to absorb yearly increases in the labour force and to reduce the current level of unemployment.[46] Optimum growth would obviously require a considerable inflow of new capital. Aubrey Dickman, Anglo-American's economic consultant, also warned that a shortage of foreign funds would lead to rising unemployment.[47] 'The demographic reality—a non-White labour force expanding at 3% pa—challenges us to reattain a growth rate of at least 5.5%. . . . It is undisputed that we cannot achieve this without foreign capital.' In the ten years to 1976, the average net capital inflow was R570m pa.

The government's latest Economic Development Programme specifically states that the reduced availability of capital inflows is a major constraint on growth. The Minister of Economic Affairs, too, emphasized that 'shortage of capital remains one of the country's biggest problems'.[48] Harry Oppenheimer, chairman of Anglo-American, stressed that SA's ability to stimulate its lagging economy was strictly limited by the balance of payments and the 'severe shortage of foreign capital'. Summing up the debate on the vital importance of foreign capital to ensure growth, the *Financial Mail* (25 November 1977) concluded: 'Yet fast growth we must have. 3% growth in GDP means virtually no increase in living standards. 4% implies growth in *per capita* income of only a little more than 1% a year—at which rate it takes more than 50 years to double the average standard of living. . . . We must have 5% or more. And for growth of 5% or more we must have foreign capital. It is really as simple as that.'

SA also continued to experience considerable difficulties in 1977 in raising loans at reasonable terms on the international monetary market. ESCOM arranged two German loans, each for 20m marks, with a three-year maturity at a rate of 8%. It also raised a Swiss loan for 80m francs for three years at 7%. Standard Bank was trying to raise a loan of up to 40m Swiss francs on the same terms. Not only were these maturities shorter than the traditional five to seven years, however, but the interest rates were considerably higher than for other borrowers (Norway, for example, managed to raise 200m Swiss francs at $3\frac{1}{4}$% for five years). Moreover, the money available on German and Swiss markets was reportedly far short of SA's needs which were minimally set at $1,000m; according to one commentator, SA 'will be lucky to obtain one-quarter of this'.[49]

Underlining the reluctance of even Swiss bankers to meet SA's loans, Robert Studer, the senior vice-president of the Union Bank of Switzerland, told a South African conference that the extent to which foreign firms would grant loans to Government and private business in SA hinged primarily on their evaluation of the investment and credit risk.[50] He added that serious concern persisted that apartheid could produce revolution, civil or underground warfare, and even open war between West and East. He said it was immaterial whether this concern was justified or not in the investment context. 'The very existence of these incalculable risks . . . both in the form of direct investments and long-term capital issues, would result in the decline of the flow of foreign capital in the future, or in it drying up completely, depending on how the situation develops.'

However, it was not simply the fear of political risks that made SA less attractive to foreign investors. The US *Business International* newsletter produced figures to show that SA had forfeited its place near the top of the world profitability league.[51] The table below, which compares rates of return on US direct foreign investment in SA and the rest of the world (in percentages), shows how the Republic's position has deteriorated, relatively and absolutely, since 1973, with a very sharp drop in profitability in 1975. For the first time in this decade, it lost its lead over Australia and was again surpassed by Brazil.

	1970	1971	1972	1973	1974	1975
Saouth Africa	16.0	11.3	10.2	18.4	17.6	8.7
Non-US world	11.2	11.9	12.2	16.4	21.6	13.2
South Africa's advantage	+4.8	−0.6	−2.0	+2.0	−4.0	−4.5

US parents' earnings divided by its net equity in and loans to foreign affiliates. Earnings comprise parents' share in affiliates' earnings, less withholding taxes, plus interest received on intercompany accounts.

Meanwhile, opinion in most Western countries hardened in 1977–78 against trading with, or investing in, SA (for details, see Foreign Affairs below). Canada became the first Western country officially to discourage trade with SA; Holland was the first whose parliament considered a Bill to authorize participation in any international sanctions campaign. West Germany restricted government security and insurance guarantees for German exporters to SA; a Swedish all-party parliamentary committee recommended the suspension of all further investment in SA; and the EEC adopted a collective policy designed to apply economic pressures. Even France, until recently Pretoria's favoured trading partner, threatened to break trade and diplomatic links if SA carried out its proposed nuclear test.

A number of British firms decided to limit their connections with SA. Drake and Scull, an engineering group with large interests in Nigeria, sold out its entire holding. So did Reed International. The multinational GEC decided to sell half its SA holding for R27.5m. The US electronic firm, Polaroid, stopped its operations entirely; the Canadian mining company, GRANEX, withdrew from SA and Namibia. The two US car manufacturers, General Motors and Ford, decided they would not increase their investment stake; at the same time, Henry Ford said he would considerably increase the sum spent on training and promoting Black workers. A number of other foreign firms decided, without publicity, not to expand their activities in the Republic.

Western banks took the lead in refusing to make any further loans to SA. In the US, these included Chase Manhattan, the Chemical Bank, the First Pennsylvania Bank and Trust, Citicorps and Wells Fargo. The First National Bank of Boston decided to make no further loans, while allowing those in existence to roll over. The British Midland Bank and the Nieuwe Rotterdam Bank also announced that they would make no further loans.

POLITICAL AFFAIRS
THE REPUBLIC'S FUTURE[52]
There was a significant departure in 1977 from earlier practices by Government spokesmen in always insisting that all was well with the Republic and that any

troubles were exaggerated by hostile critics. Even the Prime Minister, in his most reassuring statement, admitted foreseeing 'sporadic troubles', though he denied the possibility of a 'race war'. Few tried to pretend that serious difficulties did not lie ahead. The Minister of Defence, P. W. Botha, told his army that while SA was emerging from 1977 'beset with escalating international problems', it was about to enter another year 'promising even heavier seas. . . . We will, in increasing measure, be subjected to coercion, persuasion and possibly even seduction to submit to the will of the aggressor. . . . We shall not waver and we shall not succumb. What is more, we shall solve our problems in our way.'[53] The Chief of the Defence Force, Gen Magnus Malan, said: 'The attack continues because our enemy knows that only by destroying our will, will he have reached his goal. That is why he is set for a total attack against us—economically, politically, spiritually, militarily and [with] technology.'[54] He warned businessmen to start adapting for a 'war for survival'.[55] However, the 'enemy' was no longer perceived as just being 'the communist forces'; from 1977, it also included the West (see Confrontation with the West, above).

There was also a more sophisticated appreciation of the futility of earlier official policies in calling for Western help on the grounds of SA being 'a bastion against communism'. Prof Nic Rhoodie, head of the Department of Sociology at the University of Pretoria, said that in the Western world of today, the mere protestation of anti-communism was 'no longer the certificate of respectability it used to be'.[56] SA's traditional Western friends no longer regarded anti-communism as a trade-off for racism. Racism has become the 'supreme and ultimate social sin' in the second half of the 20th century; if the Whites persisted in misreading the wider international implications of this, the Republic could look forward to grave problems in the 'immediate future'. He added that while the ruling party still had the power to launch radical initiatives to reconstruct SA along democratic federal/confedural lines, it was impossible to say how much longer it would retain this power—'but most informed people seem to agree that time is running out fast'. Prof Rhoodie's brother, Eschel, the influential Secretary for Information, took a similar position when presenting his Ministry's official report to parliament.[57] He said that certain aspects of world opinion should be recognized. 'One is that the world believes that racism or any form of ethnic discrimination . . . is the greatest social evil today, and the one most fraught with potential conflict. In the 1940s, it was Nazism; from 1945–60, it was communism; since 1960, it has become racism.' Developments in SA were judged in the light of this all-prevailing theory. No amount of money or manpower would be able to promote SA's cause except by 'imaginative, large-scale moves in the implementation of Government policy to move away from racial discrimination and to structure a plurality of democracies for the country'.

A former columnist for the pro-Government *Die Transvaler*, Natie Ferreira, declared: 'Apartheid is stone dead. It cannot work. It has been written off, buried. The world has declared it a threat to peace and a crime against humanity. And calling it plural democracy is not going to help either. . . . How can the Nationalists admit after 30 years that they are wrong? It doesn't work that way. . . . Afrikaners are being asked to vote for "a war of survival". How can the Nats survive a war against the world? It doesn't make sense.'[58] Dr Jan Moolman, a former architect of apartheid, member of the Tomlinson Commission which planned the Homelands and later director of the African Institute, also declared that he could see 'no future for old-style apartheid' which was 'really an escape from our problems'.

No less remarkable was the grave warning of Prof Gerrit Viljoen, chairman of the formidable Broederbond (see below): 'We should have no illusions that we are in a critical situation and time is short'.[59] If Whites tried to retain everything they had, they ran the risk of having it taken away. Somewhat surprisingly, he added: 'I have never considered Separate Development as an ideology or a dogma. Separation was merely an instrument to achieve certain goals—orderly government, political stability from the point of view of Whites and Afrikaners, and maintenance of their identity. That means it is an open-ended road. What is going to happen as things develop is an open question.' He urged various courses of action including publication of a planned programme of change to give Blacks an idea of the future; dramatic consolidation and development of the Homelands; local self-government for urban Blacks; and an urgent look at such issues as job reservation. He envisaged SA's future as a loose confederation of Whites and Homelands and urban Blacks. 'We will have to define which political preconditions are essential and which are only useful or advantageous to ourselves,' Prof Viljoen said. 'We will have to examine which are non-negotiable and which can be phased out.' Among the non-negotiable preconditions were that Whites should continue to hold political control over their own affairs and that White and Afrikaner identity should be safeguarded. However, the broad areas of socio-economic life, such as job reservation, were negotiable: 'If, as has been said, this applies to only 3% of the labour force, one would have to ask: does the antipathy it creates not outweigh the advantages?'

There was also a greater readiness by government spokesmen to tell the White electorate that past apartheid promises and hopes could not be fulfilled. The Deputy Minister of Social Welfare and Pensions, R. N. H. Janson, told parliament that it was wishful thinking to suppose that the people of Soweto could be transferred to the Black Homelands by the year 2000; he warned that the growing force of nationalism was something that could not be suppressed 'with all the force in the world'.[60] When people were 'in trouble' they were more likely to be receptive to ideas, Piet Cillie, the editor of *Die Burger*, told the Chamber of Commerce.[61] He emphasized the need for all people to be given the prospect of freedom and full citizenship, and said he felt the present was a good time to emphasize what was 'not a new policy'. Asked whether SA had time to change, he replied that too little, too late was 'a law of political life', but ended on a distinctly gloomy note: 'If South African civilization should collapse like that in Mozambique and Angola, we should try to go down with a clean conscience. That is the sort of message which we (*Die Burger*) are bringing primarily to Afrikaner Nationalists. It is the best message we have got.'

The warning of the Roman Catholic Archbishop of Durban, Denis Hurley, was that an increasing number of Blacks were looking to Angola, Rhodesia and Mozambique, and saying 'violence is the only way for us. . . . There is nothing that men dread more than violence, yet there is nothing more *unavoidable.*'[62]

THE PROPOSED NEW CONSTITUTION

The Prime Minister outlined his proposals for a new Constitution for the Republic to the four provincial conferences of the National Party in August and September 1977, and won their separate endorsements. Vorster made it quite clear that the proposed changes would not affect the Separate Development plans for the African majority: Africans would achieve their political rights only within separate Homelands. The constitutional proposals were instead designed 'to give the Coloureds and Indians meaningful rights with regard to matters of common concern, and exclusive rights over matters of their own. They did justice to the principle of self-determination without putting the rights and future of the Whites in jeopardy. Consultation would take place between the Government and the elected leaders of the other population groups.'[63]

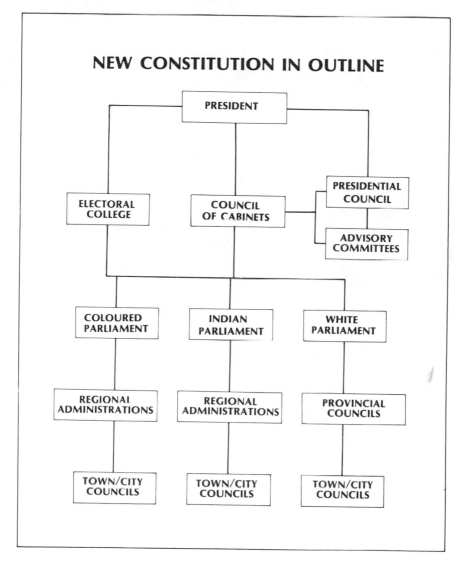

NEW CONSTITUTION IN OUTLINE

PRESIDENT

ELECTORAL COLLEGE

COUNCIL OF CABINETS

PRESIDENTIAL COUNCIL

ADVISORY COMMITTEES

COLOURED PARLIAMENT — INDIAN PARLIAMENT — WHITE PARLIAMENT

REGIONAL ADMINISTRATIONS — REGIONAL ADMINISTRATIONS — PROVINCIAL COUNCILS

TOWN/CITY COUNCILS — TOWN/CITY COUNCILS — TOWN/CITY COUNCILS

The proposals incorporated the principle of proportional representation for the Indian, Coloured and White Parliaments, as well as for the Council of Cabinets. On these principles a formula was proposed providing for 185 White members of parliament, of whom 165 were to be elected at general elections and 12 more on the basis of the proportional representation of the different parties within parliament after the election.

The detailed proposals for the new constitution were set out by the Africa Institute, as follows:

The Electoral College will consist of 88 members chosen from the White, Coloured and Indian Parliaments; it will elect the President for a term of five years and have the authority to remove him from office.

The President will chair the Cabinet Council, preside during Council meetings and open sessions of the various Parliaments; put his name to legislation affecting the common area; name a permanent deputy to act in his absence; appoint the prime ministers of the White, Coloured and Indian Parliaments; appoint the cabinet ministers of each Parliament following consultation with the leader of the ruling party; have the authority to dismiss ministers; and have the decisive say on legislation that conflicts with the common area when such matters cannot be resolved by the joint advisory committees.

The Cabinet Council will comprise the prime ministers of the White, Coloured and Indian Parliaments and a number of members from each Parliament, and will initiate and compile legislation affecting the common area for the various Parliaments. Councillors will have the right to address the various Parliaments, arrange the order papers for the various Parliaments in consultation with majority leaders in each legislature, and recommend that conflicting legislation be referred to joint advisory committees.

The Presidential Council will act in a purely advisory capacity; consist of members nominated by the various Parliaments (in relation to the size of each Parliament) as well as members nominated by the President; contain persons with specialized knowledge (members of the various Parliaments and Provincial Councils will not be eligible for membership); have a chairman appointed by the President from the ranks of its members, and advise the Cabinet Council on its own initiative or at the request of the Cabinet Council.

The White, Indian and Coloured Parliaments will legislate exclusively on matters pertaining to their own peoples and have the right to put their name, in the person of the Prime Minister, to all legislation passed (this function is currently carried out by the State President). They will consist of the following: Whites, 185 members (20 nominated, 12 on a basis of *pro-rata* party representation); Coloureds, 92 members (10 nominated, 6 on a basis of *pro-rata* party representation); Indians, 46 members (five nominated). They will share in the national Budget and have the power to impose their own taxes and levies over and above the allocation from the common treasury.

Provincial and Regional Administration: Provincial Councils will be maintained for Whites (if they so desire). Regional administrations will be established for Coloureds and Indians. They will be headed by administrators, but be without legislative authority.

Local and Municipal Development: Each race group in every town and city will elect its own council. The councils will have full local and management powers in dealing with their own affairs.

THE CONSTITUTIONAL DEBATE

The Prime Minister's proposed constitutional reforms were rejected by all the parliamentary opposition parties, as well as by most of the leaders of the Coloureds and Indians (see below) and by a number of Homeland leaders. Objections and alternative proposals for evolving an acceptable constitution were set out by the leaders of the parliamentary parties during the general election campaign. [64]

New Republic Party: 'We oppose these plans because (1) the proposed executive president usurps the sovereignty of parliament; (2) he acquires dictatorial powers in those important areas where there is dispute; (3) the flash-point in South African politics, the urban Black, is totally excluded. Proper consultation is what was done at the Turnhalle—sitting round a table and negotiating with the leaders of the various racial groups, who are elected by and responsible to their people—and not as individuals self-appointed to serve their personal ambitions.'

Progressive Federal Party, 'The reforms are both dangerous and futile. By entrenching racial divisions between White, Coloured and Indian in the constitutional structure and by excluding Blacks entirely from the decision-making process at parliamentary level, they will increase the conflict situation in SA. They take us further along the road to authoritarianism. Consultation alone is inadequate. All groups must have a say in the formulation of the constitution and decide jointly on its final form. Unless all race and other interest groups are free to choose who will represent them, a new constitution will not command their loyalty and support.'

South African Party: 'We welcome the proposed joint White/Coloured/Indian Cabinet Council as a step in the right direction. For many years we have pleaded for joint decision-making, and we see the Government's proposals as a means toward that end. This will not develop a leadership class among Coloured and Indian people, but enable them to play a greater part in SA's broader interests. Proper consultation can only take place among the leaders of the various race groups, and proper leadership can only be promoted primarily through their own institutions.'

Herstigte National Party: 'Race federation has a limited tolerance for dissent. It cannot stand the strain of religious and race differences, and either blows up, leading to violence, or makes dictatorship inevitable. The proposed State President will be a virtual dictator. Parliament will be reduced to a glorified White municipality, yet the Carters and Youngs will not be satisfied. No constitution taking different race groups into a single government has ever been acceptable to all race groups, and has ever worked. Historical realities and the inequalities of nations and races should be accepted as the basis of consultations.'

The debate over constitutional reforms, which in fact has been in progress for several years, was not confined to the Prime Minister's new proposals. The idea of SA adapting the Swiss cantonal system—first floated by the Defence Minister, P. W. Botha, in 1970—gained considerable impetus from a keynote speech made by the Minister of National Education and Sport, Dr Piet Koornhof. This was at an international conference on Accommodation in Plural Societies, organized in May 1977 by the Foreign Affairs Association, a body which stands in well with the Government. [65] As was subsequently pointed out, Koornhof's speech marked the first time that a Cabinet Minister 'did not rule out political rights in SA for Blacks living outside of their Homelands'. [66] While he stood by the 'two cornerstones' of SA's policies—'multinationalism and self-determination' (i.e. a continuation of the process of creating 'independent' Black Homelands), he said that the time had come to deal with 'the grey areas in the White part of SA':

'The concept of cultural pluralism must include basic ideas of equal opportunity for all people, respect for human dignity, and the power to control significant environmental and psychological forces impinging on people. Mutually supportive relations must not be confused with tolerance. To confuse tolerance and "mutual supportive relationships" is patronizing. Despite a bloody world history of cultural exploitation, cultures have rights paralleling those of people. Culture is the core of man's being: what he was, is and ought to be. Cultural pluralism is not an assimilative posture; it is a negation of assimilation. It is a posture which maintains that there is more than one legitimate way of being human without paying the penalties of second-class citizenship, and that this pluralism would enrich and strengthen the nation. In the South African framework, a policy of plural democracies (of which the Swiss variant is the ideal typical model) is a coalition of autonomous and mainly territorially-based units co-operating within a political system providing for "consensual decision-making" at both group and national level.

'The units in cultural pluralism will comprise mainly the White, Coloured and Indian groups. However, there are those in SA who believe that, in theory at least, Blacks legally regarded as members of permanent communities within SA may in time also be drawn into the new dispensation. There is a school of thought in SA which believes that these Blacks, as separate communities, should also be ultimately phased into the cultural pluralism orbit. Politics, especially in these times, are unpredictable and only time will prove whether this line of thought is feasible or not.

'The basic design of a cultural pluralism could embody the following: inalienable rights of each ethnic group to determine its own destiny, coupled with the right of every group to co-participate in the State's decision-making process in all matters of national importance. On the other hand, matters relating to the individual's everyday needs (those with the greatest emotive potential), and with a distinctive group content, fall within the formally demarcated preserve of decision-making institutions created specially for the purpose.

'In terms of decision-making power, therefore, the cultural pluralism will be based on two sets of political institutions, functioning both independently and complementarily. One set of institutions is group-orientated and guarantees group autonomy in matters affecting the everyday needs of the individual in his historically evolved ethnic or cultural setting. These autonomous institutions may function as group parliaments with carefully delineated legislative and decision-making competence and having jurisdiction that may also be territorially defined. The second level of decision-making power may be vested in an over-arching institution designed so that it can provide for cross-ethnic or cross-community decision-making on matters that in no way prejudice the identity or grassroots structure of the participant groups.

'The question arises whether the newly introduced Cabinet Council for White, Coloured and Indian groups could not be viewed as the beginning of the process of institutional evolution which will culminate in a sophisticated parliamentary system specially tailored to the needs of SA's multi-ethnic population structure. Cultural pluralism in this sense represents a significant departure from the Westminster parliamentary system. Cultural pluralism would allow an individual to identify with his ethnic group, participate in the decision-making power of his group, but at the same time identify at a higher level with the collective image and identity of the nation. In this context, cultural pluralism is not fundamentally incompatible with a confederalist type of politico-constitutional arrangement. Cultural pluralism, therefore, offers South African society more policy options, and thus greater constitutional and political manoeuvrability, than the present Westminster model. In the long term, cultural pluralism could evolve into a variant of the Swiss system.

In fact, pursued to their logical conclusion, the current policies of the South African Government could have but one inevitable outcome; that SA will evolve broadly in the direction of a group-differentiated cultural pluralism.'

A number of participants in the conference expressed reservations about the likely success of any cantonal system, however. While it was felt that the Swiss system might provide some useful lessons, Prof Christopher Hughes (University of Leicester) was one of those who considered it only c. 20% relevant. 'You need a uniformly sophisticated political infrastructure to expect more than 20% commonality. In SA one doesn't find this uniform sophistication, so your first priority is to build it up and provide the systems for the cantonal concept which you lack. . . . In any plural system in SA, consultation is essential, and consensus should be reached between all participating groups—otherwise the concept will merely be a means of perpetuating White controls.' This point was agreed by most of the overseas and naturally by all the non-White South African delegates.

The elder stateman among the sociologists at the conference, Harvard's Prof Talcott Parson, warned: 'Ethnicity is fraught with dangerous cultural and racial emotions—as are class distinctions in a lesser way.' It would be dangerous to base political power-sharing on ethnic grounds. Another point made by delegates was that the most pressing priority in the search for 'fair' pluralism in SA was to secure an over-arching, internal national loyalty from *all* ethnic groups. The concept of Black Homelands moving to independence also raised questions about SA's citizenship laws, to which the answers so far put forward by the South African authorities were found unacceptable by some delegates. Was it possible to talk of the Cabinet Council as a realistic platform for representation of the Coloured people when it was said that in a plural system, such Councils or Parliaments should be sovereign?

Prof Nic Rhoodie, director of the new Institute for Plural Societies at Pretoria University, emphasized that the orderly but speedy phasing out of those discriminatory practices which evolved over more than 300 years should receive the highest priority if the Whites wished to succeed in normalizing intergroup relations. . . . Only on the basis of a broad democratic South Africanism that transcends narrow sectional interests will we succeed in creating a socio-political system with which all the peoples of the Republic can identify. To this end we need institutional adjustments geared to the realities of today'.[67] Prof Gerrit Olivier of the University of Pretoria told the conference: 'Events over the last three years have removed all doubt that, if we are to survive, the ideal of a Just Society can no longer be postponed—or be subject to the approval of the lowest common denominator in the ranks of the ruling party'. (This reference underlines the point made above concerning the caucas' power of veto over the Government).

Dr Wolfgang H. Thomas, a German economist deported from SA in 1977, published his own outline for creating institutions to achieve plural democracy.[68] While not sharing the pessimism of many about the possibility of political change, he also rejected the optimism of those who saw meaningful change as already occurring.

Black South Africans were critical of the cantonal idea mainly because all the proponents of pluralist institutions (including Dr Thomas) accept the basic concept of independent Homelands. The Black People's Convention said curtly that it did not think Koornhof's ideas justified a reaction from them. Dr Manas Buthelezi, chairman of the Soweto Black Parents' Association, described cantons as 'a good idea as long as it is not going to lead to Homelands being forced into independence'.[69] He added two corollaries: Black representation in the central decision-making body dealing with matters of common interest should be on the basis of one-man one-vote. Blacks should be given a meaningful role in the setting up of the new institution via a national convention.

Chief Gatsha Buthelezi said: 'Dr Koornhof's thinking is very advanced for the corridors of power in the National Party.' But any new deal would come to naught unless the central machinery was the product of deliberations at a new national convention in which all races were represented. Vorster, however, once again firmly ruled out the possibility of holding a national all-race convention to reach a consensus on a new constitution.[70] 'You must reject this national convention now and forever,' he said in a message to the electorate.

The only leading member of the Government who came out openly against any form of federal structure was, significantly, the chief spokesman for the *verkramptes* in the ruling party, Dr Andries Treurnicht.[71] He claimed that the canton system meant accepting a form of federalism which was excluded by National Party policy, arguing that SA was not a plural society but 'a plurality of societies', each with its own nationalism. These nationalisms had to be kept apart or they would clash.

Although Alister Sparks, editor of the *Rand Daily Mail* (27 August 1977), described Vorster's proposal as 'a constitutional monstrosity', he nevertheless thought it to be 'the single most important political development since the Nationalists came to power . . . because for all its shortcomings it does one supremely important thing. It breaks the political colour bar.' Prof D. J. Kriek of the University of SA described the intention of moving away from the Westminster system as 'extremely dangerous'.[72] Dr John van Tonder, an influential senior lecturer at Potchefstroom University, said that urban Blacks would eventually have to 'share power' with the rest in the proposed 'super-Cabinet'.[73] Dr G. E. Devenish of the University of the Western Cape found many perplexing obscurities and some astonishing anomalies in the constitutional proposals, but at the same time felt that they would bring fundamental and radical changes in the political system.[74] One of their unexpected results, he suggested, would be to diminish the 'all-powerful hold that the National Party has maintained for so long on the political development of SA.' Ex-Judge Kowie Marais (see below) warned against the constitutional proposals. It was an historical fact, he said, that 'the most enduring totalitarian systems did not have their beginnings in revolution but in constitutional evolution, in a gradual blunting of public resistance to the erosion of their democratic rights'.[75]

Kite-flying a cantonal solution for SA's problems obscured a continuing parallel debate about partition as a possible way out of the racial dilemma. Considerable prominence was given to a report by two German academics, Jürgen Blenk and Klauss van der Ropp, who considered the prospect of a racially integrated society illusory and saw territorial partition as the only solution. They put forward detailed proposals to safeguard White minority interests while ensuring real political and economic independence for the Black majority.[76] According to their plan, the Republic would be divided along the Sishen-Bloemfontein-Port Elizabeth line, with the northern state Black and the southern state White (see map opposite). One usually reliable source claimed there was some evidence that partition is even being considered seriously by the government—at least as a 'solution of last resort'.[77]

THE MOOD OF AFRIKANERDOM

Outwardly at least, Afrikaners displayed a readiness to return to the *laager* of their frontier days, in reaction against their feeling of 'betrayal' by the West and the growing threat to their security. But the *laager* is no longer a practical means of surviving in a hostile environment. When the Boer trekkers drew their circle of wagons, filled the openings with thorn bush and primed their rifles, they knew

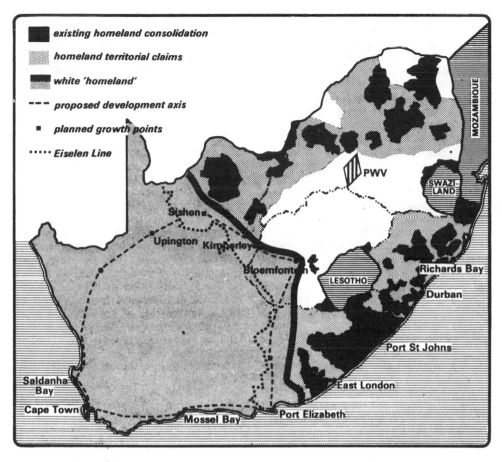

existing homeland consolidation

homeland territorial claims

white 'homeland'

- - - proposed development axis

■ planned growth points

••••• Eiselen Line

Source: Financial Mail, 19 August 1977.

with confidence that there was nobody inside the *laager* who was undependable: there was no Fifth Column. And while it is notionally possible to draw a military cordon around the borders of SA, that is not the same thing as drawing a *laager* since the great bulk of 'the enemy' is now inside. Nevertheless, this false analogy persists, though less as a physical reality than as a state of mind: a defiance of the world; a readiness to face isolation and embrace violent struggle for the sake of Boer 'survival'. The fear of the Fifth Column (as expressed by Vorster) is not of the Blacks, but of 'traitors' in the Afrikaners' own ranks.

On the eve of the general election, seven prominent Afrikaner nationalists published a collection of essays attacking the 'liberalistic element' within Afrikanerdom as the most dangerous Fifth Column.[78] Contributors to the critical essays were the Prime Minister's brother, Dr J. D. 'Koot' Vorster, Dr Andries Treurnicht, Prof Hannes Botha (who resigned as president of the South African Amateur Athletics Union because of the easing of the colour bar in sport), Prof P. S. Dreyer, and Prof G. D. Scholtz, former editor of *Die Transvaler* and author of a seminal book entitled *Het Die Afrikaner Volk 'n Toekoms*. Scholtz was particularly critical of his successor, Dr W. A. 'Wimpie' de Klerk (see below). The authors blamed the new liberalist element in Afrikanerdom for deviating from the policies of apartheid, e.g. by lessening the colour bar in sport; abandoning strict segregation in churches; contemplating repeal of the Immorality Act; weakening job reservation, and opening up social facilities to all races. Among the 'characteristics of the new Afrikaner liberalism' which Dr Treurnicht denounced were: the egalitarian dogma of individualism; tolerance of ideas other than those of Afrikanerdom; the prospect of minimum State interference in the lives of individuals; abolition of discrimination in public facilities, and support for absolute Press freedom.

At almost the opposite pole from these *verkrampte* theoreticians stands another group represented by the current editor of *Die Transvaler*. Calling for an official declaration of policy by the NP, 'Wimpie' de Klerk wrote that Nationalist policy stands irrevocably committed to the following principles: 'to respect and foster human rights for all people in SA; equal opportunities for all; one-man one-vote to guarantee autonomy (for each group) on the basis of our underlying ethnic diversity; joint participation in decision-making on matters of common concern to all groups; the elimination of colour discrimination at all levels; the free interplay of communities of different colours at those levels where we share facilities and common interests.' [79]

C. J. Alant, Professor of Sociology at the University of SA, wrote that the division of Afrikaners into *verkramptes* and *verligtes* (concepts originated by Wimpie de Klerk) was inadequate. [80] To differentiate more accurately among the different groups of Afrikaner leaders, Alant suggested four categories: the 'Standard Afrikaner' (identified with what Treurnicht calls the '*Laager* Afrikaner') who, with his clear concepts of truth, is politically and culturally aggressive; the 'Compromising Afrikaner', who is able to distinguish between God's unchanging laws and adaptable principles; the 'Liberal Afrikaner', who has broken free from the truths of the *volk* and is more of a nihilist or anarchist than a reformist or revolutionary; the 'Mature Afrikaner', who does not accept God's laws without question, but uses them as guiding principles; he remains true to the culture, history and individuality of the Afrikaner people.

The distinguished veteran educationalist, Prof E. G. Malherbe, agreed that Afrikanerdom now saw liberalism rather than the *swart gevaar* (the Black danger) as its greatest threat. [81] Liberalism and humanism were simply guises under which communism was creeping into the *laager*.

Among the Afrikaners who left the *laager* in 1977 were ex-Judge Kowie Marais, Prof Dreyer Kruger and Johan Kriel—all of whom joined the 'Progs'—and Natie Ferreira. Kowie Marais (also see PFP, below), a member of the NP since 1924 and formerly prominent in the Broederbond and Ossewa Brandwag, said that although it was clear that the whole plan of Separate Development had collapsed and no longer offered any hope, the NP advanced no alternative policy beyond promising 'change'. [82] Prof Dreyer Kruger wrote: 'It must become clear to all who are not deaf or blind that the National Party is incapable of lifting itself out of its racist framework. And any intelligent person can see that to maintain a racist approach is to head for disaster. The road on which the National Party is leading us is the road of ethnic and cultural suicide. I call upon my co-Afrikaners to leave that road, to find and open a new one. This we will be incapable of if we cling to the National Party'. [83] Johan Kriel (33) was a member of the security police who, after being converted back to Christianity, became worried about 'the ways employed to get information'. As a 'young radical Christian', he found these methods unacceptable and resigned to study for the ministry. He had hoped to stand as the PFP candidate in Stellenbosch, but deferred to his professors who argued that he could not combine a religious vocation with active political life.[84] Natie Ferreira was the political editor of the pro-Government *The Citizen* and later a columnist for *Die Transvaler*. In a series of articles, he explained how he found it impossible to achieve change from within the ranks of the ruling party.[85]

Prominent Afrikaner academics continued to speak out against apartheid policies (see Moolman and others under HNP, below). Prof J. L. Boshoff, the former rector of Turfloop University for Blacks, said that the Afrikaner had worked himself into a *cul de sac*;[86] the only way out was through consultation with the leaders of other races.[87] Prof Tjaart van der Walt, rector of Potchefstroom University, said there were two basic elements to Afrikaner nationalism: the relationship to God, and nationalism itself. He added, 'We must first be Christians, then Afrikaners. . . . Afrikaner nationalism should be inclusive not exclusive.'[88]

A remarkable group of c. 60 Afrikaner academics and students at the Potchefstroom University (the cradle of Christian National Education and of the minority Dutch Reformed Church—the *Doppers*) evolved a manifesto known as the Koinonia Declaration calling on the Government to abolish statutory prohibitions which impede free dealings between people of different races; grant equal political and economic opportunities to all races; give all racial groups a chance to voice their opinions about the proposed constitutional changes; scrap the Immorality Act; revise the Prohibition of Political Interference Act; honour freedom of speech and of the Press more scrupulously; inform the public more fully about security matters such as the recent bannings and detentions; allow detainees greater privileges, and institute all possible judicial means of avoiding another Biko case.

All those subscribing to the Koinonia Declaration are Government supporters; they have no formal organization, but meet together 'as likeminded friends to discuss the issues of the day'.[89] However, a prominent government MP, Albert Nothnagel, described this group as 'Afrikaner Jeremiahs', adding: 'The few Afrikaner propagandists of discrimination hysteria must be irrevocably shaken out of our ranks'.[90] He was one of the participants in a symposium on 'The Future of the Afrikaner' organized by the University of Cape Town Summer School.

The leaders of the *Morelig* (morning light) church group in the Free State town of Bethlehem claimed they were being persecuted and intimidated when they tried to challenge the policy of the Nederduitse Gereformeerde Kerk by distributing funds to Black missions. The Rev J. M. van Vurren was suspended; the deputy-postmaster, Tim Mattheus, suddenly transferred from the town; and all complained about receiving anonymous threatening letters.[91]

AFRIKAANS WRITERS

Prof S. A. Strauss, head of the Department of Criminal Law at the University of SA, resigned from the South African Academy for Science and Art because of its refusal to admit to membership Prof Bhadra Ranchod, an Indian with a distinguished record of work in Roman Dutch Law. The reason for the rejection was not actually stated as colour, but because he had not published enough in Afrikaans. Later, six prominent Afrikaner writers (all members of the *Afrikaans Skrywersgilde*) resigned from the Academy because of its 'inability' to reach a decision on admitting a well-known Coloured poet who writes in Afrikaans, S. V. Petersen.[92] The authors who resigned are Chris Barnard, Abraham H. de Vries, Elsa Joubert, Etienne le Roux, Jan Rabie, Leon Rousseau and F. A. Venter.

A controversial book by Prof W. S. H. du Randt, head of the Afrikaans department at the University of Port Elizabeth, brought a threat of libel action by the playwright, Athol Fugard.[93] He and Nadine Gordimer were among those accused of aiming at 'the violent overthrow of the Government'—charges they vigorously denied. He also accused the group of Afrikaner writers known as the *Sestigers* (the Sixties) of writing 'resistance verse'. Du Randt's book was made a compulsory set work for all first-year students of Afrikaans-Nederlands.

Radical Afrikaner writers again found themselves in trouble with the censor.[94] Etienne le Roux's prize-winning satiric novel, *Magersfontein, O Magersfontein*—which pokes fun at everybody from Cabinet Ministers to traffic cops—was banned on the grounds that it used 'in excess, filthy language' etc. His was the second banned Afrikaans novel, the first being *Kennis van die Aand*. In 1977, 31 Afrikaans writers formed a Writers' Guild to fight against censorship.

AFRIKANER BUSINESSMEN

Afrikaner business tycoons, who in the past had co-operated with each other against the English-dominated financial world, began to quarrel in 1977. The two biggest Afrikaner-owned financial empires—Sanlam and Volkskas—came into conflict over the acquisition of Trust Bank.[95] (Sanlam's Dr Andreas Wassenaar had been involved in a political row with the Prime Minister in 1976 over his book attacking 'state capitalism'.)[96] One inside observer saw the struggle as essentially between the Cape businessmen, who represent *verligtheid*, and the more conservative-minded Transvalers in the north. Dr Albert Wessels, one of the leading Afrikaner financiers, joined Wassenaar in his fight against what he called 'creeping socialism'.[97] He said: 'There is a tremendous amount going on behind the scenes in Nationalist Party and Afrikaner circles. There is a swing towards more liberal policies particularly among the intellectuals, the church and businessmen who will no doubt put pressure on the party leaders.'

Afrikaner business leaders also came out in support of using skilled Black workers in all sections of the economy, including administrative and supervisory jobs. Donald Masson, chairman of the Johannesburg *Afrikaanse Sakekamer* (Chamber of Commerce) said that training skilled Black workers was an economic necessity since there were simply not enough Whites to do the jobs. Some of the members of his Chamber were already employing Black managers.[98] The president of the Afrikaanse Handelsinstituut (trade institute) Jack van Wyk, said his organization stood squarely behind a policy of breaking down race discrimination in employment.[99] 'I would be sorry to see the Government running scared. We have to change. We are ostracized all over the world and should not be complacent. South Africans must realize that there must be some faults in the system and we have to put these right.'

DIE BROEDERBOND[100]

The strong influence exercised on the Government by this Afrikaner secret society was revealed by the Johannesburg *Sunday Times*, which secured evidence that the Broederbond receives highly confidential documents from the Prime Minister, and that he consults it on major policy issues, usually before coming to any final decision.[101] Nevertheless, there is some evidence of policy disagreements. In the aftermath of the Soweto riots in 1976, the society drew up a master plan to implement a 'grand strategy' of Separate Development which runs directly contrary to the Government's own decision to accept that the urban Black communities will form a permanent part of 'White SA'. Under the Broeders' plan, millions of Africans would be removed to the Homelands, the thought of urban Africans being regarded as permanent dwellers in the 'White lands' being rejected outright. The plan goes so far as to suggest that the Government should take powers to harness both the private and public sectors of the economy to make the massive transfer of population possible—and even produces a fanciful policy of persuading some of the

Western powers to underwrite a 'Marshall Plan' to facilitate this enterprise. It also outlines plans to indoctrinate English-speaking South Africans and Coloureds to accept these proposals; the blueprint talks repeatedly of the need to 'compel' compliance with the master plan.

Other secret documents show the extent to which the society has already captured most of the key posts in the South African education system—a strategic area of its activities; a special target for takeover in 1977 was Natal.[102] The Broeders were also shown to have played a role in the choice of candidates for the NP in the election campaign,[103] and to have taken a hand in deciding policy towards Rhodesia.[104]

Details about the early history of the Broederbond were revealed in an important study published by Dr E. G. Malherbe (see above).[105] He quotes a circular of 16 January 1934 in which the society's executive declared: 'Our chief concern is whether Afrikanerdom will reach its eventual goal of *baasskap* (domination) in SA. Brothers, our solution for SA's troubles is that the Afrikaner Broederbond shall rule SA.' In effect, they have been doing that for just on 30 years.

THE PRIME MINISTER'S ROLE

After 11 years in office, John Balthazzar Vorster (62) won the biggest majority ever secured by a South African Prime Minister in the elections held in November 1977. Although making no secret of the grave problems facing the Republic (especially the growing hostility of the West) or of the need for change, he made it abundantly clear that this would occur only within the narrow limits defined by himself. Blacks would walk their own political road; they could not sit in the same parliament as Whites.[106] He would 'eliminate race discrimination' but not turn SA into a multi-racial society; separation of the races would stay. Within those limits, he showed himself ready to embark on what is, for Afrikaners, radical constitutional changes—but not just yet. Typical of his style of leadership, he held his cards very close to his chest, while encouraging his ministers to stick out their necks to gauge possible political reactions to ideas formulating in his own mind. The colleague used most frequently in this role was his *verligte* Minister of National Education and Sport, Dr Piet Koornhof. Thus, when Koornhof formally declared himself in favour of reorganizing the Republic's institutions into Swiss-like cantons (see Constitutional Affairs, above), it can be taken for granted that he was flying a kite for the Prime Minister.

Apart from his preoccupation with constitutional reforms, the other major themes in Vorster's speeches were the growing confrontation with the West and the deepening threats to the Republic's security. In his 1977 New Year speech, he announced: 'If a communist onslaught should be made against SA, directly or under camouflage, then SA will have to face it alone.' With regard to the controversy in August over SA's proposed nuclear tests (see below), he invited the West to 'do its damdest', since SA would have no alternative but to say 'so far and no far-ther'.[107] In October, he said that SA could and would survive alone in the face of international pressure, including 'Russian force and American finesse'.[108] In November, he promised that English and Afrikaans-speaking South Africans would defend the Republic to 'the last man' against any attempt to take over the southern tip of Africa—not only for their own sake but 'for the sake of the free world and Christianity'.[109] While envisaging sporadic troubles breaking out, he did not 'foresee a racial war in SA, now or in the future. These tensions will pass. I don't think they will wreck SA's future one bit.'[110] Throughout 1977, he repeatedly said that his government was bracing itself to withstand international economic sanctions, but under no circumstances would it give in to US or other foreign pressures; it would resist 'blatant meddling' in the country's internal affairs.[111] Nevertheless, he lost no opportunity to meet with Western leaders to discuss the problems of the Republic.

The Prime Minister took a confident view about his government's efforts to meet African grievances. 'The Blacks in SA,' he claimed, 'have made more progress in the past five years, in all directions, than in the last two centuries.'[112] He continued to stress the crucial importance of SA achieving harmonious relations with the rest of the continent. 'We have tried for decades to sell ourselves to Europe and the Western world,' he told a meeting of the party faithful.[113] 'We will not succeed in this until we have sold ourselves to Africa, and if this happens, then we will automatically have sold ourselves to the West.' However, he was quick to add that there was a difference between 'selling ourselves to Africa' and 'selling ourselves out of Africa'.

The first full-length biography of the Prime Minister—*Vorster—the Man* by John D'Oliveira, assistant to the editor of the Johannesburg *Star* —appeared in November 1977. In it, Vorster describes the three years he spent in prison (1942–45) as a leader of the Ossewa Brandwag and an opponent of the war. 'They locked me up and forgot about me. . . . People talk about the terrors of solitary confinement. I know about it.' It might be thought strange that his own experience has had no effect on the way he treats his opponents. In an especially revealing passage, one of Vorster's closest friends, Flip le Grange, relates how he spent hours trying to convince him of the importance of adopting democratic methods and eschewing violence. 'John went away unshaken in his belief that there was no other way to serve the Afrikaner cause, to give Afrikaners control of SA. . . . Vorster argued at the time that he had no faith in democratic methods. . . .'

The foreign editor of the London *Times*, Louis Heren, who interviewed Vorster early in 1978, described him as 'a very impressive man . . . hardly likeable, but a visitor immediately feels that he is in the presence of a powerful and confident leader. . . . He reminded me of Adenauer; the impassive face, upright back, unblinking stare and the formal politenesses.'[114]

THE GOVERNMENT

The Prime Minister made few changes in his 25 January 1978 Cabinet reshuffle, but one significant move was his decision to transfer the influential Dr Connie Mulder from the Interior Ministry to head the Bantu Affairs Department, renamed the Ministry of Plural Affairs and Development. Mulder's predecessor, M. C. Botha, who had announced his decision not to stand for election, had the reputation of being an undeviating *verkrampte* and was widely unpopular among Africans. Dr Nthato Motlana, chairman of the Soweto Committee of Ten, described Botha as 'a man who would not listen to anybody. . . . He thought he knew all about Blacks.' Mulder, it seems, at least believes in real consultations with Africans (see National Party, below). A separate Ministry for Bantu Education was created, with Willem Cruywagen (57), the former Deputy Minister, in charge. The new Deputy Minister is Dr Willie Vosloo who, with his wife, devotes time during parliamentary recesses to voluntary medical work in Malawi.

The new Minister of Interior is Alwyn Schlebusch, chiefly remembered for his role as chairman of the commission of that name which in 1972–73 acted as a 'star chamber' investigating the role of the National Union of South African Students, the South African Institute of Race Relations and a number of Christian bodies.[115] The new Minister of Posts and Telecommunications, F. W. de Klerk (42), is the brother of the controversial *verligte* editor of *Die Transvaler.* The Minister of Justice, Police and Prisons, Jimmy Kruger, retained his portfolio. All ministers in the new Cabinet belong to the Broederbond except two: the Finance Minister,

Senator O. Horwood, is English-speaking and so automatically barred from membership; and Marais Steyn who, by the time he had switched from the UP to the NP, was too old to be considered. Significantly, Vorster did not promote his leading *verkrampte* apostle, Andries Treurnicht, to the Cabinet. He was again given a junior post as Deputy Minister of Education and Training.

THE GOVERNMENT (as at January 1978)

State President	Dr N. C. Diederichs
Prime Minister	John Vorster
Other Ministers:	
Defence	P. W. Botha
Transport	S. L. Muller
Labour and Mines	S. P. Botha
Bantu Development and	
Administration and	
Development and Information*	Dr C. P. Mulder
Social Welfare and Pensions,	
Posts and Telecommunications	Senator J. P. van der Spuy
National Education, Sport	
and Recreation	Dr P. G. J. Koornhof
Agriculture	H. Schoeman
Health, Planning and	
Environment	Dr S. W. van der Merwe
Finance	Senator O. P. F. Horwood
Economic Affairs	J. C. Heunis
Justice, Police and Prisons	J. T. Kruger
Indian Affairs, Community	
Development and Tourism	S. J. M. Steyn
Immigration, Public Works	
and Interior	A. L. Schlebusch
Forestry and Water	A. J. Raubenheimer
Coloured, Rehoboth and	
Nama Relations	H. H. Smit
Foreign Affairs	R. F. Botha
Education and Training	W. A. Cruywagen

* The portfolio was changed to Department of Plural Relations and Development.

PARLIAMENTARY PARTIES

The configuration of parliamentary parties changed completely on 28 June 1977 when the official opposition, the United Party, dissolved because of irreconcilable divisions within its own ranks. Formed in 1936 by two Boer War generals, J. B. M. Hertzog and Jan Christian Smuts, the UP was the governing party until May 1948. But it never fully recovered from the electoral defeat of Smuts: neither of his two successors, J. G. N. Strauss nor Sir de Villiers Graff, was able to inspire much confidence or hold the party together. In his final speech, Sir de Villiers said the UP was 'in danger of becoming irrelevant because at this critical and dangerous time in our history, we are not broadly based enough to attract sufficient support to challenge a government which has done SA irresponsible harm and has no solutions to its problems, many of which it has created itself.' UP members realigned themselves among the New Republic Party, the Progressive Federal Party and the South African Party.

THE HERENIGDE NASIONALE PARTY (NP)

While not as deeply divided as the UP, the ruling party was itself by no means united. The basic split remained between the *verkramptes* (inward-looking, narrow) and the *verligtes* (enlightened), a split kept in check only by the policies of the Prime

Minister who skilfully made concessions to the former, while encouraging the latter. The leading *verkrampte* remains Dr Andries W. Treurnicht, who failed to gain Cabinet promotion in the 1978 reshuffle.[116] The leading *verligtes* are the Foreign Minister, Pik Botha; the Minister of National Education, Sport and Recreation, Dr Piet Koornhof; and the Defence Minister, P. W. Botha. But the divisions within the ruling party were by no means confined to these two opposite groups. For example, a non-*verligte*, the Minister of Agriculture, H. Schoeman, roused considerable controversy when he declared that the 'sex across the colour line' law—the Immorality Act—was unnecessary.[117] His views were strongly criticized by Treurnicht and others.

The new Foreign Minister, Pik Botha, drew most of the lightning from the *verkramptes* over his energetic call for the scrapping of 'petty apartheid'—the minor irritants of racial discrimination—a policy also favoured by Vorster, Koornhof and P. W. Botha. They received support from a new quarter, Piet Marais, a rural Cape Province MP who called on the government to rethink its racial policies.[118] Speaking of the position of urban Blacks, he said: 'If we are honest we must say that we don't know where we are going on that issue.' He also felt that the borders of the Homelands should not be regarded as final and called for improved land consolidation. These views were strongly challenged by Treurnicht and others. But the *verkrampte* group's main target was Pik Botha himself. Quoting from his own book *Credo van 'n Afrikaner*, Treurnicht said: 'If minor apartheid is eliminated, the concept of Separate Development becomes superfluous and unnecessary. You can't make apartheid big if you kill it little by little.'[119]

Treurnicht widened these criticisms by declaring himself against the ideas of 'pluralism' voiced by at least three senior ministers (see Constitutional Affairs, above). In a speech to the conference of the South African Bureau of Race Affairs, he criticized the word 'pluralism', claiming it was dangerous to view Coloureds, Asians and Black people living outside the Homelands as part of one plural society. No Black man in a White area lacks political rights or representation; they exist among his own people in their own territory.[120] In keeping with this view, Treurnicht had strong reservations in accepting the Prime Minister's proposals for a multi-racial Cabinet. However, the strongest attack against the *verligtes* was delivered by Treurnicht and six other prominent government supporters in a volume of essays entitled *Afrikaner-Liberalisme* (see Afrikaners, above).

Another divisive issue was the Theron Commission report on the Coloured people.[121] The Cape Nationalists, under the leadership of P. W. Botha, were strongly in favour of implementing its main findings, but two pro-government papers took a critical line.[122]

Less clearly definable was the degree of support enjoyed by the influential leader of the Transvaal Nationalists, Dr Connie Mulder, regarded by many as the Prime Minister's Dauphin—though not by Vorster himself. Mulder has been less critical of the *verkramptes* (though he disagrees with them on such issues as 'pluralism') than of Pik Botha, whom he sees as a serious rival. Mulder upset the ranks by making his own independent statements on foreign affairs, such as suggesting a policy less dependent on the West and a possible warming of relations with Peking! Mulder (backed by the Police Minister, Jimmie Kruger, and Louis le Grange) came out against the 'cantonal' system of pluralism advocated by P. W. Botha and Piet Koornhof (see Constitutional Affairs, above). Mulder and Koornhof—though both advocates of 'pluralism'—also disagree about whether they mean 'plural democracies or a plural co-society'.[123]

Mulder's transfer in February 1978 from the Ministry of Interior to the strategically difficult Ministry of Bantu Affairs (which he renamed Plural

Relations) put him into the hottest seat in the country. (He retained the Ministry of Information.) Mulder defined his objectives in parliament as affording Africans 'basic human rights, majority rule and self-determination within the concept of plural democracy; paying special attention to good human relations and healthy dialogue; doing nothing which would jeopardize any group's right of self-determination or which could destroy the identity of any group. He identified the issue of urban Blacks as 'the crux of the matter'. Mulder is described as 'an ideologist but not a paternalist. His lack of paternalism is his great asset. His commitment ideologically to White survival through White control of their own future is central to his political thinking. He is willing to negotiate, and really negotiate, with officially-elected Black leaders for whatever dispensation they would like, provided it does not involve political sharing where Black numbers could outweigh Whites.'[174]

The Minister of Police, Justice and Prisons, Jimmy Kruger, lost considerable political ground over his handling of the Steve Biko affair (see below), and his generally truculent position towards critics of his policies and of the police. The Red Cross described his attitude to its attempts to visit detainees as 'arrogant'. In a single act of contrition, he told parliament on 31 January 1978 that he would be 'truly sorry if any action of his had harmed SA'.

PROGRESSIVE FEDERAL PARTY (PFP)

The PFP was formed on 5 September 1977 by a merging of the Progressive Reform Party (PRP)[125] and a section of the UP led by Japie Basson. The leader of the new party is Colin Eglin, the former leader of the Progressive Party, with Basson as deputy leader. The third member of the triumvirate is Harry Schwarz who led the former Reform Party. Although the PFP emerged as the main opposition party in the general election (see below), it still remains to be seen whether a dilution of the earlier 'Prog' principles has been necessary to accommodate the new forces. What does seem clear, however, is that relations between Schwarz and the two principal 'Prog' leaders, Colin Eglin and Helen Suzman, are not very cordial.

The PFP programme commits the party to power-sharing. Its seven basic principles are: full citizenship for all South Africans without race or colour discrimination; a new constitution for the Republic, drawn up, negotiated and agreed upon by representatives of all sections of the population; sharing of political rights by all citizens without the domination of one race by another; an open society free from compulsory separation or compulsory integration; right of all people to maintain and develop their religious, language and cultural heritage; equality of opportunity for all citizens in an economy based on free enterprise, right of every individual to the protection of his life, liberty and property and access to the judiciary in defence of these rights.[126]

A major recruit to the PFP was Kowie Marais, formerly one of the most prestigious judges in the country. At one time a rabid Afrikaner nationalist who, with Vorster, belonged to the violent anti-war movement, the Ossewabrandwag, he was expelled from the Broederbond in 1977. Marais said that Steve Biko's death in detention had caused him to become 'a complete and unequivocal enemy of the country's security legislation'.[127] Marais has also become deeply interested in Judaism, goes to synagogue on Friday evenings and wants to buy land in Israel.[128] He was elected MP for a Johannesburg constituency.

Colin Eglin, who visited President Senghor in Senegal and President Kaunda in Zambia, took a critical attitude to President Carter's policies towards SA. He complained that US actions 'give the impression that it is more concerned with punishing SA for not having changed than with helping it to change'.[129] Eglin

69

denied that the PFP stood for Black majority rule; it rejected 'the racist concept of Black majority rule' just as it rejected 'the racist concept of White minority rule'.[130]

THE NEW REPUBLIC PARTY (NRP) AND THE SOUTH AFRICAN PARTY (SAP)

The 24 MPs of the UP who refused to join the PFP agreed at first to merge with the Democratic Party of Dr Theo Gerdener (a former Nationalist Minister of Interior and proponent of confederalism) to form the NRP on 29 June 1977. But only three weeks later, Gerdener himself withdrew. Denying reports that this was because he was not chosen for a parliamentary seat, he said the new party showed an 'obvious lack of insight into the needs which are, and will remain, critically vital to the party if it is to evolve into a viable opposition, not to mention an alternative government'.[131] Myles Cadman MP was elected the new leader, but he was defeated in the general election in which the NRP won only ten seats. With the motto, 'self-rule for all', the NRP's aims are to produce a confederal constitution linking the different political units comprising a pluralist society, and to decentralize decision-making, leading to maximum self-rule and local options.

A handful of the most conservative-minded UP supporters, led by Myburgh Streicher, formed the SAP, but won only three seats in the elections.

GENERAL ELECTIONS, NOVEMBER 1977

In a surprise move on 21 September 1977, the Prime Minister announced 30 November as the date for parliamentary and provincial council elections. In seeking a fresh mandate, Vorster indicated that he wanted endorsement for his new constitutional proposals (see above). At a time when the parliamentary opposition parties were in a state of disarray, he could also hope to increase the strength of the ruling party from the 117 seats held in the old parliament of 165 members. (The new parliament would have only 161 members since, with the exception of the Walvis Bay constituency, Namibian seats would no longer be represented in the South African Assembly.) Anti-government forces saw the Prime Minister's strategy as being dictated by four major considerations: to demonstrate to the outside world that his government had overwhelming electoral support; to consolidate his personal authority over the ruling party and to demonstrate the weakness of his *verkrampte* opponents; to receive a mandate for his constitutional proposals; and to establish his new government before economic conditions deteriorated further.

The veteran Progressive MP, Ms Helen Suzman, pointed out that whatever the election results, it had to be remembered that only 20% of adult South Africans would go to the polls since voting was restricted to the 2,217,530 White electorate (of whom 1,110,667 are in the Transvaal, 678,331 in the Cape Province, 257,768 in Natal and 170,724 in the Orange Free State). The former UP MP, Japie Basson, commented: 'To be returned with the same majority, or a bigger majority, or a smaller majority, will be completely irrelevant as far as the outside world is concerned.'

The election campaign was marred by the savage murder of the government candidate in Springs, Dr Robert Smit and his wife. Although the crime was immediately attributed to Black terrorism, it was later concluded to have had no direct political motive or significance and no arrests were made. At the time of his murder, Smit—a brilliant economist—was involved in helping to arrange a R1,000m Swiss bank loan for a group of businessmen.

The NP gained the biggest electoral victory of any government in the 17 elections held since Union in 1910, winning 134 seats against the 30 of the Opposition (one seat is vacant):

| | Seats | | |
Party	% of vote	1977 election (before dissolution in brackets)	1974 election
National Party	64.8	134 (116)	122
New Republic Party	11.8	10 (23)	(UP 40)
Progressive Federal Party	16.7	17 (18)	(Progs 7)
South Africa Party	1.7	3 (6)	—
Herenigde Nasionale Party	3.2	0 (0)	0

The PFP's 17 seats made it the official opposition. Almost all its seats were won in the more affluent or middle-class areas of Johannesburg, together with a cluster in Cape Town and a single seat in Natal. The former opposition—if equated with its successor, the NRP—lost 28 seats, the ten it retained confined almost entirely to Natal. The *verkrampte* HNP did worse than ever, losing its deposits in all but two seats.

Alexander Steward, editor of *RSA World* (who reliably reflects official thinking), described the result as 'a declaration of national independence. Anglo-South Africans and Afrikaners alike are disillusioned today with the West. Association with the West, conforming to its precepts, is no longer a necessary criteria. They now see the safeguarding of their future in political action untrammelled by external influence.'[132]

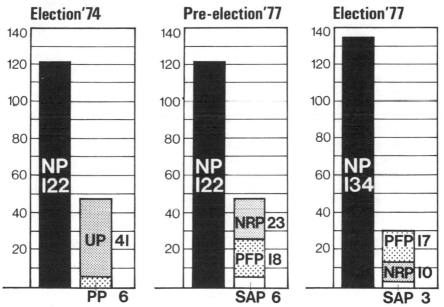

THE BLACK MOOD

The mood of SA's 21m Blacks and Coloureds can be summed up in a word: defiance. Although all the movements prominently identified with Black Consciousness—the embodiment of this mood—were banned and repressed in October 1977, this official action appears only to have increased the spirit of defiance, as was shown by the determined boycott of almost 95% of the people of Soweto in the elections for their Urban Council (see below); by the continued clandestine activities of urban Black groups all over the country; by the angry breaking off of relations with Pretoria by the Transkei government; by the KwaZulu leader, Chief Gatsha Buthelezi's refusal to restrict the membership of his Inkhata movement to Zulus only, and by unblunted attacks by Black journalists, led by Percy Qoboza, the editor of the banned *World*, after his release from detention. Addressing the Cillie Commission of Inquiry into the causes of the Soweto riots, Mpiyakhe Kumalo, a university lecturer in African languages, warned that while Whites believed there was peace in SA, superficial Black 'contentment' was really the lull before the storm.[133] Because of fear and insecurity, the average Black man 'will always remain superficially contented, yet always curse the all-powerful White man when he finds an opportunity'. Nevertheless, Percy Qoboza wrote: 'I have not to date come across any responsible Black leader who has advanced the theory that Whites are expendable and must be thrown into the sea. We have, on the contrary, over the years emphasized that Whites are South Africans and have the right to exist in a common fatherland; and that all of us, around a conference table, must devise a formula acceptable for future co-existence.'[134]

But even Qoboza said that, at 39, he considered himself on the edge of 'the older generation that is being pushed aside' in the Black Consciousness movement.[135] A reporter of the Soweto scene, Tom Duff, wrote of the mood of young Sowetans: 'Many of these youngsters hate Whites as well. One reason for this lies in Soweto's very separateness from White Johannesburg. The only Whites many of them come into contact with are West Rand Board officials and the police. They dislike both these groups and tend to see all Whites as fitting into the same category. As a reporter who has covered Soweto for more than a year, I have come across this hatred time and time again—only to see it diminish when one sits down and talks to students and convinces them that one does not fit the stereotype they have of the White man. Suspicion is replaced by a guarded friendliness when they realize that all you are interested in is listening to what they have to say. But there are those whose hatred runs very deep—especially those who have had close friends and relatives killed in the unrest.'[136] Nimrod Mkele, director of the Institute for Black Studies, wrote similarly of the spirit of young people in Soweto: 'We adults have very little to do with what is going on. . . . The kids say we are irrelevant.' The *tsotsis* (delinquents) and 'unruly elements' are the 'spawn of apartheid—children who went to school, got frustrated, couldn't finish their schooling and have ended up as unruly elements. They are unruly precisely because they did not get the training they needed and now, as a result, they can't get jobs.'

A survey of Black urban attitudes to Whites carried out by a market research company, Markinor, in the nine main urban areas around the country showed, surprisingly, that fewer Africans thought that race relations were worse in April 1977 than in September 1976.[137] (The survey was taken before the October 1977 clampdown on the Black Consciousness movement; one must also allow for inaccuracy as a result of Africans not revealing their true feelings.) In April 1977 (cf September 1976 in brackets), 37% (52%) thought relations were worsening; 12% (9%) that they were improving; 25% (19%) that they were remaining the same; 26% (20%) did not know. Only 19% (26%) felt their families would be better off in a year's time; 36% (38%) that they would be the same; 33% (31%) that they would be worse off; 12% (6%) did not know. There was a significant difference of attitude between those with jobs and those without.

What lay behind these attitudes and unrest? According to an interview in August 1977, the Prime Minister's own view was that 'Black majority rule, not grievances, was the real issue behind the continuing unrest'.[138] But he also said that there was no intention on his Government's part ever to accept majority rule for SA (see Vorster's role, above).

BLACK POLITICAL MOVEMENTS
SOWETO POLITICAL GROUPS
The Committee of Ten was among the movements banned on 19 October 1977 (see above). Nevertheless, it issued a Manifesto which rejected the 'powerless advice tribunal—the Urban Bantu Council'—and called instead for the establishment of a Soweto Local Authority to be set up and controlled by Sowetans, with a five-year plan to produce proper facilities for the city of 1.25m Blacks near Johannesburg.[139] It favoured the 'Black concept of sharing and communalism'. Its chairman was Dr Ntatho Motlana (43), who had been arrested and banned for his part in the ANC Defiance Campaign in the 1950s. Later he helped to found the BPC. Although Motlana proclaimed that 'SA will become Azania in 10 years' and is a firm believer in one-man one-vote, he was widely regarded as 'a moderate' and was invited to speak at Broederbond and other Afrikaner meetings.[140] He did not support international sanctions against SA but looked for 'friendly diplomatic pressure' from the US and other Western countries.[141] 'If they want to beat Russia to the post, they had better apply pressure. We don't want to go communist.' As the spokesman for the Committee of Ten, Motlana repeatedly expressed its willingness to sit down and negotiate with the Government about the running of Soweto's affairs. However, it was not consulted when the authorities established a new elective Urban Bantu Council for Soweto, which was overwhelmingly rejected by Sowetans.

After the banning of the Committee of Ten, the Azania People's Organization (Azapo) was formed to continue the work of propagating Black Consciousness. Its two principal leaders, Ishmael Mkhabela and Lybon Mabasa, were detained on 4 May 1978.

Six other Soweto groups were formed after the banning of the Committee of Ten: the Masingafi Party, led by Sipho Motha; the Ratepayers' Association, led by Peter Lengene; the Residents' Committee, led by M. T. Moerane; the Sofasonke Party, led by Letsatsi Radebe; the Makgotla Faction, led by Lucas Shabangu; and Mamate Dingaka, led by P. J. Majola. The first three all oppose the Government's proposed Urban Council, while the last three accept it but with qualifications.[142] Masingafi claims 10,000 members, wants the same status for Soweto as Johannesburg, and favours full political rights for Blacks in parliament. The Ratepayers demand fully-fledged municipal status and claim over 700 members. The Residents' Committee favours an autonomous city council and African representation in local and central government. It claims that individual members of its executive command wide support through the organizations they represent.

THE SA STUDENTS' ORGANIZATION (SASO)
SASO, formed in 1968 as an exclusively Black students' organization (see below), suffered from serious internal problems even before it was banned in October 1977. These difficulties are frankly discussed in Z (Vol 2, No 5), published by SSD in Cape Town. Its exile leaders have continued to maintain their organization in Botswana, Nigeria and England. One of these leaders, Tsietsi Mashinini, was reportedly caught up in a struggle between Communist and Trotskyite organizations in European student and anti-apartheid movements.[143]

At home, SASO continued to give leadership to the students' strikes in Soweto and acted as a pressure group to oppose those willing to participate in the new Soweto community council elections. It was also reported to have opened a campaign to persuade all Blacks to resign from Government bodies or as Government servants, including traffic policemen. [144] In his presidential address to the eighth conference of SASO, Diliza Mji said that 'students can never effectively contribute positively to the changing SA scene if we pursue middle-class interests'. [145] In a policy statement published in December 1977, SASO declared that 'the structures and activities of the Black Consciousness Movement (BCM) will now join those of the National Liberation Movement in ''underground'' politicization and mobilization work among the oppressed masses. Decentralization is the strength of the movement for liberation in SA, and while the legal years of BCM were useful to those organizing for liberation, they were by no means imperative. The National Liberation Movement in SA is now stronger than ever before and encompasses all individuals and organizations striving for the liberation of the oppressed masses and for the establishment of a non-racial and just society.' [146]

SASO also began to adopt a friendlier attitude to the National Union of SA Students (NUSAS). While still holding that NUSAS can 'never be wholly progressive', nevertheless, despite 'the natural constraints imposed by its constituency, NUSAS in 1977 indicates clearly that a powerful movement exists among White students and youth who promote majority rule in a non-racial and unitary SA'. [147]

BLACK PEOPLE'S CONVENTION (BPC)

The BPC's president, Kenneth Rachidi, and other members of the executive were placed in indefinite detention in Modder B prison but managed to smuggle a Christmas message from jail in December 1977 declaring: 'We are not and shall not be bothered by bannings. The struggle goes on. The BPC expresses power and solidarity with the ANC and PAC in the present detentions, trials and convictions of the ANC and PAC sons and daughters.' Before the banning, the BPC leadership refused to have discussions with Ambassador Andy Young because of the unrepresentative nature of the South Africans he was due to meet. At Biko's funeral, before his detention, Rachidi said that 'Steve Biko remains the vanguard of not only resistance, but a creator of sound and healthier alternatives'. He said that police harassment of BPC only strengthened the Black Consciousness Movement. Dr Mamphela Ramphele, described by Donald Woods as the 'Odette' of the Black Consciousness struggle, was banned for a second time in May 1977 and sent to a remote place of detention in Vendaland. [148]

INKHATA YENKULULEKO YESIZWE (INKHATA) AND THE SA BLACK ALLIANCE (SABA)

Chief Gatsha Buthelezi challenged the SA Government on two major issues in 1977: he insisted that the KwaZulu Homeland, of which he is Chief Minister, would never opt for separate independence, and that he regarded those Homeland leaders who did so as 'traitors'; and he refused to restrict his Inkhata movement to Zulu membership, insisting that it was open to all. His leadership was strengthened in February 1978 when, in the first KwaZulu elections, Inkhata won all 55 of the elected seats for the Homeland Legislative Assembly. However, Buthelezi faced two hostile demonstrations in 1977–78. In September, he called off a meeting at the university for Indians in Durban when students demonstrated against him; he angrily reminded them of the bloody Zulu-Indian riots of 1949. In March 1978, he was forced to withdraw from the funeral of Robert Mangaliso Sobukwe after being threatened with violence. The Inkhata executive, backed by the leaders of the (Coloured) Labour Party, blamed the incident on a 'small, misguided and immature clique'.

Inkhata claims to have 130,000 paid-up members. Although its Publicity Secretary, Gibson Thula, agrees that the vast majority are Zulus, he insists that a fair number are from other tribes, especially in the Free State. The Minister of Justice, Police and Prisons, Jimmy Kruger, summoned Buthelezi to a special meeting to warn him of the consequences if he refused to obey the Government's orders to restrict Inkhata's membership to Zulus. One of Buthelezi's aides subsequently released a full transcript of what had transpired. At one point, Kruger told Buthelezi that if he sought to broaden his political base beyond Zulu membership 'to a Black polarization . . . there is going to be trouble. No doubt about it, because you can understand we have got to react. We cannot sit back while Black man polarizes against White man. It will become a life and death struggle then. This is our difficulty. . . . I want to say very honestly, you are causing a very great reaction among the Whites. I am very worried that the White man will put his back to the wall and say, "No, go to hell, we do nothing for them. They want to fight, let them fight." My people did that at Blood River. They will do it again, and I don't want that. . . . It means we are going to kill each other off, and we don't want that. We want to live together in peace.'[149] Buthelezi said after his meeting with Kruger that just as the NP did not exclude other White ethnic groups from membership, he claimed the same right not to exclude other Blacks.[150]

Kruger also raised the question of whether Inkhata was linked to the outlawed ANC and PAC. Buthelezi denied the existence of any such links, although the party's colours—green, gold and black—are the same as the ANC's. However, Gibson Thula commented on another occasion: 'We would not be looking at reality if we did not admit the legitimacy of the ANC in the struggle for liberation'.

Buthelezi ignored a government order that a meeting he was to address in Soweto on 30 January 1978 should be confined to Zulus, and that he should speak only about the elections in KwaZulu. About 15,000 Sowetans of all tribes gave Buthelezi an enthusiastic welcome. He told them that Inkhata stood four-square behind the banned Committee of Ten and that it would be an 'act of treachery' for Sowetans to vote in the Urban Council elections while the Committee's leaders were in detention.[151] More pleasing to the authorities, he counselled the students to call off their school boycott and repeated his strong opposition to economic sanctions against SA since they would hurt Africans most.

Buthelezi also said on a number of occasions that he was opposed to armed violence to bring about change in SA. Speaking to Stellenbosch students, he said: 'No lasting solution can ever be based in the fire that comes through the barrel of a gun. If we rely on that fire, its flames will finally consume all of us. Because I have believed in a Christian perspective for SA all my life, I still stand—even at this late hour—for a non-violent change. I have operated within the present Government's policy, while I abhor the ideology behind it, in the hope of avoiding polarization and the resultant confrontation and conflict.' He added that there was no prospect at present that peaceful solutions for SA's problems could be found unless common ground was found between fellow South Africans and fellow Christians. 'If we cannot find common ground, more and more of our people will feel that violence is the only alternative left to the Black people of SA. Let me stress that I am merely expressing the feelings of most of my people.'[152]

Buthelezi went further than just open Inkhata's ranks to non-Zulus, however. At a meeting at the Zulu royal capital of Ulundi on 11 January 1978, he was elected chairman of a new national political movement—the South African Black Alliance (SABA)—to represent Africans, Indians and Coloureds. Associated with this move were Sonny Leon, the chairman of the (Coloured) Labour Party; N. Chinsamy, leader of the Indian Reform Party, and the Homeland leaders of Qwa-Qwa.

Inkhata's secretary, Sipho Bhengu, said: 'After the White solidarity in the White election, we ought to show our solidarity in our rejection of apartheid'. While all three parties operate within the government's separate institutional structures, all reject independence within the Separate Development plan, as well as the Prime Minister's three-tier Cabinet for Whites, Indians and Coloureds.

Buthelezi also snubbed the Government by refusing to attend the summit meeting between the Prime Minister and the Homeland leaders in October 1977. He had described the previous meeting in July as a 'time-wasting farce' and 'a dialogue of the deaf'. Buthelezi told the US ambassador to the UN, Andy Young, that the only guarantee for the future of SA was a genuine dialogue with all Black leaders, including the prisoners on Robben Island. He repeatedly said that the Zulus would 'stand alone if necessary' in opposition to the geographical fragmentation of the Republic. Pointing out that the 5.2m Zulus outnumbered the 4.3m Whites, he said: 'If necessary, we alone will ensure that Black South Africa will never be fragmented into a number of ridiculous mini-states'. [153]

LABOUR PARTY AND FREEDOM PARTY
The Labour Party, which is exclusively Coloured, seemed at one point to be divided over whether to accept the Prime Minister's constitutional proposals for a three-tier Cabinet (see Constitutional affairs, above), but in the end, it rejected them. As the major party in the Coloured Person's Representative Council, this decision hit hard at Vorster's plan. The party's annual conference in December 1977 endorsed the decision to form an alliance with Inkhata. It also came out in favour of sanctions and other forms of economic pressures against SA, and asked churches to examine their investments in businesses that practised racial discrimination. Sonny Leon was re-elected as leader of the party, David Curry as deputy-leader, and the Rev Allan Hendrickse as national chairman.

The Federal Party, which decided at its conference in January 1978 to rename itself the Freedom Party of Southern Africa, endorsed the Prime Minister's constitutional proposals. The national chairman, Dr W. J. Bergins, explained that it had done so only as a basis for further negotiations to attain full citizenship for all South Africans. Admitting that there were many difficulties still in the way, he added: 'For the first time in our history, we have the opportunity to take political decisions about our future and carry them through'. The national chairman, Willie Africa, said that if the constitutional plan were to succeed, it would have to be preceded by the removal of all discriminatory legislation.

THE REFORM PARTY
A new Indian party, led by N. Chinsamy, was formed in 1977 in opposition to the SA Indian Congress which favours the Prime Minister's constitutional proposals. The Reform Party joined in the alliance with Inkhata and the Coloured Party and believes it can win a majority in the first elections to be held for the Indian Representative Council.

CLANDESTINE MOVEMENTS
AFRICAN NATIONAL CONGRESS (ANC)
With its exile headquarters and training camp now in Mozambique, the ANC's plans for an armed struggle showed signs of becoming more active in 1977, with a number of explosions occurring inside the Republic. Its guerrilla force was also considerably strengthened by the influx of Sowetan and other youth from urban areas. In a swoop in August 1977, police discovered caches of arms, booby traps and explosives which suggest that the ANC had been successful in smuggling

weapons across the border. The police continued to track down ANC agents sent into SA to recruit and plan attacks. Nine ANC members were convicted in one trial, five of them getting life sentences (see Trials, below).

The ANC also continued to attract greater international recognition. The Swedish Government presented the ANC President, Oliver Tambo, with a cheque for £800,000 in 1977. The city of Reggio Emilia (Italy) signed a pact of solidarity with the ANC in June 1977, and a street in Holland was named after one of the ANC leaders imprisoned on Robben Island, Govan Mbeki. But most of the ANC's economic, political and military support comes from the Soviet bloc countries. An unsigned article on the Great October Revolution in the ANC organ *Sechaba* reviewed the historic connection between the ANC and the USSR.[154] It traced how the ANC moved from a position of nationalism to proletariat internationalism, as was demonstrated at the 1969 Morogoro conference. It had then been decided that 'for a revolutionary movement like ours, it is not enough simply to declare and adhere to the principles and concepts of non-racialism, but our movement must be non racial even in its physical composition without losing sight of actual historical realities of our country where the Africans are the majority, the most oppressed, the leading and most dynamic force.' (It was at Morogoro that the decision was taken to establish a working relationship between the ANC and the SA Communist Party.) The article continued: 'Our people appreciate the assistance rendered us by the socialist countries, especially by the Soviet Union . . . .'

Oliver Tambo explained in *Sechaba* the relationship between the ANC and the Black Consciousness Movement which had led to difficulties after the Soweto uprising in 1976.[155] 'In a way we started from the point of Black Consciousness too: we formed the ANC from just Africans—because the British had delivered themselves of a constitution which cut us out of power. They transferred power to the White settlers, and we had to organize ourselves to defend our rights. But we have not stayed there; we have developed to the position where we expect all the people in SA to form part of the movement for the transformation of the social, political and economic situation. Black Consciousness, looked at from this point of view, is thus a phase in the struggle. It is not outside the struggle for human rights—on the contrary—it grows into the mainstream which has been set by the ANC.

'There is no question in our struggle of Black on one side and White on the other. We've passed that stage; the world has passed that stage. There are communities where there is no separation. The world is not a Black versus White world. And we have never been fighting for a SA in which the White people will be driven into the sea. If you are being objective, then you must accept that what you are doing is to mobilize and unite all people for justice.

'But of course there are attempts to create a movement rival to ANC and to keep this movement different. There is talk about a Black Consciousness movement which is not the same as the ANC, and which has got somehow ultimate objectives different from those of the ANC. If there were such a group, it would have no future. But, in fact, many of the leading young people who have been associated with what has been called the Black Consciousness movement are themselves growing. They are learning politically; they are in ANC and they have broadened their vision of the issues in SA. And their understanding is very clear—they are no less determined to win not just gradual changes in SA, but radical immediate changes under the banner of the ANC.'

The Minister of Justice and Police, Jimmy Kruger, declared in April 1977 that the Government would stand firm on its policy that prisoners on Robben Island serving life sentences would never be released. Among those condemned to permanent penal servitude are Nelson Mandela, Govan Mbeki and Walter Sisulu. In an attempt to rebut adverse UN reports about conditions on the island, the authorities took a party of journalists on a tour of inspection, but they were not allowed to talk to the prisoners.[156]

PAN-AFRICANIST CONGRESS (PAC)

Robert Mangaliso Sobukwe, founder of the PAC, died of cancer on 27 February 1978 at the age of 53 and was buried in his home town, Graaff Reinett. He had spent the last 18 years of his life as a prisoner on Robben Island and as a banned person in Kimberley.

The PAC in exile continued in 1977 and early 1978 to suffer from the divisions which have seriously undermined it ever since the leadership was taken over by Potlako Leballo. A number of top PAC leaders were expelled during this period. Although the PAC obtains the same recognition and support from the OAU Liberation Committee as the ANC, it has little external backing except from a few African governments, notably President Amin's in Uganda and Col Gaddafy's in Libya. A PAC representative, Muhammad Nur ad-Din, declared in Tripoli that the 'successes so far achieved by the Africans would not have been possible without the revolutionary support of the Jamahiriya (Libya) and its revolutionary leader'.[157]

Disillusioned PAC members who had taken refuge in Kenya were allowed to return home in 1977. They spoke of their disappointments with the exile PAC leadership.[158] Nevertheless, the PAC has continued to recruit new members and to maintain some clandestine activity, as was shown by a number of trials (see below).

SA COMMUNIST PARTY (SACP)

Brig John Coetzee, deputy-chief of security police, said in August 1977 that responsibility for the arms caches found in SA was with the communists whose 'mastermind' was a SA exile lawyer, Joe Slovo, the husband of Ruth First. (Slovo works in Maputo as a special adviser to the Machel regime on South African affairs; his wife teaches at the local university). However, Mrs Adelaide Tambo, wife of Oliver, indignantly denied the allegation, stating it was 'a crude attempt to claim that we are communist-led'.[159]

Following the Soweto uprising, the communist theoretician who writes under the pseudonym of Z. Nkosi declared: 'The time is ripe for the injection of the element of guerrilla warfare into the SA confrontation. Nor must it be assumed that guerrilla warfare can come only to SA from across its borders. The recent events show that the scope of mass action has not been reduced to nothing by Vorster's legislative and administrative tyranny. On the contrary, we have seen that mass insurrection in the townships, in the reserves and in the country areas *is* possible, indeed now certain.'[160]

A survey entitled 'The Role of Black Consciousness in the SA Revolution' by R. S. Nyameko and G. Singh concluded: 'The national liberation movement under the ANC has the main task now of unfolding guerrilla warfare through its military wing *Umkhonto we Sizwe* as part of the political struggle to meet the violence of the state with the revolutionary counter-violence of the people. The Communist Party, as an integral part of the national liberation movement and the party of the working class, is carrying out its historic tasks in mobilizing the working people in the common struggle for the overthrow of the apartheid regime and the seizure of people's power. It is taking its rightful place in the armed struggle. The BPC, SASO, BPA and other similar organizations must be seen as important tributaries to the Great River of the liberation movement headed by the ANC . . . .' The authors added that since Soweto, 'a growing number of youth and militants have been seeking out ANC and CP contacts inside and outside the country for political guidance and military training'.[161]

OKHELA AND THE SA LIBERATION SUPPORT COMMITTEE (SALCO)

Okhela, the underground organization which sent the Afrikaans poet Breyten Breytenbach on his ill-fated clandestine mission to SA, which resulted in his being sentenced to 10 years imprisonment, believes that hostile communist influences working within the ANC were responsible for betraying him to the police. Okhela (Zulu for Spark) was formed in 1972 by a group of Afrikaners linked to Breytenbach in an attempt to establish a White lobby group within the ANC.[162] They claim that the organization was formed with the approval of ANC leaders including Oliver Tambo, but was disapproved of by the CP.

The background to this episode was given in an anonymously-written pamphlet issued by three former members of Okhela: a former SA Methodist minister, a SA army deserter, and a former SA student activist.[163] They explained the mistakes they had made and their reasons for forming a new 'open' organization—the SA Liberation Support Committee (Salco). They claimed that Okhela (formerly known as Atlas) was set up with the knowledge of two of the 13 members of the ANC executive, who apparently kept it secret from the rest. According to their version, they received ANC finance and were given access to the ANC's 'resources, skills and key contacts'. One of Okhela's apparent 'fatal' mistakes was to depend on an 'outside organization' for false documents. Henry Curiel (who was subsequently detained by the French authorities in a country hotel) was reported by the French magazine *Le Point* to have admitted supplying Breytenbach with his forged passport in the name of Christian Galeska. SA embassies in Europe were tipped off in advance that Breytenbach would be arriving in SA under this name, and security police tailed him from the moment he set foot in the Republic.

URBAN BLACKS

The new Minister of Plural Relations (formerly Bantu Administration), Dr Connie Mulder, made the following statement on 8 February 1978: 'When National Party policy is taken to its logical conclusion, there will no longer be a Black man in SA who has South African citizenship'.[164] His statement came at the second reading of the Bantu Homelands Amendment Bill which rules that no Black who declines to accept Homeland citizenship will automatically be 'given' South African citizenship; it also states that any Black out of work for four months can be sent to a 'rehabilitation' centre for a ruling on whether he will be allowed to stay in the 'White' area or be 'repatriated' to a Homeland. Such Government attempts to impose restrictive policies by defining Blacks as 'foreigners in their own land'[165] continued to clash with the political aspirations of urban Blacks who constitute a quarter of SA's total population.

It was in terms of this policy that many people interpreted continued curbs on Black business development and the dismal housing record of the White-administered Bantu Administration Boards which govern the Black townships. The housing shortage in Black urban areas was officially estimated at 170,000.[166] Although R510m would be needed to resolve the shortage, the government allocated only R100m for three years in November 1977.[167] As there are no industries, no central business districts and no freehold tenure in the townships, the Bantu Administration Boards have to rely for their income on rents and liquor sales which they control.

In reference to Soweto, Helen Suzman (PRP) blamed the West Rand Administration Board (WRAB) for providing 'progressively fewer houses each year since 1974'.[168] In that year, 1,009 houses were built; in the 1976–77 financial year, only R750,000 was spent on housing out of a total budget of R57.778m.[169] At the end of 1977, the WRAB shelved indefinitely an electrification programme for

Soweto;[170] this fed resentment against the authorities and was seen as part of the policy of preventing Black urban areas from becoming 'too comfortable'. Of the 522,000 African housing units in the urban areas, less than a quarter have electricity. In April, during demonstrations against large rent rises, the Soweto Students' Representative Council called for the resignation of the Urban Bantu Council (UBC)—which advises the Bantu Administration Board but has no power—saying it had achieved nothing and was used by the authorities to oppress the people. In June, the Council members did resign and the Council itself was officially suspended by the WRAB.

Soweto was more or less in a state of revolt against Government policies throughout 1977, most manifestly in the form of the schools boycott. The vacuum caused by the UBC resignation was filled by the Committee of Ten, made up of acknowledged community leaders: church and education figures, BPC members and leading businessmen (see Black Political Movements, above). Under the chairmanship of Dr Ntatho Motlana, the influential committee presented itself as a moderate interim group wishing to negotiate with the Central Government for the right of Blacks to own property in the township and to establish it as an autonomous city, subsidized by the Government and with a fully-elected 50-member council. The committee refused to have any dealings with the discredited WRAB. Many leading Whites, including Afrikaans academics, urged the Government to talk to the Committee of Ten.[171] The WRAB countered by saying that the Committee was not representative of the people and accused it of holding separate negotiations with a 'Committee of 13'.[172] It was later established that there was no such group. The authorities banned meetings at which the Committee of Ten planned to put its proposals to the people of Soweto. On 19 October, they banned the constituent parts of the Committee and arrested all its members (see Black Consciousness, above).

The detentions left the WRAB free to conduct an intensive campaign to win support in Soweto for the Government's new proposals for elected Community Councils, in line with the Community Councils Act No 125 passed at the end of 1977. While these would have more powers than the Urban Bantu Councils, they fell far short of being proper municipal authorities and were subject to arbitrary suspension by the Minister for Plural Relations. The Committee of Ten had strongly opposed the new councils. The SA Institute of Race Relations (SAIRR) declared that the councils would be as 'impotent' as the UBCs and 'noted with alarm' the power over urban Africans that would remain with the Minister.[173] The three White opposition parties opposed the bill as conferring 'no meaningful powers' on urban Blacks.[174] Analyses in the English-language press described the Act as giving urban Blacks additional responsibilities without the means to meet them.[175]

Only 8,000 of Soweto's 1.5m population registered to vote in the first Community Council election on 18 February 1978. Of these, only 480 actually voted. Only two of the 30 wards were contested, drawing a 5% poll; 19 wards drew no candidates at all.[176] Nevertheless, the 11 elected members were announced by the Minister to be the only legitimate representatives of Soweto. Under the Act, he had the right to appoint members to the vacant wards but chose instead to hold special by-elections. Before the by-elections, four members of the Committee of Ten, including Dr Motlana and two *World* journalists, including Percy Qoboza, were released. It was not clear at the time of writing whether this would lead to a bigger poll.

Early in 1978, the Government relented to the extent of allowing 99-year land tenure which would allow urban Africans, under the Certificate of Registered Title, to meet building society loan requirements. But it firmly ruled out freehold land ownership.

Although the types of businesses Africans are permitted to engage in were broadened, they are still barred from such enterprises as manufacturing, electrical repairs, hotels and liquor stores. Expansion is also hampered by other restrictions on businessmen such as being confined to a single site with a maximum area of 350 sq ft.[177]

THE HOMELANDS

	People	Capital	Head of Authority
Transkei Republic	Xhosa	Umtata	President Botha Sigcau Prime Minister Kaiser Matanzima
Bopthutha Tswana Republic	Tswana	Montshiwa	President Lucas Mangope
Ciskei	Xhosa	Zwelitsha	Lennox L. Sebe
Gazankulu	Shangaan and Tsonga	Giyani	Prof Hudson Ntsanwisi
KwaZulu	Zulu	Nongoma	Gatsha Buthelezi
Lebowa	North Sotho (Pedi)	Lebowakgomo	Cedric Phatudi
QwaQwa	South Sotho	Phuthadinthjaba	Kenneth Mopeli
Swazi	Swazi	Tonga	
Venda	Venda	Sibasa	Patrick Mphephu
Ndebele	Ndebele	—	—

	African	Other	De Facto Population	De Jure Population
Bophutha Tswana	1,154,200	4,000	1,158,200	2,103,000
Transkei	2,390,800	20,300	2,411,100	4,250,200
Ciskei	474,600	4,200	478,800	871,800
Gazankulu	333,000	600	333,600	814,000
KwaZulu	2,691,200	10,200	2,701,400	5,029,000
Lebowa	1,384,100	3,400	1,387,500	2,234,000
QwaQwa	90,200	300	90,500	1,698,000
South Ndebele	—	—	—	—
Swazi	208,000	600	208,600	590,000
Venda	338,700	600	339,300	449,000

POLITICAL AFFAIRS

BophuthaTswana became the second Homeland to opt for independence on 6 December 1977, the Transkei having been granted this status on 26 October 1976. In February 1977, KwaZulu opted for the second stage of self-government under the Homelands Constitution Act of 1971. All other Homelands, except for the Swazi and South Ndebele, have self-governing status. In October 1977, a Territorial Authority was established for the Ndebele and a Legislative Assembly for the Swazi, according the latter the first stage of self-government.

The Bantu Homelands Constitution Amendment Bill—defining a third stage of self-government before independence—went through its first reading in the 1977 parliamentary session. It provides for self-governing Homelands to be declared internally autonomous countries. As such, they will have additional powers, including the right to decide on the powers and designation of the head of the executive and the right to make laws concerning matters not covered in Schedule 1 of the Act 'to secure the internal peace, order and good government of the country'. However, power of veto over the exercise of these rights rests with the South African State President. Bills also have to be submitted to the Minister of Bantu

Administration and Development for possible submission to the State President before any Homeland chief executive can assent to them. Opposition MPs criticized the power of veto saying it could prevent a Homeland government from repealing apartheid legislation. The Chief Ministers of Gazankulu and Lebowa, Prof Hudson Ntsanwisi and Dr Cedric Phatudi, said they might be prepared to use the new powers to repeal the apartheid laws. QwaQwa's Chief Minister, Kenneth Mopeli, described the bill as a 'cunning plan to dangle a carrot before Homeland leaders' as a lure to independence. KwaZulu's Chief Buthelezi also dismissed the bill as political bait, even before he had heard of the veto clause.[178] The leader of the PFP, Colin Eglin, attacked the measure for doing nothing to provide a political voice for the millions of Blacks living outside the Homelands.

Friction continued between participants in the Homeland system and Blacks who regard Homeland leaders as puppets of the Pretoria regime. At Robert Sobukwe's funeral in March 1978, Chief Buthelezi was forced to leave by radicals who branded him as a 'collaborator' (see above); at the funeral of Steve Biko, the Ciskei's Chief Minister Lennox Sebe was similarly condemned.[179]

Ciskei, Venda and BophuthaTswana were granted extraordinary powers similar to those operative in the Transkei, allowing for arbitrary detention and banishment by decree. The powers are specifically designed to bolster the authority of chiefs and headmen, who remain the key Black supporters of the Homeland policy, and to curb political demonstrations.

The two major grievances felt by Homeland leaders, as well as by their critics, were the Government's determination that all Blacks should become citizens of the Homelands—irrespective of whether they ever have or ever will live there—and the allocation of new land to the Homelands. (For further discussion of these issues, see chapters on Transkei and BophuthaTswana.) The following table shows land already allocated to the Homelands, the planned final consolidation areas and the numbers of land parcels these will comprise:

	Hectares		No. of non-contiguous areas
	1976	After Consolidation	
Bophutha Tswana	3,800,000	4,043,000	6
Transkei	4,100,000	4,501,000	1
Ciskei	533,000	770,000	1
Gazankulu	675,000	741,000	3
KwaZulu	3,100,000	3,239,000	10
Lebowa	2,200,000	2,518,000	6
QwaQwa	48,000	62,000	1
South Ndebele	75,000	73,000	2
Swazi	370,000	391,000	1
Venda	650,000	668,000	3
	15,551,000	**17,006,000**	

HOMELAND ECONOMIES

The vote for Bantu Administration and Development for 1977–78 provided for a grant-in-aid to the South African Bantu Trust Fund of R216.968m, an amount over and above statutory grants payable to Homeland governments of R129.702m for the construction of access roads to the Homelands (R2.92m), for Bantu Administration in Namibia (R22.959m), and for road construction in Namibian Homelands (R2.286m). [180] The estimated State contribution to Homeland government expenditure for 1977–78 was as follows (in rand):

	Statutory Grant	Additional Grant	Administrative and Technical Assistance	Total
Bophutha Tswana	26,795,000	24,623,100	3,386,800	54,804,900
Ciskei	22,870,000	17,370,800	2,827,400	43,068,200
Gazankulu	12,454,000	3,001,500	1,614,800	17,070,300
KaNgwane (Swazi)	4,192,000	1,632,000	294,200	6,118,200
KwaZulu	45,658,000	38,233,000	3,997,800	87,888,800
Lebowa	34,238,000	13,801,600	3,381,800	51,421,400
QwaQwa	1,410,000	2,093,300	486,200	3,989,500
Venda	8,901,000	8,785,400	1,330,400	19,016,800
	156,518,000	**109,540,700**	**17,319,400**	**283,378,100**
Homelands of SWA:				
Caprivi	3,221,000	538,300	514,900	4,274,200
Ovambo	—	—	1,029,300	1,029,300
Kavango	—	—	759,400	759,400
Totals	**159,739,000**	**110,079,000**	**19,623,000**	**289,441,000**

Since its 'independence', amounts payable to the Transkei have come under the vote of Foreign Affairs. For 1977–78, they totalled R113.5m, in addition to the R44,000 for the salaries of judges seconded to the Transkeian Government.

The 1977–78 budget of the South African Bantu Trust was as follows (in rand):

Purchase of land for consolidation of Bantu areas	50,000,000
Development towards self-determination of Bantu areas (Republic)	155,514,000
Subsidizing of Bantu transport	10,733,000
Purchase of properties in independent Homelands	4,000,000
Services in Caprivi	3,623,000
Total	**223,870,000**

Figures published in the official Yearbook of the Republic (1977) show the Gross National Income (GNI) of the Homelands, excluding the Transkei, at c. R1,477.1m for the 1974–75 financial year. The estimates are shown in the first Table following. The figures represent a doubling of GNI since 1970–71 when it was estimated at R719.2m. They also reveal the continuing importance of migrant and commuter worker incomes to the Homelands' GNI. However, the theoretical contribution of these workers to GNI is greater than the actual contribution as in practice, only c. 20% of the income earned by migrants flows back in cash or kind into BophuthaTswana, Lebowa, Gazankulu and Venda, where studies have been done.[181] Where the contribution of migrant and commuter workers is large, the increase shown in the above table says more about wage rises in the White areas than Homeland development; and although R10 to R14 represents a substantial increase in weekly per capita income, it is still not enough to live on.[182]

The Yearbook offers the breakdown of GDP shown in the second Table following (in thousand Rand), although the difference between the total here and in the previous Table is not explained.

About 84% of the agriculture (which accounts for c. 21% of GDP) is non-market subsistence production. The public sector accounts for 35.9%; community, social and personal services 28.9%, and manufacturing 4.7%. Mining forms an important part of the GDPs of Lebowa and BophuthaTswana.

The GDP of the Transkei for the year 1973–74 was R131.2m, with agriculture accounting for 32.5%; community, personal and social services 26.1%, and manufacturing 15.2%. The Transkei Budget was R135.8m. The Deputy Minister of Bantu Administration said that agricultural production levels would have to rise by 1,000% to meet food requirements. While some progress was being made, retrogression of resources had not been successfully dealt with.[183]

Allowing for direct and indirect taxation of Blacks, the percentage of the Republic's GNP spent on the Homelands was 2.3%.[184] Among the priorities for Homeland development listed in the official Yearbook is 'the creation of high-speed transportation networks' between residence (in the Homelands) and place of work (in the White areas).

In 1976, there were 74 mines in the Homelands employing 64,018 Africans. Industrial investment by the private sector on the agency basis had mounted to £58.3m, creating jobs for 14,235 Africans, while Bantu Investment Corporation industries were employing c. 6,000 on a permanent basis.

Under the Promotion of the Economic Development of the Bantu Homelands Act of 1977, the name of the BIC was changed to the Corporation for Economic Development Ltd (CED). Its role was also redefined: the main changes allow for the establishment of 'national' Homeland development corporations, and for Whites, Coloureds, and Asians to become minority shareholders in 'Bantu companies'. Another CED role is to encourage overseas investment. In 1976–77, nearly 40% of all capital invested in the Homelands came from overseas sources. At April 1977, there were 15 companies with overseas shareholding established in Bophutha-Tswana, KwaZulu, Lebowa and the Ciskei, with a total investment of R11.9m.[185]

THE HOMELANDS: INTERNAL AFFAIRS
CISKEI
Unrest stemming from the June 1976 uprising in Soweto continued to simmer in the Ciskei late into 1977. There were arson outbreaks at Mdanstane and Dimbaza, and student demonstrations and disturbances in Alice and Queenstown. At Steve Biko's funeral, Ciskeian Chief Minister, Lennox Sebe, was denounced as a 'toy' of the White authorities.[186] On 30 September, extraordinary powers similar to those

GNI (million Rand)

Year	Blacks				Non-Blacks	Total	Income per capita (Rand)		
	GDP	Commuter income	Migrant worker income	Subtotal			GDP Blacks	GNI Blacks	GNI Total
Total									
1970–71	169.5	176.0	359.4	704.9	14.3	719.2	32.00	119.00	121.00
1973–74	285.7	315.3	573.3	1,174.3	17.7	1,192.0	47.00	172.00	176.00
1974–75	357.1	401.0	698.1	1,456.8	20.3	1,477.1	57.00	207.00	209.00

Source: Department of Statistics, *National Accounts of the Bantu Homelands 1969–70 to 1973–74,* March 1976.

GDP

1974–75:	Ciskei	KwaZulu	QwaQwa	Bophutha-Tswana	Lebowa	Venda	Gazan-kulu	Swazi	Total
Agriculture, forestry, hunting and fishing	9,137	30,842	463	12,612	31,331	3,684	10,047	2,574	100,690
Mining and quarrying	—	555	—	78,265	15,019	228	108	—	94,175
Manufacturing industry, electricity, gas and water, and construction	6,889	25,759	892	19,130	12,118	2,958	3,107	1,131	71,984
Wholesale and retail trade, catering and accommodation services	1,170	11,442	149	3,423	3,661	834	1,085	410	22,174
Transport, storage and communication	2,298	6,498	464	4,787	1,166	179	345	10	15,747
Financing, insurance, fixed property and business services	5,908	13,821	290	7,738	4,716	553	802	1,016	34,844
Community, social and personal services:									
Public administration	7,352	16,367	870	8,807	6,292	2,592	4,057	497	46,834
Education services	10,456	14,922	1,121	10,055	11,837	3,172	2,738	756	55,057
Health services	2,361	12,809	186	5,307	4,044	1,018	1,821	368	27,914
Other marketable services	400	2,384	94	853	910	143	254	106	5,144
Total GDP	**45,971**	**135,399**	**4,529**	**150,977**	**91,094**	**15,361**	**24,364**	**6,868**	**474,563**

Source: SA Department of Statistics, *National Accounts of the Bantu Homelands 1969–70 to 1973–74,* March 1976.

granted to the Transkei in 1960 were extended to the Ciskei under Proclamation 252 of the Native Administration Act of 1927. The powers allow for 90 days detention without trial, banishment without decree, prohibition of unauthorized meetings and heavy fines or prison sentences for showing disrespect or disobedience to chiefs and headmen who remain the instruments of official policy. 29 of the 44 elected members of the Ciskei Legislative Assembly are chiefs or headmen.

Chief Sebe said he would favour independence if the Ciskei were given all the land due to it and if other problems were resolved, but opposition politicians totally rejected independence. Chief Sebe said in January 1978 that the Ciskei would be the first Homeland to opt for 'autonomy' if the Bill proposing the third stage of self-government became law (see Political Affairs, above). Independence was likely to be the major issue in the 1978 election.

Until March 1978, refugees, eventually numbering more than 37,000, continued to pour into Thornhill and Pavet-Bushey Park areas from two Ciskei districts ceded to the Transkei.[187] Appalling conditions caused by the massive influx and initial failure of the authorities to make adequate arrangements resulted in babies dying at the rate of five a day.[188] The Ciskei Government attempted to clamp down on information, and a report that 300 people had died was denied by the Ciskeian Secretary for Health. At the end of April, officials from Oxfam and the Red Cross visited Thornhill and found that there was hardship but that the situation was being adequately dealt with.

GAZANKULU

The Chief Minister, Prof Hudson Ntsanwisi, is one of the most outspoken critics among Homeland leaders of the policy of Separate Development. The reliance of the Homeland on its migrant workforce remained exceptionally high (accounting for 77.5% of GNI in 1973–74). There were no notable developments in this Shangaan and Tsonga area in the period under review.

KANGWANE (SWAZI)

The Chief Executive Officer of the Kangwane Territorial Authority, Chief Mokholoshi Dhlamini, was removed from office on 23 June 1977 following a vote of no-confidence after he refused to sign a land consolidation proposal by Pretoria. In a Supreme Court action against the Minister of Bantu Administration and Development, Dhlamini established that it was a meeting of the Authority which had decided that he should not sign. The judge found that Dhlamini had been wrongfully deposed and that the subsequent election of Enos J. Mabuza as Chief Minister and six others was null and void.[189] In the meantime, however, Mabuza had negotiated with Pretoria for the Swazi Homeland to enter the first stage of self-government. The Kangwane Legislative Assembly was thus established under Proclamation 214 gazetted in September 1977. This allows for a 36-member Assembly, nine members being appointed by each of the four regional authorities in the area for a period of five years. No provision was made for elected members. Mabuza appealed against the ruling, but pending the appeal, the Assembly dissolved itself so that an election could be held to establish who was to be the Homeland leader.

KWAZULU

The KwaZulu Government embarked on its second phase as a 'self-governing territory within the Republic' in February 1977. The Executive Council was replaced by a Cabinet, which took over all functions except foreign affairs and defence. In the first elections early in 1978, the Inkhata movement made a clean sweep of all 26 constituencies. The only organized movement to put up candidates, Inkhata had campaigned on the rejection of independence for the Homelands and the rejection of apartheid. The main qualification to vote was possession of a Homeland certificate which most Blacks view as the first step to their loss of rights in 'White SA'. About 1.4m certificates were issued and 629,000 people registered to vote.[190] The *de jure* population is over 5m. (For details of the Inkhata movement and Gatsha Buthelezi's political activities, see above: Black Political Movements.)

The sprawling township of Kwa Mashu was incorporated in the Homeland. On 16 August 1977, the Minister of Justice confirmed that he had asked for the extension to the entire Homeland of emergency powers granted for one area troubled by faction fighting. His request was turned down.

LEBOWA

The Chief Minister, Dr Cedric Phatudi, said Blacks were not prepared to accept only 13% of the land-surface of the Republic and that it would be fatal for them to seek independence. At a Press conference in London in June 1977, he said consolidation of Lebowa—which will consist of six separate blocks under present plans—was his priority. He saw SA ultimately as a federation of multiracial states controlling their internal affairs but united under South African citizenship.

Lebowa did not oppose Pretoria's decision to create an Ndebele Homeland, though some Ndebele tribes live in Lebowa.

With elections in the offing in 1978, the split in the ruling Lebowa People's Party between factions of Phatudi and the radical former Minister of the Interior, Collins Ramusi, seemed unbreechable. A third party—the Black People's Party—emerged under the leadership of Chief S. Molepo.

NDEBELE

A Government notice gazetted on 7 October 1977 provided for the establishment of an Ndebele Tribal Authority. The move followed a request by three Ndebele tribes to secede from BophuthaTswana but was opposed by the Ndebele People's Front. The Front maintained that disputes between the Ndebele and the Homeland Authority (such as the medium of instruction in schools) could not be resolved. Following the go-ahead for the Tribal Authority, some Front members went over to the secessionists. The new Authority's jurisdiction falls in the Groblersdal area. No land has been ceded by Lebowa, but some Ndebele tribes living there may secede to the new authority.

QWAQWA

The *de facto* population of this smallest, over-populated and grossly undeveloped Homeland is now put at 180,000, thousands of poorly-paid farm workers from the southern Orange Free State having sought refuge there over the past seven years. The Chief Minister, Kenneth Mopeli, claimed that according to a preliminary census in BophuthaTswana, a further 46,000 Sotho-speaking people at Thaba 'Nchu in the Orange Free State and 12,000 in Maboloka in the Transvaal had indicated a desire to join QwaQwa. He argued that to make this possible, some land yet to be purchased for BophuthaTswana should be ceded to QwaQwa.

Mopeli has often expressed opposition to independence. In October 1977, he predicted that QwaQwa would eventually unite with Lesotho. In January 1978, the Minister of the Interior, Caswell Koekoe, said he would refuse to issue travel documents to the people of QwaQwa. 'We are not foreigners,' he said. The documents—a substitute for reference books—were agreed upon in 1977 between Pretoria and Homeland leaders, excluding Buthelezi.

VENDA

Following continued student unrest, during which the Legislative Assembly was stoned and 35 schools were closed, extraordinary powers were extended to the Homeland Authority. The Authority, composed of 42 nominated and 18 elected members, is headed by Chief Minister P. R. Mphephu, who drives a Mercedes 280SE and lives in a R140,000 house. Following reports that Venda might be the next Homeland to opt for independence, Mphephu said it would not do so until the territory had been consolidated and a sound economy developed. The opposition Vendaland Independence Party, which holds 13 of the 18 elected seats and contends that it should therefore be in power, opposes the plan for independence. Its leader, B. Mudau, accused Pretoria of 'working on' the weaker Homelands to accept independence. He also maintained that the ruling Venda National Party depended for its majority on the support of the chiefs who 'were being intimidated'.[191] In March, the opposition walked out of the Assembly following a government motion favouring the idea of a defence force.

During 1977 it was announced that Iscor would mine Venda's extensive coal reserves, paying a 3% royalty (c. R540,000 a year) to the Homeland. Iscor thus stands to save R20 a ton against the price of imported coal.

(For *BophuthaTswana* and *Transkei*, see separate chapters following.)

THE COLOURED COMMUNITY

Hope for some meaningful change in the position of the c. 2.5m Coloured people receded in April 1977 when a Government White Paper rejected 31 of the most crucial recommendations of the 1976 report of the Erica Theron Commission on the Coloured population.[192] Acceptance of the Theron proposals would have meant eventual social and economic equality for the Coloureds with the Whites and a meaningful share of political power. With these hopes dashed in April, Coloured leaders were left feeling frustrated and angry (see Black Political Movements, above). The Coloured community had other reasons to feel apprehensive about its future, especially as the architects of Separate Development apparently intended moving Coloureds far from the urban centres to 'autonomous' cities of their own—the earlier fate of the Indians. Two such 'mini-Colouredstans'—Atlantis and Mitchells Plain—were under construction several kilometres outside of Cape Town; another, Ennandale, was being developed near Johannesburg.[193]

Coloured leaders rejected the government's vision of a separate and unequal destiny for their community and began militantly to demand full representation for Coloureds in Parliament. They received considerable support in this both from the English-language Press and from Afrikaans-speaking academic and literary sources. Sonny Leon, the most representative Coloured leader (see Political Parties above), said that without a share in the legislature, his people would remain 'cut off, poor and unequal to those benefiting through their representation in Parliament. We'll reject everything which is not equal to that given to White citizens. We will not settle for second best anymore.'[194]

The opposition Federal Party, which initially was conservative and pro-apartheid, agreed to talks with Leon's Labour Party in July 1977 to resolve their differences and so enable them to present a united front to the Government. After these discussions, both parties agreed not to take part in any future political dispensation that excluded the country's urban Black population.[195] This closer identification with the African majority continued to be a feature in Coloured politics and was especially evident among Coloured youth.

In August 1977, the Government met Coloured and Indian leaders for talks on its new constitutional proposals. Afterwards, several Coloured leaders said they could not support the plan because it made no provision for urban Blacks, did not meet the needs of the Coloured people, led to no meaningful sharing of power, and was simply an extension of the Separate Development policy.[196] Leon said in September that he believed the whole nation should be consulted if the Government wanted to change the country's constitution, and he called for a Coloured Representative Council election to test Coloured opinion on the Government's new proposals. When the Prime Minister refused to allow the elections, Leon said he was not surprised; Vorster had refused because he knew what the response would be and wanted to avoid embarrassment.

A memorandum prepared by the Ministry of Coloured Relations and leaked to the Press in November spelled out the Government's plans for a 'Coloured parliament', which clearly would have plenty of work, but little real power.[197] It would not be able to repeal or amend many measures which Coloureds find repugnant such as the Group Areas laws, race classification, separate amenities and prohibitions on mixed marriages. The parliament would control police, prisons and community development in 'Coloured areas'—but on Pretoria's terms. It would issue business and trading licences, but not for arms, ammunition or explosives. It would be able to make laws relating to recreational and cultural facilities and would also issue dog licences. Other areas within its competence would be industry and mining (subject to many conditions), public works and social security, but not hospitals. It would legislate on Coloured education, but not at university level.

THE INDIAN COMMUNITY
Provision was made early in 1977 for the half-elected, half government-appointed SA Indian Council (SAIC) to become a fully elected body. Despite being compulsory, registration of voters (all Indians over 18) was slow and an amendment act had to be introduced to extend the SAIC's term of office. By September 1977, a year after registration had begun, only 230,000 of the 400,000 entitled to vote had registered. By mid-March 1978, the election had still not been held. The Department of Indian Affairs explained the delay in terms of its own inexperience and the lack of established Indian political parties; but some Indians also objected to the idea of voting for a racially-constituted body. During 1977, the Natal Indian Congress and the Transvaal Action Committee decided to co-ordinate their political efforts to oppose the elections. SAIC members who had opposed a majority decision to participate on a trial basis in Vorster's inter-Cabinet Council (see Constitution, above) formed the Reform Party. With aims similar to the Coloured Labour Party, it proposed to use the SAIC as a platform from which to air grievances and expose short-term concessions likely to lead to 'long-term suffering'.[198]

DEFENCE AND SECURITY
SA's defence budget for 1976–77 of R1.654 bn was marginally cut in 1977–78 to R1.53 bn due to the cancellation by France of the order for corvettes and submarines. At the same time, the Defence Minister, P. W. Botha, announced that he expected the 1978–79 Defence budget to rise to R2 bn. The estimated defence budgets for 1972–73 to 1975–76 were respectively: R335.336m, R472.022m, R702m and R948m. These figures do not reveal the actual total cost of defence spending, however. For example, the South African Defence Force (SADF) received an additional R112m in 1976 and R81m in 1977 from special accounts.[199] Also not reflected in the budget are the votes for BOSS and PISCO, as well as for the Armaments' Corporation (see below). The stockpiling of arms and oil has accounted for a large part of defence spending increases over the last few years (see above: SA

vs the International Community). The Defence White Paper also shows discrepancies in money voted and actual expenditure from 1975–78.[200]

	1975–76	1976–77	1977–78
Operating Costs	R 568.5m	R 709.5m	R 984.6m
Capital Costs	R 475m	R 698.1m	R 955.8m
Total	R 1,043.5m	R 1,407m	R 1,940.4m

The estimated percentage of total State expenditure spent on defence was 15 in 1975–76, 17 in 1976–77 and 19 in 1977–78. The estimated percentage in relation to GNP was 4.1, 4.9 and 5.1 over the same years respectively. This rising defence expenditure has put SA into the top league of the world's arms spenders: only the US and UK spend more of GNP on defence than SA.

The following figures indicate how costs of weapons and training have escalated: the cost of a Mirage fighter rose from R900,000 in 1967 to R2m in 1977. It now costs R1m to train a Mirage pilot.[201] The cost of training an armoured vehicle officer to the rank of major is estimated at R77,000, while that of training a national serviceman for one year is R4,000. In ten years, the price of combat radios has increased sixfold, to R6,000; combat vehicles now cost R200,000 each and combat tanks R1m.

The Defence White Paper of April 1977 proposed doubling the length of national service to 24 months. As the Defence Minister explained: 'We must prepare for the worst'. As a result, the number of national servicemen will increase to 126,000 in 1978. It was also proposed to increase the size of the Permanent Force, which in 1977 comprised 7% of defence manpower; national servicemen accounted for 6.6%, the Citizen Force for 54.9%, and civilians 3.1%.

The White Paper also recommended strengthening the Air Force by building 100 Mirage F-1 fighters and by speeding up production of Impala-2s, the South African version of the Italian Aermacchi 326M dual trainer. More than 50 Mirage IIIs were delivered by Dassault before the French arms ban was announced.[202] On the other hand, France's refusal to deliver four warships set back the naval expansion programme as it is not clear to what extent local shipyards will be able to build substitute warships in future. During a visit to SA in 1977, Adr Elmo Zumwalt, former US Chief of Naval Operations, said that the South African Navy was not able to defend the country's sea lanes.[203]

The Defence Minister announced that SA was to build a new army base at Phalaborwa in north-east Transvaal, 50 km from the Mozambique border, and a new air base at Hoedspruit, 40 km further south near the Kruger game reserve. A combat school for brigade manoeuvres is to be established at Sishen in the Northern Cape, near the Namibian border. It will also provide training for conventional warfare.[204]

South African defence chiefs rejected a proposal by 300 immigrants to form their own army unit, on the grounds that it would be 'too élitist'. Members of the group are known as the *Germanischer Freikorps*; most are German and many served in Hitler's army.[205]

The Defence Act was amended in 1977 'to conform with the modern-day concepts of war'. The Defence Minister explained that the present Act was based on the old international law concepts of war or the state of war, but that SA was 'currently faced with conditions which posed as big a threat to it as war'.

The Defence Minister rejected proposals to give a bigger role to Blacks, Indians and Coloureds in the army. While SA, 'like Israel', had to maintain 'a people's army', he said he did not intend to create bigger units manned by 'people of colour'.

However, Blacks and Coloureds might be useful to the commandos, in which case they would be armed to protect themselves for specific purposes. But he warned that arms could not simply be distributed on a large scale without the strictest regulations governing storage. [206] The demand for a larger role for non-White troops was first made by the army chief, Gen Magnus Malan, and was supported by the commando leaders. He said that the loyalty of those under arms was above suspicion: 'You find that Black, Brown, and White soldiers are fighting side by side in the operational area against our common enemy'. [207] Malan disclosed that 20% of SA's military forces in the operational area were Black.

DEFENCE STRATEGY

The 47-year old Chief of the Defence Force, Gen Magnus Malan, announced a new military strategy in two interviews early in 1977. [208] He referred in particular to Mao Tse-tung's concept of 'total war' as revealing the essential character of revolutionary strategy since the end of World War II. The implication was that every activity of the State must be seen and understood as a funtion of total war. He also accepted a second Maoist concept—the protracted war of low intensity—and revealed that the army was working towards something like a 'game plan within the restrictions inherent in our democratic system'. He added that SA had carefully considered the strategic models developed by other countries but, while borrowing from them, had formulated its own strategy. The time had come for a 'rethink of all our national resources'. His own strategy meant 'a national reorientation aimed at survival, while at the same time ensuring the continued advancement of the well being of all South Africans'.

Gen Malan's ideas were incorporated into the 1977 Defence White Paper which called for a 'total national strategy' for defence: 'whether we wish to accept it or not', SA is already at war. In preparing plans for a six-mile deep 'no go' area along its entire frontier, a Bill was presented to Parliament in March 1978 to allow the army to clear areas of people and buildings.

The SADF Director-General (Resources), Maj-Gen Neil Webster, said that if an independent Namibia were to become a Marxist state under Swapo, it would have to be regarded as a potentially hostile base; preparations against that eventuality were being made. [209] He added: 'As long as Marxism succeeds in impersonating African liberation, nationalism and solidarity . . . SA will be obliged to look upon its neighbours as potentially inimical.' According to Maj-Gen G. J. J. Boshoff, the Chief of Army Logistics, however, the real weak link in SA's defences was the Republic's troubled race relations: 'We will never be able to withstand modern threats unless all the nations of SA strive for solidarity and form a solid communal front against outside attack'. [210]

THE SOUTH AFRICAN ARMAMENTS' MANUFACTURING CORPORATION (ARMSCOR)

This State-controlled consortium, whose budget is not disclosed, is responsible for co-ordinating the total arms manufacturing industry in the country. It also owns and operates its own aircraft and other weapons' factories and, as of April 1978, decided to enter the capital market on its own account for the first time. The chairman, Commandant Pieter Marais, said that SA would continue to manufacture foreign weapons under licence despite the Security Council ban. This would include the French Mirage fighters, Panhard armoured cars and the Italian Aermacchi's Impala. [211] He said that the revocation of these licences would only help SA, because modifications to planes or tanks could then be made without payment to the licencee.

THE BUREAU OF STATE SECURITY (BOSS) AND THE PARLIAMENTARY INTERNAL SECURITY COMMISSION (PISCOM)

BOSS was set up in 1961 and later given its own statute enabling it to act as an independent authority. In 1977 it also received its own coat-of-arms. BOSS's chief function is to collect, collate and interpret external intelligence material and to advise the Prime Minister; its 1977 budget was R12.086m. Its head until mid-1978 was Gen Hendrik van den Bergh, a close friend of Vorster's; they were detained together as enemies of the State during World War II. BOSS was given new powers under a Bill introduced in May 1978 which, *inter alia*, provides heavy penalties for anybody claiming to be a BOSS agent. The deputy-head of BOSS, Alexander van Wyk, admitted in June 1977 that its agents had been working in the UK, US and other countries for over five years. 'All countries,' he said, 'have intelligence services.'[212] A parallel body, PISCOM, deals only with internal security.

THE RISING TOLL OF VIOLENCE

Internal and external violence directly affecting the Republic's security rose significantly in 1977—and even more in the first half of 1978. With the disclosure by Brig C. F. Zietsman, chief of the Security Police, that 4,000 guerrillas were being trained for action against SA (see above), the security outlook looked dark. The White Paper of April 1977 warned that 'insurgents from neighbouring States' could be expected to 'cross the borders and politically indoctrinate and even intimidate the local population'. It disclosed that between April 1975 and April 1978, 33 members of the security forces had died in Namibia—most of them in accidents; 53 civilians were killed by insurgents and 233 Swapo guerrillas were shot. In October 1977, in one clash alone, five members of the security forces and 61 guerrillas were killed. The biggest operation of all, accounting for hundreds of deaths among Namibian civilian and Swapo forces in Angola, occurred in April 1978 (see chapter on Namibia).

The increasing threat from armed insurgents is indicated by the following catalogue of incidents:

AUGUST 1977: Three armed black guerrillas were held after crossing into SA from Angola with supplies of arms. Two of a contingent of 18 guerrillas were arrested; the others went into hiding. Paul Langa, chairman of a subcommittee of the SSRC in Soweto, was accused of leading a suicide squad which had set off explosions at Jabulani police station, a nightclub and a house in Soweto; he was jailed for 25 years. The Minister of Police said he had information that the ANC and the communists had infiltrated the Black Consciousness movement. The Security Police announced on 29 August that they had 'smashed terrorist bases' close to Durban and in places around Johannesburg, seizing Russian-manufactured arms including machine-guns, rocket-launchers, grenades, explosives, booby-traps and ammunition. An undisclosed number of 'terrorists' were arrested in this operation. The police laid responsibility for the network of caught agents on Joe Slovo, the leader-in-exile of the South African Communist Party; Jack Hodgson, described as the sabotage adviser to the ANC; and Ronnie Kassler, a former Natal University student and 'technical adviser to the ANC'.[213]

SEPTEMBER 1977: A Black security policeman who had played a leading part in exposing the secret network uncovered in August was killed by automatic gunfire in Durban. The Germiston police station was damaged by a bomb. After two Whites were machine-gunned to death and armed caches were found in several Black townships in the Transvaal, two men alleged to be ANC guerrillas were arrested. A cell of insurgents was captured on the Swaziland border; one of its members who escaped arrest, a teacher, Nicholas Molokwana, was shot dead in a house in Soweto after a gunbattle. Concern was expressed over 'the danger of urban terrorism'.[214]

NOVEMBER 1977: A skirmish with guerrillas occurred near Pongola (Natal); one guerrilla was killed. Police said they had seized hand-grenades and Russian sub-machine guns, and were pursuing the insurgents along the Natal-Swaziland border. A bomb explosion in the Carlton Centre in the heart of Johannesburg wounded 16 people.

DECEMBER 1977: Another bomb exploded in the Germiston police station.

FEBRUARY 1978: A bomb was defused in the basement of a Johannesburg block of offices; police said it consisted of 12 slabs of Soviet-made TNT.

MARCH 1978: A bomb exploded outside the Port Elizabeth headquarters of the Bantu Affairs Administration Board, killing one and injuring three. Security police found explosives and hand grenades in Soweto which had earlier been stolen from an army base. Brig Zietsman announced a number of arrests in Soweto after the discovery of another cache of arms. (Also see Trials, below.)

ARMED FORCES

Total armed forces number 55,000, including 38,400 conscripts. Defence expenditure in 1977–78 was R1.65 bn ($1.9 bn). Military service is compulsory for 24 months. The Army of 41,000 includes 34,000 conscripts and 2,100 women, and has one corps and two headquarters divisions; five signals regiments; one armoured brigade; one mechanized brigade (with one forming); four motorized brigades; two parachute battalions; eight field and two medium artillery regiments; nine light anti-aircraft artillery regiments and nine field engineer squadrons. (The last seven formations are cadre units, forming two divisions when brought to full strength on mobilization of Citizen Force.) It is equipped with some 150 Centurion, 20 Comet medium, and M-41 light tanks; 1,600 Eland (AML-60/-90) armoured cars; 230 scout cars including Ferret, M-3A1; 280 Saracen, Ratel armoured personnel carriers; 500 light armoured personnel carriers including Hippo and Rhino; 25-pounder, 105mm self-propelled howitzers, 25-pounder, 105mm, 5.5-in and 155mm guns/howitzers; 81mm and 120mm mortars; 17-pounder and 90mm anti-tank guns; 105mm recoilless rifles; SS-11 and ENTAC anti-tank guided weapons; 204GK 20mm, K-63 twin 35mm, L/70 40mm and 3.7-in anti-aircraft guns; 18 Cactus (Crotale) and 54 Tigercat surface-to-air missiles. There are 130,000 active reservists who serve 30 days per year for eight years.

The Navy numbers 5,500, including 1,400 conscripts, and has three Daphne-class submarines; one destroyer with two Wasp anti-submarine warfare helicopters; three anti-submarine warfare frigates (three with one Wasp helicopter); one escort minesweeper (training ship); six coastal minesweepers and two patrol craft (ex-British Ford-class). Two Agosta-class submarines, two Type A69 frigates, six guided-missile fast patrol boats, six corvettes with Gabriel II and Exocet surface-to-surface missiles are on order. There is a 10,500-strong Citizen reserve force with one destroyer, two frigates and seven minesweepers.

The 8,500-strong Air Force includes 3,000 conscripts and has 362 combat air-craft. There are two light bomber squadrons, one with six Canberra B(I)12, three T4, one with nine Buccaneer S50; two ground-attack fighter squadrons with 32 Mirage F-1A; one fighter/reconnaissance squadron with 27 Mirage IIICZ/BZ/RZ; one interceptor squadron with 16 Mirage F-1CZ; two maritime reconnaissance squadrons with seven Shackleton MR3 and 19 Piaggio P166S; four transport squadrons with seven C-130B, one L-100-20; 15 L-100-30; nine Transall C-160Z; 30 C-47; five DC-4; one Viscount 781; seven HS-125 and seven Swearingen Merlin IVA; four helicopter squadrons, two with 40 Alouette III, one with 25 SA-330 Puma and one with 15 SA-321L Super Frelon; one fleet of 11 Wasp (naval assigned); and two communications and liaison squadrons (army assigned) with 22 Cessna 185A/D/E, 40 AM-3C Bosbok and 20 C-4M Kudu. Operational trainers include 29 Mirage IIIEZ/DZ/D2Z, 12 F-86, 150 MB-326 Impala I, 22 Impala II and 30 Vampire; other training aircraft include 100 Harvard (some armed), C-47 aircraft and Alouette II/III helicopters. There are 50 Impala II and 20 Kudu on order. A reserve Citizen Force of 25,000 has six squadrons equipped with 75 Impala I/II, 10 Harvard and T-6G.

The paramilitary forces are comprised of 90,000 Commandos in infantry battalion-type units grouped in formations of five or more with local industrial and rural protection duties. Members do 12 months' initial and 19 days' annual training. There are also 13 Air Commando squadrons with private aircraft and 35,500 South African Police of which 19,500 are Whites and 16,000 non-Whites.[215]

NUCLEAR POWER

With extensive supplies of uranium, advanced technology[216] and a method of producing enriched uranium in a new pilot plant near Pretoria, SA allegedly stood on the brink of becoming the world's seventh nuclear power in August 1977, but was prevented from achieving this status by the unusual collaboration of Russia, France, the US, the UK and West Germany (see SA vs the West, above). Previous setbacks had included President Carter's clampdown on export licences for shipping enriched uranium to SA in April 1977: the order had already been pending for two years. In July, Britain rejected SA's offers to make up a shortfall of uranium supplies.[217] With a bitter loss of prestige, SA was ousted from its seat on the International Atomic Energy Agency in June.

On 6 August, Russia informed the American President that SA was about to explode a nuclear device in the Kalahari desert. Moscow also informed Paris, London and Bonn, as well as the world public through Tass. The White House had already photographed an apparent test site in the Kalahari desert—a massive excavation surrounded by outbuildings—and Administration experts corroborated that SA might explode a bomb within a matter of weeks.[218] France sent a stiff warning to SA (see Foreign Affairs, below); so did the UK and West Germany. On 21 August, SA made a statement that it 'did not have nor did it intend to develop a nuclear explosive device for any purpose, peaceful or otherwise'.[219] Nevertheless Britain and France continued to sound warnings and Washington let it be known that it was considering a total ban on American exports of nuclear fuel to SA until it adhered to the Nuclear Non-proliferation Treaty and opened the pilot enrichment plant at Pelindaba to international inspection.[220] (The enriched uranium supplies to the American-built Safari-1 reactor are carefully controlled, and the US did not suspect that any fuel had been diverted for illicit purposes.) Further proof of SA's nuclear expertise came in September when the Council for Scientific and Industrial Research (CSIR) announced that it would build an advanced-technology nuclear particle accelerator.

Although much domestic political capital was made out of SA's sudden nuclear potential and much bravado expressed as to how it would be used, the Minister of Foreign Affairs later affirmed that SA intended to use nuclear energy for peaceful purposes. But at the end of September, satellite pictures showed that the testing site had still not been dismantled. By the same time, intelligence information had ruled out the possibility that the site was a diamond mine or a non-nuclear missile test range.[221]

Amid fears in December that SA might still go ahead with a nuclear explosion, the US publicly threatened to end nuclear co-operation with Pretoria unless it signed the Nuclear Non-proliferation Treaty.[222] SA replied that it would agree to stay out of the nuclear club only if the West guaranteed to back the country's resistance to 'Russian expansionary ambitions'.[223]

In December, the Uranium Enrichment Corporation awarded a £305m contract to build its much-publicized commercial enrichment plant for nuclear fuel. The decision to make SA invulnerable to fuel boycotts was almost certainly prompted by fears tht US enrichment fuels needed for the two French-built reactors at Koeberg nuclear power station would not be delivered. The President of the Atomic Energy Board, Dr Ampie Roux, said that SA was rapidly catching up to Canada to become the world's second largest producer of uranium. In ten years, it would be able to supply its own enriched uranium requirements and build its own nuclear power stations.

There was much speculation about how SA had achieved its nuclear breakthrough. One version was that the West Germans had collaborated; this suspicion was based on documents stolen from the South African embassy in West Germany.[224] The ANC, which held the sensitive documents, interpreted them as a conspiracy by Right-wing forces in both countries to get access to the bomb. However, Zdenek Cervenka and Barbara Rogers suggested that it was rather the reckless salesmanship of big business.[225] With its cheap electric power, SA could test the energy-hungry jet-nozzle process and perfect it, making the method more commercially viable. In return, West German industrialists expected equipment contracts and a steady supply of uranium. Another suggestion was that the Israelis were co-operating with SA in nuclear development.

French protest groups demonstrated in December 1977 in advance of the arrival of c. 40 South African nuclear technicians and their families. The technicians were to take training courses at the Super-Phoenix nuclear project and power stations at Bourgoin.

In early 1978, the South African Government proposed drastic increases in penalties to prevent unauthorized disclosures about nuclear installations in the country.

SOCIAL, LEGAL AND INDUSTRIAL AFFAIRS
WAGES
Surveys published in 1977 showed that from 1970 to 1976, wages for African workers increased faster than for Whites and that the ratio between Black and White incomes was decreasing. However, because Black wages started from such a small base, the actual increase in cash was small, and in fact the absolute difference between Black and White *per capita* incomes actually increased. For instance, the mean annual income of a Black factory worker in 1976 was just below R1,500, while the average for a White worker was R6,850.[226] While the African share of total income increased from 26% in 1970 to 32% in 1975, the distribution of incomes among Blacks seemed to have widened.[227]

White wage increases, especially in government service, suffered most from galloping inflation, but in practically every sector of Black employment, the average income was still below the breadline. In early 1977, the Government cut subsidies on maize, sugar and milk; coal and paraffin also went up in price. According to one estimate, these increases pushed up the cost of living of the poorest people in the Republic by 20%.[228] In Soweto alone, it was estimated that the cost of living was rising at an annual rate of 25–30%. Statistics gathered in June 1976 showed African monthly earnings were on average R109 in manufacturing and construction, R91 in the motor trade, R84 in the wholesale trade, R75 in local authorities, R70 in the retail trade, R51 in the hotel trade and R151 in banking.[229] According to the quarterly report of the Department of Statistics published in January 1978, Black workers earned an average of R120 a month during the last quarter of 1976 (cf R535 of the average White worker). This average African wage is below the urban breadline of R130 per month established by Prof J. Potgieter in October 1976. The Johannesburg Chamber of Commerce put the Soweto breadline (for May 1977) at R152 a month, and calculated that it had risen by a staggering 10.3% between November 1976 and February 1977, the highest rise in six years.[230] The Central Bantu Labour Board argued in November that a Black worker with four children on the Witwatersrand (the gold mining area centred on Johannesburg) needed at least R166.75 per month to live.[231]

The latest official statistics show that during the five years 1972–76, African wages rose more than twice as fast as those of Whites. The average monthly wage for African workers at the end of 1976 was almost one-quarter of the average monthly White wage; in 1972, it was only one-seventh.

Compound inflation from 1972 to the end of 1976 soared to 54.2%, but the average wages of all South Africans rose faster: Blacks by 150%, Asians by 97.3%, Coloureds by 79.2% and Whites by 70.7%. Average increases in the manufacturing sector were 73.7% for Black workers, 64.6% for Asians, 46.7% for Whites and 38.4% for Coloureds. The lowest increases were paid by the hotel, transport and building trades.[232]

Working with *per capita* incomes, the economist Jill Nattrass revealed an enormous wage gap. In 1975, the average *per capita* income for Black workers was R19.58 per month—one-eleventh of the average White *per capita* income of R209.16. This was a slight improvement on the 13:1 ratio in 1970, when the figures were R9.25 for Blacks and R124.42 for Whites. Nattrass' calculations show that from 1970 to 1975, average real wages for Blacks increased by 6.6% a year, and for Whites by 1%. This was reflected by a decrease in the absolute wage-gap from 1973 to 1975 in terms of 1970 prices. (Market Research Africa data showed that in absolute terms, the wage gap between White and African earnings grew from R143.50 in 1973 to R169.50 in 1975).[233]

The *Financial Mail* showed that because of the effect of inflation from 1970 to 1976, average White pay in Government service decreased in real terms from R282 to R254, while average African pay in real terms grew from R45 to R83—a drop in the ratio of 6:1 in 1970 to 3:1 in 1976. In the manufacturing sector, the real absolute wage gap remained fairly constant, though the ratio of White to African earnings dropped considerably. Average White pay in real terms grew from R307 to R340 in manufacturing, while Africans' grew from R52 to R79. The average real income of White employees rose at a rate of 1.3% a year from 1970 to 1975, while that of Blacks went up 8%.[234] The following table shows the percentage change in real earnings for all races:

Race group	1971	1972	1973	1974	1975	1976
Whites	3.8	(0.2)	(0.6)	2.1	(0.6)	(1.9)
Coloureds	7.7	2.2	3.7	0.7	1.4	(0.8)
Indians	9.4	3.6	3.5	2.1	3.5	4.4
Africans	3.0	4.5	7.4	11.5	11.7	5.1

Source: Trends and Afrikaanse Handelsinstituut.
Change over previous year in non-agricultural sectors (decreases shown in parenthesis).

The White slice of SA's cake is declining at 1.4% annually, according to MRA figures.[235] If this trend continues, it will still take another quarter of a century before SA's income distribution resembles that of the UK; i.e. before the wealthiest 15% receive 35% of the country's total income. In 1975, 16.8% had 67% of the cake. Figures for the year up to June 1977 show that Black pay rose by 16.5%, while

White pay remained below the 11% rise in the cost of living. [236]

The president of the Transvaal Chamber of Industries said he thought foreign-controlled companies had taken a lead in the improvement of wages and working conditions since 1973. [237] The Department of Trade confirmed that South African subsidiaries of British firms were improving Black wages and other conditions of employment. [238] The then Minister of the Interior, Dr Connie Mulder, said that closing the wage gap in all aspects of the State service would cost R164.9m a year. But another source estimated that R43m a year would be sufficient to give equal pay to equally qualified doctors, nurses, university lecturers, Department of Justice prosecutors, policemen, soldiers, teachers and post office officials. [239]

EMPLOYERS

South African employers entered 1977 somewhat shocked out of the complacency nurtured during the boom years. The foreign investment drain was starting to escalate, threats of boycotts were mounting, and the 1976 township riots and worker stay-aways were still a frightening memory. A mood of self-examination filtered down from leaders of big business, and human rights' consciousness was given much publicity. Millions of rands were pledged by businesses to the Urban Foundation for projects to improve the quality of African life. A Code of Employment practice, proposed at the end of 1976, was published at the end of 1977 with the support of 90% of organized commerce and industry. The Code commits employers to eliminate discrimination 'within the evolving legal framework' in the areas of selection and advancement, wages and fringe benefits. It asks them to recognize the basic rights of workers in collective bargaining and lawful strikes. However, the Code skirted the question of Black trade unions and made no commitment to a viable living wage.

At the annual Association of Chambers of Commerce (Assocom) congress in October 1977, businessmen affirmed their wish to see the end of racial discrimination. One motion called for a five or ten year socio-economic plan, the creation of a Black middle class, and constructive means to improve Black education.

Employers troubled by a dearth of African skilled labour set much store by the Wiehahn and Riekert Commissions which started investigating the whole gamut of African labour legislation (see Job Reservation and Trade Unions, below).

The Oppenheimer Anglo-American Corporation clashed with unions over its policy to integrate the workforce and allow African advancement (see Mine Labour, below).

EMPLOYMENT

African unemployment was one of the most pressing economic and social problems of 1977, with estimates of up to 2m jobless or seriously under-employed. As shown below, surveys varied widely in calculating the actual number and percentage of unemployed as well as the numbers of economically active Africans. According to Prof P. J. van der Merwe, African employment and under-employment stood at 1.424m or 23.2% of the African workforce at the end of 1976. He estimated that 27,000 lost their jobs each month up to July 1977, when the number in both categories stood at 1.586m. Building, shipbuilding, textiles and vehicle manufacturing were the areas most affected. Between 1970 and 1976, 40% of the increase of the African labour force in the White areas—85% in the Bantustans—were unemployed. Dr Wim de Villiers, chairman of General Mining, projected that 2.8m jobs would have to be created by 1980. With unemployment increasing by roughly 200,000 a year, this suggests at least 2m unemployed in 1977. [240] At the end of 1977, the Development Studies Research Group at Natal University put the total unemployment rate for all races at 22% of the economically active population. The rate for Blacks would be slightly higher.

Another survey estimated that 200,000 Blacks (18.8%) were unemployed in Johannesburg, Pretoria and the East and West Rand. Of these, 80% had been out of work for more than a month, and more than half for six months. Africans in the Cape Peninsula were worse hit because legislation decrees that Coloured people must be given preference.[241] In June 1977, it was estimated that the slump in the construction industry in the Western Cape had caused c. 11,000 building workers to be laid off. There were also 30% fewer artisans and labourers in the industry than there had been in 1976.[242]

The Government appeared to take a complacent attitude to the problem of Black unemployment—at least in its public statements. In July, the Finance Minister said that while the Government was keeping a close watch on the unemployment problem, its severity had been overstated. In January 1978, the Minister of Labour announced that there were only 129,000 unemployed Africans. When official statistics were published a few days later, the figure was five times higher (but even so, much lower than any other estimates), at 634,000 Africans or 12.4% of the total economically active Black population which was estimated at 5,110,000. Labour experts said the survey did not reflect the number of seriously under-employed Blacks. Criticism was also levelled at the four criteria for unemployment used in the government survey. The first, that he or she must not have worked for more than five hours in the previous seven days, would exclude an unemployed person living on his family's smallholding and giving a hand there. Many demographers believed that the under-employed, who might work a few hours each week to eke out an existence, formed a large part of the economically active population, but they were ignored by the official statistics.[243]

Black women were worst hit by unemployment. The government survey calculated unemployed women at 19.4% of the economically active population, as against 9.4% unemployed men. The national organizer of Domestic Workers' and Employers' Project, Sue Gordon, said there had been a 50% increase in the number of women seeking jobs through her non-profit employment service from January to July 1977. Many were laid off from the factories and now seeking domestic work.

Many of the jobless Africans were unable to draw unemployment money since the Act excludes the following from social security: farm and domestic workers; Africans on the gold and coal mines if they are fed by an employer; all foreign workers on contract; all Africans employed in rural areas unless they work in a factory; all Africans who earn less than R10.50 a week.[244] Migrant workers were obliged to claim in their 'home' areas. Another difficulty was the negligence of some employers who failed to register their workers. Many Africans entitled to unemployment pay complained to the Black Sash Advice Bureau that they experienced bureaucratic delays and even obstruction when they claimed benefits.

While millions suffered as a result of unemployment, a survey showed that the number of Black graduates was hardly enough to fill existing jobs in the Transvaal alone. For instance, 485 teaching posts were filled, but another 3,054 remained vacant.[245] In the private sector, there was a big demand for personnel and training officers and chemists. The Stellenbosch Bureau for Economic Research (BER) pointed out that the number of firms reporting skilled labour shortages had risen from 33% to 41% during 1977.

The view that more and more Africans were occupying skilled, technical and managerial positions in SA was shown to be a myth (see Table below).[246] According to Department of Labour manpower surveys, the proportion of Africans in almost every class of skilled position dropped between April 1975 and April 1977. A problem in comparing the figures is that the 1977 survey excluded the Transkei, but the *Financial Mail* calculated that African participation in administrative, executive and managerial posts dropped from 2% to 0.4% in two years. As the latest occupants of these jobs, Africans may have been the first to be laid off.

However, labour forecasts showed that the Black skilled workforce would outstrip the White in the next few years. Given a growth rate of 5% a year, 56,900 or 70% of artisans and technically skilled workers would be Black by 1981.[247]

The lack of skilled labour was caused in part by the drop in White immigration.[248] But the excess of unskilled labour was caused mainly by mechanization.[249] Even with an upswing in the economy, this will remain a major problem.

AFRICAN AND WHITE PARTICIPATION IN SKILLED, TECHNICAL AND MANAGERIAL POSITIONS

	Administrative, Executive and Managerial		Professional, Semi-professional and Technical		Artisans and Apprentices
	African	White	African	White	African
April 1975	2.9%	94%	29%	60%	2.5%
April 1977*	0.4%	97%	26%	61%	2.1%

*The Transkei was not included in the 1977 Manpower Survey. Totals not equalling 100 indicate Coloured and Asian participation.
Source: Department of Labour Statistics.

TRADE UNIONS

For the first time in its 25-year history, the Trade Union Council of SA (TUCSA), representing 63,000 Whites and 150,000 Coloureds and Asians, elected a Coloured man as its president in September 1977. He is Ronnie Webb, general-secretary of the Motor Industry Combined Workers' Union. At the same conference, three small unions pulled out of TUCSA—evidence of continuing disunity.

In evidence to the Wiehahn Commission into labour legislation, TUCSA asked that all laws be non-discriminatory. Blacks should be allowed full trade union rights, although unions in turn could retain their ethnic identity. Since 1973, TUCSA has been trying to provide a trade union vehicle for Blacks by organizing parallel unions under the wing of the registered movement (Blacks are prohibited from induction into registered unions: see *ACR* 1976–77 pp. B834f). However, TUCSA's former general-secretary, Arthur Grobbelaar, admitted in April 1977 that progress in parallel unionism had been disappointing. He blamed this on fear of possible action by the authorities and the fact that the rank-and-file were often apprehensive of being swamped by large numbers of Blacks.[250]

The bulk of White trade unionists confirmed their prejudice against Blacks when the right-wing Confederation of Labour, representing 193,000 Whites in 25 unions, told the Wiehahn Commission that it was in favour of job reservation and opposed to Black unionization except in the Bantustans.[251] Earlier, observers had thought the Confederation was softening its attitudes. Instead, the Mine Workers' Union (MWU) general-secretary, Arrie Paulus, threatened to disaffiliate if the Confederation dropped its stand against Black 'infiltration'. At its conference in February 1978, the Confederation confirmed its support for job reservation unless other safeguards were offered. It also rejected a proposal that would have admitted racially mixed unions into its ranks.[252]

Black trade unions limped into 1977 in the restrictive atmosphere of 24 recent bannings, police and labour department pressure, White unions' mistrust and employers' nervousness. Black unions had no legal bargaining channels. Independent Black unions especially had an uphill struggle getting employers to listen to their demands. An even greater setback was the passing of the Bantu Labour Relations Regulation Amendment Bill which enabled African workers to negotiate binding wage agreements—not through unions, but through liaison committees composing 50% of workers. These, together with works' committees, were the Government's answer to the threat of union power. Bargaining by liaison committees was of course restricted to factory level and had no independent power base.

Many employers, nervously looking for a way to make concessions after the spontaneous strikes of 1973 and the unrest and political stay-at-homes of 1976, took this legislation as a lead on how to deal with the growing Black union movement—ignore it. For instance, when the three-year agreement between the British company, Smith & Nephew, and the National Union of Textile Workers came to an end in July 1977 (the first agreement negotiated by any company with a Black union), the company told its workers it was no longer prepared to recognize the union and wanted to deal with them through the liaison committee. This brought international criticism; the Council for Industrial Workers of the Witwatersrand also complained that the liaison committee was unrepresentative of the workers.[253] Another British firm, United Transport Holdings, refused recognition to an unregistered union. The general-secretary of the Transport and Allied Workers' Union, Clement Montso, was detained by security police for several hours after asking for an interview with the manager.

1977 brought further examples of intimidation of union officials by employers. Four workers at Kelloggs (SA) were sacked after fighting for a registered works' committee as a basis for their union. A Unilever shop steward was fired after he had approached management about organizing facilities.[254] Unions also alleged that police were carrying out a nationwide probe of the independent Black trade union movement. A statement issued by ten unions in September charged that police (or men who claimed to be police) were engaged in questioning workers, apparently interested in a proposed federation of Black workers. 1977 also saw quick police action against strikers. In one incident, 30 labourers of the Witbank coal agency were fined or given three months after being found guilty of striking. Miners at the Cornelia colliery were sent back to the reserves after a strike. 186 workers of Scottford Mills were remanded in custody for ten days after refusing to start work during a pay dispute.

However some employers showed a more positive response to Black unions, and Black trade union officials said that 1977 had been the best year ever.[255] One of the trend-setting employers was Sir Harry Oppenheimer, Anglo-American Corporation chairman, whose remark, 'There is nothing in law to prevent employers from recognizing Black unions and negotiating with them,' was given wide publicity. In terms of Anglo-American's policy documents, Anglo companies are expected to deal with African unions which approach them.[256] Anglo favours a two-tier system in which unions and works' committees both play a part. One subsidiary, Zinchem, foresaw that liaison committees would deal with purely local matters, while pay scales would be negotiated by the union. Zac de Beer, executive director of Anglo-American, warned of the danger of separate unions leading to racial friction and said that integrated unions were preferable. Another Anglo policy document indicated a move to integrate the work force in the mines, which would shift power away from the White unions (see mine labour). Another multinational employer, Leyland, actually asked Ronnie Webb to organize its Black workers at Elandsfontein—having repeatedly refused an independent Black union these facilities in the past.[257] Webb said that he had no trouble finding 12 to 15 motor component firms which had 'no objection' to his organizing their employees.[258] Two eastern

Cape multinationals, Ford and SKF, changed their attitudes to recognition of Black unions. Ford Motors agreed to operate a check-off system once the Black union in its Port Elizabeth assembly plant succeeded in registering a majority of the workers.

The Institute for Industrial Relations—formed in 1976 but still relatively inactive—claimed in October 1977 that membership was growing. It now includes 30 companies, 18 unions (half of them Black) and a number of co-ordinating bodies. The director, Sam van Coller, claimed a softening of attitudes between management and unions as well as a marginal improvement in relations between Black and non-Black unions.

Early in 1977, the National Union of Motor Assembly and Rubber Workers, which had recently left TUCSA, organized a meeting of unregistered African unions with the idea of setting up a Federation of Black Unions. The unregistered unions endorsed the principle of federation and agreed to set up a feasibility committee. However four years of mutual recrimination among the various union groupings—plus suspicion of the registered unions—proved too great a stumbling block. At a meeting in September 1977, the federation attempts were postponed.

JOB RESERVATION

The general feeling was that 1977 marked the beginning of the end of statutory discrimination in commerce and industry, with 18 job reservation determinations scrapped by December, and with the Riekert and Wiehahn commissions investigating the whole gamut of African labour legislation. Unions committed to the protection of the White worker were worried, whereas Government critics feared that only the most outmoded racial measures were being attended to as a cosmetic operation to forestall future unrest and remove some obstacles slowing economic recovery. Although 25 job reservations were still enshrined in Section 77 of the Industrial Conciliation Act and many other discriminatory labour laws remained in force, the year passed in a mood of seeming Government flexibility as Vorster repeated his intention to do away with 'restrictive measures'.[259]

With the shortage of skilled labour in many jobs reserved for Whites, vacancies multiplied and—in defiance of Proclamation No R1260[260]—hundreds of Black managers worked in White areas.[261] However, in mid-year, the then Minister of Bantu Administration, M. C. Botha, refused to grant permission for the training and use of Black managers in urban areas. Amid adverse publicity, Botha softened and said he was willing to consider guidelines prepared by the Association of Chambers of Commerce (Assocom) on the use of Black managers in White areas 'where there is a preponderance of Black customers and a totality of Black employees'. In the focus on Black job advancement, however, it emerged that management in general was more interested in window-dressing promotions than with real advancement and responsibility.[262]

One group to escape the ministrations of Bantu Administration were African attorneys. Notices to vacate city offices and to remove themselves to the Homelands were withdrawn after representations by the Association of Law Societies.

The Industrial Tribunal completed a probe into existing job reservation determinations in September 1977 when the Labour Minister announced that most of the trade unions had agreed that the determinations should be withdrawn. By December, all except five had been suspended or scrapped. Determination 27 on the mines and 28 in the building industry—both strongly supported by the White unions—were among those remaining. It was suggested that a different mechanism for the protection of White workers would be introduced to placate the Confederation of Labour and particularly the Mine Workers' Union—possibly a seniority system whereby present incumbents would be favoured in cases of advancement and retrenchment.[263] However, it was pointed out that jobs no longer protected were of little interest to Whites who had moved out of them long ago; Indians and Coloureds were now mainly affected. The major bars to African upward mobility were in fact other discriminatory laws like the Apprenticeship Act and practices like closed shop industrial agreements.

The Wiehahn Commission's brief encompassed mainly the commercial and manufacturing sectors, but was later widened to look at the Mines and Works Act. Discriminatory laws like the Shops and Offices Act, the Factories Act and the Bantu Building Workers' Act were expected to be affected by the report.

A second commission was appointed in August under the Prime Minister's economic adviser, Piet Riekert, to look at a wide range of laws affecting the position of the urban African in the labour market. Vorster promised that the laws would be reviewed with a view to eliminating bottlenecks experienced by both employer and employee. Many of these affected African job opportunities in the urban areas, and some contributed to unemployment.[264]

MINE LABOUR

In the first quarter of 1977 there was a drop in gold output of c. 250,000 ounces, mainly because of an acute shortage of workers in the first month.[265] However from mid-February, recruits flowed in to such an extent that by May an estimated 7,000 to 10,000 had to be turned away, and underground strength stood at 100.45%. One of the reasons given for the labour instability was the growing number of Black South Africans recruited on six-month contracts as the complement of foreign workers on long-term contracts declined. Mozambique labour dropped from 84,733 in April 1976 to 38,244 a year later. Malawian labour virtually dried up; only 207 Malawians were on the mines in April 1977, though the number rose quite significantly again by the end of the year. At the end of April, the South African labour component stood at 51.62%—38.5% from the Bantustans and Transkei (see Table). The Employment Bureau of Africa (Teba) succeeded in its attempt to increase the proportion of South Africans on the mines largely because of the vast unemployment in the country. However, despite unemployment, mining remained so unpopular with urban Africans that Teba had to close its Soweto office.

SOURCE OF MINE LABOUR*

Foreign		South Africa (including Transkei) 'White Areas'	
Mozambique	38,244	Cape	23,846
Malawi	207	OFS	14,644
Rhodesia	24,727	Transvaal	11,029
Botswana	24,810	Natal	5,394
Lesotho	99,964		**54,913**
Swaziland	11,756	'African Areas'	
Kavango	2,166	Transkei	96,999
Caprivi	325	Ciskei	18,206
Angola	1,247	Bophutha Tswana	20,091
	203,446	KwaZulu	12,327
		Lebowa	6,543
		Venda	1,821
		Ndebele	70
		Gazankulu	1,657
		QwaQwa	3,725
		Swazi 'Homeland'	655
		Others	83
			162,177
		Total	**420,536**

*Strength at the end of April 1977 of mines which are members of the Chamber of Mines.
Source: The Financial Mail, 5 August 1977.

In an attempt to stabilize the workforce, Teba started issuing 'employment guarantee certificates' to miners in February 1977. These entitled men who had worked 45 weeks on the mines to be rehired automatically if they returned within six months. Part of the reason for the decline in foreign labour was that only those with previous experience were being hired. Lesotho, with more workers than any other area, was worried by the new policy.

The pace of Black wage rises on the mines has been slowing down: a 37.5% hike in 1975 decreased to 13.6% in 1976 and to only 6% in July 1977. The last was barely half the current rate of inflation. But the Chamber of Mines said the Black miners were cushioned against inflation to some extent by the provision of free board and lodging. It pointed to the fivefold increase in wages from 1971 to 1976, saying there had been little or no improvement in productivity.[266] It also argued that wage increases seemed to encourage migrants, who are part of a dual economy, to opt for shorter contracts.[267] Monthly average earnings of White miners in 1977 were R843 including all benefits.

According to the Chamber of Mines, there were 389,350 Africans working under its umbrella in the gold mines and 73,515 on the coal fields in June 1977. Surface workers constituted about a third of the Black component on collieries and a quarter in the gold mines.

The interim report of the Franzen Commission of Enquiry, set up after the 1976 Mine Workers' Union (MWU) dispute, came out strongly against the argument that the mines could afford a five-day week: mines lying idle for two days a week would cause a 6.1% drop in gold production and cost the collieries R28.2m. The report endorsed an 11-shift fortnight experiment, which would be tried for a year to assess its effect on production. It suggested that a system should gradually be phased in where mines operated for seven days a week, but miners only worked five shifts. Goldfields chairman, Adriaan Louw, blamed the 11-shift fortnight for a drop in production, but Arrie Paulus, MWU secretary-general, charged the mine management with sabotaging production to thwart the five-day week.

The Anglo-American Corporation, which employs more than 300,000 mineworkers, conducted a study which showed up the serious conflict between Black and White miners. White miners were seen as enemies because they did no hard labour, but got more pay and insisted on blind obedience.[268] This report annoyed Arrie Paulus, the champion of job reservation. He remained on the attack all year and apparently succeeded in his efforts to retain job reservation Determination 27 (see above). Anglo also prepared a secret working paper setting out a strategy for shifting the balance of power away from the White union so that negotiations on job changes could take place leading to an integrated workforce.[269] The document was leaked to Paulus' newspaper, *The Mineworker*, and he reacted by holding mass meetings.

Anglo was also at odds with other more conservative mining houses in 1977. The Chamber of Mines battled to achieve consensus for its evidence to the Wiehahn Commission. Conservatives wanted migrant miners to be represented by mine level committees only, while Anglo felt full trade union rights would help the industry achieve a unified industrial relations structure.[270]

LEGAL AFFAIRS
By the end of 1976, SA had such a welter of security legislation that a Professor of Law at the University of Cape Town remarked that, legally, it was impossible to distinguish between times of normality and emergency.[271] More specifically, during the unrest following the 1960 Sharpeville shootings, emergency regulations were issued to cover the following: the control and dispersal of gatherings, preventive

detention, prevention of the dissemination of subversive statements, suppression of subversive associations, and detention for interrogation. By mid-1976, all these emergency measures were covered by ordinary legislation.

Security and related legislation introduced during 1977 was less spectacular than in past years. New laws seemed aimed at closing administrative loopholes, entrenching executive power and eliminating whatever 'obstacles' might occur in a situation of unrest.

The Criminal Procedure Bill aroused much criticism. It replaced the Criminal Procedure Act of 1955, which was the closest SA ever came to adopting a charter of human rights. The new Bill empowered judges or judicial officers to examine an accused person before the actual trial. This effectively replaced SA's 'innocent until proved guilty' system of criminal justice with the continental inquisitorial system— but without the checks and balances which European countries have developed. The Bill also provided for the 'protection' of witnesses by detention for up to six months, with no access to legal advice. Clause 217 of the Bill deals with the challenging of confessions. Defence must now prove that confessions were not made freely and voluntarily, whereas previously the onus was on the State. The only witnesses an accused can call are the police who interrogated him. Opposition spokesmen said the Bill introduced into criminal procedure serious deviations of principle which were consistently loaded against the accused who, without legal representation, could easily incriminate himself in pre-trial interrogation.

Another contentious piece of legislation was the Lower Courts Amendment Bill, which aimed at dealing with the greater numbers of people awaiting trial under the Terrorism Act. This gave regional magistrates jurisdiction to hear terrorism and sabotage cases and impose sentences of up to ten years and fines of up to R10,000. Previously sabotage and 'terrorism' trials were heard exclusively by judges in the Supreme Courts; regional courts had been restricted to cases involving fines of up to R1,500 or sentences of three years. Critics of this new law argued that it was wrong to bring cases of a serious political nature before the lower courts. Besides being public servants, magistrates were less qualified to deal with the sensitive and subjective issues sometimes involved.

The Indemnity Act exempted police from legal action for anything that occurred during riots between 16 June 1976 and the commencement of the Act. This made it impossible for complainants to obtain redress or compensation. One observer said the Act was 'yet another measure limiting civil rights'.

The Reservation of Public Amenities Amendment Bill empowered the Minister of Community Development to direct any person who has control of any public amenity to reserve it for a particular racial group.

An outcry greeted the Bantu Laws Amendment Bill which doubled the fines for contraventions of the hated pass laws. The maximum was raised to R100 or three months' imprisonment. This came soon after the Viljoen Commission of Inquiry into the penal system had recommended that pass offenders not be classified as criminals (see above). Opposition spokesmen termed the Bill 'a dangerous and reckless measure'. Helen Suzman warned that the higher fines were likely to increase racial friction: 'I do not believe that there is a single commission of inquiry since influx control was first implemented that has not pointed out that the pass laws were one of the greatest causes of racial friction'. She said the measure would put more people into the already 'bursting' jails 'for the crime of looking for work'.[272]

During 1976 there were a few cases where squatters successfully took action against the demolition of their shacks, but the Prevention of Illegal Squatting Act of 1977 removed all their legal safeguards and grounds of appeal. After the Act came into operation, thousands of squatters in the Cape Peninsula had their homes demolished despite public concern and appeals to the authorities. In terms of this Act no court order, judgement or other relief to prevent the demolition of a squatters' structure may be sought in a civil court unless the squatter can prove he owns the land! Further, the landowner (often the State) does not have to give notice of his intention to demolish any shack erected on his land without his consent. The Act also brought the Coloured people within the orbit of influx control for the first time, as it became a heavily punishable offence for employers to take on any worker who could not produce a certificate indicating he had 'suitable' housing.

Another repressive law, the Community Councils Bill, *inter alia* legalized the 'Makgotla' system of tribal justice which has existed unofficially in many African townships. This meant that chiefs and headmen dealing with criminal and civil cases which involved Africans only could publicly administer flogging to males under the age of 30. The Bill also abolished the Urban Bantu Councils and made provision for them to be replaced by community councils, which were to be elected on a tribal basis. This followed the resignation of the Soweto UBC (see above: Black Students).

The Publications Amendment Act further extended the powers of the Minister of Police to deal with internal disorder and terrorism, and included an extension of censorship powers. 'Perhaps the most disquieting feature of this Act,' said Dr Kenneth Hughes, chairman of the Civil Rights League, 'is the apparently harmless provision repealing a section of the amended Act and thus bringing professional and scientific publications and religious journals within its ambit.' Since the Act became law, the statement of the Nyanga Ministers' Fraternal (about police brutality) and of the Christian Institute's pamphlet 'Torture in South Africa' have been banned. [273]

The Minister of Economic Affairs announced that the government had the power, under the National Supplies Procurement Act of 1970, to compel foreign and local companies in SA to manufacture military supplies. All that was necessary was the promulgation of certain sections of the Act by placing a notice in the Government Gazette. [274]

After the Nationalist landslide election victory, the new Minister of Plural Affairs, Dr Connie Mulder, introduced two controversial apartheid Bills. The first was yet another Bantu Laws Amendment Bill, which the Press dubbed the 'idle' Bantu law'. Mulder explained that it was to keep 'idle and work-shy Bantu in check'. In terms of the Bill, urban Blacks face arrest if they are unemployed for more than 122 days in any calendar year. The four months of unemployment need not be consecutive. Penalties for the 'idle' include detention in a rehabilitation centre or farm colony, where 'prescribed labour' would have to be carried out, or deportation to a work settlement in a Bantustan. Helen Suzman said the Bill made it a crime to be out of work and introduced a form of forced labour. [275] The other new law, the Bantu Citizenship Amendment Bill, ensured that those relinquishing their Bantustan citizenship would not automatically become South African citizens. In a burst of candour, Mulder said he did not wish to hide the Government's ultimate goal in passing such legislation: a country in which no Black person would have South African citizenship. [276]

In January 1978, the International Commission of Jurists criticized the new National Welfare Bill, which made it an offence for any organization to provide social welfare services unless it had a registration certificate. It also became a criminal offence for any person to give instruction in social work unless registered as a social worker. Another Bill the Commission criticized made it an offence for anyone to collect contributions from the public with a view to promoting any object relating to the rendering of material aid to any other person. [277] The President of the

SRC of the University of Cape Town, Steve Kahanowitz, said that if these Bills became law, they would effectively prevent any student involvement in the Black community. Many students voluntarily involved in literacy, legal aid and many other projects would become classified as social workers and have to obtain Government approval for their work.

PRISONS

SA's prison population is more than twice that of Britain, and one of the highest in the Western world. In the year ended 30 June 1976, there were 273,393 sentenced prisoners and 243,967 awaiting trial, the latter an increase of 55,471 over the previous year.[278] The unit cost per prisoner per day was put at R12.27, excluding capital expenditure.[279]

Of the total number of sentenced prisoners of all races, 65% were Africans jailed for periods of four months and less. The report of the Commission of Inquiry into the penal system, chaired by Mr Justice Viljoen, attributed the high number of African prisoners to the poverty of their social, economic and political conditions and the high number of offences they are subject to under influx control, curfew and township laws.[280] There were 178 prisoners in 1976 under sentence of death.[281] Of these, 109 were new admissions. Sixty convicts were executed; 21 had their sentences commuted; eight appealed successfully; two were sent for re-trials; one committed suicide, and 86 were still in their condemned cells at the end of 1976.

Corporal punishment was administered to 2,251 prisoners, including a large number of juveniles found guilty of charges relating to civil unrest. In one case a number of children under 14 received eight cuts each for attending an illegal gathering.

There were 391 deaths in prison: 13 were said to have committed suicide, 11 to have died accidentally and 14 while trying to escape.[282] The Minister of Police revealed that 117 police detainees had died, 28 of 'natural causes', 21 by 'committing suicide', and 20 of wounds sustained during their arrest or in attempts to escape.[283]

Police shot 605 people 'in the course of their duties', killing 195.[284] These figures do not include people shot during civil disturbances. The overwhelming number of those killed were Africans 'attempting to escape'. Helen Suzman MP deplored this 'alarming tendency' to shoot people trying to escape.[285]

After two children aged 13 sustained bullet wounds while being held on housebreaking charges, a policeman was suspended and the charges withdrawn. During 1975–76, 236 policemen were convicted of crimes ranging from assault to murder; eight had previous convictions.[286] Only two of those with previous convictions were among the 16 subsequently discharged from the force.

Evidence of police violence and torture was given in a number of trials (see below). An order was issued by a Natal Court restraining the Minister of Police, the Natal Attorney-General and various police officers from assaulting or molesting prisoners;[287] this followed an interdict by three prisoners who claimed they were tortured with an electric-shock machine. Two policemen from Rehoboth Police Station in Namibia, defending themselves against charges that they had tortured and assaulted suspects, claimed that such methods were common.[288] A notice gazetted in June 1977 made it an offence under the prison regulations for a warder to assault a prisoner.[289] The International Red Cross sent its report on prison conditions in SA to the Government in 1977, but by prior agreement it was not made public.

DETENTIONS

At 30 November 1977, 714 people were being held in detention without trial.[290] The Minister of Police and Justice told Parliament that 240 people were being held under Section Six of the Terrorism Act which allows for them to be detained indefinitely and incommunicado. Another 64 were being held under Section Ten of the Internal Security Act, which allows for the detention of witnesses and people considered a threat to 'public order'.[291] The Minister told a party congress that since June 1976, 2,430 people had been detained. Of these, 817 had been tried and convicted; 118 were awaiting trial; 372 were under investigation, and 135 were held in preventive detention. The remaining 988 were presumably released without having been charged.

Questioned in Parliament by Helen Suzman, the Minister said 236 males and 23 females under 18 years had been detained. Reports showed that children under 16 had been held in solitary confinement, some of them only ten years old. Ms Suzman said the Act was being used 'ruthlessly and with abandon' against people who were not terrorists. Prof John Dugard said the use of the Terrorism Act against children emphasized its abhorrent nature, which deviated from all the principles of criminal justice. Parents and relatives of many of the detained, including the children, were not informed of their whereabouts.

Members of such organizations as BPC and SASO, school-children and students, community leaders, churchmen and journalists were among those detained. 12 Black journalists were arrested. *World* editor Percy Qoboza and *Weekend World* news editor Aggrey Klaaste (see above) were released in March 1978 without any explanation, after nearly five months in detention.

Of 662 people being held without trial at the end of September 1977, 224 had been in detention for between six and 12 months, and 97 for more than a year. Thebani Phantsi was detained without trial for three periods totalling 513 days between October 1975 and March 1977; he was again detained on 9 June 1977. On 8 June, the BPC regional chairman, Mapapa George Wanchope, was re-detained in Soweto after 279 days in solitary confinement in 1976.

At least 24 people detained in the Transkei since independence were still held at the end of November 1977. T. Mosala was 'found dead' in his cell in November 1976. No explanation was given.

Apart from two youths who died in police custody after their arrest in the Soweto unrest, 19 people are known to have died while detained by the security police between March 1976 and November 1977. Five of these were described by inquest magistrates as suicides. Nine died by 'hanging'; three by 'jumping or falling' from upper storeys of interrogation blocks; four from 'natural causes'; one from 'brain injury', and one from 'hypertension and spontaneous intracerebral haemorrhage'. None of these deaths was found to have been caused by the 'act or omission of any living person'. In several cases, evidence was given of other wounds on the deceased, unexplained by the official causes of death. In the one remaining case, that of Joseph Mdluli, four security policemen were tried but acquitted on charges of culpable homicide. In July 1977, Mr Justice Howard, presiding in a Terrorism Act trial, said of Mdluli's death: 'The most probable explanation is that all or most [of the wounds] were inflicted by the security police'.

At the inquest into the death following brain injury of the Black Consciousness leader, Steve Biko, the magistrate found that no one was responsible, and that his injury probably occurred during a 'scuffle' with policemen trying to restrain him. The finding evoked world-wide publicity and condemnation. British and US legal observers who attended the inquest were highly critical of the police investigations into the death and of the magistrate's finding. Prof Louis Pollak, dean of the Law School at Pennsylvania University, said in his report that the inquest left him 'with no doubt' that Biko's death was caused by injuries inflicted by unidentified members of the security police.[292]

Numerous calls for an independent commission of inquiry into the deaths of detainees—which now number 43 since the introduction of security legislation in 1961—were ignored or rejected by the authorities.

Reports on the torture of detainees were issued by Amnesty International, the South African Institute of Race Relations (SAIRR), the Anti-Apartheid Movement and the African National Congress. [293] Amnesty found that torture was used by the security police on 'almost a routine basis' and that by failing to remedy the situation, the Government appeared to condone it. The SAIRR report gathered together torture claims by 115 prisoners and detailed sworn affidavits of political prisoners—all previously published material. Tortures described included electric shocks, the tying of weights to the testicles, throttling, the placing of a plastic bag over the head to induce suffocation, beatings and whippings, the enforced wearing of shoes containing small stones, being made to sit on an imaginary chair until the muscles collapsed, and threats of death or of being thrown from upstairs windows. The report was banned in SA.

TRIALS

There were 45 trials under the 1967 Terrorism Act in 1977—more than double the all-time record of the previous year. [294] In addition, there were 38 trials under the sabotage laws, involving 257 accused, of whom 144 were acquitted or had their charges withdrawn. Many of the sabotage cases arose from damage done during civil unrest. Under all security laws, 144 people were convicted in the course of 95 trials and sentenced to a total of 898 years in prison.

In the major political trial of 1977, 11 men and a woman faced 79 charges under the Terrorism and Internal Security Acts. It was alleged that they were members or supporters of the ANC, the South African Communist Party or *Umkhonto We Sizwe* (the ANC's military wing); that they had conspired in the distribution of pamphlets urging the overthrow of the government; had recruited people as ANC members or for overseas training; had smuggled arms into SA; committed acts of sabotage and infiltrated organizations. The State opened its case in the Pretoria Supreme Court in June and 100 witnesses proceeded to give evidence. But on 2 November the judge died and a re-trial had to be ordered.

In July, nine men were found guilty under the Terrorism Act on charges of seeking recruits for the ANC to undergo military training outside the country. During the hearing in Pietermaritzburg, two State witnesses, Frans Kunene and Harold Nxasana, said they had agreed to give police evidence only after violence was used against them. Police denied the allegations, but the defence attorney said that the evidence of witnesses detained under Section Six of the Terrorism Act needed careful evaluation, as such witnesses could be held in solitary confinement for long periods and interrogated until they made statements that satisfied the police.

Five of the accused—H. Gwala, A. Zaba, J. Nene, M. Meyiwa and Z. Mdalose—were sentenced to life imprisonment. J. Nduli was jailed for 18 years; C. Ndhlovu and V. Magubane for 15 years, and A. Ndebele for seven years. Leave to appeal was refused. A tenth accused, William Khanyile, was earlier found not guilty and discharged.

20 students of the University of Zululand were acquitted in July of charges arising from R500,000 damage caused to university property on 17 and 18 June 1976 following a student mass meeting. 29 students had been detained as State witnesses for periods of between six and 11 months before the trial. At the hearing in Durban, these witnesses claimed that police had mistreated them in order to obtain the statements they wanted. The police denied the allegations, but at the close of the

hearing the State counsel conceded that the witnesses had not been satisfactory and the State was found not to be in a position to seek a conviction on the merits of the case.

In March, three men were sentenced to jail under the Terrorism Act in the Grahamstown Supreme Court. Walter Tshikila pleaded guilty to being a PAC office-bearer, to inciting people to leave the country for military training, and to giving lectures on the PAC. Joseph Madyo and Dumile Ndwandwa also pleaded guilty to being PAC members and to trying to leave the country to undergo military training. Mr Justice Kannemeyer said that although Tshikila had been motivated by his political ideals and had not acted for personal gain, no State could tolerate organizations aiming to overthrow it by force. Tshikila, who had previously spent six years on Robben Island for PAC activities, was jailed for 13 years, and the others for five years each.

Six men were convicted in November on charges of making and possessing explosives, hiding ammunition in Soweto, attempting to blow up the Johannesburg-Vereeniging railway line, belonging to the ANC, and recruiting and attending lectures on bomb-making. The trial arose from the discovery of explosives on the railway line and explosions in January 1977 which demolished a Soweto house used as a bomb-factory. John Phala and John Thabo were sentenced to 30 years in prison; Phillip Khoza to 15 years; Letsie Mashinini and Bafuma Nkosi to 13 years, and Solomon Musi to five years.

Mondy Motloung (20) and Solomon Mahlangu (21) appeared in the Johannesburg Regional Court in August on two charges of murder, two of attempted murder and five charges under the Terrorism Act. Their trial arose from the death of two White men during a machine-pistol and grenade attack on a warehouse in Johannesburg on 13 June 1977. They were accused of having been ANC members, of having left SA to undergo military training, and of returning to commit acts endangering law and order. At their first appearance, they pleaded not guilty but refused to answer questions because they were not represented. After a postponement, the defence successfully applied for Motloung to be sent for mental observation as he had sustained brain damage during his arrest. He was subsequently found unfit to stand trial. In March 1978, Mahlangu was sentenced to death by Mr Justice Theron, even though he had not done the shooting or thrown the grenade. Mahlangu, who was recruited into the ANC shortly after the June 1976 unrest in Soweto, was lead from the dock giving the Black Power salute.

In January 1978, the trial of 18 Blacks accused of furthering the aims of the banned PAC opened in the Bethal Circuit Court in camera. Among the accused was a 65-year old PAC founder-member, Zeph Mothopeng, who has already served a sentence on Robben Island. On the list of 86 alleged co-conspirators—including PAC founding president, Robert Sobukwe—were the names of four detainees who have since died in security police detention. The trial judge refused a defence counsel application for US and Swedish diplomats to attend as observers.

BANNINGS
In the continuing purge of Government opponents, the number of banned people increased during 1977; at the end of 1976, 146 people were officially banned.[295] Of these, 11 had banning orders against them renewed for a third time. Such orders, which severely curtail freedom of movement and speech, are imposed on people considered a danger to the State who cannot be convicted of any crime. During the year Ms Winnie Mandela, living in Soweto under a banning order, was served with a new order restricting her to a small town in the Orange Free State. (For other detentions, see the Events of October, above.)

EDUCATION: WHITE STUDENTS

Black student organizations continued to refuse to have any contact with White students during 1977; among White students themselves, the Afrikaanse Studente Bond (ASB) refused to communicate with the National Union of Students (NUSAS), which operates only on English-speaking campuses. The steady and general drift into a conservative White unity movement was also apparent at the English-medium universities—formerly renowned for their outspoken criticism of apartheid.

NUSAS, traditionally the focus for student opposition, started 1977 seriously weakened. The organization had all but collapsed during 1976, both because of the Okhela affair (see above: Clandestine Movements) and because of a concerted conservative assault on what was seen as an unrepresentative Left-wing controlling clique. In fact, since 1974 the English-speaking student political scene has stagnated seriously due to such Government attacks as the Schlebusch and Van Wyk de Vries Commissions (see *ACR* 1973–74, pp. B447–49), to regular bannings of student leaders, and finally to the Affected Organizations Act which cut off 75% of NUSAS' funds. [296] Also, virtually every student newspaper published since 16 June 1976 has been banned.

NUSAS' main activity during 1977 was to promote the theme of 'White Africanism' which NUSAS president Nicholas Haysom described as a process designed to 'free English-speaking students of the last remnants of their colonial mentality'. [297] The idea was to encourage English-speaking students to develop an African identity rather than to think of themselves as displaced Europeans or aspirant Americans. Proponents of the idea admitted that 'White Africanism' was a response to Black Consciousness: 'Whites are experiencing a deep crisis of identity in the face of Black nationalism'. [298] Another aim of the 'White Africanism' campaign was to inculcate a commitment to SA and thus stem the flow of students leaving the country. Because many young people opposed to apartheid felt increasingly ineffectual, they were leaving SA as soon as they completed their degrees.

Some students disillusioned with NUSAS formed radical movements such as the Students' Africa Movement (SAM) at the University of the Witwatersrand (Wits) and Students for Social Democracy (SSD) at the University of Cape Town. Their newspapers, *CRISIS* and *Z* respectively, contained analysis of the South African situation and appeared fairly regularly, despite official harassment.

A major feature of 1977 student politics was the activity of conservative student elements. For instance, the ASB denounced as unpatriotic and disloyal the commemmoration by some students on NUSAS campuses of the 16 June 1976 Soweto protest. At Wits, a mock graveyard with miniature crosses planted on the library lawns was attacked by conservatives who poured petrol over the crosses and set them alight. [299] Rhodesian Societies were also set up at three NUSAS campuses 'to counter propaganda' against the Smith regime. Although these societies denied any governmental links, they made extensive use of the Rhodesian consulate telex facilities and covered the campuses with pro-Rhodesian propaganda portraying 'terrorist' atrocities against fellow Blacks. In another incident, scores of students at Wits applauded when the detention of 20 Black and White student leaders by the security police was announced. The detained included five from Wits, one of whom was the NUSAS secretary-general.

SAFESS (the South African Federation of English-Speaking Students), which first appeared during 1976, produced regular issues of its *Campus Independent* newspaper in which it constantly took the offensive against 'subversive' influences on the campuses. The SAFESS group, which played a major part in the 1976 anti-NUSAS campaign, has never been elected by any student group. It is allegedly financed by BOSS, but members refused to say more than that their backers were 'big business'.[300]

At the beginning of 1978 the new NUSAS president, Auret van Heerden, toured the English-speaking campuses. Pointing to the increasing fragmentation among English, Afrikaans and Black students, he said that Black Consciousness had 'developed into a form of reverse racism that was more destructive than constructive'.[301]

EDUCATION: BLACK STUDENTS

The Government's new deal for Black education, announced at the end of 1976,[302] failed to end the widespread boycotts of exams, burnings of schools and books, and other forms of student protest that had continued unabated since the Soweto crisis in June 1976. 1977 began with c. 200,000 Black pupils and students throughout the country boycotting lectures. Only a small percentage took advantage of the Government's offer to hold supplementary examinations in March, and the situation continued to deteriorate. In Soweto, the majority of secondary school students boycotted classes, and one after another the schools closed down. Sporadic arson attempts at Black schools and police violence against pupils also occurred throughout the year and into 1978.

Police harassment of student leaders was unrelenting. On New Year's Day 1977, four top members of the Soweto Students' Representative Council (SSRC) were arrested. The SSRC president, Sydney Khotso Seathlolo (18), was shot and wounded by police during a car chase in mid-January; he then fled into Botswana. His predecessor and founder president of the SSRC, Tsietsi Mashinini, had fled five months previously with a R500 reward on his head. Daniel Sechaba Montsitsi (20) took over from Seathlolo and brought the SSRC into full-scale involvement with the community. Under his leadership, the SSRC resisted and succeeded in blocking massive rent increases in Soweto.

On 10 June 1977, while arranging services to commemorate the first anniversary of the Soweto student rising, Sechaba and 17 other SSRC members were arrested. Trofomo Somo (18) then assumed the leadership and continued the campaign against Bantu Education. He called on all school boards to resign. (These Government-appointed boards are an important and very unpopular part of Bantu Education. Most schooling in Soweto is organized along tribal lines, with pupils having to attend schools of their own ethnic group.) Within a few days of the SSRC's new campaign, the boards did begin resigning. After most of them had taken this step, the Government announced that it would administer 40 of Soweto's 42 high schools directly.

In August, teachers resigned in their hundreds. They said that Bantu Education was inadequate, and they were angry about police harassment of themselves and their pupils.[303] Students in Soweto and many towns all over SA mounted daily demonstrations at this time. In Pretoria, c. 20,000 students were involved in the boycott which forced a total shutdown of schools in the capital's Black townships. School attendance in Cape Town fell to c. 50%. Some students were shot during demonstrations and arson attempts, and many were arrested and charged with public violence.[304]

The student leader Montsitsi 'disappeared' while in detention. Police refused to allow his mother even to collect his dirty clothing. Police Commandant, Gen Gert Prinsloo, told the family that he could not say where their son was because he could not 'keep track of all people detained'.[305]

The situation in September was summed up as follows: 'Education in Soweto is dead for the moment. There are virtually no pupils now, and soon there won't be any teachers.'[306] Some 600 teachers—almost half of those employed in Soweto—had resigned. In an attempt to break the deadlock, the Bantu Education Department (BED) attempted to reopen the schools, but only c. 100 students registered.

In November 1977, the Government dropped leaflets on Black townships urging students to write their examinations and parents to accompany their children to school to try to stop intimidation. In these leaflets, the Government said students not writing the examinations would have to repeat the school year. One leaflet read: 'In your area bright students are also determined to sit for their examinations. Dropouts know they cannot pass. These dropouts will try to prevent the bright students from sitting for their examinations.'[307] During exam time, many stayaway schoolchildren were rounded up in police raids: 474 were arrested in Port Elizabeth and c. 100 in Pretoria's Atteridgeville township. The local police chief said they had been picked up because they were 'in need of care'; each child's case would be studied to establish whether he or she should be committed to an institution.[308]

1977 closed with many thousands of Black pupils not having sat for an examination since December 1975. The boycotts from June 1976 had brought education to a standstill in various parts of the country while also keeping the political temperature in the townships close to boiling point.

The prognosis for 1978 was not encouraging, the Prime Minister's response being limited to making ministerial changes and dropping the term 'Bantu': the Bantu Education Department would be renamed the Department of Education and Training. Moreover, the new Deputy Minister of Education, Dr Andries Treurnicht (see above) announced in Parliament in February 1978 that Black education would definitely not be integrated into a single national education system. He denied that there was 'general chaos' in Black education, stated that Bantu education was 'of the highest standard' and added that what trouble there was had been caused by a 'mastermind' behind intimidators who aimed at replacing the present political system with Black majority rule.[309] In fact, at the time of Dr Treurnicht's speech, there were nightly arson attempts on schools in the Black townships around Port Elizabeth where more than 40,000 students were boycotting schools. In the Transvaal, many thousands of pupils were roaming the streets. The newly-formed Soweto Students' League was holding meetings outside schools at which young people sang freedom songs while burning application forms for student registration.[310] Of Soweto's c. 170,000 students, less than 3,000 turned up to register.

Throughout the year, Government spokesmen praised their education record and policy in fulsome terms. Dr Connie Mulder said that SA should get the Nobel prize for the work it had done in uplifting and educating Black peoples.[311] Jaap Strydom, the man seconded to sort out Soweto's school rebellions, claimed that the students' call for an end to Bantu Education was no more than a plea for better teachers. The Minister of Police, James Kruger, asked: 'Why have so many Blacks matriculated and gone on to take university degrees in the last 15 years if the standards of Bantu Education are as inferior as alleged?'

In fact, very few Blacks have matriculated and taken degrees, Disregarding 1976 and 1977 (because of the massive boycotts), fewer than 0.25% of the African school population reached the final year of secondary schooling (matric); in the 1975 matric examination, only 0.09% obtained university passes (see Table). Statistically, there have indeed been improvements, but only in relative terms.

The BED stated that at the end of 1973, a total of 5,097 degrees had been awarded to Africans since the first of them graduated in SA. During 1973, the Department of Statistics estimated that the total African population was 16,217,000. Thus only 0.03% of the entire African population had obtained degrees by 1973.

Year	Total no in school	No in matric	No to gain university entrance
1962	1,678,388	968 (0.06%)	146 (0.009%)
1965	1,957,836	1,405 (0.07%)	323 (0.016%)
1970	2,748,650	2,938 (0.11%)	1,009 (0.04%)
1972	3,101,821	4,814 (0.16%)	1,801 (0.06%)
1973	3,302,476	5,736 (0.17%)	1,860 (0.06%)
1974	3,513,957	6,732 (0.19%)	2,058 (0.06%)
1975	3,731,455	9,009 (0.24%)	3,481 (0.09%)

Source: Race Relations News, October 1977.

Another interesting statistic—bearing in mind that Blacks outnumber Whites by 4:1—is that in 1977, 86.13% of university students were White and only 6.6% Black. [312]

During October 1977, Black medical students at the University of Natal decided to boycott all academic activities, including examinations. This followed a Cabinet announcement that Black students would be phased out of the medical school. 94 of the Black students (of 274 Africans, 325 Indians and 24 Coloureds enrolled) were in their final year and risked sacrificing six years of study and their whole future careers as qualified doctors. After this determined display of solidarity, there was an official announcement that Black students would be allowed to remain at the medical school, although those who had taken part in the four-week boycott would probably lose their bursaries. [313] The reason for the proposed phase-out was that the Government wanted all Black students to study at a new medical school being built near Pretoria.

At other Black universities, hundreds of politically active students were expelled during 1977—more than 1,000 from the University of the North alone after demonstrations following the expulsion of a member of the SRC. [314]

POPULATION REMOVALS

By the end of 1977, only a little over half of all Africans remained outside the Bantustans—which comprise c. 13% of SA's land area. According to one commentator, the 1980 census is likely to show that there are more Africans in the Bantustans than in the common area. [315] The Government also assumed new powers to send unemployed Africans to work in Bantustan settlements (see above: Legal Affairs).

1977 saw the clearance of several 'black spots' in the Transvaal (such as Marabastad in Pretoria and Alexandra township in Johannesburg). But the most systematic application of the Government's policy of removing Africans was in the Western Cape where tens of thousands of squatter families had their homes destroyed, and many 'illegal Bantu' were regularly deported to the Ciskei and Transkei (see chapter on Transkei).

Much of the Cape Province is a 'Coloured Preference Area'. Consequently, no family housing has been built for Africans in this area for more than a decade, and firms wishing to employ Africans have to prove that they are unable to find suitable Coloured labour. The result of this policy is that thousands of Africans are employed illegally (because they are desperate for work and thus often accept lower wages than Coloureds); they have to live in shacks in the bush because there is no housing available for them. Other African squatters are migrant labourers who have permission to work, but whose wives are in the Cape illegally. Some are Xhosa workers who have left the single men's hostels provided by the Government and gone 'underground' in the squatter camps because they fear being forced to take out Transkei 'citizenship' and then made to leave the urban area. [316]

A 1974 Government survey estimated that there were 200,000 squatters in the greater Cape Town area.[317] In 1977, the figure was nearer 250,000, of whom c. 200,000 were Coloureds—some with good jobs such as clerks or artisans and earning up to R400 a month. The majority of this large workforce was essential to Cape production, but there was simply no housing for them. For Coloureds, the waiting period for city council housing was seven years.

Squatter shacks were built amid the sand dunes and bushes of the Cape flatlands of foraged wood, sheets of corrugated iron and cardboard boxes. There was no sewage system, refuse removal or running water. Larger camps generally elected committees to initiate community projects, but when camps grew in size they also attracted the attention of the authorities and were then demolished. During 1976 and 1977, committees were elected at most camps to fight against the demolition orders and enlist public support for their cause. In some cases squatters were actually successful in getting legal protection to prevent the destruction of their homes.

In early February 1977, the Ministry of Community Development served notice on the c. 10,000 residents of Modderdam that it intended to demolish the camp within a week. The Modderdam squatters, many of them veterans of earlier bulldozings, fought the decision, appealing to liberal politicians, community leaders and the Press. Two busloads of residents went one Sunday and petitioned outside a church service attended by the State President. A major controversy developed and for a few months the Bantu Administration Department (BAD) left the squatters alone. In June 1977, however, the Prevention of Illegal Squatting Amendment Act was gazetted (see Legal Affairs), virtually blocking access to the courts. Speaking in Parliament, the PFP spokesman, Dr F. van Zyl Slabbert, predicted that once the Act became law, it would herald an 'open season on squatters'.

His prophecy was soon fulfilled. Demolition of Modderdam camp began during the first week of August. During the five-day operation, police used dogs and teargas on several occasions to disperse protesting crowds of squatters, students and members of the public. An Anglican priest, the Rev David Russell (see bannings), and two White social workers were arrested at the camp when they lay down in the path of a bulldozer. Many of the African residents who were supposed to be 'repatriated' to the Transkei and Ciskei simply disappeared. Some were absorbed into the African townships of Langa, Guguletu and Nyanga; others set up home on the bushy slopes of Table Mountain. (A survey conducted before the demolition by the Cape Flats Committee for Interim Accommodation, CFCIA, showed that only 1.2% of the Coloured residents and 12.3% of the African residents were born outside the Cape.)[318]

A fortnight after the demolition of Modderdam, the bulldozers moved in on nearby Werkgenot camp, which had been demolished once before in November 1975. Churches in the élite White suburbs set up 'tent cities' in their grounds, but the authorities soon removed these as well. Shelter, a fund-raising organization for squatters established in March 1977, had raised c. R200,000 by August and was planning to build low-cost housing for the homeless.[319] A few families were housed by Shelter during 1977.

Following the destruction of Werkgenot, even Afrikaner churchmen joined in condemning the Government's actions. A group of 16 Nederduitse Gereformeerde Kerk pastors publicly asked the authorities to stop demolishing shacks and show more compassion.[320] However the National Party made it clear that it would not relent in its campaign against squatters and 'illegal' African residents. The Deputy Minister of Bantu Affairs, W. A. Cruywagen, told the Cape Congress of the National Party: 'I am going to turn the tap tighter'.[321] Indeed, at the beginning of January 1978, he ordered the demolition of Unibel camp, home of more than

10,000 people. A large police contingent protected the demolishers as they razed the camp. [322]

RELIGIOUS AFFAIRS

Official action against individuals and church organizations opposed to apartheid reached a climax on 19 October when the Christian Institute was declared an unlawful organization and its leading officials were banned (see above). The authorities acted against various other churchmen, including four who were detained under the Terroism Act. The South African Council of Churches strongly condemned the detentions. By June 1977, the Council's fund set up to aid people suffering the consequences of civil disturbances (such as imprisonment or bereavement) had raised R1.2m.

At the beginning of 1977, a major Church-State clash seemed likely when the Catholic Church began to implement a decision to integrate its private schools. This process began in Natal, but the Administrators of the Cape and Transvaal threatened action against schools that admitted Blacks. [323] Following subsequent talks between the Church and the authorities, the matter was suspended pending Cabinet consideration of the question. It was reported in March 1978 that the Cabinet had given the Catholic schools permission to integrate, but without making a public statement because of likely opposition by government supporters. [324]

The explosive issue of conscientious objection was again raised when the Catholic Bishops' Conference urged the State to provide an alternative for people who saw national service with the armed forces as participation in 'unjust oppression'. Several churches and church bodies supported the resolution. [325]

Moves were made in Johannesburg and Pretoria to stop mixed or Black church services in White areas when officials informed local authorities that permits were required under the Group Areas Act.

Calvanist professors, students and clergymen—who are largely National Party supporters—urged the government to put Christian convictions before party policy. In a nine-page declaration, they condemned oppressive government measures and called for the security police to be kept under strict judicial supervision to 'prevent another Biko case'. [326]

HEALTH

In April 1977, the Government cut subsidies on basic foodstuffs by R40m to R130m for 1977–78. Opposition MPs condemned the cuts as 'indirect taxation of the poor'. A survey published in the December issue of the *SA Medical Journal* showed that in a Transkei village, 36% of the children under five were suffering from malnutrition and 30% died before they were two. At 53,829 cases, the number of TB notifications in 1976 was down on the 1975 figure. However, the South African National Tuberculosis Association (SANTA) pointed out that investigation into the incidence of TB had been confined by staff and money shortages and by disruption of the health services due to civil unrest. SANTA believes the incidence is five to ten times more than the official figure. [327]

Following allegations in 1977 of maltreatment of Blacks in mental hospitals, [328] the International Red Cross accepted a Government invitation to carry out an investigation. The Minister of Health later announced that the delegation had found no Blacks in mental hospitals for other than medical reasons, but stated that the kind of investigation conducted could not produce general or definite conclusions. [329] SA was named among countries where doctors were alleged to have collaborated in the torture of political detainees. A list of 17 doctors in various countries was presented at an international symposium of medical practitioners arranged by Amnesty International. The symposium agreed on a course of investigation of the allegations.[330]

PRESS

Government action against the Press during the year provoked criticism both within the country and internationally. The Government already exercised formidable control of the Press through its powers to ban individuals, organizations and publications, through its veto on the publication of information relating to prisons and defence, as well as through its range of security legislation. But early in 1977, it threatened to introduce statutory controls in the form of the Newspaper Bill which contained provisions for a Press Code and a Press Council headed by a Government appointee with powers to fine and imprison individuals and close down newspapers.[331] The Bill was conditionally suspended for a year following representations by the Newspaper Press Union. Newspaper owners were given the chance 'to get their own house in order' under their own revised Press Code and Press Council.[332] The revision allows complaints to be made direct to the Press Council, which has powers to impose fines of up to R10,000.

Between its inception in April and 18 July, c. 70 complaints—many of them relating to the use of particular words—were placed before the Press Council. Under the chairmanship of ex-Justice O. Galgut, the Council rapidly gained a reputation for judgements that were severely restrictive.[333] Increasingly, editorial decisions were first referred to lawyers, and journalists had to consider that anything they reported which seriously clashed with Government policies could land them before the Council. A tendency appeared in some papers to down-page stories that might get them into trouble under the incitement clauses of the Code (these could concern Black unrest, for instance). In an article on Press restrictions, Benjamin Pogrund, assistant editor of the *Rand Daily Mail*, wrote that the Code—many of whose categories are sweeping and ill-defined—'in practice inhibits newspapers from free publication'.[334] The London *Daily Telegraph* correspondent reported that the impartiality of the Council was being questioned, and that observers believed that it was out to convince the Government that no further legislation was necessary.[335]

Even so, the Prime Minister and other Ministers continued to warn newspapers that the government would not hesitate to close down those that 'threatened law and order'. The editor of the *World*, Percy Qoboza, was twice warned about his strongly anti-Government line. He replied by pointing out that the *World* had never been challenged before the Press Council or a court of law.[336] On 19 October the *World,* the country's second largest newspaper, and its sister paper, the *Weekend World*, were banned in terms of the Internal Security Act (see above: The Events of October 1977). Another victim of the Press purge was the *Daily Dispatch* editor Donald Woods, then also the London *Observer*'s South African correspondent and a longstanding critic of the government. He was banned after campaigning for a full judicial inquiry into the death of Steve Biko. His subsequent flight from SA received international publicity.

Newspaper circulations and advertising volumes generally showed a marked decline in 1977. The economic depression, the advent of commercial television and overtrading were blamed.

In February 1978, it was announced that the pro-Government English-language daily, the *Citizen*, had been sold by Louis Luyt to the African International Publishing Co (Pty) Ltd which publishes *To the Point*. Identified as members of the consortium were the 'Emperor of Austria and King of Hungary', Dr Otto von Hapsburg; the publisher of the *Saturday Evening Post*, Dr Beurt Sevaas; and a

Dallas attorney, David A. Witts. The president of the Panax Corporation, John P. McGoff, denied that he had an interest in the paper.

TELEVISION AND RADIO

Radio and television—whose current affairs programmes promote official policies and interpret events only from the Government's viewpoint—are not subject to the code administered by the Press Council. There were two critical appraisals of the bias evident in SABC broadcasting in 1977. One, a detailed record of propaganda techniques, noted that in seven days of radio listening, 40 statements by Government members and officials were broadcast as against two by Opposition MPs—neither of the latter being political.[337] The other survey recorded that in one week during the election campaign, Government spokesmen had 24 minutes of television time as against five minutes 15 seconds given to the main Opposition PRP Party.[338] Several politicians also condemned the SABC for promoting the sectional interests of the National Party,[339] and in October the Coloured Persons Representative Council banned the SABC from covering the rest of its session because of its biased reporting. According to the annual report of the SABC tabled in Parliament, the television service 'made a point of stressing the need for spiritual, economic and military preparedness'.[340]

The Minister for National Education gave the operating costs of SABC TV at R39.965m in 1976, excluding capital and loan redemption expenditure.

SPORT

In February 1978, the way seemed largely cleared for integration on the sports fields when the Minister of Sport, Dr Piet Koornhof, wrote in a letter to the International Tennis Federation: 'No permit or other legal permission is needed by any player on any court in SA, and no permit or other legal permission is required to join any club'.[341] This was taken by sports bodies—without any immediate official contradiction—to apply to all sports. Many Government supporters strongly disapprove of Dr Koornhof's policies (see the Mood of Afrikanerdom, above). He himself told the pre-election party congress in the Cape that 'mixed sport at club level remains contrary to Government policy'.

Further relaxations announced by the Minister allowed for permission to be given annually to provincial and national sporting bodies for mixed audiences to attend their events. Formerly, permission was required for each event, and clubs had to apply for 'international' status to serve drinks to people of all races. However, the option of applying for the relaxations is left at the discretion of individual clubs. A fairer distribution of Government funds for sports among the race groups was also promised; in 1975–76, more than 60% of such funds went to the White group.

Despite the increase in multiracial sport, SA's isolation has increased. In 1976, it was suspended by the International Amateur Athletics Association, the Club International Pisca Sportive, the International Football Federation and the International Softball Federation. The Common Market countries were reported to be preparing to make a unified stand against apartheid in sport,[342] and the Commonwealth Prime Ministers meeting in 1977 included a statement on sporting relations with SA in their final communiqué (see pp. C48–49).

The influence of non-racial sports bodies inside the country was strengthened in December 1976 by the acceptance of their co-ordinating body, the South African Council for Sport (SACOS), as a member of the Supreme Council for Sport in Africa, which has been largely instrumental in excluding SA from international sport. However, the formation in October 1977 of the Black People's Sports Council, which proposes cutting all sports contact with Whites until a 'normal' society has been established, may introduce a split into the non-racial SACOS at a time when the all-White sports bodies have come to accept that SACOS virtually held a veto on whether SA would be readmitted to international sport. [343]

IMMIGRATION AND EMIGRATION

Large-scale White emigration in 1977 gave SA its first net loss since 1960, the number leaving the country exceeding new immigrants by 1,170. The figure would have been much higher but for a heavy influx of 8,077 White Rhodesians. During the year, 26,000 Whites left SA and 24,822 came to settle. The figures do not reflect the considerable number of people who left the country without declaring themselves as emigrants. The South African Medical Association expressed concern over the departure of at least 225 and possibly 250 doctors in 1977. [344]

POPULATION

Department of Statistics mid-year 1977 estimates put the total population at 26,126,000 (24,033,000 excluding the Transkei). Whites number 4,320,000, c. 16% of the total. The African total is 18,629,000 (2,078,000 in the Transkei), more than 71% of the population. Coloureds form the third largest group, with 2,434,000. The Indian community numbers 746,000.

David Dewar, Senior Lecturer in the Department of Urban and Regional Planning at the University of Cape Town, provided the following figures to indicate the scope of urban African problems: [345]

1) By the year 2000, the African population will have more than doubled from a 1970 figure of 15m to 37m, or from 70% to 74% of the total. By 2020, it will have increased to 63m or 77% of the total.

2) If White immigration does not occur at the projected rate of 30,000 a year, Coloureds will also outnumber Whites by c. 2010.

3) 'The most critical implication is that, because there is a direct correlation between race and income in SA, the vast majority of this staggering increase will be amongst the poorest people.'

4) By the year 2000, 93% of Whites, 86% of Coloureds, 92% of Indians and 75% of Africans will be urbanized. This implies a growth in urban population from 12m to 40m, of which 34m will be Black. Total urban population in 'White' areas will thus more than double.

5) Africans are coming onto the job market at a rate of 203,000 a year— 105,000 from the Homelands and 98,000 from 'White' areas. In the last 15 years, 120,000 decentralized jobs have been created—only one half of one year's job requirements.

6) If Separate Development is even 50% successful, essential services will have to increase threefold in order to maintain present minimal developmental levels.

7) These projections mean that, in the next 24 years, SA will have to provide more housing and more services in the urban areas than have been produced in the last 300 years merely to maintain existing standards. This means that four more cities the size of the Pretoria-Witwatersrand-Vereeniging region or 11 the size of Cape Town or Durban will have to be built.

Another permutation of SA's demographic problems was offered by Dr P. S. Hattingh of the Africa Institute, who said that one Black baby was born every minute in SA as against one White baby every six minutes. [346] He used this graphic figure to show that the time taken for the Black increase to equal the entire White population is becoming steadily shorter. In the years before Union in 1910, it was nearly 17 years. By the 1960, it was less than nine years. By the year 2020, it will be down to five-and-a-half years. Putting it another way, Dr Hattingh stated that in

1921, Whites formed 21% of the total population. In 1970 it was 17%; by the year 2020, only 11.2%. He pointed out that those who hope White immigration will help restore the balance face certain disillusionment. If 30,000 White immigrants were to enter SA in a year, they would be equalled within 24 days by the Black population increase. In 1977 more White immigrants were leaving than arriving; meanwhile the Black population was going up by 1,250 a day..

Dr Hattingh noted that official policy still aims at reversing the flow of Blacks from the Homelands to White-controlled areas. (The Cabinet Committee investigating the position of Blacks in 'White' SA has set itself the ultimate goal of settling these Blacks in the Homelands.) Referring to a recent prediction by the Deputy Minister of Bantu Administration that 72% of all Blacks will be living in the Homelands by the turn of the century, he said that for this to be fulfilled, the flow from the Homelands would have to cease and 30,000 Blacks return each year from the urban areas. This would require the creation of thousands of new jobs in the Homelands each year. But studies by Prof P. J. van der Merwe of Pretoria University showed that in the last six months of 1976, unemployment in the Homelands rose by 38,000.

FOREIGN AFFAIRS

SA's foreign policy has two principal aims: to maintain its political, economic and military ties with the West, and to develop its economic and political ties with Africa. Until 1976, SA could count on support from enough Western governments to make any threat of international isolation seem remote; until 1975, its policy of seeking detente with Africa had also looked promising. But the South African army's intervention in Angola[347] stopped detente in its tracks, after which links were confined to only five significant African countries: Ivory Coast, Malawi, Senegal, Gabon and Zaire. In September 1977, President Senghor announced in an interview with *Le Monde* that he too had 'renounced all forms of contact with Mr Vorster and his political friends'.

Relations with the West as a whole became strained in 1977—to the point where South Africans began to treat the West as an enemy and the Carter Administration as the greatest danger of all (see Areas of Confrontation, above). Pretoria was particularly shattered by the switch in policy of its closest European ally, France, which in the past had supplied it with sophisticated weapons and some nuclear technology. The only non-African countries which did not join the overtly hostile ranks were Israel, Iran and Japan, each for its own particular reasons. Israel felt aggrieved by the Afro-Asian resolution at the UN equating Zionism with racism; it needed to maintain its links with South African Jewry and its trade with SA. Nevertheless, it too reluctantly announced its decision to observe the UN arms embargo. Iran's policies reflected the idiosyncratic views of the Shah and his passionate fear of Soviet penetration into the Red Sea and the Indian Ocean. Japan's interest was purely economic. None of these motives offered a solid basis on which to build a reliable relationship.

Up to 1977, SA had concentrated its main effort in persuading the West to back its policies; it had relied to a large extent on Western nations (especially France) to help build its bridges into Africa. In May 1977, Vorster finally seemed to realize that the opposite was true; as his critics had been saying for years, the road to 'winning over' the West lay through Africa. If enough Africans could be persuaded to side with SA, Western nations would find it easier to come to terms with Pretoria (see the Prime Minister's role, above). But how to win over Africa while pursuing apartheid at home? That remains the central dilemma of the Republic's foreign policy, whose solution became even more remote with 'independent' Transkei's breaking off of relations with Pretoria early in 1978.

Nevertheless, Vorster saw two gleams of hope. After his meeting with the US Vice-President in Vienna in May, he returned home with the message that 'a new spirit is dawning in the world, especially among the younger generation . . . a spirit of conservative realism'.[348] He had no doubt that this tendency would continue to grow and eventually dominate the world scene. SA was thus committed to waiting for the 'eventual' rise of youthful conservatism in the West. The second chink of light was that 'for the first time in many years, the initiative in Africa has passed from the hands of the Marxist militants to the moderates; it is the Kremlin and its agents which are now on the defensive and in danger of being discredited openly and totally'.[349] Moderate African leaders around the continent were allegedly waiting in the wings impatient to join an alliance with SA and the West to repel the Russians. Somewhat contradictorily much of SA's propaganda was geared towards accusing the West of standing by passively while the Communists were busy taking over the continent.

RELATIONS WITH AFRICA

SA's policy of detente in the continent rests on the assumption of the anti-communist-minded African leaders' willingness to sink their differences with the Republic over its apartheid policies in order to enlist its support in forcing a Russian retreat from Africa. According to the Information Minister, the ultimate divide will be between pro-communist and anti-communist countries.[350] 'Luckily, the majority of African countries are led by moderates who say they are proud to include SA as an African state.' Mulder added that detente was by no means dead, and claimed (without specifying) 18 'open contacts' with African and Middle East states. 'We must maintain contact in Africa. We must maintain our role in Africa if we want to progress and carve our future in Africa.' He envisaged SA taking its place in an 'economic and military bloc' of African countries opposed to Marxism.

Apart from the neighbouring states of Botswana, Lesotho and Swaziland, the only 'open contacts' SA had in 1977 were with Ivory Coast and Malawi. Vorster met President Houphouet-Boigny in Geneva in May after his talks with Mondale. In a joint statement, both sides expressed determination 'to contribute to the efforts of the international community towards the development of peaceful solutions to the problems of southern Africa'.[351] SA's Foreign Minister, Pik Botha, also met the Ivorian President in Geneva in September, and a few days later visited President Banda in Malawi. He said his visits had one purpose: 'To continue to establish ourselves in Africa, to reach African leaders, to try to eliminate misunderstanding concerning . . . the basic aims of our policies. We'll continue to do so. We'll never give up hope because we know there are also moderate and reasonable African leaders as there are White leaders everywhere in the world. We don't distinguish in that respect at all.'[352]

By far the most serious setback to SA's position in Africa was the new stand taken by Nigeria in compelling foreign firms to choose between doing business with it or with the apartheid Republic (see Areas of Confrontation above, and Relations with Britain below).

The principal channel for South African relations with Black Africa is provided by trade. The South African Department of Customs and Excise disclosed in May 1977 that between 1966 and 1976, exports to other parts of Africa rose by R256m to R453m—an increase of 130%. Imports rose by R181m to R310m, an increase of 141%. Since 1964, no breakdown has been given of African countries' dealing with SA, but it is accepted that the bulk of the trade is in fact with Rhodesia.[353] The South African Foreign Trade Organization said in October 1977 that c. 12% of

SA's total export trade is with the rest of Africa. [354] Another area of trade is with the 'hostage' countries in and around the Republic—Botswana, Swaziland and Lesotho, who are linked to the South African economic system through the Southern African Customs' Agreement. SA's payments on account of customs and excise were just under R43m in 1976. Botswana has 50,000 migrants working in SA, Swaziland 30,000, and Lesotho 140,000. [355]

Zambia, which was forced to trade with SA after the closing of the Rhodesian border, has reduced its imports from K35.8m in the first ten months of 1975 to K30.9m in the same period in 1976. Zaire, on the other hand, has steadily increased its commercial links with SA. Imports reached R40m in 1976, mainly oil, food-stuffs, chemical and mining equipment and manufactured goods—shipped through Rhodesia and Zambia. It has also made public its arrangements to ship 125,000 tons of copper to Japan through Port Elizabeth. Although SA provided R20m in credits, Zaire has seriously defaulted on payments. Mauritius continues to be a major South African trading partner; 90% of its tourists are from the Republic. The other two sizable markets for South African goods are Gabon and Ivory Coast, followed by Senegal and the Central African Empire. All these countries conceal their actual trade figures. [356]

Mozambique continued pragmatically to accept the need to maintain the economic links established with SA by the Portuguese. The Republic still provides considerable technical assistance to keep the Mozambique railways and the Beira port in operation. However, the number of Mozambique migrants working in South African mines has decreased from 100,000 in 1973—28% of the total South African mine labour force—to c. 34,000. Under the original Mozambique Convention, the Maputo regime is paid part of the wages earned by its workers in gold at the preferential price of $42.22 an ounce; but the South African Finance Minister announced that this would change when the Convention comes up for renewal in 1978. He made this statement to an irate questioner who wanted to know how much longer 'huge profits' were to be made by 'the terrorists that are shooting our relatives in Rhodesia'. [357] The R600m Cabora Bassa hydroelectric plant is due for completion by early 1979, although the ZAMCO consortium has been supplying 960 mw to the South African electric grid system since March 1977. This was due to increase to 1,440 mw in January 1978. Difficulties still abound, however. The chairman of *Hidroelectrica de Cabora Bassa* (HCB), Antonio Martins, outlined the need for 'a better spirit of co-operation' to solve the diverse problems connected with the project'. [358] The final price has not yet been agreed, with the Portuguese partners insisting on a much higher figure than the 0.3 c/k WH worked out years ago.

Relations with Angola continue to be bad, with SA allegedly giving military support to the Unita rebel forces and Angola providing bases for Swapo guerrillas. SA's major concern is over the role of the Russians and especially the Cubans in Angola, and any help they may be giving Swapo in arms and training. These troubled relations reached a climax in May 1978 when the South African army made an attack against Swapo villages and bases deep inside Angola (see essay, 'Crisis in Southern Africa'). Angola still holds seven South African soldiers as prisoners of war. The South African Defence Minister told Parliament in April 1978 that he personally saw American aircraft delivering arms to Angolan bases held by South African troops during the civil war in 1975-76. [359] The statement was officially denied by Washington. Botha also said that SA's military intervention had taken place with the full knowledge and encouragement of the US which had 'recklessly left us in the lurch'. According to Botha, that story had still to be told. [360]

RELATIONS WITH RHODESIA

The Prime Minister showed some willingness to co-operate with the UK and US in promoting their peace initiative in Rhodesia, but he reiterated that he was not prepared to apply any pressures on the Smith regime. Vorster claimed to have told Andrew Young: 'If they [the UN] think they can pressure me into pressuring Smith, then they have another guess coming because I won't do it'. [361] His Foreign Minister said SA's role was not to interfere in Rhodesia, but to use its good offices so that the various parties could discuss the situation in a calm atmosphere. [362] However, SA continued to supply Rhodesia with all its arms, and there were reports that it was training Rhodesian pilots to fly Mirages, which are built under French licence in SA. Hundreds of South African volunteers also joined up to fight in Rhodesia. In June 1977, the Foreign Minister carried a message to Washington from Ian Smith outlining the 'internal settlement' later negotiated in Salisbury which SA strongly supported. Vorster told his parliament that he saw the 'internal settlement' rather than the Anglo-American negotiations with the Patriotic Front as the best means of getting agreement. [363] However, privately and publicly he urged that Joshua Nkomo be brought into the transition arrangement. The Foreign Minister said that it had to be accepted that there could no longer be a solution without 'losers' who would keep on fighting for a time; but after a Rhodesian Government had been duly elected, he was confident that the fighting would slacken. [364]

POLICY TOWARDS NAMIBIA

Despite his obdurate public stand against pressures from the West, Vorster showed considerable flexibility in responding to the five Western Security Council members' initiative over Namibia. The US, UK, France, West Germany and Canada—who formed the so-called Contact Group—continued to negotiate between SA and Swapo for an agreed settlement on Namibia's independence (see essay, 'The Crisis in Southern Africa'). At his first meeting with the Contact Group in Cape Town in April 1977, Vorster said that while he was willing to talk to anybody, he was firmly committed to the Turnhalle proposals for an 'internal settlement'. [365] But under pressure from the Contact Group, he backed away from this position and postponed implementing Turnhalle. Similarly, while consistently ruling out a handover of the territory to 'Marxist Swapo'—or even negotiations with the organization—the Group continued to mediate between the two sides. [366]

Just when the Western plan was about to be presented to the Security Council—where it was assured of strong African backing—SA launched a major military attack on 4 May 1978 supposedly against Swapo's base camp at Cassinga, over 100 km inside Angola. This resulted in delaying the presentation of the Contact Group's plan. There are two possible explanations for Vorster's decision to allow the army to act. First, that he needed to reassure the *verkramptes* in his own ranks (who were critical of the 'sell-out' of the Turnhalle agreement) and took the risk that the attack would not scupper the Western plan. The second explanation (not necessarily contradictory to the first) is that the South African army wanted to weaken Swapo's military build-up in Angola before it withdrew the bulk of its forces from Namibia, as was required under the agreement. (For a fuller discussion of SA's policy, see chapter on Namibia.) By July 1978, SA and Swapo had both come round to accepting the Western proposals, and the Security Council had endorsed them.

RELATIONS WITH BRITAIN

Britain joined the other major Western powers in November 1977 to veto a Security

Council proposal to apply economic sanctions against SA, having previously voted in favour of a mandatory arms embargo. Nonetheless, British policy moved considerably closer to accepting the possibility of selective sanctions under certain circumstances. The Chancellor of the Exchequer, Dennis Healey, told Parliament in November 1977 that 'the Government intends to discourage investment by British industry in SA'.[367] The junior minister at the Board of Trade advised businessmen to take a careful look at the figures showing that British exports were much higher to Black Africa than to SA: Nigeria alone bought £774m worth of British goods in 1976, which was £100m more than SA; the whole of Black Africa bought almost £2,500m in 1976. The Foreign Secretary, Dr David Owen, argued in a number of speeches that in considering an appropriate policy to follow in Africa, Britain's moral principles and economic interests coincided.[368] He agreed fully with President Carter that the question of human rights was a legitimate subject for international concern, but stated that Britain's domestic economy ruled out support for economic sanctions against SA. However, he promised to 'take a hard look' at any new investment.[369] The Liberal Party conference adopted a motion in September 1977 urging government action to limit investment in SA.

More surprising were the tougher attitudes adopted by Tory leaders. Lord Carrington, the party's leader in the House of Lords, said in October 1977 after consulting with Margaret Thatcher, that SA's 'friends in the West' had been 'saddened, bewildered and horrified by Pretoria's latest spate of repression'; their support could not 'be taken for granted'.[370] He warned that 'unless progress is made in the field of human freedom and personal liberty, the end sooner or later will be catastrophic—not just for SA and the South Africans, but for all of us in the free world'. After visiting SA, Lord Carrington said that those who warned the West of its interests in the face of communist expansion 'must surely remember that to enlist Western support, SA has to produce the conditions in which that support can be forthcoming among those of us who wish to help'.[371] John Davies, the Tory Shadow Foreign Secretary and a longstanding friend of SA, said he believed SA's future lay in abandoning apartheid. He added that if Vorster said that this was impossible, he would tell him that he risked totally breaking 'the bridges with people like me'.[372] Lord Home advised SA to 'bring responsible Africans into the administration and the government'.[373] In another speech, he said he wished the South African Government would be less insensitive, because they made it almost impossible for their friends to help them.[374]

The Confederation of British Industries expressed unhappiness with aspects of the Code of Conduct for British firms operating in SA, which had been agreed by the EEC.[375] Its spokesman, John Whitehorn, said the CBI 'still has significant reservations about the document'.[376]

Meanwhile, Britain's exports to SA continued to drop. In 1974, the UK took second place to West Germany as the biggest exporter to SA. In 1976, it was in third place, after West Germany and the US. SA's imports from the UK in 1976 totalled R1,031m, c. R63m below 1975 levels. As a supplier of SA imports (barring arms and oil), the UK's share fell from 19.7% in 1975 to 17.5% in 1976 (cf 27.3% in 1966).[377] (Also see Economic Affairs, below.)

RELATIONS WITH UNITED STATES
The strategic bond between SA and the US—whereby a smaller power gives its allegiance to a major power in exchange for military protection—snapped in 1977.[378] This decisive change in relationship was formally acknowledged by Vorster

in his 1977 New Year's speech in which he stated that if SA came under attack from the communists, they would have to fight alone (see Prime Minister's Role, above). When this kind of break normally occurs, the small power shifts its allegiance elsewhere—but SA has nowhere else to go, despite some ludicrous ministerial references to China. Nor was there much comfort for SA from its super-hawk friends in the Nato lobby. Even Admiral Elmo Zumwalt, former US Chief of Naval Operations who favours military links with SA, said during a visit to the Republic: 'I believe that anyone who believes in the Christian religion should work towards full equality, and that discrimination is wrong. . . .'[379] He added that it was difficult for Western governments to counter Soviet moves because of the 'disagreement' most of them have with SA's political policies; 'this largely checkmates the motivation of these governments to worry about the strategic c :ctives of the Soviets'.

/orster supported the view of his Foreign Minister, Pik Botha, that the US had come a greater enemy of SA than Russia.[380] Russia, Vorster explained, 'wanted to ll us off by force, while the US wants to strangle us with finesse'. The break, he dded, had come in January 1977—when the Carter Administration took office. It became irreparable in May when Vice-President Mondale 'demanded in Vienna' that SA 'adopt a one-man one-vote system'. Although the Americans had not yet supported economic sanctions, Vorster said it was always at the back of their mind: 'It was said to us in no uncertain terms that if we don't reach a one-man one-vote situation, then sanctions will be forthcoming'.

The confrontation between Mondale and Vorster in Vienna was clearly decisive.[381] Vorster apparently came away convinced that Mondale had issued an ultimatum over one-man one-vote, although Mondale tried to explain that this was not so. In a carefully worded interview with Benjamin Pogrund, he said the US would not insist on one-man one-vote if the people of SA settled on some other means of bringing about 'full political participation' by all races. 'We don't have an answer or a prescription,' he said.[382]

When the US Secretary of State, Cyrus Vance, was asked about his attitude to one-man one-vote, he answered: 'We feel that all South Africans should ultimately have a part to play in the political life of their country. That is what we have said. But we have also said: "We cannot tell you how to do this, or what the timetable is. That's up to you to decide." It's more complicated than just one-man one-vote.'[383]

When the South African Foreign Minister went to Washington in June 1977 to seek clarification of US policy, he argued that the US should evaluate SA in the African context (i.e. compare the Black South Africans' condition to that of Africans elsewhere in the continent). Furthermore, the Americans should recognize SA's role in southern Africa's economic development; refrain from threatening US corporations established in SA; refrain from embargoing equipment needed to defend the sea lanes around the Cape; and recognize the efforts SA was making to bring about change.[384] At the end of his visit, he said it had been 'a week of hell'.[385]

In September, Vorster told American businessmen that SA and the US were still drifting apart because Washington had decided 'to hammer us'.[386] He accused the US of following a selective policy: 'Name me the African country upon which I must model my country in order to be acceptable to you,' he said. After the strong international reactions to the crackdown on the Black Consciousness movement in October (see above), Vorster said that if the US wanted to review its relations with SA 'that is Mr Carter's business. As far as I am concerned, I am not interested. . . . It is totally irrelevant. For ten months, the Carter Administration has been trying to make policy for us. It will be nice for a change if they make their own policy.'[387] Although Ambassador Young said the US was opposed to banning nuclear fuel to SA,[388] Pretoria disclosed in November that there had been a 27-month delay in receiving a consignment of enriched uranium fuel elements from the US.[389] This was because of SA's refusal to sign the Nuclear Non-Proliferation Treaty (see Nuclear Power, above).

A new element crept into South African foreign policy statements after the strong Western reactions to the October clampdown: the US was blamed for the growing violence and repression in southern Africa. The Minister of Justice, James Kruger, was the first to say that the US had to bear 'a lot of the responsibility' for the action he took in banning the Black Consciousness movements and newspapers. Expanding on this statement in an interview with the *New York Times*, he said it was an incentive for people to take to violence if they felt they were backed up by a major power like the US.[390] 'I wish the US would stay completely out of this area. I think we would have been nearer to a solution to our problems by now if they had not entered this arena at all. Sooner or later you will have to bear the responsibility for the conflict situation that you are in fact now encouraging in southern Africa. Blacks and Whites are going to suffer immensely if America continues along this road.'[391]

The South African Government's attempt to portray America as ignorant of the Republic's affairs yet intent on destroying it was dealt a severe blow by Louis Gerber, who had helped to establish the SA Foundation and had set up its offices in Washington. (The Foundation's task is to present as positive a picture of SA as possible to the West.) In 1977, Gerber decided to run as a Progressive Reform Party candidate and gave these impressions of his experience as a South African lobbyist in the US: 'There is simply no animosity towards SA or South Africans, Black, White or brown, as such. The whole weight of American criticism and disapproval is directed at the odious apparatus of apartheid and the successive South African governments which have legalized and institutionalized it. Whatever cynics may say, Americans feel sincerely and often strongly about human rights. They have a deeply ingrained, if sometimes rather naive, sense of justice and political morality. When the objectives of that moral drive happen to coincide with America's strategic and economic interests—as they do in Africa—the present South African regime can expect a rough time. No wonder they seem to be more frightened of the US than they are of Russia.'[392]

Reports were current during 1977 of strong differences among US policymakers, with the President's national security adviser, Zbigniew Brzezinski, and the ambassador to the US, Andy Young, taking opposite sides. Vice-President Mondale went out of his way to emphasize that 'the policy that we have developed in SA—and in all of Africa—has been heavily influenced by the advice and counsel of Andrew Young'.[393] In the same interview, he said that the US refusal to endorse economic sanctions against SA was taken 'with very careful attention to Andrew Young's advice'.

Although there were clearly differences in style and priorities between Young and Brzezinski, there was, at least initially, a common approach to SA. In 1976, Brzezinski told Stephen Barber: 'We shall place on the active agenda of international discussions the question of what ought to be the future arrangements within some form of South African confederation which would permit the coexistence of Africans who happen to be both Black and White. It's an enormously complex problem, the apartheid issue. It's quite likely we are going to have a situation that will be more emotional than the Middle East.'[394]

After an interview with Brzezinski, Jonathan Power wrote: 'He gave the most forceful and ringing commitment to one-man one-vote in SA we have heard since Vice-President Mondale confronted Mr Vorster in Vienna in May. . . .'[395] Young's basic approach was summed up in a speech he made to South African business leaders in Johannesburg on 21 May 1977, of which the nub was the following: 'The battle that SA faces is not a military battle at all and will never be a military battle. The battle is in fact an economic battle. It's a battle which results in a sense out of a competition between systems. If we believe in a free market system as the best means of producing change of a revolutionary nature throughout this world and especially on the African continent, it would seem that all citizens have to be included in that change and in that free market system. And if in fact they are locked out of that system, they have no choice but to choose alternative systems. So I would hope that in addition to thinking about day-to-day economic problems and the profit margin . . . that there would also be some long range thinking. Not to fight to the death, but to share the life and abundance that has been produced by Western technology in this nation. . . .' [396]

At conferences in Africa and at the UN, Young repeatedly declared himself against automatic support for movements of violence. 'Armed struggle,' he said, 'is not as successful as everybody thinks it is. . . . Liberation fighters would probably never be able to overthrow the South African Government by force.' [397] Though opposing the withdrawal of Western investment in SA, he agreed that 'business has been a part of the mechanism of oppression, but it does not have to be. Frankly, I think the challenge to Western European and American businessmen in SA is to develop a Black middle class that is capable of running the country.' [398] On the issue of sanctions, he said he would 'love to avoid them', but in the eventuality that we have to turn to sanctions, 'they ought to be tied to specific aims'. [399] Blanket sanctions would make SA 'more stubborn'. He was also blunt about the tough measures the Carter Administration might take if SA forced a confrontation. 'I can see them even forcing us into the armed struggle'—not directly perhaps. [400]

American business reacted in three different ways to the confrontation between the US and SA. The majority of the 300–350 US companies with interests in the Republic decided not to withdraw their investment, but to endorse a Statement of Principles promoting racial equality drawn up by the Rev Leon Sullivan, a Baptist minister from Philadelphia and a director of General Motors. By April 1978, 84 firms had endorsed the Sullivan principles. A second group launched an American Chamber of Commerce in Johannesburg with a view to fostering further trade and commerce between the two countries. [401] It claimed to have the support of 130 companies, including Esso Standard SA Ltd. John L. Caldwell, manager of the US Chamber of Commerce's international division, said it hoped to get across to Washington 'a more balanced view of what American business is doing in SA'. [402] For the first time in its history, Du Pont, the world's largest explosive group, gave a licence to a South African firm to manufacture explosives under Du Pont's name. A third much smaller group decided to withdraw altogether or to begin to disinvest. Polaroid, the leading US camera and film manufacturer, pulled out after dismissing its distributor for selling film and equipment to the South African Defence Force and the Bantu Reference Bureaux (pass offices). [403] The second and third largest US commercial banks announced that they would use their loan regulations to prod SA into changing its policies. David Rockefeller, chairman of Chase Manhattan Bank, announced that it would apply a new Code of Ethics to ban loans benefiting apartheid. Walter Writson, chairman of Citibank, said that it regarded apartheid as having a negative effect on SA's economy and so would continue to moderate its business activities in the Republic. [404]

Henry Ford announced in January 1978 that his firm—whose c. £70m investment represents the biggest US stake in the Republic—intended to stay in SA, but had no plans for expansion. However, over $1m was being allocated to greatly increase the training and education programmes for Ford's Black employees. The company also declared that it intended to end segregated eating facilities by 1978, to seek approval substantially to increase the number of Blacks in supervisory jobs, and to ask the government to appoint a commission of inquiry with a view to removing all racial discriminatory laws from labour practices. They also recognized the Black trade union and agreed to operate a check-off system for it. Ford's announcement was deliberately misrepresented in SA, where it was publicized as a declaration for 'expansion'.[405]

The Senate Foreign Relations sub-committee on Africa, headed by Senator Dick Clark, recommended that the US take active steps to discourage further US investments in SA.[406] Clark said that the aim of the new policy should not necessarily be to get US corporations to withdraw from SA, but to 'foster specific and meaningful changes in the role which US corporate interests have traditionally played in SA'.

A more active lobby developed in the US in 1977 to persuade American investors (especially church bodies and universities) to sell their South African share holdings. A survey of this lobby's activities was presented by Prexy Nesbit, Coordinator of the Committee to Oppose Bank Loans to SA, to the UN Centre Against Apartheid.[407]

The US issued detailed instructions in early 1978 to extend the existing arms embargo against SA to include all items—from computers to fuel tanks—if intended directly or indirectly for military or police purposes.[408] At the same time, the US Commerce Department ordered an internal investigation into US and South African commercial regulations.

According to the US Department of Commerce *Survey of Current Business*, US companies operating in SA account for almost 40% of American investment in Africa.[409] The survey reveals that the book value of direct American investment in other countries totalled $137,244m at the end of 1976. Of this, $4,467m was invested in Africa and $1,665m in SA. The latter figure is 1.2% of the total and 37.3% of US investment in Africa. Other African countries lag far behind. US investment in Libya at the end of 1976 was only $362m; in Liberia $348m, and in Nigeria $341m. But there was only a $9m increase in 1976 in the equity (other than reinvested earnings) and intra-company loans of US subsidiaries in SA (cf $256m rise in Africa as a whole). These companies' reinvested earnings (earnings net of gross dividends) amounted to $73m in 1976 as against less than $30m in Liberia and Nigeria, and a total of $584m for the continent. Remittances of $125m from SA were proportionately far lower than those from some other African countries (cf $177m from Libya and $174m from Nigeria). The value of South African gold and other mining shares owned by US investors was estimated at c. R2,000m, which exceeds the value of all direct US investment in SA. US investors own c. 25-30% of all South African gold shares, whose total market value is over R6,000m.[410]

RELATIONS WITH EEC

The European Community's nine members, who had begun to establish a common front on South African problems in 1976, continued this trend in 1977. While the initiative for a West European consensus came largely from the British Foreign Secretary, he received strong support from Holland, Denmark and—what was new—from West Germany. In July, the Nine Foreign Ministers agreed to Dr Owen's proposals to explore practical ways by which European companies in SA could be used as a lever to help bring about economic and social change. The London *Daily Telegraph*'s Common Market correspondent wrote on 13 July that this move 'could prove to be an historic first step towards using [the EEC's] economic weight to bring about changes in SA's racial policies'.

Though at first reluctant to accept the idea of an EEC Code of Conduct for European firms operating in SA, the French eventually supported the Code which was adopted on 20 September 1977.[411] Some critics felt that it did not go far enough and that it could not be properly supervised;[412] others, including the Confederation of British Industries and French and West German industrialists, that the Code went too far. Patronat, the main French employers' organization, clashed head-on with the Quai d'Orsay, which explained that 'the main purpose of the Code is to create a climate conducive to some form of dialogue with African States which have a personal feeling for the racial situation in SA'.[413] Although admitting the difficulty of compelling firms to observe the Code, a Quai d'Orsay spokesman said: 'One should not underestimate the French Government's capacity to act legally in the case of firms found guilty of serious infringements of the Code'.[414] The East Asiatic Company of Denmark, the biggest Scandinavian employer in SA, set an early example by adopting the six principles of the Rev Sullivan's US Code (see above). The SA Foreign Minister said that while his government welcomed enlightened labour practices, it resented the EEC's high moral tone and felt that the Code would be credible only if it were applied world-wide.[415]

After the clampdown on the Black Consciousness movement in October 1977, the nine EEC countries issued a joint Note condemning SA's actions. In a five-page reply, Pretoria denounced this 'flagrant interference' in the Republic's affairs. The South African ambassador in Paris was summoned to the Quai d'Orsay to receive a separate French protest. In a new departure, Paris radio (25 October 1977) said: 'It is the South African Government which is deliberately choosing the path of political terror'.

In November 1977, the EEC took two major decisions. First, the Nine agreed not to recognize the new 'independent' Republic of BophuthaTswana, since the creation of Bantustans was 'an integral part of the policy of apartheid, which the Nine have condemned on many occasions'. Second, the Nine agreed to continue to study the possibility of a ban on new investment in SA, curbs on export credit guarantees, and other measures in the trade and cultural fields,[416] although it decided not to go beyond the arms embargo and the Code of Conduct for the moment. A tougher stand was foreshadowed during November 1977 in preventing South African subsidiaries of European companies from being forced to supply arms and weapons or spare parts for them (see above) and thus contravene the UN arms embargo. The issue was how the European countries could legally enforce their Code against firms which were being compelled under South African law to deliver certain products to the army and police.[417]

With the ending of Britain's five-year transition period as a member of the EEC (during which time the former Imperial Preference system had operated), SA braced itself to meet the full weight of EEC protectionism. This was expected to hit SA's fruit and wine exporters in particular.[418] In a good year, South African fruit is capable of earning over R200m in foreign exchange, while wine earnings are c. R45m. While there appears to be some flexibility in negotiating over fruit (since much of it is produced at different seasons from European and Mediterranean crops), the French and Italian wine lobby is totally opposed to concessions to non-associates.

RELATIONS WITH FRANCE

The French decision to support the UN arms embargo and to cancel its contract to supply two submarines and two corvettes (see Defence, above) was seen by one observer as 'the lowest watermark ever in SA's ebbing international fortunes'.[419]

Although France's turnabout affected arms supplies and diplomatic support, the French retained and even planned to expand their non-military trade links.

Paris dealt a number of hard knocks to Pretoria in quick succession in 1977. In August, it took a strong initiative in denouncing SA's plans for testing a nuclear device—a sensitive issue because France had defied world opinion in supplying SA with a nuclear plant to help meet its energy needs (see Nuclear Power, above). Paris went so far as to threaten a diplomatic break and economic sanctions if SA went ahead with the nuclear test. The French Foreign Minister icily rejected SA's denials that it was planning any test except for peaceful purposes; he announced that he had evidence to prove the allegations.[420] Only a week earlier, he had said in Lusaka that while France regarded apartheid as 'a stupid policy', it did not believe in using force to bring about change. In October, the Quai d'Orsay summoned the South African ambassador to receive a strong protest over the wholesale banning of the Black Consciousness movement.

SA's Finance Minister, Senator Horwood, angered the French twice in September 1977. To start with, he referred to Louis de Guiringaud as 'this new little French Foreign Minister who fled when confronted with a demonstration by a few Blacks in Dar es Salaam'.[421] Later he insisted that SA felt free to use its nuclear technology for any purpose it chose'. Both statements required diplomatic apologies.

Trade figures published in February 1978 show that SA has become France's third biggest African supplier after Algeria and Ivory Coast and that the trade balance has swung in SA's favour. French exports to SA totalled FF 2,439m in 1977, and imports FF 2,470m (the latter being a 60.6% jump over 1976 when imports were worth FF 1,538m). France's biggest imports from SA were coal (FF 764m), wool and skins (FF 195m) and citrus fruit (FF 184m). French exports to SA increased tenfold from 1966 to 1976, and South African exports fourfold. Total French investment in SA is estimated at R200m. As a spin-off from the nuclear power station sale, a long-term contract was signed in July 1976 between the French Atomic Energy Commission and Randfontein Estates to deliver 900 tonnes of uranium oxide a year for ten years. The French also provided a $100m interest-free loan to develop the mine.[422] Nevertheless, Desmond Colborne, the South African Foundation representative in Paris, said in response to a question about how French businessmen feel about investing in SA: 'The question they ask is—does SA have a future? How long can we go on doing business with it? They feel pretty safe about five years.'[423]

No figures on arms sales to SA have ever been published, but fairly detailed lists are available of equipment supplied.[424] The French Defence Minister said in October 1977 that no new arms contracts had been signed for more than a year, nor had new arms been shipped. M. Bourges admitted, however, that SA was producing some French military equipment under licence, such as Mirage F-1 fighter bombers and Panhard armoured cars, and that, having sold the licences, France no longer had any say. But the problem is not quite as simple as this, according to informed sources.[425] Two kinds of licensing agreements have been concluded by France and SA. The one covering the Mirage F-1 provides for the construction of a maximum of 75 aircraft, with French officials ensuring that this ceiling·is not exceeded. In the case of land equipment, on the other hand, SA is entitled to produce an unlimited quantity.

RELATIONS WITH WEST GERMANY
Bonn played a more active part with its Nato allies in applying political pressures on SA, both through its membership of the Contact Group for Namibia and through the EEC (see above).[426] At the end of November 1977, Bonn decided to limit the

number of government-backed export guarantees for goods to SA. In addition, future guarantees were made dependent on West German firms signing a declaration of willingness to abide by the EEC Code of Conduct and an undertaking that no foods would be re-exported to Rhodesia. In the 18 months up to November 1977, guarantees for exports to SA had risen to a total of c. DM 2.8 bn. Among the ventures guaranteed by the Government were supplies by Deutsche Babcock for a strategically important coal liquifying project, Sasol 2, worth £129m; machinery for two coalfired power stations, worth £35m, and a car plant worth £9m.

Bonn addressed a memorandum to the OAU early in 1977 categorically refuting allegations that it had any military or nuclear deals of any kind with SA.[427] However, in December 1977, the West German Economics Minister admitted that six powerful marine engines had been sold to SA for coastal patrol vessels. He said they did not have a specifically military character and so did not require an export permit.

During 1977, Nigeria replaced SA as Germany's biggest market in Africa. Germany's biggest African import markets are Libya, Algeria and SA in that order.

RELATIONS WITH OTHER EUROPEAN COUNTRIES
The Belgian government supported EEC policies towards SA, its Foreign Minister taking a firm line in support of the arms embargo (see EEC above). Before attending the World Conference for Action against Apartheid in Lagos, M. Simonet said that the EEC was planning to use 'the power of economic pressure' to help end apartheid.[428] On the other hand, a Belgian Chamber of Commerce was established in SA in June 1977, with the encouragement of Belgium's commercial attaché. Belgium is a major export market for SA goods, with sales worth R217m in 1976, a 80.8% increase over 1975.

The troubled relations of the majority of Afrikaners with the Dutch motherland continued in 1977. The Dutch parliament discussed a Bill to allow the government to support economic sanctions against any country, a measure especially meant for SA. An unusual feature of the Bill is that it proposes to lift the immunity on Dutch citizens living abroad; this would make them subject to jurisdiction in the Netherlands if they offended against the proposals in the Bill. There were 41,671 Dutch citizens living in SA in 1977. The government also froze a 26-year old cultural agreement with SA and suspended a longstanding State subsidy for Dutch immigrants to SA. The Prime Minister received the ANC leader, Oliver Tambo, and presented him with R180,000 in humanitarian aid; a street in Holland was named after Govan Mbeki, one of the Robben Island prisoners. Holland refused an export licence for a Fokker-28 Fellowship aircraft for Namibia. The largest Dutch trade union, the Industrie-Bond NVV, has played an active role in encouraging a boycott of SA, and an official inquiry was launched into the South African dealings of Philips, the multinational electronics firm. The Amsterdam-Rotterdam Bank decided against making any further loans to SA.

A significantly tougher attitude has been taken by Swiss bankers to SA. Robert Studer, a senior vice-president of the Union Bank of Switzerland, warned the South African government that the flow of foreign capital could decline further or even dry up altogether if its race policies were not 'softened'.[429]

Spain decided in 1978 to launch a South African export drive, concentrating on machinery for the rubber and plastics industries and electronics.

RELATIONS WITH THE NORDIC COUNTRIES
All four Nordic countries have been prominently involved in supporting the anti-apartheid movement and have voted consistently for UN pressures against SA.

Sweden still provides the cutting edge for this Nordic thrust despite the change from the traditional Social Democratic government to a Conservative-Liberal coalition. The new government gave £800,000 to the ANC as humanitarian aid in 1977; it also appointed an all-party commission to examine the role of Swedish firms in SA. Preliminary indications suggest that Sweden may become the first European country to stop further investment in SA and to control the use of profits earned there available for reinvestment. In September 1977, Sweden's ambassador to the UN, Ms Karin Söder, proposed that the Security Council resort to sanctions to eliminate the threat to peace in the region and that all new investments in SA be banned. The former Prime Minister, Olof Palme, led a Socialist International delegation to southern Africa in 1977 and recommended a seven-point programme of action. This would end all military co-operation, licences and transfer of technology, including in the nuclear sphere; prohibition of capital exports and of new investment in SA; and support for the liberation movements and for the victims of apartheid.[430]

RELATIONS WITH COMMONWEALTH COUNTRIES
The Commonwealth Prime Ministers' meeting in 1977 adopted a series of strongly critical resolutions condemning South African policies and supporting international action.[431]

Pierre Trudeau's government became the first in the West to cut off all official commercial links with SA, maintaining only diplomatic ties. The External Affairs Minister, Don Jamieson, announced on 19 December 1977 that Canada wanted Black South Africans to win equal rights without bloodshed. He added that while there were other countries which violated human rights, SA's was the only established government structure making 'decisions affecting humans on the basis of race and colour'.[432] Canada withdrew all its Trade Commissioners from SA, ended all government loans to finance trade deals, and proposed to establish a Code of Ethics for Canadian firms wishing to remain in SA.

The Canadian opposition strongly criticized Prime Minister Trudeau's decision. The move put into jeopardy the annual sale to Canada of 215,000 tons of sugar worth R2m. Canada's trade with SA was worth $300m in 1976. In 1977, Canada's exports to SA were worth $71m, while imports totalled $98m. It was estimated that in 1978, Canadian exports to SA would drop by 20% and imports by 32%

The Canadian international mining company, Granex, withdrew from SA in November 1977. Part of the Granby Mining Corporation (its parent company being Zapata of the US), it was also involved with a West German consortium in a copper mine in Namibia. A Granex spokesman said that factors influencing the decision to withdraw were complex, but that political considerations were involved. "We were given an indication from our Canadian managers that they felt there wasn't enough "positive development" going on in SA's political scene.'[433]

Australia's Prime Minister dismissed Senator Glen Sheil within 24 hours of appointing him as Minister for Veterans' Affairs because of a statement that he would like to see apartheid introduced into Australia.

RELATIONS WITH COMMUNIST COUNTRIES
The South African army displayed three Cuban prisoners taken during SA's military intervention in Angola in 1976. The sergeant and two privates said they had asked to appear before the press conference to reassure their families that they were alive and well cared for.

A high-level mission from Poland visited SA in March 1977 to study the advanced technology used in the new coal-to-ammonia complex installed by AECI.

A former KGB officer, Capt Aleksei Myagkov arrived in SA in March 1977. He told a press conference that White and Black KGB agents were active in southern Africa, having been trained in Samerkand. He said that Soviet aims in SA were political, econmic and strategic.

The Soviet Union donated funds to the OAU to establish a radio station for the use of African liberation movements.

RELATIONS WITH JAPAN

Japan's mineral trade with SA has largely enabled the Republic to build and maintain its two new ports at Saldanha and Richard's Bay.[434] Japan takes c. 40% of Saldanha's iron ore and has long-term contracts for coking coal from Richard's Bay. However, trade relations between the two countries became more difficult in 1977, partly because of Japan's wish to cut down on its coal imports, which stood at 383,000 tons in 1975. Japan also insisted that the extremely high prices being charged for South African chrome ore be considerably reduced in 1978.

The Kansai Electric Power Company has a contract to buy 500 tons of uranium from Namibia in 1977–78, 600 tons in 1979–80 and 1,000 tons annually from 1981 to 1986.

The South African oil-from-coal complex, Sasol, sold its unique method for upgrading poorer quality coal to a Japanese consortium.

RELATIONS WITH LATIN AMERICA

The South African Press reported in April 1977 that an official of the Bolivian Ministry of the Interior, Guido Strauss, had announced that his ministry was interested in importing thousands of Whites from SA, Namibia and Rhodesia.[435] This was denied a few months later by the Bolivian President who described the report as 'an international plot'. He added that Bolivia, like any other country which has a true concept of what a human being is, refused to open its arms to citizens who believe in discrimination.[436]

Andean countries were described as attractive areas for a South African export drive by the South African Federation of Trade Organization's Latin American area manager, R. Kerr Martin. He said that South African machinery, especially for the mining industry, was well suited to those countries.[437] The first contract of Fedmis' phosphoric plant was placed in Brazil, where the South African construction industry also has links. The National Process Industries began negotiations for a R57m fertilizer plant in Paraguay. Concor is part of a consortium engaged in a R300m irrigation plant in Peru, for which SA has contributed a R30m loan through its parastatal Industrial Development Corporation.[438]

Argentine's Foreign Minister, Oscar Montes, told the Italian news agency Ansa (3 October 1977) that his country, along with other countries of the southern cone of South America, was engaged in conversations with SA for the defence of the South Atlantic. He added that while no military treaty had yet been signed, there were 'good intentions' of doing so. According to Montes, the US was not involved in the negotiations.

RELATIONS WITH IRAN

Iran has remained one of SA's most valuable economic allies, supplying it with between 90–95% of its vital oil imports and retaining a direct interest in the Republic's major coal-into-oil industry, Sasol.[439] Iran is also an increasingly important market for South African exports. Under a contract signed in March 1978, BMW (SA) will export 1,650 cars to Iran during the coming year. SA also completed the last part of a valuable order for agricultural implements supplied by John Deere.

The Shah's sister, Princess Shams Pahlavi, visited SA in March 1978 to lay flowers on the grave of her father, King Reza Shah Pahlavi, who died in Johannesburg where he was exiled by the Allied forces in World War II.

However, there were some signs of possible changes in Iran's policies in 1977–78. Tehran opened diplomatic relations with Nigeria, and the Lagos Press (with Government support) raised the question of the Shah's ties with SA; the OAU also attacked Iran's links with the Republic. Iran's ambassador at the UN voted in favour of boycott proposals against SA which were submitted by the Africa Group. Similarly, when the Shah visited Bulgaria in May 1978, he signed a joint communiqué stressing the two countries' support for 'the peoples of Zimbabwe, Namibia and SA in their just struggle'.

RELATIONS WITH ISRAEL

A Kenya newspaper report commented on the Israel-SA connection as follows: 'They make strange bedfellows: the Jewish State built on the ashes of Nazi persecution and 3,000 years of racial discrimination, and the apartheid regime led by former sympathizers of Hitler's Germany. But both countries are drawn toward each other by the hostility each faces from the powerful Afro-Arab bloc, by economic and military boycotts and by a feeling in each country that any friend is better than none at all.'[440]

Israel's greatly expanding economic and other relations with SA were vigorously defended in a speech by its ambassador in SA, I. D. Unna: 'The growth of SA-Israeli trade relations—from the meagre dimensions of roughly $3m less than 10 years ago to a balanced trade of well over $80m today—is indicative of a very healthy ongoing relationship. Obviously Israeli industrialists would not embark on ventures in SA if they did not have full confidence in the country's future. Special mention should be made of the ties between the Council of Scientific and Industrial Research (CSIR) in SA and the National Council of Research and Development in Israel. Hostile quarters constantly speak of the sinister Pretoria-Jerusalem axis. Let me tell you in all frankness, there is nothing sinister and there is nothing which causes us any embarrassment whatsoever.

'South African and Israeli scientists are co-operating in the fight against soil erosion; they are investigating the question of recycling of waste water; they are co-operating in the development of horticulture and cultivation of various kinds; they are exchanging medical information. It should hardly be necessary for me to emphasize that the good relations which now exist between our two countries do not imply my country's approval of your domestic structure. If Israel is not as articulate as some people expect us to be, it is because we feel that the approval or the rejection of the manner in which SA attempts to solve her domestic problems is primarily a matter for the people of SA. But let me assure you that we are not disinterested or indifferent spectators, and that we view your efforts to remove discrimination from your internal social scene as vital. For just as you here in SA have an interest in peace and stability in the Middle East, we regard peace and stability in your part of the world as immensely important to us.'[441]

A more critical attitude towards apartheid was expressed by Israel's ambassador to the UN, Gen Chaim Herzog, in a statement to the General Assembly on 17 November 1977: '. . . The policies of apartheid are as abhorrent to Israel and the Jewish people as any other form of racism. As Prime Minister Begin said just a few days ago: "We are anti-racist. And we told this time and again to SA and the whole world." '

According to the Johannesburg *Star* (11 February 1978), an Israeli delegation led by the Minister of Finance, Simcha Erlich, supported the idea that Israel should be used as 'a bridgehead into the Common Market and the US for South African goods'. A delegation of Israeli academics who visited SA in September 1977 had earlier proposed the setting up of subsidiary or joint venture companies which would enable SA to take advantage of the free trade agreement between Israel, the EEC and the US.[442] Prof Tamir Agnom was reported to have disclosed how SA steel was entering the EEC through Israel by a joint venture of Koor Metal Industries of Israel and the SA parastatal ISCOR.[443] South African iron and steel imports to Israel have soared from R1.2m in 1970 to over R17m in 1975 and R21.2m in 1976. Exports for the first five months of 1977 amounted to R5.2m. SA and Israel also have an agreement for the supply of 500,000 to 800,000 (possibly rising to 1m) tons of steam coal a year to the Hadera power station. First deliveries are due to be made in 1980.[444]

When the Israeli Finance Minister, Simcha Erlich, visited SA in February 1978, two agreements were signed: one obviating double taxation and the other covering investments, bonds and commercial relations. Erlich said during his visit: 'I can point out with satisfaction that we have achieved far-reaching gains in our talks with the Government of SA'.[445] After meeting with the South African Minister of Economic Affairs, a delegation of Israeli industrialists declared that it would be possible to treble present trade levels between the two countries.[446]

While neither country mentioned military deals, there were a number of seemingly well-informed reports about them. Robert Moss, who writes with authority on South African military matters, reported: 'While South African engineers sit in Haifa, watching the construction of a new type of Israeli missile boat, equipped with a helicopter carrier deck, Israeli technicians are hard at work along SA's borders, erecting an electrified "wall" and laying a carpet of electronic sensors.

'Perhaps the most dramatic example of the military importance of SA's understanding with Israel is the development of Israel's home-made tank, the Chariot. Although detailed comparisons of its performance with that of Nato tanks have not been published, the Israelis believe that the new type of armour plating that they have fitted to the Chariot is far superior to that currently used by the world's other armies. It has been reinforced by the injection of a chemical mix into special steels. Once they had developed the formula, the Israelis had the problem of importing the right steel. The Americans refused to supply their needs, and brought pressure to bear on West European suppliers to do likewise. At this point the South Africans came forward. They delivered the special steels that the Israelis needed, and in return, the Israelis agreed to refit their armoured vehicles—from Centurion tanks to Panhard armoured cars—with the new armour plating.

'The Israelis have helped SA's military programme in many other ways. The South Africans have taken delivery of three of Israel's home-made Reshef-class missile boats, and will get three more. Israeli technicians are helping to revamp SA's air force. The most closely guarded secret of all remains the full extent of Israel's co-operation in SA's nuclear programme. But there is little doubt that SA would not have been able to move so quickly towards the testing of a nuclear device without substantial Israeli scientific help.'[447]

A South African businessman revealed that the South African-made mini-helicopter, the 'Scorpion' would be assembled in the Israeli plant of Chemavir Masok and exported commercially to Common Market countries.[448] According to another report, Israel has supplied SA with three patrol boats valued at $100m, together with Gabriel sea-to-sea missiles for six South African-built corvettes.[449] There was also a report that Israel had supplied SA with rifles, mortars, electronic equipment and licences to make both the Uzi submachine gun and the 65-ft Dabur class patrol boat.[450]

A respected Washington columnist wrote in November 1977: 'Israel is one of the world's most courageous democracies and SA is an appalling model of racist repression. But these two countries have been carrying on a curious relationship based on the fact that both feel isolated and vulnerable to outside pressures'.[451] He added that the Carter Administration was privately urging Israeli officials that 'the South African connection could be disastrous to them in both international and domestic American terms'.

Immediately after the Security Council's mandatory arms embargo in November 1977, Gen Dayan said that Israel would stand by SA despite its condemnation by the UN. He added: 'SA has always been a friend of Israel and we will not abandon it because of President Carter's position.'[452] However, in December, Israel sent a Note to the UN Secretary-General saying it would be 'guided' by the Security Council resolution; on 4 April 1978, a new Note stated that Israel would comply with the embargo.

Israel's involvement with SA was not without critics at home. The powerful trade union federation, Histadrut, announced in February 1978 that it would dissolve its partnership with South African interests in two joint investment companies.[453] A leading Labour Party member, Asher Maniv, strongly attacked Israel's policy at the 29th Zionist Congress. Pushed to defend himself, the Finance Minister replied that, given its situation, Israel could not choose its friends.[454]

Arab and Soviet critics extensively exploited the 'alliance between Tel Aviv and Pretoria'.[455]

ECONOMIC AFFAIRS (1.696 Rand = £1 sterling)

SA's economy suffered another recessionary year in 1977, although there were some indications in 1978 that it is on the road to recovery, at least in the short term.[456] Real economic growth was achieved in 1977, though at a relatively unimpressive rate of between 1-2%. Faster growth was precluded by the difficulty of attracting new foreign investment (see SA versus the International Community, above). Other key indicators, such as balance of payments, value of exports and volume of agricultural production, fared better in 1977 than in 1976. The major problem with such indicators, however, is that by their very nature they depict short-term results without providing much information on underlying long-term developments. Where stability is increasingly at risk—as underlined by the outflow of capital and of professionally skilled people—such underlying developments are of great importance.

ECONOMIC PERFORMANCE AND THE ROLE OF NEW CAPITAL

On the basis of the state of business activity in 1977-78, a significant increase in investment in SA is unlikely before 1979, and with industry already running at an excess capacity of 25%, it is doubtful whether there can be a substantial turn-around in investment before 1980. Prospects for below normal growth for some five years will significantly dampen SA's performance, and as exports are unlikely to continue increasing at the high rates achieved in 1976, the economy's growth potential will automatically diminish.

A banker provided the following analysis of SA's economic future: SA's future growth can also be harmed by political developments in the subcontinent. If, as seems likely, the political outlook remains clouded, direct foreign investment and the country's ability to raise long-term loans abroad would be affected. In these circumstances, the balance of payments will remain a problem for reasons unconnected with business cycle movements. The outcome of such developments could be tighter control of imports. Also, since there is a direct link between the growth rate of the economy and the level of imports, the authorities would have to keep a tight rein on monetary and fiscal policy with an object of keeping economic growth low. Hence there is a very real possibility that the longer term cycle of relatively slow growth that started in 1969 will extend into the next decade. Low growth expectations would, in turn, significantly affect investment plans by both the public and the private sector. In addition, investment outlays may be further diminished by features typical for an economy subjected to political pressure. These include relatively high and increasing rates of taxation, high interest rates, tighter exchange controls and a general tendency towards more direct government intervention in the economy. This analysis of recent investment trends and the economy's difficult future growth environment permits the drawing of a number of important conclusions:

The ratio of investment to GDP, which had risen sharply on account of the infrastructure boom, will tend to decline. Apart from the large amount of infrastructure already provided in the past eight years and the probability that for the time being government will not allow its spending to grow unchecked, the large excess capacity of non-primary sectors will diminish the amount of investment capital required. Many industrial companies subject to direct foreign control may also grow slower than in recent years due to a desire to limit the growth in country exposure in an uncertain political climate.

A central problem in the medium-term will not be a shortage of capital investment as such, but how to make better use of existing investments. The main factor to constrain economic growth is likely to be the availability of foreign exchange. Given SA's high import intensity, any shortages of foreign exchange, as a consequence of diminished capital flows which may result from lacking confidence and political factors, would limit the ability to import and consequently the overall growth rate. Import controls and export incentives are therefore likely to be used in the medium-term to use existing resources more efficiently.

In the private sector, investment spending for imports displacement is likely to gain momentum. In the foreseeable future, it is likely to become more difficult to import non-essential consumer and capital goods, leading to specific measures to protect and enhance domestic manufacture.

Public sector investment spending is likely to switch from 'normal' infrastructure spending to 'strategic' investments, because of a changing social and political climate. Investments of this nature include projects already underway such as the oil-from-coal plant and petrochemical complex of Sasol II, the nuclear power station at Koeberg, various energy related projects, military expenditure, as well as social investments such as the electrification of Black urban townships, plus substantial efforts in Black housing, schooling and technical training.

Broad implications, on a sectoral basis, are that mining, electricity, gas and water, and to some extent manufacturing, are likely to generate above average investment growth. Increases in these sectors will be counterbalanced by lower growth rates in agriculture, finance and insurance, fixed property and general government.'[457]

STATE CONTROL OF ECONOMY

The publication of *Assault on Private Enterprise* by Dr A. D. Wassenaar, one of the biggest Afrikaner tycoons,[458] opened up a debate on the extent to which South Africa's economy is State-controlled. The growth of bureaucracy and the extent of State intervention in industry were also analysed by Martin Creamer, who reached the following conclusions: the total number of people employed by the Government is nearing the million mark, with total earnings over R2,000m. This excludes the many thousands with jobs in the 25 State corporations, 22 agricultural control boards, 29 prison boards and the host of advisory, statutory and other boards and semi-state bodies. Ministers consistently refuse to provide any information about these bodies, their number, staff, pay and total costs. Appointments are made directly by Ministers or the State President. There is no open competition on merit. Nor do State corporations advertise jobs for general managers and managing directors, who earn enormous salaries. According to a public administration expert, reports rendered to Parliament are useless for control purposes. They don't give salaries, directors' fees or budgets.

There is hardly a facet of industry in which the State corporations do not have an interest—ranging from steel and aluminium to property development, fishing, filming, advertising, publishing and supermarkets. Iscor has not only nationalised the iron and steel industry, but also has huge interests in engineering as well as hunting resorts, farms, country clubs and hotels. 'It adds up to an empire of hair-raising proportions.' The Armaments Corporation has doubled its numbers of subsidiaries in ten years. The Industrial Development Corporation's offspring include Sasol, Foskor and the Aluminium Corporation, as well as all the Development Corporations. The Fisheries Development Corporation has a stake in five public companies and four private businesses. Sasol has reached into property development and coal mining.

The public corporations tend mostly to run at a loss. Analysts say Parliament has lost control of these corporations, and they have become a law unto themselves.[459]

NATIONAL ACCOUNTS

SA experienced one of its lowest growth years of the post-war period from 30 June 1976 to 30 June 1977 when total GDP at constant prices grew only 1%. The bulk of the GDP increase was concentrated in agriculture and non-gold mining (see below). Manufacturing and construction, on the other hand, suffered off-years in 1976–77; the total value of manufacturing activity declined c. 4.5%, and construction fell by an alarming 10%. The recession was also evidenced in the wholesale, retail and motor trade sectors which suffered a 7% loss in 1976–77. Production capacity went unfilled as demand for various manufactures failed to increase—indeed decreased in many cases—and wholesale and retail sales were adversely affected.

Real aggregate domestic demand, as measured by real gross domestic expenditure, continued to decline—a trend which began in 1974. Deterioration was by another 3.5% in 1976–77. This situation was further aggravated by the 8% decline in real gross domestic fixed investment in the year under review.

AGRICULTURE

According to estimates by the Department of Agricultural Economics and Marketing, farmers enjoyed a particularly good year in 1976–77. Farmers' gross income jumped c. 24.5% (from R2,723m to R3,389m), while the volume of agricultural production rose c. 12.4% in 1976–77 over the previous year. Besides the increase in volume, the growth in farmers' gross income was attributable in large part to higher producer prices.

Wheat production, as measured by quantity marketed by producers, expanded 31.9% in the first eight months of 1977 compared to the corresponding period in 1976. The quantity of Koring wheat marketed from January through August 1977 amounted to c. 130m bags of 90 kg each, the total for the first eight months of 1976 having been only c. 98m bags. Curiously, the quantities of Koring wheat milled into flour and meal products do not correlate with the above listed figures for total wheat marketed. In fact, flour and meal products amounted to 0.1% less in the first eight months of 1977 compared to the corresponding period in 1976, when they totalled 3,052,200 bags.

Grain sorghum production, as measured by quantities marketed, jumped a remarkable 62.4%, from 2.96m bags in 1975–76 to 4.80m in 1976–77. This quantitative leap can only partly be explained by the fact that attractive prices induced producers to market more and store less of their crop. This was indicated by the fact that average month-end stocks of grain sorghum fell 5.9% from 2.09m bags in 1975–76 to 1.97m bags in 1976–77. The most likely explanation for the tremendous growth in production is either higher productivity or more cultivated acreage or a combination of both.

Maize production is a major exception to an otherwise growth year for agriculture, with quantities marketed plummeting 26.5% from 81.0m bags in 1975–76 to 59.6m in 1976–77. In contrast to grain sorghum, average month-end stocks of maize also fell 12.7%, from an average of 47.9m bags in 1975–76 to 41.8m bags one year later.

The wool clip in 1977–78 was expected to increase 2.1% to 101.7m kg (cf 99.6m kg in 1976–77). However, it is unlikely that proceeds will exceed the 1976–77 total because of lesser anticipated world demand and relatively low wool prices.

Depressed world prices also lessened the impact of a 14.4% growth in sugar cane production in 1976–77 when an estimated 19.2m tonnes was reached.

MINING

Minerals, base metals and precious stones continued to lead SA's exports in 1977; their importance to the economy in general cannot be exaggerated. SA ranks first in the world in both production and reserves of chrome ore, andalusite group minerals, gold, platinum group metals and vanadium; it also ranks in the top two in both production and reserves of manganese ore.

The most spectacular development in the mining sector between 1975 and 1977 was the growth in exports of coal and iron ore by nearly eight times. These unprecedented increases were greatly facilitated by the commissioning of two new harbours with rail links: Saldanha, on the west coast of Cape Province, for iron ore; and Richard's Bay, in Natal, for coal from Transvaal (see above, Foreign Affairs: Japan). Overall production of iron ore doubled in the first six months of 1977 compared with the first half of 1976, reaching a level of 12.52m tons. In the same period in 1977, revenue from sales of iron ore nearly quadrupled to R100.2m (from R25.4m for the first half of 1976). Coal production also increased considerably though not as dramatically as iron ore. In the first half of 1977, coal production totalled 42.2m tons—17.2% above the same period in 1976. Sales jumped 79.2% for the same half-year periods, reaching R375m in the first six months of 1977.

Total gold production in the first half of 1977 amounted to 392,964 kg, a rise of 12.4% over a similar period in 1976. Gold sales, too, expanded by 6.8% in the first half of 1977 over the corresponding period in 1976, for a total of R1,284m.

The increase in production of silver outpaced that of gold. Production totalled 58,855 kg in the first half of 1977, an increase of 36.7% over the same period in 1976. Because of depressed silver prices, however, only an 0.8% growth for a total of R5.2m was achieved in the first half of 1977.

Chrome production in the first half of 1977 totalled 1.57m tons, an increase of 34.8% over the first half of 1976. Earnings from sales in these respective periods more than doubled, to R46.6m. Copper production climbed to 109,000 tons in the first half of 1977—an increase of 17.3% over the same period in 1976. Sales of copper expanded 38.4% in the first half of 1977, for a total of R113.3m.

Production of manganese ore rose 4.3% for a total of 2.63m tons in the first half of 1977 compared with the same period in 1976. However, unfavourable world prices for manganese ore led to an actual decline in sales revenue of 2.2% between these two half-yearly periods, from R57.8m to R56.6m.

Diamond mining yielded 2.829m carats in the first five months of 1977, for total earnings of R107.8m. These figures compare favourably with the 1976 calendar year totals of 7.023m carats and R215.1m respectively.

BUDGET

The 1978–79 Budget, like that of 1977–78, was intended to stabilize rather than expand the trouble-ridden economy. Government expenditure is intended to grow 9.1% to R9,811m; with inflation hovering around 10%, however, government spending could actually decline in real terms. Certainly the government sector's share of GDP should fall relative to other sectors.

In line with such limited increases in expenditure, a new tax structure was introduced which cut personal income taxes by 10%, but at the same time instituted a 4% general sales tax. Subsidies for essential food items were simultaneously introduced in order to ease the transition between the old and new methods of taxation for low-income earners whose consuming habits are relatively inelastic. On balance, this change from direct to indirect taxation should yield greater revenue for the government. By reducing the rate of taxes for higher income, it should also encourage production, consumption and savings in the long term.

Other major features of the 1978–79 Budget include stimulation of the labour-intensive construction industry, emphasis on Black housing and education, a reduction in the rate of growth of defence spending (particularly for foreign-produced material), and temporary relief measures for low-income groups.

Total revenue is expected to reach R7,668m, leaving a deficit before borrowing of R2,143m—an increase of 10.4%. Financing requirements will grow to R3,897m, or 22.2% more than in 1977–78. The bulk of this financing—R2,945m or 75.6%—is expected to be raised from domestic loans. Foreign loans are scheduled to total R75m, c. 34% more than in the previous year but still only 1.9% of total financing requirements.

BALANCE OF PAYMENTS

Dr T. W. de Jongh, Governor of the South African Reserve Bank, said in his annual report that the most favourable development in the year ended June 1977 'was the marked improvement in the current account of the balance of payments, from a deficit of R2,039m in 1975–76 to only R199m in 1976–77'.[460] He added that the current balance was transformed from a peak deficit of R2,529m in the first quarter of 1976 to a surplus of R1,277m in the second quarter of 1977. Given that economic policy was aimed primarily at improving the balance of payments and reducing inflation, it can be argued that at least the first of these objectives was achieved.[461]

The improvement in the current balance was attributable to a number of developments, including the increase in merchandise exports. Higher prices in international commodity markets for a wide range of items contributed to a 25% growth in merchandise exports in 1975–76, followed by 33% growth in 1976–77. At the same time, the balance of payments was favourably affected by an actual decrease in the value of merchandise imports beginning in the first quarter of 1976. The fall in imports reflects the recessionary character of SA's economy in the past few years, particularly in terms of reduced demand and the decline in real gross domestic expenditure. The continued expansion of oil imports was attributable largely to stockpiling (see SA versus International Opinion, above). Declines in the import of machinery and electrical equipment more than offset the growth in the value of oil imports, thus further confirming the pessimism of investors who have apparently decided that capital-intensive investment is either uneconomic or too risky in the prevailing business climate. The improvement in the current account was considered less satisfactory when it became apparent that the outflow of both short and long-term capital could not simply be attributed to seasonal fluctuation.

FOREIGN TRADE

For the first time in ten years, SA enjoyed an apparent trade surplus in 1977. However, the official figures do not include gold exports nor arms or oil imports. These notable exceptions aside, trade surplus reached R676.3m, a turnabout of R2,055m from 1976. Exports rose 29.2% to R5,803m in 1977; at the same time, imports fell 12.6% from R5,870m to R5,126m.

Exports of transport equipment soared by c. 51% and machinery and electrical machinery by c. 33% in 1977. In addition, exports of live animals and animal products, minerals, chemicals, precious stones and metals, and base metals all rose considerably in 1977. Imports of machinery and transport equipment in turn declined c. 15% and 19% respectively. Most other import items also fell in 1977, with the important exceptions of certain precious stones and vegetable products.

The UK remained SA's most important market in 1977. Exports to the UK still more than double in value those to the second largest market, which for the first half of 1977 was the US. Japan fell from being SA's second most valuable market in 1975 and 1976 to being third for the first half of 1977. Exports to African states, which are officially unspecified, continue to make up a sizable proportion of the country's total export trade (for further details, see Foreign Affairs, above).

The US, which first became SA's largest supplier in 1976, still led through the first half of 1977, though the half-year figures amount to only 42.3% of the full 1976 total—reflecting SA's recent cutback in imports. West Germany and the UK were the second and third largest supplier countries respectively through the first six months of 1977, as they were throughout 1976.

MONEY AND BANKING

At the end of 1977, SA's international reserves totalled $829m, down from $940m at the end of 1976 and from $1,216m at the end of 1975. Gold reserves also reflected this trend, falling from $727m at the end of 1975 to $515m at the end of 1976 and $413m at the end of 1977. Reserves in the form of SDRs have remained comparatively constant, at $48m at the end of 1977. Foreign exchange reserve holdings amounted to $368 at the end of 1977.

The South African Reserve Bank had foreign assets of R909m at the end of November 1977; claims on government totalled R1,945m, and claims on deposit money banks R261m. The Reserve Bank's total of reserve money reached R1,695m at this same time; foreign liabilities totalled R889m, while government deposits fell slightly to R1,290m.

Deposit money banks held R498m in reserves at the end of November 1977; foreign assets totalled R138m and claims on government reached R2,953m. Claims on the private sector dropped for the second straight month to R9,231m.

The IMF monetary survey of SA listed net foreign assets at –R543m at the end of November 1977; domestic credit (of which 27.68% represented net claims on the government and 72.32% claims on the private sector) stood at R12,788m at this time. The money supply rose to R4,488m and the quasi-money supply to R7,942 at the end of November 1977.

GOVERNMENT FINANCE (million Rand)

	1975	1976	1977 (Jan–Sept)
Deficit (–) or Surplus	–1,679	–1,979	–1,014
Revenue	5,417	6,313	5,263
Expenditure	7,096	8,292	6,277
Financing			
Net Domestic Borrowing	1,617	1,683	1,349
Net Foreign Borrowing	257	450	29
Use of Cash Balances	–197	–153	–367
Domestic Debt	9,065	10,761	12,108
Foreign Debt	918	1,345	1,377

Source: IMF, *International Financial Statistics.*

OVERSEAS DEBT (as at 17 November 1976)

Government Foreign Borrowing:

	'000
Deutschmarks	1,080,735
US dollars	470,820
Swiss francs	148,000
Sterling	10,330
Dutch Guilders	22,500
European units of accounts	16,300
European currency units	23,000

Source: *Financial Mail.*

Guaranteed External Debt:

	'000
Deutschmarks	2,727,517
Swiss francs	757,346
US dollars	473,582
Sterling	86,648
Dutch guilders	50,000
European units of account	26,430
Maltese pounds	5,000

BALANCE OF PAYMENTS (million US dollars)

	1975	1976	1977 (first half)
A Goods, Services and Transfers	–2,444	–1,967	469
Exports of Merchandise, fob	8,446	8,217	5,040
Imports of Merchandise, fob	–9,174	–8,572	–3,889
Exports of Services	1,910	1,706	864
Imports of Services	3,816	–3,446	–1,619
Private Unrequited Transfers, net	58	20	19
Government Unrequited Transfers, net	131	109	54
B Long-Term Capital, nie	2,175	875	–121
C Short-Term Capital, nie	–174	302	–16
D Errors and Omissions	–113	61	–349
Total (A through D)	**–557**	**–730**	**–18**
Reserves and Related Items	557	730	18

NATIONAL ACCOUNTS (million Rand)

	1975	1976	1977* (Jan–Sept.)
Exports	7,388	8,359	10,094
Government Consumption	3,715	4,463	4,972
Gross Fixed Capital Formation	7,758	8,801	8,886
Increase in Stocks	599	–369	–338
Private Consumption	14,787	16,658	18,996
Less: Imports	–8,119	–8,790	–8,691
Gross Domestic Product	**25,924**	**29,121**	**33,904**
Less: Net Factor Payments Abroad	–1,220	–1,392	—
Gross National Expenditure = GNP	**24,704**	**27,729**	—
National Income, Market Prices	22,660	25,336	—
GDP at 1970 Prices	15,368	15,566	—

*Quarterly data seasonally adjusted at annual rates.

Source (of two preceding tables): IMF, *International Financial Statistics.*

THE STATE REVENUE ACCOUNT (million Rand)

	Revised figure 1977–78	Budget figure 1978–79	% change
Total expenditure	8,990	9,811	9.1
Total revenue	7,049	7,668	8.8
Deficit (before borrowing)	1,941	2,143	10.4
Financing Requirement	**3,190**	**3,897**	**22.2**
Financing			
Domestic loans			
Public Debt Commissioners	761	650	
Re-investment of maturing stock		1,230	
New stock issues	1,968	750	
Non-marketable debt		315	
Foreign loans	56	75	
Loan levies	464	480	
Transfer from Stabilisation Account	—	355	
Transfer of cash balance from previous year	71	42	
	3,320	**3,897**	
Balance	**130**	**—**	

Source: Financial Mail, 31 March 1978.

BUDGET ALLOCATIONS (thousand Rand)

Department	Total estimated Exp. 1977–78	Final estimates 1976–77	% change
State President	365	365	+ 8.5
Parliament	5,861	5,482	+ 7
Prime Minister	12,817	12,420	+ 3.2
Defence	1,654,000	1,364,000	+ 21.3
Foreign Affairs	147,444	21,496	+ 585.2
Bantu Administration and Development	610,271	672,987	−9.3
Bantu Education	117,419	77,885	+ 50.7
Transport	150,225	143,008	+ 5
Labour	21,503	19,500	+ 10.3
Mines	168,001	180,806	−7.1
Information	15,370	14,100	+ 9
Interior	9,100	8,242	+ 10.4
Public Service Commission	10,330	9,960	+ 3.7
Government Printing Works	13,350	12,960	+ 3
Social Welfare and Pensions	370,000	353,984	+ 4.6
National Education	303,934	264,277	+ 15
Sport and Recreation	2,705	2,480	+ 12.7
Agricultural Economics and Marketing	175,408	226,808	−20.1
Agricultural Credit and Land Tenure	50,260	48,415	+ 9.1
Agricultural Technical Services	66,000	61,652	+ 7.1
Health	136,983	121,760	+ 12.5
Planning and the Environment	55,386	51,105	+ 8.4
Statistics	5,510	4,882	+ 14
Treasury	3,119,736	2,814,598	+ 10.8
South African Mint	1,594	1,654	−3.7
Inland Revenue	18,500	16,000	+ 15.6
Customs and Excise	8,919	50,720	−82.4
Audit	4,700	4,267	+ 10.1
Commerce	52,161	48,632	+ 7.3
Industries	253,686	297,160	−14.6
Justice	44,700	40,150	+ 11.3
Police	204,000	185,629	+ 9.9
Prisons	80,750	73,826	+ 9.4
Indian Affairs	84,049	71,641	+ 19.8

	Total estimated Exp. 1977–78	Final estimates 1976–77	% change
Community Development	267,773	224,500	+ 19.3
Tourism	6,550	5,872	+ 11.5
Public Works	264,652	216,027	+ 22.5
Immigration	11,524	11,503	+ 0.1
Water Affairs	160,400	160,107	+ 0.1
Forestry	38,939	31,745	+ 22.7
Coloured, Rehoboth and Nama relations	235,230	214,864	+ 9.5
Total	**8,960,105**	**8,147,350**	**+ 10**

Source: *Africa Research Bulletin*, 15 March–14 April 1977.

MINERAL PRODUCTION, 1976 (as percentage of total Western world and total world production)

	Western world rank	Western world production %	World rank	World production %
Platinum group metals	1	86	1	48
Gold	1	75	1	59
Vanadium	1	58	1	46
Chrome ore	1	41	2	26
Manganese ore	1	40	2	24
Andalusite group metals	1	36	1	30
Antimony	1	33	1	22
Vermiculite	2	39	—	—
Diamonds	2	23	3	18
Asbestos	2	18	3	9
Uranium (U_3O_8)	3	13	4	9
Coal	5	6	8	3
Phosphate	5	2	7	1
Fluorspar	7	6	10	5
Nickel	7	3	9	3
Copper	8	3	10	2
Iron ore	10	2	12	1
Tin	10	2	12	1
Silver	13	1	16	1
Zinc	15	2	21	1
Lead	36	0.05	46	0.03

Source: SA Department of Mines; *Financial Mail*, 20 May 1977.

DIRECTION OF TRADE (millions of US dollars)

Major Purchasers	1975	1976	1977 (Jan.–June)
United Kingdom	1,255.0	1,146.6	773.0
United States	589.7	526.8	378.9
Japan	664.9	592.0	327.1
Africa, not specified	573.1	521.1	291.5
West Germany	601.8	543.8	264.5
Belgium	162.4	224.7	119.8
France	155.6	170.6	108.0
Italy	124.8	165.1	97.0
Asia, not specified	105.9	113.4	84.7
Netherlands	120.3	143.6	78.0
Total (including others)	**8,864.8**	**7,874.1**	**4,594.5**

Major Suppliers

United States	1,340.8	1,458.2	616.9
West Germany	1,409.2	1,217.5	513.8
United Kingdom	1,493.9	1,185.3	488.2
Japan	840.3	690.5	330.9
Africa, not specified	344.3	356.3	175.3
France	335.4	294.7	150.4
Italy	275.9	243.7	92.4
Netherlands	192.5	170.4	70.6
Switzerland	192.5	142.4	67.8
Asia, not specified	105.5	133.7	59.7
Total (including others)	**7,591.2**	**6,769.4**	**2,941.4**

Source: IMF, *Direction of Trade.*

FOREIGN TRADE BY SECTORS (million Rand)

	Exports		Change (up)	Imports		Change (down)
	1976	*1977*	*(%)*	*1976*	*1977*	*(%)*
Footwear	1.1	2.1	90.9	16.0	12.8	20.0
Mineral products	247.4	446.0	80.3	48.9	48.3	1.2
Misc. manufactured articles	1.1	1.9	72.7	23.5	20.1	14.5
Wood articles	6.5	11.2	72.3	29.7	16.7	43.8
Machinery	66.9	105.9	58.3	1,052.1	837.2	20.4
Animals/products	49.1	68.6	39.7	18.8	17.8	5.3
Base metals/articles	352.3	475.1	34.9	198.0	161.1	18.6
Vehicles	29.0	39.1	34.8	669.1	471.4	29.5
Resins	10.6	14.2	34.0	129.3	107.4	16.9
Chemical products	78.8	105.0	33.2	238.7	241.6	+ 1.2
Pearls/precious stones	456.7	592.5	29.7	29.5	33.5	+ 13.6
Paper-making	42.7	53.9	26.2	90.7	81.3	10.4
Raw hides/leather goods	33.8	41.5	22.8	15.3	12.2	20.3
Textiles/articles	124.5	147.4	18.4	236.4	182.0	23.0
Unclassified goods	142.2	154.0	8.3	30.8	23.0	25.3
Optical	8.6	8.4	−2.3	106.8	97.3	8.9
Stone	8.0	7.8	−2.5	38.2	28.8	24.6
Animal/vegetable fats	12.6	12.0	−4.8	18.7	20.9	11.8
Prepared food	232.6	198.5	−14.7	45.5	46.0	+ 1.1
Vegetable products	274.3	190.1	−30.7	63.4	93.2	+ 47.0
Artworks	6.2	1.0	−83.9	12.2	2.0	83.6
Total	**2,185.0**	**2,676.2**	**+ 22.5**	**3,111.6**	**2,554.6**	**−17.9**

Source: Financial Gazette, 12 August 1977.

NOTES

(Unless otherwise indicated in first reference, all newspapers and journals quoted are published in SA.)

1. See *Africa Contemporary Record (ACR)* 1976–77, pp. B787ff, and all previous volumes of *ACR* from 1968–69 to 1975–76.
2. *Financial Mail (FM)*, 25 November 1977.
3. The *Observer*, London; 1 January 1978.
4. *Ibid*, 2 January 1977.
5. See Anthony Delius in *Rand Daily Mail (RDM)*, 24 May 1977.
6. The *Observer*, 18 and 25 September 1977.
7. For an excellent account see Michael Savage's paper 'The Costs of Apartheid', reproduced by the UN Centre Against Apartheid, *Notes and Documents*, No 27/77, September 1977.
8. See *The Times*, London; 15 May 1978.
9. Radio Johannesburg, 8 April 1978.
10. *Ibid*, 20 March 1978.

11. The *Star*, 2 April 1978.
12. *FM*, 21 October 1977.
13. *The Times*, 3 June 1978.
14. *FM*, 25 November 1977.
15. *Sunday Tribune*, 10 July 1977.
16. See *ACR* 1975–76, p. A46; 1974–75, pp. B428, B435, B440, B466; 1973–74, pp. B417, B422; 1972–73, p. B372; 1971–72, p. B333; 1970–71, p. B500; 1969–70, p. B285; 1968–69, pp. 290, 306, 329.
17. See UN Centre Against Apartheid, *Notes and Documents*, October 1977.
18. See Bob Hitchock's profile of Percy Qoboza in *RDM*, 20 October 1977.
19. Donald Woods, *Steve Biko* (London and New York: Paddington Press, 1978).
20. *RDM*, 20 October 1977.
21. *Die Beeld*, 20 October 1977.
22. *RDM*, 22 October 1977.
23. The *Observer*, 23 October 1977.
24. Quoted in the *Star*, 22 October 1977.
25. *The Times*, 24 October 1977.
26. *Ibid*, 25 October 1977.
27. *Ibid*.
28. The *Star*, 22 October 1977.
29. *Ibid*, 11 March 1978.
30. *RDM*, 20 April 1977.
31. *The Star*, 28 January 1978.
32. See *ACR* 1975–76, pp. A3ff.
33. See *ACR* 1975–76, pp. A39ff; 1974–75, pp. A3ff.
34. *Daily Telegraph*, 24 October 1977.
35. For text of statements, see Documents section, pp. C31–42.
36. The *Star*, 11 March 1978.
37. *Sunday Times*, London; 11 September 1977.
38. *Ibid*.
39. *RDM*, 16 September 1977.
40. *Daily Telegraph*, 12 October 1977.
41. *FM*, 11 November 1977.
42. The *Star*, 25 February 1978.
43. *RDM*, 21 October 1977.
44. The *Star*, 26 November 1977.
45. *FM*, 7 October 1977.
46. *FM*, 21 October 1977.
47. *FM*, 25 November 1977.
48. Radio Johannesburg, 8 April 1978.
49. *RDM*, 2 February 1978.
50. *RDM*, 12 November 1977.
51. *FM*, 21 January 1977.
52. For stocktaking of the Republic's future, see *ACR* 1976–77, pp. B794–96, and all previous volumes of *ACR*.
53. Quoted in the *Star*, 17 December 1977.
54. *Ibid*.
55. *RDM*, 8 September 1977.
56. *RDM*, 20 January 1978.
57. The *Star*, 7 May 1978.
58. *RDM*, 30 November 1977.
59. *Sunday Times (ST)*, 6 March 1977.
60. The *Star*, 25 June 1977.
61. *RDM*, 19 November 1977.
62. The *Star*, 11 June 1977.
63. *Ibid*, 22 November 1977.
64. *Ibid*.
65. The speeches delivered at the Conference can be found in a special edition of *Plural Society* published in Pretoria by the Africa Institute (Vol 15, No 16–17) 1977.
66. *To the Point*, Brussels; 10 June 1977.
67. The *Star*, 28 May 1977.
68. Wolfgang H. Thomas, *Plural Democracy* (Johannesburg: SA Institute of Race Relations, 1977).
69. *RDM*, 26 May 1977.

70. *RDM,* 24 November 1977.
71. The *Star,* 11 June 1977.
72. *Ibid,* 12 November 1977.
73. *RDM,* 13 May 1977.
74. *ST,* 15 January 1978.
75. *RDM,* 17 November 1977.
76. Their proposals were first published in *Aussenpolitik,* Hamburg (3/1976), and reproduced in the *SA Journal of African Affairs* (Vol 7, No 1), 1977.
77. *FM,* 19 August 1977.
78. *Afrikaner Liberalism* (Pretoria: Boekenhout Uitgewers, 1977).
79. *ST,* 19 July 1977.
80. The *Star,* 11 March 1978.
81. *Ibid,* 14 May 1978.
82. *ST,* 17 April 1977.
83. *Ibid.* Also see *ACR* 1976–77, p. B798.
84. *ST,* 23 October 1977
85. See *RDM,* 5, 12 and 22 November 1977.
86. See *ACR* 1976–77, p. B799.
87. *ST,* 19 June 1977.
88. The *Star,* 11 June 1977.
89. *RDM,* 26 November 1977.
90. *RDM,* 6 February 1977.
91. *ST,* 22 May 1977.
92. *Ibid,* 30 October 1977.
93. *Deur Grens en Tyd: 'n Werkboek vir die Afrikaanse Literatuur Geskiedenis Opvoedkundige en Inligting-sisteeme* (Pretoria, 1977).
94. See *ACR* 1974–75, p. B461; 1975–76, p. B575.
95. *FM,* 16 December 1977.
96. See *ACR* 1976–77, pp. B802–3.
97. *RDM,* 30 September 1977.
98. *RDM,* 23 July 1977.
99. *Ibid.*
100. See *ACR* 1972–73, p. B366; 1973–74, p. B411; 1974–75, p. B427; 1975–76, p. B575.
101. *ST,* 22 and 29 January 1978.
102. *Ibid,* 7 January 1978.
103. *Ibid,* 9 October 1977.
104. *Ibid,* 22 January 1978.
105. *Education in South Africa,* Vol 2 (Cape Town: Juta, 1977).
106. *FM,* 22 April 1977.
107. The *Star,* 28 January 1978.
108. *Daily Telegraph,* 24 October 1977.
109. *The Times,* 23 November 1977.
110. *RDM,* 14 November 1977.
111. *International Herald-Tribune (IHT),* Paris; 19 September 1977.
112. *Ibid.*
113. *RDM,* 2 May 1977.
114. *The Times,* 18 February 1978.
115. See *ACR* 1973–74, pp. B447–49.
116. See *ACR* 1969–70, p. B274; 1970–71, p. B489; 1971–72, p. B325; 1972–73, p. B363; 1973–74, pp. B408, 413; 1974–75, p. B422; 1975–76, p. B569; 1976–77, pp. B801, B806, B808–9, B818.
117. The *Star,* 9 July 1977.
118. *ST,* 17 April 1977.
119. *RDM,* 8 April 1977.
120. *ST,* 19 July 1977.
121. See *ACR* 1976–77, pp. B825–26.
122. See Fleur de Villiers, *Sunday Times,* 26 June 1977.
123. See Harald Pakendorf, *Sunday Times,* 26 June 1977.
124. John Patten in the *Star,* 25 February 1978.
125. See *ACR* 1976–77, pp. B809–10.
126. For full programme, see *RDM,* 6 September 1977.
127. *RDM,* 20 September 1977.
128. *ST,* 13 November 1977.
129. *Ibid,* 30 October 1977.
130. *Ibid.*

131. *RDM*, 24 July 1977.
132. SA Broadcasting Corporation, 2 December 1977.
133. *RDM*, 20 March 1977.
134. The *New York Times*, 21 October 1977.
135. *IHT*, 24 October 1977.
136. The *Star*, 15 October 1977.
137. *Ibid*, 4 June 1977.
138. Quoted by Dr E. E. Mahabane, President of the SA Institute of Race Relations in *The Road Ahead* (Johannesburg: SAIRR, 1978).
139. For manifesto and history of Committee of Ten, see *SA Outlook*, Cape Town; November 1977.
140. *RDM*, 16 October 1977.
141. *Christian Science Monitor*, Boston; 24 October 1977.
142. *RDM*, 15 November 1977.
143. David Beresford in the *Sunday Times*, 12 June 1977.
144. *The Guardian*, Manchester; 25 July 1977.
145. *SASO Bulletin* (Vol 1, No 1), June 1977. Published in Durban.
146. *Apartheid* (Vol 1, No 3), December 1977. Published by International University Exchange Fund (IUEF) in Geneva.
147. *Ibid.*
148. The *Observer*, 15 May 1977.
149. *RDM*, 22 September 1977.
150. *RDM*, 20 September 1977.
151. *RDM*, 30 January 1978, and the *Star*, 4 February 1978.
152. The *Star*, 11 March 1978.
153. *RDM*, 12 November 1977.
154. *Sechaba* (Vol 11, 4th Qtr), 1977. Published by the ANC in Dar es Salaam; printed in Neubrandenburg, East Germany.
155. *Ibid.*
156. *RDM*, 27 April 1978.
157. Arab Revolutionary News Agency (ARNA), Tripoli; 15 June 1977.
158. *ST*, 6 February 1977.
159. *Daily Mail*, London; 30 August 1977.
160. *The African Communist*, No 68, 1977. Published in London.
161. *Ibid.*
162. See David Beresford in the *ST*, 10 April 1977.
163. *Towards an Understanding of the Role of Whites in the South African Struggle* (London: SALSCOM, Box 2190, 1977).
164. *Daily Telegraph*, 9 February 1978.
165. Chief Gatsha Buthelezi, *The Post*, 6 November 1977.
166. SAIRR *1977 Survey*, p. 398.
167. *FM*, 11 November 1977.
168. *RDM*, 14 November; *FM*, 16 September 1977.
169. SA National Assembly 1977 *Hansard* 3, col 207.
170. *FM*, 25 November 1977.
171. *ST*, 31 July 1977.
172. *RDM*, 28 July 1977.
173. SAIRR *1977 Survey*, p. 382.
174. *Hansard* 21, cols 11227–30; 11233.
175. *ST*, 22 May 1977.
176. The *Star*, 18 February 1978.
177. *FT*, 22 February 1978.
178. SAIRR *1977 Survey* p. 320.
179. *RDM*, 4 October 1977.
180. RP 2 and 5 1977.
181. *1976 Benbo Economic Review* for Lebowa, Venda, Gazankulu and BophuthaTswana.
182. *FM*, 1 July 1977.
183. *Government Gazette*, No 5777, 19 October 1977.
184. *SA Year Book 1977*, ch 14.
185. Bantu Investment Corporation (BIC), *Annual Report 1976*, p. 78.
186. *RDM*, 4 October 1977.
187. *Hansard* 7, col 621.
188. *RDM—extra*, 5 June 1977.
189. *RDM*, 11 November 1977.
190. *The Times*, 20 February 1978.

191. *RDM*, 25 January 1978 and 24 August 1977.
192. See *ACR* 1976–77, p. B826f.
193. *FM*, 13 May 1977.
194. The *Star*, 30 April 1977.
195. *The Guardian*, 7 July 1977.
196. *RDM*, 24 August, 20 and 27 September 1977.
197. *FM*, 18 November 1977.
198. The *Star*, 23 March 1977.
199. *RDM*, 31 March 1977.
200. *To the Point*, 15 April 1977.
201. *ST*, 27 March 1977.
202. *Sunday Telegraph*, London; 23 January 1977.
203. *RDM*, 1 November 1977.
204. *Daily Telegraph*, 29 September 1977.
205. *RDM*, 23 April 1977.
206. *ST*, 22 January 1978.
207. *RDM*, 24 October 1977.
208. *ST*, 13 February and 13 March 1977.
209. The *Star*, 20 October 1977.
210. *Ibid*, 30 April 1977.
211. *RDM*, 12 January 1978.
212. *ST*, 24 July 1977.
213. *RDM*, 29 August 1977.
214. *The Times*, 28 September 1977.
215. *The Military Balance 1977–78* (London: International Institute for Strategic Studies).
216. *The Guardian*, 24 August 1977.
217. The *Star*, 2 July 1977.
218. *The Guardian*, 29 August 1977.
219. *White House Report*, Washington; 25 October 1977.
220. *The Guardian*, 25 August 1977.
221. *Ibid*, 28 September 1977.
222. *FT*, 21 December 1977.
223. *Daily Telegraph*, 12 September 1977.
224. The *Observer*, 14 August 1977.
225. *The Nuclear Axis*, Document No 8 presented at the South Africa Hearing, Oslo, 12–13 October 1977.
226. The *Star*, 14 January 1978.
227. *FM*, 16 September 1977.
228. *The Natal Mercury*, 14 April 1977.
229. *FM*, 19 November 1976.
230. *FM*, 27 May 1977.
231. *FM*, 25 November 1977.
232. The *Star*, 14 January 1978.
233. Market Research Africa quoted in *FM*, 6 May 1977.
234. *FM*, 16 September 1977.
235. *FM*, 6 May 1977.
236. The *Star*, 31 December 1977.
237. *Ibid*, 12 March 1977.
238. *RDM*, 19 December 1977.
239. *ST*, 15 May 1977.
240. *FM*, 10 February 1978.
241. *Weekend Argus*, 14 May 1977.
242. *Cape Times*, 15 June 1977.
243. *FM*, 10 February 1978.
244. *RDM*, 11 January 1977.
245. *Cape Times*, 18 July 1977.
246. *FM*, 17 February 1978.
247. The *Star*, 9 July 1977.
248. *FM*, 30 December 1977.
249. *FM*, 11 February 1977.
250. *FM*, 1 April 1977.
251. *FM*, 14 October 1977.
252. *FM*, 24 February 1978.
253. *RDM*, 25 July 1977.
254. *FM*, 30 December 1977.

255. The *Star*, 31 December 1977.
256. *FM*, 21 October 1977.
257. *FM*, 2 December 1977.
258. The *Star*, 31 December 1977.
259. *FM*, 29 July 1977.
260. *Government Gazette*, 7 August 1970.
261. The *Star*, 23 July 1977.
262. *FM*, 16 September 1977.
263. The *Star*, 17 and 31 December 1977.
264. *FM*, 19 August 1977.
265. The *Star*, 23 April 1977.
266. *FM*, 5 August 1977.
267. The *Star*, 23 April 1977.
268. *Cape Times*, 14 May 1977.
269. *FM*, 18 November 1977.
270. *FM*, 21 October 1977.
271. Prof W. H. B. Dean, quoted in *RDM*, 16 November 1976.
272. *Progress*, July 1977.
273. Civil Rights League *1976–77 Annual Report*, presented at the annual general meeting, 17 October 1977.
274. *ST*, 6 November 1977.
275. *The Guardian*, 8 February 1978.
276. *The Economist*, London; 18 February 1978.
277. Agence France Presse (AFP), Geneva; 4 January 1978.
278. Commissioner of Prisons Report, RP 46/1977, p. 23.
279. *Hansard* 14, col 1056.
280. RP 78/1976.
281. Commissioner of Prisons Report, p. 26.
282. *Ibid*.
283. *Hansard* 5, cols 456–66.
284. *Hansard* 9, col 708.
285. *Hansard* 10, col 4495.
286. *Hansard* 9, col 709.
287. *Sunday Express*, London; 23 January 1977; *Natal Mercury*, 26 February 1977.
288. *RDM*, 16 March 1977.
289. GN 968 Gazette 5575.
290. SAIRR *1977 Survey*, p. 144.
291. United Press International, 10 February 1977.
292. The *Star*, 11 March 1978.
293. 'Torture in SA', SAIRR *1977 Survey*; 'Repression, Torture and Death', ANC, June 1977.
294. SAIRR *1977 Survey*, p. 131.
295. Minister of Police, *Hansard*, col 83.
296. Southern African News Agency (SANA), Geneva; May 1977.
297. *Ibid*.
298. *Crisis*, (Johannesburg: University of the Witwatersrand, April 1977).
299. *Apartheid* (Vol 1, No 2), July 1977.
300. SANA, May 1977.
301. The *Star*, airmail weekly edition, 11 March 1978.
302. See *ACR* 1976–77, p. B842.
303. *FM*, 9 September 1977.
304. *Anti-Apartheid News*, London; September 1977.
305. *Ibid*.
306. *FM*, 9 September 1977.
307. Associated Press (AP) telex from Johannesburg, 6 November 1977.
308. AFP, telex from Johannesburg, 10 November 1977.
309. The *Star*, weekly airmail edition, 18 February 1978.
310. *Ibid*.
311. *Ibid*, 30 April 1977.
312. The Minister's quote, the table and statistical information all from *Race Relations News*, October 1977.
313. *Anti-Apartheid News*, December 1977.
314. *Ibid*, November·1977.
315. *FM*, 17 February 1978.
316. Evidence submitted by John Gaetswe, general-secretary of the South African Congress

of Trade Unions, to the hearing on SA, Oslo; 12 October 1977.
317. *Southern Africa*, US; June–July 1977.
318. *Civil Rights Newsletter* (Vol XXI, No 3), 4 April 1977. Published in Cape Town.
319. Information supplied to *ACR* by Dr Kenneth Hughes, chairman of the Civil Rights League.
320. *The Argus*, 31 August 1977.
321. *The Guardian*, 26 August 1977.
322. *Ibid*, 17 January 1978.
323. *ST*, 23 January 1977.
324. The *Observer*, 26 March 1978.
325. *RDM*, 7, 8, 10, 18 February 1977.
326. *The Times*, 24 November 1977.
327. SA National Tuberculosis Association, *Annual Report 1976*.
328. WHO Report, *Apartheid and Mental Health*, March 1977.
329. *RDM*, 7 July 1977.
330. *The Times*, 13 March 1978.
331. *RDM*, 11 March 1977.
332. *ST*, 3 April 1977.
333. *RDM*, 17 October 1977.
334. *RDM*, 30 November 1977.
335. *Daily Telegraph*, 18 October 1977.
336. *RDM*, 29 August 1977.
337. *Sunday Tribune*, 21 August 1977.
338. *ST*, 6 November 1977.
339. *Hansard* 16, col 7839; *FM*, 7 October 1977.
340. The *Star*, 18 April 1977.
341. *The Guardian*, 24 February 1978.
342. The *Star*, weekly airmail edition, 18 March 1978.
343. *Daily Dispatch*, 13 August 1977.
344. The *Star*, 18 March 1978.
345. *FM*, 3 December 1976.
346. *Bulletin of the Africa Institute of SA*, No 6 and 7, 1977.
347. See *ACR* 1975–76, pp. A3ff.
348. SA Broadcasting Corporation, 27 May 1977.
349. *Ibid*, 1 May 1978.
350. *ST*, 15 May 1978.
351. *RDM*, 23 May 1978.
352. The *Star*, 24 September 1977.
353. *RDM*, 9 May 1977.
354. *Daily Telegraph*, 1 October 1977.
355. *FM*, 9 December 1977 and 6 January 1978.
356. See *Africa*, London; February 1978.
357. The *Star*, 5 November 1977.
358. *FM*, 28 October 1977.
359. The *Star*, 22 April 1978.
360. *The Guardian*, 19 April 1978.
361. *IHT*, 19 September 1977.
362. *The Times*, 28 July 1977.
363. *Ibid*, 30 January 1978.
364. *Ibid*, 28 July 1977.
365. *RDM*, 8 April 1977.
366. *The Times*, 31 January 1978.
367. *FM*, 25 November 1977.
368. For text of Dr Owen's speech, see Documents section, pp. C19–21. Also see essay on 'Britain's Year in Africa'.
369. *The Times*, 26 May 1977.
370. *The Guardian*, 26 October 1977.
371. *Financial Times (FT)*, London; 27 October 1977.
372. *RDM*, 26 October 1977.
373. *The Times*, 9 November 1977.
374. *Ibid*, 11 November 1977.
375. For Code of Conduct, see Documents section, pp. C53–55.
376. *The Times*, 28 September 1977.
377. *FT*, 10 May 1978 and 24 June 1977.
378. See Ken Owen, 'The Pistol to our Heads' in *ST*, 29 May 1977.

379. Interview with Willem Steenkamp in the *Cape Times.*
380. The *Star*, 15 October 1977. Also see Vorster's comment in TV interview with ABC; quoted in *RDM*, 24 October 1977.
381. For full text of Mondale's speech, see Documents section, pp. C27–31.
382. *RDM*, 18 October 1977.
383. Meeting with editors of *US News and World Report*, Bureau of Public Affairs Office of Media Services, 31 October 1977.
384. See Prof Donald Baker, 'Washington-Pretoria Confrontation', *Africa Institute Bulletin*, Nos 9 and 10, 1977.
385. *FT*, 25 June 1977.
386. *IHT*, 28 September 1977.
387. *The Guardian*, 21 October 1977.
388. *The Times*, 31 October 1977.
389. *ST*, 27 November 1977.
390. Quoted in *RDM*, 24 October 1977.
391. *Newsweek*, Washington; 5 December 1977.
392. *RDM*, 25 October 1977.
393. 'Meet the Press', 8 November 1977.
394. *ST*, 15 May 1977.
395. *IHT*, 21 October 1977.
396. For full text, see *Race Relations News* (Johannesburg: SAIRR), July 1977.
397. *Daily Telegraph*, 24 June 1978.
398. Swedish TV, 18 November 1977.
399. *FT*, 27 May 1977.
400. The *Observer*, 22 May 1977.
401. *The Washington Post*, 24 November 1977.
402. *Ibid.*
403. *RDM*, 23 November 1977.
404. *IHT*, 2 November 1977; and *FT*, 2 November 1977.
405. See *X-Ray*, March/April 1978, Africa Bureau, London; and *FT*, 15 March 1978.
406. *FT*, 26 January 1978.
407. See *Notes and Documents* 32/77, December 1977.
408. *FT*, 24 February 1978.
409. *FM*, 30 September 1977.
410. *RDM*, 1 February 1978.
411. For text of Code of Conduct, see Documents section, pp. C53–55.
412. See *FM*, 15 July, 2 and 23 September and 14 October 1977; *FT*, 22 September 1977.
413. *FM*, 14 October 1977.
414. *Ibid.*
415. *RDM*, 27 September 1977.
416. *The Times*, 23 November 1977.
417. *RDM*, 19 November 1977.
418. *FT*, 6 September 1977; *RDM*, 30 December 1977; *FM*, 6 January 1978.
419. *FM*, 11 November 1977.
420. *The Guardian*, 23 August 1977.
421. *RDM*, 2 September 1977.
422. *FT*, 6 July 1977.
423. *FM*, 20 May 1977.
424. See 'France and South Africa' in *Notes and Documents*, UN Centre Against Apartheid, December 1977.
425. *FT*, 28 October 1977.
426. See essay on West Germany in Africa in this volume.
427. For text see *German International*, Bonn Foreign Ministry, March 1977.
428. *FM*, 26 August 1977.
429. *RDM*, 12 November 1977.
430. For full report see *Socialist Affairs*, November/December 1977; 88 High Street, London NW8.
431. See Documents section, pp. C44–49.
432. *New York Times*, 20 December 1977.
433. The *Star*, 5 November 1977.
434. *The Economist*, London; 25 February 1978.
435. The *Star*, 23 April 1977.
436. Radio Panama City, 27 July 1977.
437. The *Star*, 19 February 1977.
438. *Ibid*, 11 December 1976.

439. Memorandum to OAU on 'Oil Supplies to SA' by the Haslemere Group, 16 Mecklenburgh Sq, London WC1; December 1977.
440. *Daily Nation*, Nairobi; 15 December 1977.
441. The *Star*, 14 May 1977.
442. *RDM*, 13 September 1977.
443. *FT*, 10 October 1977.
444. *Ibid*, 21 February 1978.
445. Israel Home Service, 10 February 1978. Also see *FT*, 6 February 1978.
446. The *Star*, 18 March 1978.
447. *Daily Telegraph*, 5 November 1977.
448. The *Star*, 3 December 1977.
449. John F. Burns in *IHT*, 28 October 1977.
450. *Newsweek*, 12 September 1977.
451. *The Sun*, Washington; 21 November 1977.
452. *The Guardian*, 7 November 1977.
453. *FT*, 22 February 1978.
454. *Daily Telegraph*, 22 February 1978.
455. See, for example, S. Astakhov in *International Affairs*, No 8, 1977, pp. 62–66.
456. For background, see *ACR* 1976–77, pp. B855–63.
457. *Standard Bank Review*, August 1977.
458. See *ACR* 1976–77, p. B802.
459. Quoted in *Progress*, Cape Town; February 1977.
460. *RDM*, 24 August 1977.
461. See SA Reserve Bank, *Annual Report 1977*, p. 17.

BophuthaTswana

The BophuthaTswana flag was hoisted over Mmabatho, near Mafeking, on 6 December 1977 in an 'independence' ceremony which, like that of Transkei a little over a year before, was boycotted by the international community.[1] Only SA, the Transkei and two other Homelands, Ciskei and Venda, were represented.

However, the BophuthaTswana President, Chief Lucas Manyane Mangope, did not refer to the absence of representatives from the outside world in his 'independence' address. Mangope, the driving force behind the decision to opt for independence from Pretoria, was preoccupied with another problem—land. His new State consists of seven pieces of territory scattered across three of SA's four provinces. That these seven pieces were scheduled to be reduced to six under plans to 'consolidate' BophuthaTswana was of little comfort.

He told his audience in independence stadium that self-respect made it impossible to deny 'well-founded bitterness' because of the fragmented nature of BophuthaTswana. 'To us and the rest of the whole world, excepting Pretoria, it would seem logical that our greater independence necessarily means greater consolidation. . . . Even with all the bitterness it arouses in our Tswana ranks, it is absolutely essential that the serious issue of consolidation be raised here and now. Whether we like it or not, it is a shadow that looms over all the revelry and rejoicing of our festivities.'[2] Conceding that 'independence' suffered from a fatal credibility gap because of the fragmented nature of the territory, Mangope added: 'It is not at all surprising, I am afraid, that in overseas capitals they show me a map of the bits and pieces of BophuthaTswana and add the sarcastic remark, "Did you say independence? Please forgive our mirth. We thought you were joking."'

Nevertheless, Mangope expressed the hope that BophuthaTswana's 'independence' would contribute to resolving SA's race problem—not in the negative sense of reducing the number of Blacks in SA, but in the positive sense of improving race relations. '. . . There can be no doubt in the mind of anybody who understands the predicament of SA that by far the greatest promise of our independence lies in the field of human relations. Let us therefore all dedicate ourselves in this hour of independence to the greatest and noblest service anyone can render unto SA. It is this, my compatriots and friends: to let this hour go down in history as marking the beginning of the end of racial discrimination in SA.'[3]

Pledging his fledgling state to the path of non-racialism, Mangope continued: 'Inasmuch as we succeed in setting a worthy example of non-discrimination, our road to greater independence is fully vindicated. Inasmuch as we fail in cutting out the cancer of discrimination from our flesh, we are putting ourselves, by our own free choice, into the chains of spiritual slavery.'

Although BophuthaTswana was conceived as an ethnic Homeland for the Tswana—BophuthaTswana means the 'gathering in' of the Tswana people—Mangope believed it would contribute to the dignity and well being of all Black South Africans. Replying to President Nico Diederichs at a banquet on the eve of independence, Mangope said: 'There was only one goal consistently before my eyes and an absolutely clear one: to win a place in the sun for my people—and that means not only for the Tswanas but for all the Black people of SA.'[4] The tone and central thesis of Mangope's speeches were similar to those of the Transkei leader, Paramount Chief Kaiser Matanzima, when he led Transkei to independence on 26

October 1976. Cardinal to the justification of accepting Pretoria-style independence was the hope that it would help eliminate race discrimination in two ways: 1) by creating an enclave or series of enclaves within the former boundaries of SA in which non-racialism would be the order of the day; and 2) by making the independent Homeland a psychological catalyst for change within the whole region.

However, not even BophuthaTswana's most staunch advocates can feel very optimistic, at least about the immediate future of the infant state. The most hopeful scenario would be eventual triumph over its problems and escape from its present isolation in the international community. Two essential factors underline its unenviable position: the refusal of the outside world to accord recognition, and the unpopularity of Mangope and his Ministers among articulate and politically-conscious urban Blacks, even his own Tswana people. The OAU, for instance, has rejected BophuthaTswana's independence as a 'sham which amounts to nothing more than balkanization'.[5] Without the OAU's sanction, the likelihood of recognition from any country apart from SA and Transkei is minimal. Moreover, a recent poll showed that less than 3% of urban Blacks favoured Mangope as a leader above his rivals,[6] a rating well below the 20% proportion of Soweto's population which is Tswana.[7]

Mangope's supporters and sympathizers believe, however, that he can win credibility by speaking up strongly on behalf of Black South Africans, and in this way win their support and eventually that of the international community. But there is little evidence that speaking out on their behalf cancels Blacks' animosity to Bantustan leaders whose gestures of solidarity are often rejected with contempt. When a man of the calibre of Dr Nthato Motlana, chairman of the Soweto Committee of Ten, cannot get a South African passport to attend an international conference in Europe because he is Tswana-speaking, all the bitterness of 'betrayal' is rekindled. It was Motlana who predicted that a time would come when Blacks would simply ignore the boundaries set up by independent Homelands and reunite SA or, as he would put it, Azania.[8]

POLITICAL AFFAIRS
THE LAND QUESTION
The territory allocated to BophuthaTswana was to all intents and purposes the Tswana share of the nearly 64,000 sq mi (c. 168,850 sq km) set aside for 'natives' under the 1913 and 1936 Land Acts.[9] The Tswana people were one of the eight 'Bantu national units' recognized as eligible for self-government under the Promotion of Bantu Self-Government Act of 1959.

From the time he became Chief Executive Councillor of the Tswana Territorial Authority in 1969 and was elected Chief Minister in 1971, Mangope has persistently campaigned against the existing distribution of land in SA between Whites and Blacks: more than 86% for the former and less than 14% for the latter, even though Blacks constitute more than 70% of the population against less than 20% for Whites. Not only was it unfair, Mangope contended, but a totally unsuitable basis on which to establish 'independent' Homelands.

'In our country,' Mangope said in January 1974, 'the country of our birth, there must be more fair and just sharing of the land. It is a principle from which we can never deviate. We reject outright the present attempts to make the 1936 Land Act the basis of settling this issue. This law was introduced to increase the then native reserves or, if one prefers to put it that way, to solve the then native problem. In no way did the law claim or intend to provide additional areas for future independent sovereign states. In terms of the present policy, therefore, this law has no relevance whatsoever in respect of Homeland consolidation negotiations.'[10]

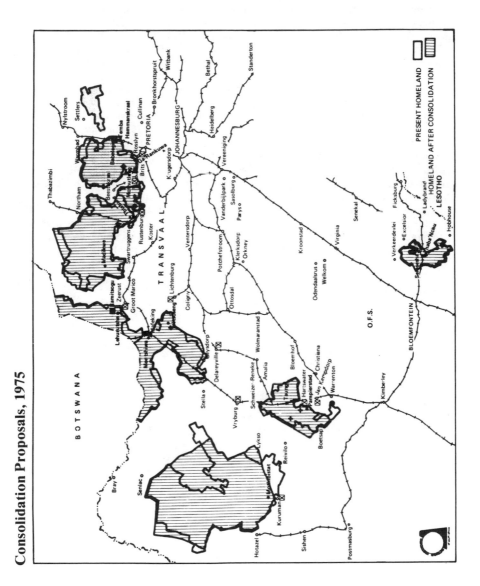

Consolidation Proposals, 1975

PRESENT HOMELAND

HOMELAND AFTER CONSOLIDATION

Mangope's position was clear: independence on the basis of the 1936 Land Act was out of the question. But Prime Minister Vorster was equally adamant in refusing to go beyond the 1936 Land Act: 'If a Homeland does not want to become independent as a result of the fact that I do not want to give it more land, then that is its affair.'[11] The BophuthaTswana Legislative Assembly's counter-proposals were for the creation of a single block of Tswana territory by adding chunks of White-owned territory and towns where Tswanas predominate to the Tswana reserves.[12]

Between 1973 and 1975, Mangope stuck to his stand of no independence without a new and fairer land deal—a position endorsed by his fellow Homeland leaders with the exception, from March 1974, of Matanzima. He broke ranks to negotiate for independence unilaterally with the aim of getting the best deal possible within the 1936 Land Act, while at the same time reserving the right to demand land over and above the 1936 Act after independence. Although Mangope was initially hostile to Matanzima's decision,[13] he decided to follow suit in late 1975 when he summoned a meeting of Tswana chiefs, headmen and their representatives to Mafeking on 4 November. When the question was put of whether or not to opt for 'independence', they decided in favour by 155 votes to five.[14] Later, on 9 November, Mangope was given a unanimous mandate to negotiate for independence by his ruling Democratic Party—even if BophuthaTswana's land demands were not met.

Mangope gave several reasons for his decision, among them his belief that 'independence' would be a spur to development of BophuthaTswana, an incentive to better race relations and 'an antidote to the slave mentality' of some Tswanas.[15] 'The experience of seven years of partial self-rule tells us we need a final say in all

BophuthaTswana (black areas) within South Africa

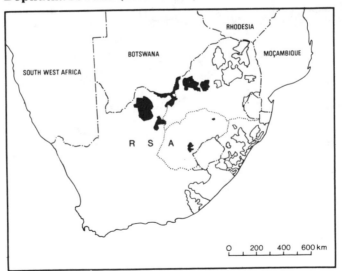

matters that affect us,' he said. 'Only when this House has a full and final say can we engage ourselves in the development of BophuthaTswana.' After arguing that goodwill between Tswanas and White South Africans would 'grow and flourish and bear even better fruit' after 'independence', he added: 'Those who oppose our move to independence must be seen to be suffering the effects of a long-term bondage. They have so been indoctrinated that they do not believe there is any chance whatsoever to escape.[16] The opposition BophuthaTswana National Seoposengwe Party (BNSP), at whom these remarks were directed, had boycotted the session of the Assembly where the decision was taken in protest that independence should be discussed separately from the land question.

Mangope later gave further reasons for his decision: independence could be used as a lever to end race discrimination in SA;[17] independence would be used as a basis from which to continue the drive for more land.[18] At a special congress of his ruling party in July 1976, Mangope warned of the danger of bloodshed if the land issue were not settled equitably.[19] It is also possible that Mangope may have been influenced by another consideration: that if he negotiated with Pretoria sooner rather than later, he might be able to get a better deal within the 1936 Land Act.

In fact, there was some evidence that Matanzima's decision to negotiate with Vorster on land unilaterally, rather than in concert with his fellow Homeland leaders, had brought him some reward. Vorster himself hinted strongly that Matanzima had been given the coveted Glen Grey area as a *quid pro quo* during Transkei's negotiations with Pretoria.[20] As some of BophuthaTswana's own territory was itself claimed by the North Sotho Homeland of Lebowa in the Hammanskraal area north of Pretoria, Mangope may have hoped that in his case too part of this land would be formally ceded to an independent BophuthaTswana.

In this regard, it is important to note that Transkei and BophuthaTswana both did relatively well under the 1936 Land Act, receiving between them 84,960 of the land ceded to or earmarked for Blacks—50.32% of the total. Comparing land distribution with the Black population, it emerges that the Tswana people, who constitute less than 12% of the total (1.7m out of c. 15m), obtained nearly 24% of the land.[21] Although these figures do not take account of the quality of the land, which is drier in the western parts where the Tswana are mainly concentrated, they may help to explain Mangope's decision to opt for independence.

RACIAL AND TRIBAL DISCRIMINATION

In his reply to President Diederichs at the 'independence' banquet in Mmabatho, Mangope asked for the success or failure of his new state to be measured by a single yardstick: whether or not it would lead to 'even greater victories over the evil of racial discrimination'. As if to demonstrate his determination to set Bophutha-Tswana firmly on a non-racial path, Mangope announced the appointment of two Whites to top positions in his Government. Dr D. J. Kriel, an Afrikaner, was named as Minister of Health, and Hendrik van Zyl as consultant to the Department of Agriculture.[22]

The Republic of BophuthaTswana Constitution Act, adopted on the first day of 'independence', contained a Declaration of Fundamental Rights, enforceable by the Supreme Court. According to one of its most important clauses, 'All people shall be equal before the law and no one may, because of his sex, descent, his race, his language, his origin or his religious beliefs, be favoured or prejudiced.'[23] In a state where one-third of the *de facto* population are not Tswanas, the declaration and the power of the courts to enforce it was obviously important, more so to Black minorities within BophuthaTswana than to Whites, the former being both more numerous and less powerful. Blacks who are not Tswanas numbered more than

294,000 of the total Homeland population of 904,000 in 1970. Whites numbered fewer than 2,000.[24]

The schedule of South African laws automatically repealed by the BophuthaTswana Constitution Act included some of SA's most overtly racial measures. Among them were the Group Areas Act, which forces people of different races to live in different areas; the Coloured Person's Representative Act, which provides for a separate political institution for the Coloured people; and the Prohibition of Political Interference Act, which forbids persons of one race from 'interfering' in the political affairs of another. But there were some notable exceptions, including laws which have been condemned throughout the world. These included the Population Registration Act, which provides for compulsory registration according to race; the Mixed Marriages Act, which forbids inter-racial marriages; and the Immorality Act, which prohibits sex between the races.

Somewhat inconsistently, the Mangope Government's commitment to human rights did not include the right to mother-tongue instruction for the Pedi-speaking Ndebeles near Hammanskraal (the Bapedi predominate in the neighbouring Venda Homeland). Similar accusations of 'tribalism' were made against Mangope's administration by the leaders of the QwaQwa Homeland on behalf of the Basotho living at Thaba 'Nchu in the Orange Free State.

More important · was the provision in the Status of BophuthaTswana Act depriving all Tswanas of their South African citizenship, irrespective of whether or not they were living permanently in the White-designated part of the Republic (see below). According to the 1970 census, about two-thirds of all Tswanas live outside their designated Homeland. For many, therefore, BophuthaTswana's independence was felt to be a threat to their rightful claims to South African citizenship; Mangope's protestations about non-racialism, however sincerely meant, rang hollow in their ears.

THE CITIZENSHIP ISSUE

The Status of Transkei Act of 1976 unequivocally spelt out Pretoria's policy on independence.[25] The essential condition was that all Blacks associated with the Homeland through descent, language or culture would lose South African citizenship and become citizens of the newly-independent Homeland, even if they had lived in White-designated SA for generations. The Act aroused Black indignation and anger as the then Dean of Johannesburg, the Rt-Revd Desmond Tutu, warned it would.[26] Mangope and his Cabinet thus had forewarning of what to expect when they set out on the same path to independence. The burning down of the BophuthaTswana Legislative Assembly in August 1976 was a clear sign that the feelings of Black youth were running dangerously high.[27]

There were various indications that Mangope and his lieutenants wanted to forestall criticism on the citizenship issue, however. As early as June 1976, Amos Kgomongwe, secretary-general of the ruling DP, said that the Tswana Cabinet was opposed to forcing BophuthaTswana citizenship on Tswanas living in White-designated SA.[28] The Cabinet's stand was that BophuthaTswana citizenship should be optional for Tswanas living outside its borders. Later, at the end of July 1976, a special conference of Mangope's DP unanimously rejected the Bantu Homelands' Citizenship Act of 1970 which, for internal purposes, made all Blacks in SA citizens of one Homeland or another—whether they liked it or not. The conference declared: 'An independent BophuthaTswana will have her own citizenship act, in terms of which citizenship will be optional'.[29] This rejection was interpreted as evidence that Mangope would not be signatory to a law modelled on the Status of Transkei Act.

In the event, however, publication of the Status of BophuthaTswana Act in May 1977 revealed that Mangope had not succeeded where Matanzima failed. Its citizenship clause was almost identical to that of the Transkei, listing five categories of persons who would 'cease to be South African citizens' on independence. In effect, all those of Tswana origin would become citizens of the new state at the cost of their South African citizenship. Blacks born after independence would also become BophuthaTswana citizens, even if only one parent was. Blacks who identified themselves 'culturally or otherwise' with any of the peoples of BophuthaTswana would similarly become citizens of the new state. The only Tswanas to escape the law were those who were citizens of another Homeland.

There was, however, one difference between the BophuthaTswana and Transkei Acts: clause 6 (3) of the former provided machinery for BophuthaTswana citizens to renounce their new citizenship after independence—with the implicit assumption that the renunciation would be in favour of regaining their South African citizenship. There was no equivalent in the Transkei Act. Mangope, who had insisted on the clause's inclusion, was reported to have believed initially that it secured the right of Tswanas to choose between the two citizenships. But in fact the clause did nothing of the kind. It simply stipulated that BophuthaTswana citizenship could be renounced 'on conditions agreed upon between the Government of the Republic of SA and the Government of BophuthaTswana'. Given that the *raison d'être* for granting independence was to 'solve' the political problem by depriving Blacks of South African citizenship, Pretoria would certainly never agree to mass renunciation by BophuthaTswana citizens of their new status in favour of their old.

After Mangope had been alerted to the failure of 6 (3) to make BophuthaTswana citizenship optional for Tswanas, he tried to extract a more meaningful concession from Pretoria by threatening to withdraw from the independence negotiations altogether. To give maximum impact to this threat, he released a letter to White opposition parties which said in part: 'To us as a Cabinet, section 6 (3) of the Status of BophuthaTswana Act, 1977 cannot be read in isolation, but always with section 6 (1), which causes BophuthaTswana people to cease to be citizens of SA. . . . For us to agree to BophuthaTswana becoming independent, clause 6 (3) must be amended in the current parliamentary session to provide that such people automatically regain the citizenship of SA which they lose in terms of section 6 (1) of the Act. Unless this amendment is effected in the current parliamentary session, the resolution of the BophuthaTswana Legislative Assembly empowering the Cabinet to negotiate with SA for independence will be frustrated, as we are not prepared to accept independence at all costs.'[30]

Mangope's condition was not met; clause 6 (3) was not amended. The then Minister of Bantu Administration, M. C. Botha, ignored Mangope's threat, insisting that if any changes were necessary, they could be made after the parliamentary session—i.e. after the Status Act had become law.[31] Botha thus called Mangope's bluff, and it was Mangope who backed down.

Mangope met with Vorster and Botha for further talks on independence at the end of June 1977. Although no agreement was reached and tension was manifest,[32] it was agreed to hold more talks on citizenship. One point should have been abundantly clear to Mangope: Pretoria would not budge in any meaningful sense, no matter how much he cajoled, threatened or pleaded. Mangope's response was to go on the offensive—verbally. He publicly accused Pretoria of attempting to deceive BophuthaTswana into accepting an independence which reeked of 'fraud and disgrace', which was designed to cater for 'certain White people's evil dreams and continued *baasskap*, privilege and discrimination'.[33] But Vorster was unperturbed, riposting that the choice to become independent had been Mangope's, and that his statements were inimical to Tswana interests.[34]

Independence talks continued, with Mangope meeting Botha in July. Agreement was reached on some land issues, although not on the pivotal question of the 1936 Land Act. He then met Vorster in August and in a joint communiqué undertook to give a 'final' decision on independence after consulting his party caucus.[35] On 16 September, the BophuthaTswana Democratic Party declared it would accept independence on the target date, 6 December, provided agreement was reached on citizenship and land issues.[36] In October, when Mangope again met Vorster, a joint statement was issued announcing that the outstanding issues between the two parties had been resolved, and that agreements would be formally signed on 15 November.[37] Mangope was ambiguous in his explanation of what had in fact been agreed: he said that the citizenship issue had been resolved 'under the circumstances', and BophuthaTswana citizens 'should' be able to renounce their citizenship if they wished and regain South African citizenship.[38]

It soon became clear, however, that the citizenship dispute had been won by Vorster. BophuthaTswana citizens could renounce their citizenship and regain South African citizenship only on two conditions: (1) Pretoria would have to agree to restore South African citizenship; (2) a non-independent Homeland would have to agree to accept the Tswana concerned. With Pretoria holding a veto, there was no likelihood of large numbers of Tswanas regaining their citizenship. The stipulation that a non-independent Homeland accept the Tswana concerned was cardinal, as Homelands still within SA confer a subsidiary internal citizenship on Blacks for internal purposes. Thus Mangope's citizenship deal—the essentials of which were confirmed by the Bantu Homelands' Citizenship Amendment Act of 1978—meant that Tswanas were no better off than Blacks of Transkei origin. They were stripped of South African citizenship without their consent and given only the narrowest of theoretical opportunities of regaining a second-class form of it.

The implications of the deal were implicit in the 1970 census figures which showed that only c. 610,500 Tswanas lived in the Homelands as against more than 1.1m in White-designated SA.[39] Of the former, more than 10,000 lived in Homelands set aside for other ethnic groups. This meant that only a little over a third of the Tswana were living in BophuthaTswana, a less favourable situation than pertained in Transkei. Botha updated the figures in Parliament, putting the proportion of Tswana in BophuthaTswana at between 39 and 40%.[40] Even so, when BophuthaTswana achieved its new status, most of its citizens lived outside its borders. These people had not endorsed Mangope's independence decision, although they were deprived of South African citizenship as a consequence.

INTERNAL DISSENT

Within BophuthaTswana itself, centrifugal forces threatening the new state include the secessionist movements of the Ndebele and Basotho. Although the Ndebele in the Hammanskraal area went so far as to refuse to fly the new Republic's flag, their opposition was temporarily stilled by the deposition of their chieftainess.[41] But few doubt their continuing hostility to being included in the Tswana Homeland. The Basotho, particularly at Thaba 'Nchu where they outnumber the Tswana, are actively encouraged to pull out of BophuthaTswåna by the Basotho Homeland of QwaQwa. Under the terms of an agreement reached between the two Homelands, BophuthaTswana will give land to QwaQwa to accommodate those Basotho who wish to leave, the size of the land depending on the numbers involved.[42] But the issue is emotional and still far from settled. The general state of tension was shown by the arrest of c. 300 Basotho 'squatters' by Tswana police in Thaba 'Nchu and the imprisonment of over 200 others.[43] The fact that these 200 are in South African jails under an agreement signed between BophuthaTswana and SA hardly improves Mangope's image among the Basotho, Ndebele and other of his opponents.

Associated with these secessionist movements is the problem of the Winterveld squatters—thousands of non-Tswanas who have settled outside the townships of Garankuwa and Mabopane, just over 20 miles from Pretoria. The squatters, who outnumber residents in the two townships by 270,000 to 139,000,[44] moved in to be close to Pretoria in the hope of finding work and subsequently found themselves part of an 'independent' Homeland. Mangope has talked of either introducing influx control or of 'resettling the squatters'; they in turn accuse Mangope's administration of tribal discrimination and some have flirted with the idea of a UDI against BophuthaTswana. These threats and counter-threats have made for incipient violence in the area.

Such problems tend to increase Mangope's dependence on Pretoria. In fact, one of the agreements signed between the two governments specifically commits SA to help with the 'resettlement' of people 'squatting in the Winterveld and Thaba 'Nchu areas'. It provides for expropriation of land if there is resistance from land owners.

THE AUGUST 1977 ELECTIONS
BophuthaTswana went to the polls from 22 to 24 August 1977, with all Tswanas over the age of 18 eligible to vote. One important difference from the last general election held in October 1972 was that more than twice the number of popularly-elected seats in the Legislative Assembly were at stake—48 against 24. This increase meant there were equal numbers of members elected to those nominated by chiefs and headmen in the regional authorities. Mangope won an even more decisive election victory in 1977 than five years before, capturing 43 of the 48 seats. As his Democratic Party had already secured 47 out of the 48 nominated members, Mangope controlled 90 of the 96 seats when the Legislative Assembly reconvened as the 'National Assembly' on 6 December.

With their crucial control of half the National Assembly members, Tswana chiefs and headmen are obviously vulnerable to political pressure from Mangope's administration. Not only are they paid by the administration, but under the Bantu Homelands Constitution Act are also appointed and dismissed by it.[45] So it was not altogether surprising that all but one of the members nominated by the traditional leaders supported Mangope.

The Opposition complained about the way in which the dice had been loaded against it in the popular elections as well. These were conducted under regulations laid down by Proclamation R47 of 1977. Clause 39, which deals with illiterate voters, states that these should name candidates of their choice 'by word of mouth' to the polling officer, and that he should put crosses next to the chosen candidates 'in the presence of two witnesses'. In a situation of illiterate electors not having a secret vote in the strict sense of the term and being at least theoretically vulnerable to pressure (even though polling officers are bound to secrecy under the Proclamation), there is no guarantee of elections being free. Since illiterate voters account for at least half of the electorate,[46] the absence of a fully secret vote has serious implications—especially in the context of Proclamation R174 of 1977. Published on 19 August, this extended emergency powers to the Government, including special protection of chiefs and headmen against 'subversive or intimidating statements or actions'. The protection clause made it an offence for Tswanas to treat their chiefs and headmen with 'disrespect, contempt or ridicule'. Special powers were granted to chiefs and headmen to enforce these and other provisions in the Proclamation. Their judicial powers included the right to sentence offenders to a fine of R200 (or four head of large stock or 20 head of small stock), or to imprisonment of up to three months.

As if the extraordinary powers granted chiefs and headmen and the regulations governing illiterate voters were not enough, even further scepticism surrounded the August elections. This related to other special powers which enabled the authorities to ban all meetings unless expressly authorized by the local magistrate; to prohibit any person or categories of persons from entering or leaving defined areas; and to detain people without trial.

The low level of participation in the election raised further questions. Fewer people registered and voted than in 1972, although between the 1970 census and mid-1976, the population had risen by c. 400,000—from c. 1.7m to 2.1m. Relevant figures for the 1972 and 1977 elections respectively were: registered voters—424,000 and 375,000;[47] actual voters—168,023 and 157,273.[48] The poor turnout was more surprising because the number of popularly-elected seats had doubled. Despite 'independence' being the issue at stake, only c. 13% of those eligible actually bothered both to register and vote.[49] At least one plausible reason for this result was that many Tswanas voted against independence 'with their feet'; others may not have voted in the belief that Mangope would win whatever happened.

The articulate opposition to BophuthaTswana's 'independence' functioned outside the Homeland framework and was partly rooted in the Black Consciousness movement.[50] With its slogan of 'One Azania, One Nation', the movement was firmly opposed to the fragmentation of SA into Bantustans. On 23 July 1977, 13 Black Consciousness organizations sent an open letter to Mangope, urging him not to 'sell the souls of his people' by accepting 'independence'.[51] Tacitly acknowledging its unpopularity, Mangope's ruling party did not even organize election rallies in Soweto, despite its large number of Tswana inhabitants. A meeting on the East Rand was cancelled after Mangope and fellow Cabinet members were attacked by stone-throwing youths at Ikageng, a small township near Potchefstroom.

Dr C. J. Maritz's summary of the election issues gives an accurate idea of what those who backed Mangope actually voted for. He wrote: 'Independence would not be brought about at any cost. The BophuthaTswana Democratic Party refused to accept Tswana living in the White areas as citizens, and insisted that they be given the choice of exercising their citizenship.'[52]

THE CABINET (as at 1 April 1978)

President and Minister of Economic Affairs	Chief L. M. Mangope.
Other Ministers:	
Law and Order	T. A. Gaelejwe
Education	M. Setlogelo
Urban Affairs and Land Tenure	D. C. Mokale
Transport, Works and Communication	Chief B. L. M. Motsatsi
Agriculture	Chief E. M. Mokgoko
Internal Affairs	A. M. Kgomongwe
Foreign Affairs	T. M. Molatlhwa
Health and Social Welfare	Dr J. R. Kriel
Deputy Ministers	Chief S. G. Ntuane
	Chief T. V. Makapan
	Chief S. V. Suping
Ex-Officio Member	Expert in Agriculture, H. van Zyl
Speaker	M. S. E. Motshumi
Deputy Speaker	Chief J. E. T. L. Mamogale

Population (1970)

Geographical distribution (thousands)

'White' area	1,108.8
BophuthaTswana	600.2
Lebowa	9.2
KwaZulu	0.4
Venda	0.2
Ciskei	0.1
Transkei	0.1
QwaQwa	0.1
Gazankulu	0.1
Swazi	0.1
Total of Tswana origin	1,719.3

Language

Language groups within BophuthaTswana

Group	% of population
Tswana	67.0
North Sotho	7.4
Shangana	6.3
South Ndebele	3.2
Xhosa	3.1
South Sotho	3.0
Zulu	3.0
Swazi	1.0
Venda	0.6
Other	4.3

ECONOMIC AFFAIRS (1.64 Rand = £1 sterling)

Under the 'independence agreement', from 1978–79 onwards, the South African Minister of Foreign Affairs, in consultation with the Minister of Finance, will pay the following amounts to BophuthaTswana: (1) Amounts equivalent to the taxes and other moneys paid by BophuthaTswana citizens in SA during the year concerned. (2) An amount not exceeding the sum of the amounts appropriated during the 1977–78 financial year by Parliament and the provinces of the Cape, Orange Free State and Transvaal. (3) During the 1978–79 financial year, BophuthaTswana will receive an amount, determined by the Minister of Finance, which will be required to carry on services for which the BophuthaTswana Government becomes responsible on independence, less any revenue accruing from these services. Parliament may appropriate further amounts from the State Revenue Fund for BophuthaTswana state property, including the Post Office, Railways and Harbours Administrations, and the Provincial Administrations of the Cape, Orange Free State and Transvaal, which is used in connection with services for which BophuthaTswana becomes responsible, may be transferred to BophuthaTswana or its nominee.

BophuthaTswana's financial dependence on SA is illustrated by the last 'pre-independence' Budget. Of the total of R72m, R59m or 82% came from SA as against only R13m from within the territory itself.[53] The introduction of new departments after independence, including Foreign Affairs and Defence, has accentuated this dependency, in spite of an agreement to pay BophuthaTswana its share under the Customs Union Agreement. The dependence is not only financial but also economic, which is reflected in several ways. More than 75% of the Tswana labour force is in SA against an overall average of 63.9% of Tswanas who live in SA.[54] As the semi-official Bureau for Economic Research re Bantu Development has noted: 'Of the economically active section of the population (16–64), there is a tremendous flow, particularly of males, to the White area.[55] One consequence is that most of the money earned by Tswanas is spent in SA to the detriment of BophuthaTswana's economic growth potential. Of the total purchasing power of Tswanas of R275m in 1976, only c. R87m, less than 33%, was spent in BophuthaTswana. Commuters (people living in the Homeland but working in SA) and migrant labourers account for nearly two-thirds of the per capita income of R231 a year.[56]

Mangope hopes that platinum mines near Rustenburg will provide part of the answer to his economic problems. But it is not as simple as that. Revenue not available to BophuthaTswana before 'independence' but accruing to it afterwards will be deducted from the money made available by SA. Furthermore, as the noted South African economist, Dr Erich Leistner, has warned, platinum prices are liable to change sharply in response to international demand.[57] The hope of quick solutions will almost certainly prove illusory. Even barring adverse political pressures, BophuthaTswana seems destined to be tied to a long-term economic strategy, particularly in agriculture which—with forestry—accounts for nearly half of the employment in the Homeland.

The first 'post-independence' Budget, presented on 13 March 1978, was set at R180m, an increase of 64% over the previous year.

COMPARISON OF COMPONENTS OF GDP IN 1969–70 AND 1973–74

	1969–70	1973–74
Mining and quarrying contribution, as percentage of total market production	53*	58
Manufacturing contribution as percentage of total market production	2.5	6
All agricultural production as a percentage of total GDP	14	11
'Big' farming as percentage of total agricultural output	11	8

*It declined to 46% in two of the intervening years.

MINING UNDERTAKINGS, 1974

Ore	No. of mines	Total employment	Area
Asbestos	3	533	Ganyesa, Thlaping-Thlaro
Chrome	3	122	Rustenburg, Marico
Granite	8	894	Brits, Marico
Calcite	1	15	Moretele
Limestone	4	438	Taung
Manganese	1	412	Lehurutshe
Platinum	3	58,349	Mankwe, Bafokeng
Vanadium	1	275	Odi
Fluorspar	1	35	Odi

CROP YIELDS 1967–74

		Maize		Wheat	
		dryland	irrigated	dryland	irrigated
1967	bags	4.2	6.9	4.9	18.0
1969	per ha	2.0	8.5	3.2	15.2
1974	tons per ha	0.9	0.4	0.6	1.5

Source (for all tables): The Black Homelands of SA (Pretoria: Malan and Hatting, 1976).

NOTES

(Unless otherwise indicated, all newspapers quoted are South African.)

1. See *Africa Contemporary Record (ACR)* 1976–77, pp. B877–96. For previous references to BophuthaTswana, see all editions of *ACR* 1970–71 to 1976–77.
2. Mangope's independence speech (photostat copy).
3. *Ibid.*
4. Mangope's speech at independence banquet (photostat copy).
5. *Rand Daily Mail (RDM)*, 3 December 1977.
6. *Ibid*, 12 June 1977.
7. Official estimate of Soweto's population by West Rand Administration Board, which administers Soweto.
8. Author's personal notes of Motlana speech, 31 May 1978.
9. M. Horrell, *Legislation and Race Relations* (Johannesburg: SAIRR, 1971), p. 48.
10. Speech delivered by Mangope at Race Relations conference in Cape Town, January 1975 (roneo copy).

11. Quoted in P. Laurence, *Transkei: South Africa's Politics of Partition* (Ravan Press, 1976), p. 74.
12. SAIRR *1973 Survey*, p. 155.
13. Personal interviews by author with Homeland leaders.
14. *RDM*, 5 November 1976.
15. Mangope's speech to the Legislative Assembly (photostat copy).
16. *Ibid.*
17. SAIRR *1976 Survey*, p. 249.
18. *RDM*, 2 August 1976.
19. *Ibid.*
20. SA House of Assembly Debates, No 10, 1978; cols 4389–4401.
21. *Africa Institute Bulletin*, Vol 15 Nos 9–10 (1977), p. 268.
22. *RDM*, 7 December 1978.
23. Republic of BophuthaTswana Constitution Act, Chapter 2, Clause 9.
24. *SA Journal of African Affairs*, Vol 7 (1977), p. 176.
25. For Constitution, see *ACR* 1976–77, pp. C117–140.
26. Laurence, *op cit* p. 123.
27. See *ACR* 1976–77, p. B824.
28. *RDM*, 29 June 1976.
29. *RDM*, 2 August 1976.
30. South African House of Assembly Debates, Vol 77, 1977; cols 8684 and 8685.
31. *Ibid*, col 8691.
32. Personal interview by author with one of BophuthaTswana's legal advisers.
33. *RDM*, 2 July 1977.
34. *Ibid*, 4 July 1977.
35. SAIRR *1977 Survey*, p. 227.
36. *RDM*, 17 September 1977.
37. *Die Transvaler*, 12 October 1977.
38. *RDM*, 12 October 1977.
39. M. Horrell, *The African Homelands* (SAIRR, 1973), p. 37.
40. South African House of Assembly Debates, Vol 77, 1977; col 8635.
41. See *ACR* 1976–77, p. B824.
42. Author's copy of a 'secret agreement' between BophuthaTswana and QwaQwa.
43. *RDM*, 12 May 1977.
44. *SA Journal of African Affairs*, Vol 7, No 2 (1977), p. 195.
45. Interview by author with liaison officer of Department of Bantu Administration.
46. SAIRR *1971 Survey*, p. 264.
47. *RDM*, 16 August 1977.
48. *African Institute Bulletin*, Vol 15, Nos 9–10 (1977).
49. *RDM*, 2 September 1977.
50. See chapter on SA: 'SA vs Black Consciousness'.
51. *RDM*, 25 July 1977.
52. *RDM*, 3 December 1977.
53. *Africa Institute Bulletin*, Vol 15, Nos 9–10 (1977), p. 247.
54. *BophuthaTswana Economic Revue*, (Benbo, 1973), p. 23.
55. *Ibid.*
56. *African Institute Bulletin*, Vol 15, Nos 9–10 (1977), p. 270.
57. *Ibid*, p. 49.

Transkei

The tensions and frustrations inherent in Transkei's unique position—as SA's first 'independent' Homeland Republic, recognized by no country except SA—finally exploded in April 1978, having simmered and boiled by turn throughout 1977. On 10 April, the Chief Minister, Kaiser Matanzima announced his Government's decision to break diplomatic relations with Pretoria and gave South African diplomats less than a month to leave. At the same time he threatened to sustain a 'passive war' against SA. Typically perhaps, the precipitating issue was Matanzima's demand that the enclave of East Griqualand (see map below), which now separates two areas of Transkei, should be given to his Homeland instead of being transferred from the Cape Province to Natal, as Pretoria proposed. The Xhosa nationalist ambitions of the Chief Minister and his brother, George, are acknowledged as perhaps the principal determinant in their policies; both dream of uniting all Xhosa-speaking people in an independent Black state between the Fish river and the Kei. East Griqualand represents one piece of the lands yet to be encompassed before the dream can become reality.

That it was this land issue which precipitated the break is a measure of the continuing dominance in Transkei politics of the Matanzima brothers. Throughout 1977, there were other issues of extreme importance—in principle and practice—concerning the consequences of Transkei's claims to independence upon which the government clashed repeatedly and unsuccessfully with the South Africans; but none of these was seen as warranting a complete break. Basically this reflects the difference between two tendencies in Transkei's governing élite: those who see the fulfilment of Xhosa nationalism as the most vital aspect and aim of the territory's 'independence', and those whose ultimate objective is political freedom for all Blacks in the South African Republic.

For those more preoccupied by Black than Xhosa nationalism, the two most important issues over which Transkei fought and lost during 1977 were the related questions of South African citizenship and the treatment of Transkei nationals in the South African Republic. No concessions were made by SA on the citizenship issue;[1] this meant that the South African authorities continued to treat all Blacks whom *they* regarded of Transkeian origin as citizens of that country, ignoring Transkei's directive that no one could be forced to take Transkei nationality against his will. For example, when the South African authorities destroyed squatter townships near Cape Town (see SA chapter: Population Removals), they expelled all Blacks whom they chose to regard as Transkeians, regardless of whether they had opted for citizenship. For its part, Transkei could only object to the precipitate timing of the operation, which it claimed gave no opportunity to make provision for the reception of the displaced persons. The hard truth, which the Transkei government was to learn, was that the South African government is in a position to enforce its interpretation of the citizenship law, regardless of the policies stated by Umtata.

The other issue—the status of Transkeians in SA—was equally decisively settled by Pretoria on its own terms; it simply made no meaningful concessions. Transkei took the position that as an independent State, its citizens were entitled to the same rights as those of any other independent State, including exemption from the pass laws and the right to buy property. However, SA regards Transkei citizens in the same light as those of Lesotho, Botswana or any other neighbouring *African* State, who are subject to all of SA's racial laws.

Transkei's greatest disappointment to date has been its failure to make any progress in breaking down the international boycott of non-recognition. Some countries—notably in Western Europe and Africa—allowed Transkei ministers and officials entry on Transkei passports; but others, including Botswana, turned back Transkei passport-holders. Despite a series of international visits and much eloquent advocacy on the part of Foreign Minister Digby Koyana, recognition remained out of reach—even after Transkei's break ith SA. (Suggestions that this was merely a plot between Umtata and Pretoria to win OAU recognition show little understanding of the real temper of the Transkei leaders.) The UN and the OAU remained adamant in their advocacy that Transkei should be shunned by the international community. The South African Department of Information report to parliament in February 1978 disclosed that it had spent R500,000 on an advertising campaign in support of Transkei's independence.[2] Among the less obvious consequences was Transkei's exclusion from world sport—and hence its total isolation in this field, since it is no longer eligible to play in SA's provincial sporting leagues.

Transkei's first independence anniversary was celebrated on 26 October 1977 with an address by the Prime Minister in which he spoke to 5,000 Transkeians of his optimism about the country's future. Despite the lack of diplomatic recognition, he said the Department of Foreign Affairs received regular enquiries from companies interested in investing capital, and was 'inundated' with applications for jobs and visas. He promised legislation to repeal all discriminatory laws and disclosed that defence and security would get a big slice of the 1978 Budget.[3] The Transkei's ambassador in Pretoria, Professor Mhaleni Njisane, cancelled a party to celebrate Independence Day on the grounds that many of those he had invited were in prison following the clampdown on the Black Consciousness movement in mid-October. A week before the anniversary, SA's Foreign Minister, Roelof (Pik) Botha, handed over a 76-room Presidential Palace to Transkei's Head of State, Chief Botha Sigcau. Built at a cost of c. R1.8m, it was a gift from the South African Republic.[4]

RELATIONS WITH SOUTH AFRICA
During 1977, Transkei's relations with SA soured steadily over a number of major as well as minor issues. Consulates were established in six South African cities; the consuls were allowed to purchase luxurious homes in White areas and send their children to White schools. But the issues of land and the treatment of Transkeians in SA (see below) created constant open hostility between the two countries. Transkei's ambassador in Pretoria, Mhaleni Njisane, and a minister in the embassy, T. F. Matshob, published strong attacks on the South African government, complaining that in matters relating to Transkei citizens, they still had to deal with the South African Bantu Administration Department instead of with the Ministry of Foreign Affairs. In November, Transkei's official representative in New York, Ngqondi Masimini, supported 'the strongest possible sanctions against SA'.[5] He wrote: 'I must applaud the world's reaction to the recent series of outrages in SA. . . . The Republic of Transkei joins its fellow nations in condemning the brutal action of SA'. However, he went on to make a plea for Transkei's 'separate identity'; otherwise 'the 3m innocent citizens of Transkei would also be punished by world action against SA'. Chief Matanzima immediately denied that Transkei supported sanctions; but Masimini maintained that his letter had been cleared by the Transkei government.

The Finance Minister, Tsepo Letlaka, and the Foreign Minister, Digby Koyana, both criticized the South African government, making it clear that they were aligned with 'other nations opposed to SA's race policies' and with their 'fellow-oppressed' inside SA. One of the leaders of the South African opposition Progressive Federal Party, Harry Schwartz, also came in for bitter criticism by the Matanzima brothers for his suggestion that South African passports should be issued to Transkeians who wanted to travel abroad, since their own passports were not recognized. Speaking in the Assembly, Matanzima said that Transkei had relations with other countries, but 'this fact need not be broadcast for a *herrenvolk* member like Mr Schwartz'. Under no circumstances, he said, would Trankeians travel abroad using South African passports.[6]

Transkei's ambassador to SA, Prof Njisane, said in an interview with the *Sunday Times* (Johannesburg, 1 May 1977) that Transkei would be prepared to surrender its full independence if racial equality were recognized throughout SA. 'Transkei would be prepared, after a negotiated agreement, to enter into a new union or federation of states in which everyone would have equal rights—such as the canton system of Switzerland.' This was the first time that an official Transkeian spokesman had even suggested any retreat from full independence.

Three South Africans practising as naturopaths in Umtata were deported at 24 hours' notice in July 1977. No reasons were given.[7]

When the row with SA came to the boil in March 1978, Chief Matanzima announced that he would invite 'all people of SA to attend a conference of the oppressed [in Umtata] some time this year'. Opening his party's congress, he said Transkei, which was accessible to the outside world from all directions, was looking to the West for assistance, but if that was not forthcoming 'we will turn to the Middle East and even to the Far East'.[8]

Earlier, when the South African Prime Minister paid an official visit to Transkei in January 1977, it was announced that the two Governments would periodically hold meetings to discuss matters of mutual concern. In mid-September, Chief Matanzima paid an official return visit to SA after which he said that his talks with Vorster had been frank and 'brutal at times'.

THE LAND ISSUE: BREAK OF RELATIONS

As early as March 1977, the Prime Minister gave a warning of the importance to his Government's relations with SA of the 'return of Transkei lands'. Opening the annual congress of the ruling Transkei National Independence Party (TNIP), he said: 'It is my hope that there will be a negotiated settlement on this issue as I shudder to contemplate the consequences of the only alternative method of settlement—an armed struggle.' He referred not only to East Griqualand but to the districts between Port Edward and Port Shepstone, as well as Harding in Natal, and Elliot and Maclear in the Eastern Cape. The call was taken up in an emergency debate in the Assembly at the end of March. The leader of the Opposition, Cromwell Diko, joined in threatening desperate consequences, including a request to the Russians for arms and assistance 'if the land issue is not settled'.[9] The Opposition supported a Government resolution calling for the unilateral annexation of the Ciskei to make a complete Xhosa 'Homeland'.[10]

The Steyn Committee of Inquiry into the East Griqualand Issue recommended in May 1977 that for the sake of administrative convenience, the area should be transferred to Natal. Ever since Union, it has formed part of the Cape Province. Repeated representations and threats from Umtata resulted only in the cryptic South African response that it 'did not share Transkei's views', but that it was studying the documents in support of their claim. In April 1978, a Bill was adopted by the South African Parliament effecting the transfer of the district from the Cape to Natal, thus precipitating the break. East Griqualand contains c. 7,000 Whites, who asked for the transfer to Natal; c. 6,000 Coloureds, the original 'Griqua' inhabitants of the area, who argued against the transfer since they fear an influx of Indians from Natal, who are barred from the Cape; and c. 40,000 Xhosas, who supported the Transkei government's claim.[11]

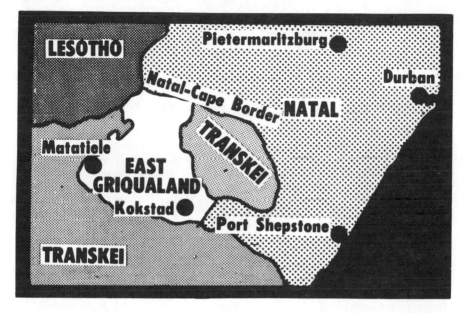

The text of Transkei's statement 'severing all diplomatic relations' with SA on 10 April 1978 read in part as follows: 'The reason for this grave step is that SA has just enacted legislation transferring districts collectively known as East Griqualand to the Natal Province of SA. East Griqualand was an integral part of the Transkei while it was a British territory, along with the other British protectorates now known as Swaziland, Lesotho and Botswana. In 1910, without the consent of the people of Transkei, their country was handed over to the Union of South Africa. In 1976, when Transkei negotiated its complete independence from SA, they made it abundantly clear that the territorial integrity of their boundaries must be restored. Despite protracted negotiations, the Republic of SA unilaterally decided to ignore this fact.'

Chief Matanzima followed up this announcement with a threatening statement: 'We shall now launch a passive war against this action of the South African government to strongly show our objection and demonstrate to the world that this territory must be restored to our country.'

CITIZENSHIP AND TREATMENT OF TRANSKEI NATIONALS

There was considerable confusion throughout 1977 about the status both of Transkei citizens who wished to remain in SA, and about urban Xhosa-speaking people who did not wish to become Transkei citizens and who had previously attained the status necessary for permission to remain in an urban area under the Bantu Urban Areas Act of 1945. The Transkei government claimed that its citizenship would not be forced on anyone who did not voluntarily seek it. However, cases constantly came to light of Xhosa-speakers—some of them with links to the

Ciskei rather than Transkei—being compelled by South African officials to apply for Transkei citizenship when they applied for reference (pass) books, without which no African can live and work in SA. Transkei's ambassador to SA said that Transkei documents would not be issued to people who were being forced to apply for them.[12] Questioned about cases documented by Black Sash and other organizations, the South African authorities claimed first that Xhosa-speakers were not being refused South African reference books and work-seekers' permits,[13] and later that cases brought to its attention by the Transkei authorities were being investigated. The plight of SA's Xhosa-speakers was summed up by Leslie Xinwa, a columnist on the *Daily Despatch* (14 January 1977). Referring to the case of an African born in Johannesburg who became unemployed and was forced 'back' to the Transkei (with which he had no links), Xinwa wrote: 'The attitude of the Transkei government . . . is that their law makes citizenship open to those who want it. But the law that empowered Transkei to be an independent state included the very citizenship issue that is forcing Blacks who do not know where Transkei is to be members of a state they do not know. . . .'

The treatment of Transkeian citizens resident in the Republic was the subject of equally confusing claims and counter-claims. Prof Njisane told the *Sunday Times* (20 February 1977) that a meeting between Transkei and South African Cabinet Ministers the week before had agreed to grant Transkei citizens the same status as White aliens. 'We were assured they would no longer fall under the regulations of the Department of Bantu Administration, but like White aliens, would be the concern of the Departments of Foreign Affairs and the Interior. The report was immediately denied by the Minister for Community Development, Marais Steyn. The Department's deputy-secretary, V. Schoeman, said the *Sunday Times* report had been irresponsible and added: 'There is no difference in the position of Transkeians and that of persons in Soweto. It cannot possibly be otherwise.' Despite these denials, no ministry was actually prepared to spell out the Republic's policy towards Transkei citizens. By implication, however, it became increasingly clear that SA intends to continue applying all its racial laws to them. Thus, arrests under the pass laws continued, and those in breach of the laws were sent to Transkei as though it were just one of the other Homelands. Prof Njisane complained that 'no privileges have come with independence, and that people are not given any real incentives to become Transkei citizens'.[14] This complaint was borne out by a spokesman for the Bantu Administration Department who pointed out that in the pre-independence agreements between SA and Transkei, it was stipulated that Transkeians working in the Republic would be 'subject to the prevailing laws of SA'.[15] Chief Matanzima always denied this, but SA's interpretation has nevertheless prevailed.

During the latter part of 1977, when large numbers of people were cleared from squatter camps in the Cape, the Bantu Administration Department announced that some of these people would be 'repatriated' to Transkei. Its Foreign Minister, Digby Koyana angrily rejected 'the concept of people being dumped in an independent Transkei at the whim of the South African government'. He warned that the basis for friendship between Transkei and SA was fast diminishing and added that if the squatters were 'repatriated', there would be a 'confrontation between the two governments'. In fact, the great majority of the Black squatters were sent back to Transkei, though many immediately returned illegally. Prof Njisane said in September that his government did not have the resources to house or provide work for a large influx of squatters, and that Transkei's rulers were beginning to doubt the wisdom of having opted for independence.[16] The following day, he sent a telegram to the Department of Foreign Affairs calling for its intervention to stop harassment of squatters. Three days later, he still had no reply and commented that the South African authorities had never even contacted his government on the squatter issue. [17]

POLITICAL AFFAIRS
Paramount Chief Kaiser Matanzima's ruling Transkei National Independence Party (TNIP) maintained its overall majority in the National Assembly. But in March 1977, its Chief Whip, Pascoe Ludidi, crossed the floor to join the Opposition. A month later, he was reported to have sought asylum in Lesotho because he feared detention. [18] The Transkei People's Freedom Party (TPFP) formed by Cromwell Diko, another defector from the TNIP, was recognized as the official Opposition, though it had fewer members in the Assembly than the Democratic Party. The first congress of the TPFP collapsed when it was attended by only three people. [19] The Democratic Party leader, Hector Ncokazi, and officials of his party repeatedly came into conflict with the authorities and were imprisoned (see Detainees, below). The Democratic Party's constitution was changed to omit its previous opposition to Transkei's independence (the new security law making such opposition treasonable). [20] However, in January 1977—before the new laws were mooted—Ncokazi called on the UN to impose economic sanctions against SA to bring about political change, and praised the UN and the OAU for their opposition to SA's Homelands policy. [21] Cromwell Diko also described Transkei's independence as 'a sham', because 'Transkeians in possession of citizenship documents are treated like slaves in SA'. [22]

Several political activists in addition to Pascoe Ludidi were reported to have left Transkei as refugees in 1977. They included a medical practitioner, Dr J. Mlandu, who asked for asylum in Lesotho in July. In May, there were reports that several school children opposed to Transkei independence had arrived in Botswana as refugees.

On 7 September, the first multi-racial elections to be held in Transkei took place when towns throughout the Homeland elected councils. In most of the larger towns, multi-racial councils were elected. In Umtata, a group of five Whites and five Africans running as a team won the ten seats. Early predictions that Port St Johns would elect an all-White council proved incorrect when an African woman (the only woman to stand) won one of the six seats. In Idutywa four Africans and four Whites were elected, and in Engcobo six Whites and two Africans. Percentage polls were quite high—65% in Engcobo, 54% in Idutywa, but a low 30.5% in Umtata.

Stella Sigcau, daughter of the Transkei's President, resigned her post as Minister of the Interior in November 1977. Her resignation had reportedly been demanded by the Prime Minister because she was pregnant, though unmarried. [23] H. Pamla, former Deputy-Minister of Health, was given her post, and was in turn replaced by Chief T. D. T. Ndamase. Although Ndamase comes from the same Pondo area as the dismissed minister, 16 members of the ruling party crossed the floor after her resignation.

A former Pan-Africanist Congress (PAC) member, Ngqondi Masimini, returned to Transkei using the good offices of the Transkei government to transit across SA. On his return, Masimini said: 'We only hear about Transkei from SA and this source is immediately rejected. . . . When Transkei is given a chance to put its own case, its independence will be viewed differently.' Masimini works in the US and is married to an American, but said he was considering settling in Transkei. (Both the Minister of Finance, Tsepo Letlaka, and Transkei's ambassador in Pretoria, Mhaleni Njisane, were also former prominent leaders of the PAC.)

DEFENCE AND SECURITY

In May 1977, the Prime Minister announced the introduction of a voluntary six-month national service scheme aimed at building up a reserve force, adding that a five-year development plan for the army was already in operation. At the end of July, the first 54 volunteers began their basic training. In January 1978, Transkei ordered the 27 South African army advisers attached to Transkei's 320-strong army to leave the country. No reasons, or any time limit, were announced. (There was speculation that the move was the result of Transkei's quarrel with SA over the demolition of shanty areas in Cape Town and the repatriation of squatters.) In announcing the expulsion of the army advisers, Chief Matanzima said that Transkeians needing training would thenceforth get it outside the Transkei, but he did not say where. He added that Transkei would continue to depend on SA for its supply of arms. [24]

LAWS

During the first sitting of the Transkeian National Assembly, two controversial laws concerning security were passed. The first was the Transkei Public Security Act which repealed all security laws applicable in SA (including the Suppression of Communism Act, the Internal Security Act, the Riotous Assemblies Act, the Unlawful Organizations Act, and also the Transkei Emergency Laws contained in Proclamation R400). However, many of the measures provided for in these Acts are incorporated in the new legislation. In terms of this Act, 1) anyone propagating or disseminating views that Transkei, or parts of Transkei, should form another country or part of another country, will be guilty of a treasonable offence and liable to penalties ranging from five years' imprisonment to the death sentence. (Originally, Chief Matanzima stated that this clause would be retrospective to 26 October 1976, but this is not in fact the case.) 2) It is an offence to harbour or help terrorists, the maximum penalty being death. 3) It is an offence to make statements or commit acts causing hostility between population groups. 4) It is an offence to belong to certain organizations declared unlawful by the State President. 5) The State President may authorize a chief to banish any person to another area, either permanently or for a specified period. 6) He may order a tribe or part of a tribe to be removed, without warning, to another area if he considers it to be in the public interest. 7) The Minister of Justice may ban gatherings of more than ten people, prevent individuals from attending certain gatherings and declare a State of Emergency if he deems it necessary. 8) Provision is made for the banning of persons, for detention without trial, and for the arrest without warrant of any person for interrogation purposes, after which arrest there may be no recourse to the courts to obtain the release of such person.

The Opposition leader, Cromwell Diko, opposition politicians in SA and legal experts all sharply criticized these security measures, warning that they could only further harm Transkei's tenuous international position. The legislation nevertheless went through virtually unchanged. Only one clause which maintained the banning of organizations prohibited in SA (including the ANC and PAC) was dropped: the Minister of Justice, Chief George Matanzima, said that the reason for this was that it would be inappropriate for an independent Transkei to continue the actions of SA.

The second controversial piece of legislation was the Intelligence Service and State Security Council Act which provides for the establishment of the Transkei Intelligence Service (TIS). This will take over the functions and duties of SA's Bureau of State Security and be directly responsible to the Prime Minister. Its functions are to collect and evaluate information relating to national security, and to detect, identify and advise the Prime Minister of any threat or potential threat to the security of Transkei. The Act will operate under a special Intelligence Service Account, which will be determined and directed by the Prime Minister and will be confidential. The Act also provides for the establishment of a State Security Council, which will formulate national policy and strategy with regard to the security of Transkei.

The Transkei Publications Act provides for censorship committees appointed by the Department of the Interior from a list of suitably qualified people. These committees will check the infiltration of undesirable literature, films and public entertainments. The Minister of the Interior said that it was intended to uphold the Christian convictions of the Transkeian people.

A motion proposed by a Government MP, H. Kentane, calling for the repeal of the Immorality Act, was passed in the National Assembly, although legislation to this effect was not introduced. Some months later, a White man and an African woman were married in a civil ceremony, apparently in the belief that the Immorality and Mixed Marriages Acts had been repealed in Transkei. Although the marriage was technically illegal, as these Acts are still on the statute book of Transkei, the Commissioner of Police, Brig E. Cwele, said that infringements of the two laws had been deliberately ignored since the passing of the above-mentioned motion and in accordance with Transkei's stated policy of non-racialism. [25]

EXTRADITION

An extradition agreement was signed between Umtata and Pretoria in December 1977. This contains a proviso covering political offenders whose extradition may be refused; excluded altogether are those offences under military law which are not offences under ordinary criminal law. [26]

MAGISTRATES

The Minister of Justice, Dr George Matanzima, disclosed in October that White officials seconded from SA comprise half the number of magistrates in Transkei's 28 districts. He said that the tempo of training local magistrates would have to be accelerated. [27]

DETAINEES

A number of officials of the opposition Democratic Party arrested before independence were released in February 1977. They included P. S. Fadana, a former Robben Island prisoner, who immediately held a Press conference and made a spirited attack on the Transkei government. 'Nobody,' he said, can change my ideas by putting me in prison; only a bullet can do that.' He stated that none of the detainees had been charged with a crime, and claimed they had only been detained to keep them out of the way during the elections. [28] He also said that the opposition's predictions about Transkei's independence making many Xhosas stateless had been proved right. A few weeks later, he was again detained.

Hector Ncokazi, the leader of the Democratic Party (see above), was also released. In a more cautious statement, he said that his party's policy on Transkei's independence might have to be re-examined 'in view of impending legislation'—a reference to the Public Security Act which makes it a treasonable offence to question Transkei's independent status. [29] Ncokazi was also re-detained in August along with another nine opposition officials, but all were released in October after having 'answered all questions put to them satisfactorily', according to the head of the security police, Major M. Ngceba. Ncokazi said he had been asked to write a letter of apology to the Minister of Justice: 'I told him in no uncertain terms that I would never apologize to a politician.'[39] In January 1978, after stating that Transkei was 'cursed with the worst government in the history of mankind', Ncokazi was again arrested under the new security laws. If charged, his remarks could be construed as treason and as such carry the death penalty.'[31]

A member of the Transkei Assembly and a headman, James Dinizulu, was sentenced to 180 days in prison for extortion and assault on two of his 'subjects'.[32]

THE GOVERNMENT (as at 1 June 1978)

Head of State	Paramount Chief Botha Sigcau
Prime Minister, Minister of Defence and Public Services	Chief Kaiser Daliwonga Matanzima
Deputy-Premier, Minister of Justice, Police and Prisons	Chief George Matanzima
Other Ministers:	
Finance	Tsepo T. Letlaka
Foreign Affairs	Digby Koyana*
Commerce, Industry and Tourism	Ramsay Madikizela
Interior and Social Services	H. Pamla
Local Government and Land Tenure	Chief George Ndabankulu
Posts and Telecommunications and Transport	Armstrong Jonas
Education	Walker Silas Mbanga
Health and Welfare	Rev Gladwin Vika
Agriculture and Forestry	Saul Ndzumo
Public Works and Energy	Herbert Mlonyeni
Deputy Ministers:	
Agriculture and Forestry	E. Z. Booi
Health	Chief T. D. T. Ndamase
Education	Mr Kakudi

* Koyana was made Minister of Justice in July 1978.

SOCIAL AFFAIRS

The Prime Minister threatened in January 1978 to 'take over' the Methodist Church in Transkei, breaking its links with the Methodist Church of SA and forming an independent Transkei entity. His action was prompted by a report that some clergy at the Church's annual conference had been unhappy about recognizing Transkei's independence.

The Foreign Minister announced in November that 'Arabs and Indians' would be welcome to settle in Transkei. Representatives of Indian organizations in SA, including the teachers' association, welcomed the move. For the first time, Indians will be able to own property in Transkei if they become citizens.

A Transkei attorney and former Robben Island prisoner, Louis Mtshizana, was told in an Orange Free State hotel that he would have to eat in the kitchen as the dining room was for Whites only. The Prime Minister was himself asked to leave a White cafe while travelling with his entourage in the northern Cape; but he refused to move until he was served with the meal he had ordered.

The three children of the Minister of Finance, T. T. Letlaka, were admitted to the formerly Whites-only Umtata High School, which is run by the Cape Provincial Administration by mutual agreement between the governments of Transkei and SA. Several primary schools, previously all-White began to admit Black children in 1977.

(For population, see chapter on SA: Population.)

FOREIGN RELATIONS
RELATIONS WITH LESOTHO
Transkei continued to deny Lesotho's accusation, first made in December 1976, that the border between the two countries had been closed. [33] When a UN delegation went to Maseru in January 1977 to examine Lesotho's aid needs in the light of the 'border closure', it did not respond to a letter from Transkei's Foreign Minister asking that the border closure claim be thoroughly explored and that the mission visit Transkei as well. [34] Digby Koyana led an official party to the border when the UN team was due to visit there, but it failed to turn up. [35] In October 1977, the Prime Minister of Lesotho stated that parts of Transkei 'belonged' to his country—a claim angrily dismissed by Matanzima who taunted Chief Jonathan with having no right to speak for Lesotho since he had not even been elected. (This was a reference to the 1970 Lesotho elections which Chief Jonathan's ruling party was alleged to have lost, after which the Constitution was torn up.)

SOUTHERN AFRICAN CUSTOMS AREA
Transkei was not formally admitted to the Southern African Customs Area or to the Rand Monetary Area Commission, because Lesotho, Swaziland and Botswana have all refused to recognize its independent statehood. [36] Nevertheless, it is treated by SA as though it were a member of both organizations.

ATTITUDE OF THE OAU
A Transkei delegation which flew to Libreville in June 1977 in an attempt to get a hearing at the OAU conference was prevented from entering Gabon. The OAU repeated its call for all States to refuse to recognize Transkei or any other Bantustan declared independent by the Pretoria regime.

ACTIVITIES IN THE UNITED STATES
N. Masimini arrived in Washington in July 1977 to represent Transkei in the US as 'Minister-at-large'. Although he achieved registration as a 'foreign agent', the US government made it clear (through its consul in Durban) that this did not imply recognition of Transkei, but was simply a legal requirement of the Department of Justice which registered all lobbyists for foreign interests. Masimini lived in Washington, not as a Transkei government official, but as a resident alien married to a US citizen.

OTHER FOREIGN RELATIONS
An official delegation from Ecuador visited Transkei in April 1977. Its leader, Vice-Admiral Aurelio Maldonado Mino, delivered a message from the Ecadorian President which expressed the hope that Transkei's 'crusade for sovereignty' would receive 'deserved and just support'. He also invited Chief Matanzima to visit Ecuador, but discussions between the two governments did not lead to any official links.

A Transkei delegation visited Taiwan in May 1977 to discuss possible diplomatic links; but although Taiwan expressed willingness to co-operate on practical matters, official recognition was not forthcoming.

France's veteran Right-wing leader, Prof Jacques Soustelle, visited Transkei briefly during a tour of SA. After meeting the Prime Minister and his Cabinet, he announced that he was impressed with the region's development and would put more pressure on his government to recognize Transkei. [37]

Although Transkei has failed to achieve diplomatic recognition, it did win a measure of foreign economic co-operation (see below).

ECONOMIC AFFAIRS (1.60 Rand = £1 sterling)

Before the break in diplomatic relations with SA, Transkei had negotiated its annual grant of R113.5m (£70.9m), which constitutes over a third of the 1978 Budget. This grant has remained constant over the past two years. The Transkei's other substantial foreign earning comes from the South African Customs Union. One of the greatest weaknesses of the Transkei is that although essentially a pastoral society, according to official figures it needs to import 90% of its food from SA. (For a fuller survey of the structure of Transkei's economy, see *ACR* 1976–77, pp. B891–94).

The debate about the Homeland's economic viability continues. Dr G. M. E. Leistner, director of the Africa Institute of SA, pointed to the extreme seriousness of Transkei's unemployment problem. Between 1973 and 1975, 84.5% of those entering the labour market for the first time had to choose, in his words, between 'unemployment and migration', Prof Newell M. Stultz of Brown University (R.I.) also emphasized that chronic mass unemployment is a central economic fact of Transkei.[38] The symbiotic work/labour relationship admittedly had benefits for both SA and Transkei, but not equal benefits. '. . . Unlike SA herself, Transkei cannot put all or even most of her own people to work when they leave the field of subsistence agriculture—which from the standpoint of unemployment has long been fully saturated.' According to Stultz, Transkei's domestic income has never accounted for more than 24.2% of annual revenues; the balance has come from Pretoria, varying from 61.9% of total income in 1965–66 to a high of 77.4% in 1974–75.

1978 BUDGET

The Transkei's second Budget, presented in April 1978, provides for an increase of one-third in government spending over the previous year, from R205m to R240m. Over R100m represents the immediate cost of capital spending in the current year, mainly on roads and bridges (R23m), industrial projects (R20m), agriculture and forestry (R17.3m), the new university (R10m) and administrative buildings (R8m).

Plans for immediate development include R34m for an integrated health scheme, R20m for four housing projects and R8m for airport extensions. The most ambitious programme is the Mngazana harbour and free port, the first stage of which will cost c. R125m (see below).

FOREIGN INVESTMENT

In the course of his Budget speech in April 1978, the Finance Minister said that the Government had succeeded in securing international loan funds for its long-term investments. In addition to the South African grant of R113.5m, he was budgeting for a deficit of R96.8m, which would be raised on the international capital markets. Although he gave no further details, unconfirmed reports from Transkei said a loan for £100m (R167m) was negotiated with 'a pool of overseas investors' through a US brokerage firm.[39]

Transkei raised a R16m loan on the South African capital market in October 1977 despite predictions of failure (since backing by the South African government would have been 'constitutionally improper'). The loan was marginally oversubscribed at a rate substantially higher than for those loans backed by SA.[40]

A French company, *Grand Travaux de Marseilles*, was contracted to carry out preliminary investigations into the development of Transkei's proposed free port at the Mngazana river mouth; c. 20 km south of Port St Johns. Chief Matanzima announced that a commercial and industrial town would be developed around the harbour.

An American company, the Intermagnetics Corporation of America, planned to build a R1m plant at Umtata in conjunction with the Transkei Development Corporation (TDC). The plant was expected to commence production in February 1978 and manufacture 20m tape cassettes a year. The American company intended buying 70% of the output.

Two Black American lobbyists, Andrew Hatcher and Jay Parker, were engaged in trying to persuade American businessmen to invest in Transkei. Hatcher announced in January 1978 that some textile companies were showing an interest.

A feasibility study for large expansion of the timber and pulp industry in Transkei is being undertaken by a Johannesburg firm of consultants. The project would involve considerable afforestation, a new pulp mill and a railway. Iran was reported to have shown an interest in financing the pulp mill.[41]

INDUSTRY

There are now 18 industries in Umtata, whose population has grown from 21,000 to 33,000 in seven years.[42] Some 12,500 Transkeians are employed in industry throughout the Homeland. Of the R97m invested in industrial development, R37.5m derived from 'SA and foreign investors', while the rest came from the Transkei Development Corporation. The R13m contract for the first phase of the new Transkei University outside Umtata was awarded to the SA company, Murray and Stewart. Other large contracts due to be awarded are for the construction of a new hospital, several hydroelectric schemes, large housing developments and new sewerage and water services for Umtata.

COMMUNICATIONS

Transkei Airways was inaugurated in February 1978 and will run regular services between Umtata and Johannesburg.

NOTES

(Unless otherwise stated, all papers quoted are South African.)

1. See *Africa Contemporary Record (ACR)* 1976–77, pp. B881–83.
2. The *Star*, 18 February 1978.
3. *Rand Daily Mail (RDM)*, 27 October 1977.
4. *Africa Research Bulletin (ARB)*, Exeter; 1–31 October 1977.
5. In a letter to the *New York Times*, 8 November 1977.
6. The *Star*, 26 March 1977.
7. *Ibid*, 2 July 1977.
8. *Ibid*, 18 March 1978.
9. *Daily Telegraph*, London; 31 March 1977.
10. The *Star*, 26 March 1977.
11. *RDM*, 19 May 1977.
12. *Ibid*, 8 January 1977.
13. South African National Assembly 1977 *Hansard*, No 3, col 186.
14. *Sunday Times*, London; 30 January 1977.
15. *RDM*, 31 January 1977.
16. The *Star*, 9 September 1977.
17. *RDM*, 14 September 1977.
18. *1977 Survey of Race Relations* (Johannesburg: South African Institute of Race Relations).
19. *RDM*, 7 March 1977.
20. *Ibid*, 2 June 1977.
21. *Ibid*, 4 January 1977.
22. *Daily Despatch*, 21 February 1977.
23. *Sunday Times*, 13 November 1977.
24. *Daily Telegraph*, 23 January 1978.

25. *RDM*, 19 August 1977.
26. *ARB*, 1–31 December 1977.
27. *RDM*, 6 October 1977.
28. *Daily News*, 12 February 1977.
29. *RDM*, 26 February 1977.
30. *RDM*, 20 October 1977.
31. *The Guardian*, Manchester; 24 January 1978.
32. *RDM*, 12 December 1977.
33. See *ACR* 1976–77, p. B755–58.
34. *Daily Despatch*, 8 February 1977.
35. *Daily News*, 3 February 1977.
36. *Daily Despatch*, 19 February 1977.
37. SA Broadcasting Corporation, 5 July 1977.
38. Africa Institute, *Bulletin* (No 6 and 7) 1977.
39. *Financial Times*, London; 20 April 1978.
40. *RDM*, 17 October 1977.
41. *Sunday Tribune*, 20 February 1977.
42. The *Star*, 20 August 1977.

PART III:

Namibia

Namibia

The prolonged crisis over Namibia's independence reached a crucial and probably final stage during 1977 and early 1978, with a combination of major political developments.[1] These included intensive Western and African diplomatic activity designed to secure an internationally acceptable settlement; SA's agreement to a decolonization formula involving the holding of national elections with Swapo participation and the appointment of an Administrator-General to co-operate with the UN during the interim period leading to elections; growing internal tension and serious outbreaks of violence between supporters of rival Namibian political parties; and a considerable escalation of the 12-year guerrilla war waged by Swapo across Namibia's northern border from its bases in Angola; finally, in late July 1978, the Security Council adopted the Western plan for the territory's independence, after both Swapo and SA had separately approved the proposals. However, SA was angered by a separate resolution declaring Walvis Bay to be an integral part of Namibia.

POLITICAL AFFAIRS
NEGOTIATIONS FOR A SETTLEMENT
Although SA suspended its attempt unilaterally to implement an 'internal settlement' as proposed by the Turnhalle Constitutional Conference,[2] it remained deeply opposed to the possible emergence of a radical, Swapo-controlled government in Windhoek, which it perceived as a threat to its own strategic security and economic interests. However, the Vorster regime proved willing to co-operate with the diplomatic initiative launched in April 1977 by the five Western members of the UN Security Council—Britain, Canada, France, West Germany and the US—who formed the so-called Contact Group to negotiate bilaterally with SA and Swapo. Although not a formal UN initiative, the Western powers based their diplomacy on the unanimous Security Council resolution of January 1976 (385) which had called for the holding of national elections under UN supervision and control, and the withdrawal of SA's military forces from the territory.[3] This was an important factor in gaining the support of the five Front-line African States for the initiative, as well as of Nigeria, whose support was increasingly viewed by Western policy-makers as crucial. Although suspicious of Western motives and anxious about any possible undermining of its status as the 'sole authentic representative of the Namibian people' (as established by the UN General Assembly in 1973), Swapo's external leadership also agreed to co-operate. It calculated that the major trading partners of SA could bring real pressure to bear on Pretoria to move towards acceptance of UN resolutions on Namibia; it was also urged to participate by the Front-line Presidents.

The Contact Group or 'Gang of Five', as it came to be known (affectionately by friends, scornfully to Pretoria), was led by Don McHenry, a Black American diplomat on the US Mission to the UN who had previously made a study of the role of American firms in the Republic.[4] Its first visit to SA and Namibia was made in April 1977 and by mid-year the outline of a possible compromise formula had emerged. SA reluctantly concluded that a Turnhalle Interim Government—based on the ethnic, three-tier constitutional structure agreed in March 1977—would stand no chance of external recognition. No less important was the collective stand on the issue by all the major Western powers including France and West Germany.

181

Although the Republic's military hierarchy remained confident of its ability to repel a major Swapo offensive, even if this involved conventional military support from Cuban forces in Angola, SA clearly understood that it would receive no diplomatic protection from the Western powers against possible moves by the Security Council to widen sanctions. Both Pretoria and Swapo were anxious about the size and location of a residual South African military presence in the period preceding elections for independence. Other stumbling-blocks to agreement were the status of Walvis Bay, Namibia's only deep-water port which was not part of the German mandated territory before World War I;[5] the powers of the UN representative; and control over the police during the transition to independence.

In June 1977, following a third round of talks with the Contact Group, Vorster announced that a (Turnhalle) Interim Government would not be established, although he re-emphasized his support for the Turnhalle's policies as being in the best interests of 'the peoples of South West Africa'. Instead, he declared SA's intention to appoint an Administrator-General to head the civil administration in Namibia during an interim period leading to elections in time for the scheduled independence date of 31 December 1978. On 6 July, Judge Marthinus Steyn (57) was named to the post, with effect from 31 August 1977. Under the SWA Constitution Act passed in June 1977, he was provided with power, subject to the ultimate authority of the South African State President, to repeal or amend existing South African legislation in force in the territory, as well as assume responsibility for the range of governmental activities controlled directly by Ministries in Pretoria since 1969. However, at the same time, Vorster repeated that Walvis Bay and the 12 offshore Penguin Islands were outside the terms of the Western proposals and would remain under South African jurisdiction. On 31 August, Walvis Bay was formally annexed by proclamation in the Government Gazette and again placed under the administration of the Cape Province (as it had been between the 1880s and 1921 when SA assumed its mandate over the territory). Swapo initially opposed Judge Steyn's appointment and denounced the annexation, but under pressure from the Front-line Presidents still continued to negotiate with the Contact Group.

After two further rounds of talks, the Western proposals were finally published in January 1978 and included the following key elements: the cessation of hostilities; the phased withdrawal of the estimated 20,000 South African troops and their replacement by a UN force; the appointment of a UN representative and establishment of a 'neutral' civilian administrator by SA who would jointly organize the holding of 'free and fair' elections by universal suffrage; the repeal of discriminatory legislation and security laws inhibiting free political activity and movement: the release of political prisoners held in Namibia; and the unrestricted return of Namibian exiles to participate fully in the elections.

These proposals formed the agenda of the high-level 'proximity talks' held in New York in early February, attended by South African Foreign Minister R. F. 'Pik' Botha, and a Swapo delegation headed by Sam Nujoma and members of Swapo's internal national executive committee. The talks adjourned after two days following the precipitate withdrawal of the South African Foreign Minister, apparently under the impression that the West was prepared to back Swapo over its demand for the inclusion of Walvis Bay in the future Namibian state. Negotiations were continued at a lower level with both parties, however, and in March a 'final version' of the Western proposals was announced, just prior to the holding of a UN General Assembly special session on Namibia.

The 'Proposal for a Settlement of the Namibia Situation', a 12-paragraph document (reproduced on pp. C211–15), provided for the establishment by the UN Security Council of a UN Transition Assistance Group, UNTAG, composed of civilians and military, to be headed by a UN Special Representative (not named but thought likely to be the UN Commissioner for Namibia, Maarthi Ahtisaari). UNTAG would have the joint task of monitoring both the ceasefire in the guerrilla war and the reduction of South African forces within a 12-week period commencing from its establishment. The South African forces were to be slimmed to 1,500 and stationed in Grootfontein and Oshivello (Ovamboland), while Swapo's forces would be confined to their bases in Angola. The second stage would be a four-month campaign leading to the election of a Namibian Constituent Assembly, with the task of approving an independence constitution for the territory. While existing citizen forces, commandos and ethnic units were to be disarmed, the South African Police were to retain 'primary responsibility' for law and order. The electoral procedures were to be devised jointly by the UN Special Representative and the Administrator-General, with the campaign commencing only after the former had approved of all measures taken. The proposals made no mention of the status of Walvis Bay, but in a covering Note, the Western countries said that this was an issue that should be negotiated bilaterally between an independent Namibia and SA. UN sources predicted that a force of c. 5,000 UN troops and a civilian staff of c. 1,000 would be required.

SA's acceptance of these proposals was announced by Vorster on 25 April 1978, although there were reports of opposition within the South African Cabinet led by P. W. Botha, the Defence Minister, and Connie Mulder, the Minister for Plural Affairs and Information. Vorster stressed that he had found it possible to agree to the proposals only after assurances that there would be no withdrawal of South African troops until the cessation of all hostilities within Namibia, the exclusion of Walvis Bay from the terms of the agreement, and the right of the Administrator-General to remain at the head of the civilian administration until the election of the Constituent Assembly. His claim that the 1,500 troops could remain in Namibia if requested to do so by the Constituent Assembly was denied by Western diplomats who stressed that the South African Army should be withdrawn automatically within one week of the election result. The announcement was widely interpreted as a diplomatic coup for SA, placing the onus for a peaceful settlement on Swapo.

The Swapo leadership had made a number of concessions at the February 1978 talks, particularly in dropping its previous demand for the immediate withdrawal of all South African troops. However, it remained critical of a number of features of the Western proposals, mainly what it regarded as the continuing ambiguity of the precise powers to be exercised by the Special Representative on the ground, and his relationship with the Administrator-General. Swapo also insisted that the 1,500 South African troops should be stationed to the south, suggesting Karasburg as an appropriate locality, and rejected the idea of bilateral negotiations over Walvis Bay. The Swapo leadership feared that the Rooikop military base just outside the port might be used to reinforce the South African military presence, and that in the event of a Swapo election victory, Pretoria might simply refuse to hand over the port to Namibian jurisdiction.

Swapo continued to delay a formal response to the Western proposals pending further 'clarifications'. What was widely seen as a make-or-break meeting between Sam Nujoma and the five Western Foreign Ministers in New York was cancelled by Swapo after South African troops carried out a major strike against Swapo bases in Angola on 4 May 1978. In a bombing and paratroop attack, c. 500 Namibians, mainly refugees, were killed at Cassinga, the iron-ore mining town 150 miles from the border. Although the raid was unanimously condemned by the Security Council, Swapo's Central Committee immediately recalled its delegation to Angola and announced the indefinite postponement of further negotiations. The raid was justified by SA as a response to an upsurge of activity by Swapo guerrillas since the start of 1978, including abductions and killings of civilians regarded as collaborators with Pretoria,[6] but was widely interpreted as an attempt to provoke Swapo into abandoning further negotiations.

However by the end of May 1978, there were renewed attempts by the Front-line States—particularly Tanzania and Zambia—to urge Swapo to return to the negotiating table. The Angolan government, too, anxious to remove the threat to its stability caused by the South African military presence in Namibia, had indicated its readiness to co-operate in implementing the Western proposals. In a bid to break the deadlock, President Nyerere ordered the release of Andreas Shipanga, the former Swapo Information Secretary, and ten other Swapo members arrested in June 1976.[7] This was because Pretoria had insisted that the release of Swapo political prisoners in SA (including Hermann Toivo ja Toivo, incarcerated on Robben Island since 1968) correspond with the release of other Swapo detainees in Zambia and Tanzania. Nyerere's action forced Swapo to face up to the divisions revealed at the time of Shipanga's arrest.

Although a majority of the external leadership remained committed to a dual strategy of diplomatic pressures and guerrilla warfare, a powerful faction on the Central Committee headed by Peter Mueshihange, the Secretary for Foreign Affairs, favoured abandonment of the negotiations and reliance on a military solution. During 1977 there was a build-up in the flow of supplies and equipment from the Soviet Union and Eastern Europe, with the Cubans providing combat training. By early 1978, Swapo was estimated to have 5–10,000 trained guerrillas.

Swapo's difficulties in formulating a final response to the Western proposals and its deep mistrust of South African motives were reinforced not only by the Cassinga attack, but also by a series of repressive measures taken by the Administrator-General after the assassination on 27 March 1978 of the Herero leader, Chief Clemens Kapuuo, one of Swapo's most vehement opponents and chairman of the Democratic Turnhalle Alliance (see below). The killing came as the culmination of several weeks of street violence in the Katutura township outside Windhoek, and of fights at political meetings organized by Swapo and DTA. In fact, the increasing polarization of the Black population—with a third factor introduced by the middle-of-the-road Namibia National Front (NNF) and by influential Black church organizations—was a new feature to emerge during 1977. Although Swapo denied any involvement in the killing of Kapuuo, who was shot by two unknown assailants, and claimed that most of the violence was being fomented by armed groups of DTA supporters, up to 40 Swapo members, including some on the National Executive, were arrested or had gone into exile by the end of April 1978.

On 19 April, Judge Steyn, who had previously relaxed the stringent security regulations in the north, took emergency powers enabling him to order detentions without trial and to bar appeals by those affected. That all those arrested under these powers were Swapo members cast the first doubts about Judge Steyn's ability to retain his 'neutrality' in a situation of growing political tension. His earlier repeal of the Immorality and Mixed Marriages Act, together with abolition of the pass laws and much of the influx control regulations, had indicated his commitment to preparing the ground for the holding of internationally-supervised elections and had been welcomed by most Namibian political organizations. However, the return to emergency powers was condemned not only by Swapo, but also by the NNF and the Lutheran Church leadership.

Further uncertainty was caused by instant demands by the DTA leaders that SA should implement the Western proposals without waiting for Swapo's agreement. At the end of May 1978, Vorster informed the Contact Group of his intention to proceed with the registration of political parties and electors in Namibia unless the negotiations were brought to a rapid conclusion.

THE POLITICS OF THE WHITE COMMUNITIES
Namibia's 32,000 White voters participated in a referendum in May 1977 on the question: 'Are you in favour of the establishment of an interim government and independence for the territory of South West Africa in accordance with the principles accepted by the constitutional conference?' About 61% voted affirmatively, and only c. 1,700 against.

Under the terms of Proclamation 264 of 30 September 1977, White Namibians lost their right of direct representation in the South African Parliament and did not vote in the 1977 South African elections. Since 1949, they have had the right to elect six MPs.

The National Party (NP) decided to break its links with SA's ruling party in September 1977. At its annual congress in late September, Dirk Mudge challenged A. H. du Plessis for the leadership; after being defeated by 141 votes to 135, he led 75 delegates in a walk-out[8] In October, du Plessis gave his support to the removal of all racial legislation which, as a former Senator in Cape Town, he had once staunchly upheld. He said that as far as he was concerned, racially discriminatory laws which in any way hampered 'the co-operation pattern we envisage for the territory should be removed'.[9] The NP offered to form an anti-Swapo alliance with other parties in future elections.

Having left the NP, Mudge and his supporters established an all-White Republican Party on 21 October 1977 which pledged to abolish all racially discriminatory practices. Mudge's stated goal was to unite all Whites in a political movement that would bring multi-racialism to Namibia.[10] In November, the Republican Party entered into an alliance with ten Turnhalle delegations; Mudge was elected chairman and Chief Kapuuo president (see below). A lifelong member of the Afrikaner National Party and former member of the militant Ossewabrandwag, Mudge (with Kapuuo) had masterminded the Turnhalle conference.

Under the leadership of a prominent barrister, Bryan O'Linn, the former United Party of SWA became the Federal Party and later merged with the NNF (see below).

NEW POLITICAL PARTIES
The Democratic Turnhalle Alliance (DTA) was formed on 5 November 1977 with the banding together of the following parties (the names of their leaders being given in parentheses): National Unity Democratic Organization or NUDO (C. Kapuuo); National Democratic Party (Pastor C. Ndjoba); Republic Party (D. F. Mudge); SWA People's Democratic United Front or SWAPDUF (E. H. L. Christy); Labour Party (A. J. F. Kloppers); Rehoboth Baster Association (Dr B. J. Africa); Caprivi Alliance (Kaptein M. Mamili); Tswana Alliance (P. Tibinyane); Bushman Alliance (G. Kashe); Kavango Alliance (A. Majavero); Nama Alliance (D. Luipert).

The DTA's 13-point Programme of Principles recognizes the supremacy of God 'in the fortunes of countries and nations'; aims at Namibia's independence based on a constitutional order which will enable all individuals and groups to assert themselves 'in moral and material spheres' and will eliminate domination; advocates the rule of law; upholds a free economic system, and endorses the Turnhalle constitution.[11]

After the assassination of DTA president Chief Kapuuo in March 1978, his successor as chief of the Herero tribe, Kuaima Riruako, attacked the very foundation of the DTA, insisting that it must become a political party instead of an ethnic coalition.

The Namibia National Front (NNF) was formed through the merging of the following groups (with their leaders given in parentheses): National Independence Party (Charlie Hartung), Federal Party (Adv Bryan O'Linn), Swanu (Gerson Veii), Damara Council (Justus Garoeb), and the Mbanderus (Chief Munjuku). Presenting itself as a centrist bloc, the NNF published a manifesto advocating complete multi-racialism and rejecting both the DTA's 'heavy emphasis on enthnicity and race' and the Turnhalle constitution, the latter because it 'retains the two most important elements of the principle of apartheid'—compulsory classification of all according to ethnicity, and the exercise of the franchise within ethnic communities.[12] The main NNF office-holders are president, Justus Garoeb; vice-president, Gerson Veii; secretary-general, Bryan O'Linn; chairman, C. I. Stanley; national treasurer, J. S. Kirkpatrick; information secretary, R. V. Rukoro; national organizer, K. B. Black; secretary for foreign affairs, C. Hartung; secretary for education and culture, J. Tjozongoro; secretary for interior, M. Nuvauva; vice secretary-general, S. N. Goabab; vice-chairmen, A. K. Kangueehi and B. de Klerk.

Prof Mburuma Kerina, a former Swapo supporter, announced in early 1978 that a new party (still unnamed) would be formed by the merger of the Young Pioneers (described as a moderate non-racial youth movement) and the Rehoboth-based Liberation Party led by Hans Diegaardt. Others associated with this move are Dr Lukas de Vries, president of the influential Unified Evangelical Church of SWA, and Paul Helmuth, a former Swapo exile.[13]

THE HOMELANDS

Despite agreement by the Turnhalle conference and SA that their plan for a second tier of government should be abandoned, the authorities continued to establish ethnic councils. However, an attempt to form a Herero Legislative Assembly was boycotted in May 1977 by Chief Kapuuo and others on the grounds that they were opposed to 'a Bantustan'. Elections held in October 1977 for a Kaptein of the Rehobothers to head the Rehoboth Self-Governing Council were narrowly won by Dr Ben Africa over Hans Diegaardt of the more conservative Rehoboth Liberation Party. There was a large demonstration in July 1977 led by acting Damaras' chief Justus Garoeb and the NNF to oppose the election of a Damara Representative Council.

THE SOUTH WEST AFRICA PEOPLE'S ORGANIZATION (SWAPO)
(For Swapo's role in the negotiations for a settlement, see above.)

Swapo held an annual meeting of its Central Committee in Lubango (Angola) from 21–24 September 1977 in the presence of the Presidents of Angola and Guinea-Bissau. Its 17-point 'Lubango Declaration' paid tribute to the 'brilliant victories and successes scored over the enemy forces' by the People's Liberation Army of Namibia (PLAN), but deplored the fact that the situation in the territory was deteriorating. A tribute was paid to the 'unflinching and disinterested material, moral and political support' given by the five Front-line African countries. It also thanked 'all the socialist countries, Nordic countries, the Netherlands and all other progressive and peace-loving nations' for their support.

Sam Nujomo said on 28 February 1978 that Swapo was not interested in 'majority rule' but rather in 'fighting to seize power by revolution'. The statement was seized upon by the South African Prime Minister to support his view that Swapo was not genuinely involved in the search for a peaceful settlement. However, Swapo's vice-president, Misheck Muyongo, subsequently explained: 'We are not fighting for majority rule as interpreted by the South African regime. We are fighting for independence for the people of our country where there will be no division of our country into sectors as the South African fascist regime is trying to do. . . . We are fighting for real and genuine majority rule where the power will be in the hands of the people of Namibia.'[14]

After his release from prison, Andreas Shipanga (see above) formed a body known as Swapo-Democrats, with himself as president. It seeks power on the basis of reconciliation of tribal and ethnic groups; opposes Nujomo whom it claims has abandoned democratic principles; and accepts the Western plan as a basis for pre-independence elections.[15] The Swapo-Democrats announced an alliance with the NNF.

SWAPO'S LEADERSHIP (as at 1 June 1977)

President	Sam Nujoma*
Vice-President	Misheck Muyongo*
National Chairman	David Meroro*
Administrative Secretary	Moses M. Garoeb*
Secretary for Foreign Relations	Peter Mueshihange*
Secretary of Defence	Peter Nanyemba*
Deputy-Secretary of Defence	Richard Kapelwa*
National Treasurer	Lucas Pohamba*
Secretary for Information and Publicity	Peter Katjavivi
Deputy-Secretary for Information and Publicity	Jesaya Nyamu
Secretary for Education and Culture	Linekela Kalenga
Secretary for Economic Affairs	Ben Amadhila
Secretary for Transport	Maxton Joseph
Secretary for Legal Affairs	Dr Ernest Tjiriange
Secretary for Labour	John ya Otto*
Organizing Secretary	Homateni Kaluenya*
Secretary for Health and Social Welfare	Dr Iyambo Indongo
Deputy-Secretary for Health and Social Welfare	Dr Libertine Amadhi
Secretary for Women's Council	Vacant
Secretary for Youth	Vacant
Chairman of Elders' Council	Simon S. Kaukungua
Deputy-Chairman of Elders' Council	Jackson Mazasi

*Member of the Executive Committee

POLITICAL ECONOMY OF SWAPO

During 1976 and 1977, Swapo presented a fairly complete political economic strategy (including policy formulation and forward planning) in two documents entitled 'Political Programme' and 'Swapo National Programme'.[16] The emergent strategy is distinctively Namibian, by no means a carbon copy of that of any other African movement, let alone an extra-continental import. However, it does have substantial similarities with the 1967–71 evolution of Tanzanian political economic strategy on the one hand, and on the immediate pre-independence transitional planning of Frelimo on the other. There is a clear commitment to socialism and a clear rejection of African capitalist strategies as pursued in Kenya or Botswana. But equally evident is the preservation of tactical freedom to choose sequences and timings, and a realization that a socialist transition is a long-term operation which must begin with selected structural changes.

Swapo's programme includes 'bringing all major means of production and exchange into the ownership of the people' and 'planning and development . . . governed by the principles of scientific socialism'. Private ownership of non-productive assets (e.g. dwelling houses, savings accounts) 'justly acquired' is guaranteed. Renegotiation of arrangements (presumably joint ventures) is set out as the main short and medium-term approach to the large-scale private sector. SA state and corporate assets (presumably mines developed since 1966 and possibly banks) are the immediate targets for nationalization of man-made assets. Land, minerals and fishing rights (over a 200-mile zone) are to be taken into state ownership, with use to be allocated by the state to selected public sector, joint venture or private sector operating units (including peasant households).

'Comprehensive agrarian reform aimed at giving the land to the tillers' is stated as a precondition for rural development. Colonial land rights are to be abolished, although negotiation of continued use of some land by some existing settler ranchers is envisaged. Peasant and rancher co-operatives and state farms are both seen as future forms of rural production organization—large private Namibian ranches are not. Self-sufficiency in food and major increases in rural incomes are central targets.

'The abolition of all forms of exploitation of man by man . . . and aggrandizement of wealth and power by individuals, groups or classes' is central to Swapo strategy for equality, provision of services and income distribution. The elimination of inequality between town and country and between region and region is a specific target. Surveillance of prices and prevention of 'parasitic' means of making profits are stressed, as is the programmatic creation of broader opportunities for full, productive and justly remunerated employment. The latter is tied to provisions for non-discriminatory wage and salary scales and to protection of workers' economic, organizational and management participation rights. The strong emphasis on workers' organizations and especially trade unions appears to flow from Swapo's longstanding base in the 'contract' labour sector and the heritage of the 1971–72 strikes. The 'contract' labour system is to be abolished.

Provision of basic services (particularly in health and education), attainment of self-sufficiency in food production, reduction of rural-urban inequalities and effective workers' organizations are seen both as ends and means. In the short term, their purpose is to increase output and in particular to raise the incomes and living standards of the poorest Namibians. But they are also seen as means to the long term end of ensuring participation and political control adequate to sustain a transition to socialism. As goals, they represent more specific articulation of the Swapo motto: 'One Nation, One Namibia'.

Swapo's development of detailed policy proposals, and especially of steps to their implementation, has so far necessarily been limited. Permanently liberated areas in Namibia remain very few and small. Fairly widespread rural medical service provision has been carried out inside the northern part of the country, but basic education and agriculture programmes have been almost totally limited to the refugee and liberation force sites in Angola and Zambia. Moreover, the demands of internal attempts at political mobilization, the armed struggle along the border and the external struggle to build support have placed very heavy burdens on the limited number of highly trained Namibians.

In 1977, a number of steps were taken toward detailed policy definition and implementation. The medical services began conducting studies of Namibian health facility and health problem patterns based on interviews with Namibians in Zambia. A training programme for telecommunications personnel was begun under International Telecommunications Organization auspices at the Zambia Posts and Telecommunications College in Ndola. Existing external scholarship placements were expanded and new programmes negotiated. The research programme of the UN Institute for Namibia was brought to bear on several planning problems in conjunction with Swapo.

In 1978, Swapo began to have each of its sections and units draw up surveys of requirements and proposals for initial national programmes and targets for the immediate post-independence period. These are seen as inputs into a national pre-planning exercise leading to political decisions on interim targets and particular areas in which to seek personnel or resources from co-operating organizations. At the same time, there has been reform and strengthening of labour organization and political education of workers. The stress is on developing a basic data bank and programme proposals from Namibians, and of establishing the main interim targets through Swapo political channels before seeking major external personnel or resource commitments for planning and programming. This is both deliberate and significant. Swapo is not autarchist, but it believes that if foreign personnel dominate the data collection and alternative formulation process without a prior Namibian-determined framework, the process is likely to become one of technical domination rather than technical assistance whatever their or Swapo's intentions. Indeed, among the areas of particular concern to Swapo is how to select and control foreign personnel in terms of their basic sympathy, reliability and willingness to carry out Namibian goals as well as in terms of their technical competence.

DEFENCE AND SECURITY
Claims made by Swapo and SA about the scale of fighting in Namibia varied greatly. According to Maj-Gen Wally Black, the South African Army Director-General of Operations, casualties suffered by his forces at the end of November 1977 were down 10% from 1976. He did not give figures. South African communiqués announced the deaths of 16 soldiers; the number of wounded are never given. The General said that there were between 250–300 guerrillas operating in the territory, with a further 2,200 in camps in Angola and 800 in Zambia. He said that although Swapo guerrillas were being trained by Cubans, 'they are by no means good soldiers'. Swapo had changed its tactics and was now operating in large groups of between 40–50, but still favoured hit-and-run attacks. He claimed that the South African Air Force had flown 12,000 hours in direct support of operations, with the loss of only one pilot.

According to a South African White Paper on Defence tabled early in 1977, a total of 231 Swapo guerrillas had been killed and many captured since 1 April 1975. During the same period, South African losses had been 33, while Black Namibians allegedly killed by Swapo numbered 53.

On the other hand, Swapo claimed in December 1977 that in one 'historic battle' alone, 82 South African soldiers had been killed. It denied a South African claim that 61 Swapo guerrillas died in a two-day battle in October.

(Also see chapter on SA, under Defence and Security.)

POLITICAL TRIALS AND ASSASSINATIONS
A successful appeal was made against the controversial trial in 1977 of six Swapo members. [17] Four of the accused, including two women who had been given long sentences, were acquitted by the South African Appeal Court which upheld their complaints of serious irregularities at their trial.

Victor Nkandi, a Swapo supporter, was formally accused in October 1977 of being implicated in the murder of the Ovambo Chief Minister Philemon Elifas in 1975. The trial was not completed by early 1978. F. N. Nangola was the first Swapo member to be executed. He was hanged in May 1977, after being found guilty of killing four Whites. Nangola had been shot during his arrest and at his trial was a paraplegic.

The Ovambo Minister of Health and Welfare, Toivo Shiyaga, was shot dead on 7

February 1978. Clemens Kapuuo, Chief of the Herero and leader of the DTA, was assassinated in late March 1978. He was succeeded—in the former capacity only—by Chief Kuaima Riruako (see above).

SOCIAL AFFAIRS
The system of Bantu education was abolished in December 1977. Henceforth all children will follow the same curriculum in schools.

The slack in the economy, security problems and the removal of residence and movement restrictions (as part of SA's attempt to create an internationally acceptable face for an internal settlement) have caused sharp rises in open urban unemployment.[18] Until recently, this was probably under 20,000 simply because unemployed Africans were sent back to 'reserves' and the real total of 60,000–75,000 *de facto* jobless was not visible,[19] a situation which seems to have changed radically in the last months of 1977 and the beginning of 1978.

(For other social affairs, see below: Economic Affairs.)

POPULATION
According to 1977 estimate, Namibia's total population is 1.25m. The last official figures, relating to 1974, gave the total number of inhabitants as 852,000, broken down as follows: Ovambo 396,000 (46%); White 99,000 (11.6%); Damara 75,000 (8.8%); Herero 56,000 (6.6%); Kavango 56,000 (6.6%); Nama 37,000 (4.3%); Coloured 32,000 (3.8%); East Caprivian 29,000 (3.4%); Bushmen 26,000 (3.0%); Rehoboth Baster 19,000 (2.2%); Kaokolander 7,000 (0.8%); Tswana 5,000 (0.6%); Other 15,000 (1.8%).

INTERNATIONAL AFFAIRS
Namibia continued to be a major issue at the UN and at most international conferences throughout 1977. The UN General Assembly considered two reports in October, both of which called for the implementation of Security Council decisions. Sam Nujomo was allowed to address the Assembly and gave his support to the Western initiative to achieve a settlement, but insisted on the withdrawal of all South African troops before elections were held. The Assembly adopted a comprehensive resolution on Namibia on 4 November under six headings: Implementation of the Nationhood Programme for Namibia; UN Fund for Namibia; Dissemination of Information on Namibia; Situation in Namibia resulting from the Illegal Occupation of the Territory by SA; Action by Inter-governmental and Non-governmental Organizations with respect to Namibia; and Intensification and Co-ordination of UN Action in support of Namibia. The FAO voted in November to admit Namibia to membership.

The OAU summit in Libreville in July 1977 endorsed its previous resolutions on Namibia. The country also featured largely at the two international conferences held during 1977 at Maputo and Lagos to discuss international action against SA.[20]

West Germany announced in October 1977 that it would close its consulate in Windhoek. There are 8,000 German nationals and between 10–20,000 South African citizens of German extraction in the territory.

ECONOMIC AFFAIRS (1.64 Rand = £1 sterling)
The continuing uncertainty about Namibia's independence affected economic prospects, with many potential investors clearly reluctant to commit themselves to large-scale developments, despite the discovery of further important uranium deposits in the region of the Rossing uranium mine as well as the existence of promising diamond deposits in the Huns Mountains region in the south. The

Contact Group's proposals of April 1978 and their acceptance by SA were received with enthusiasm by most major investors in Namibia.[21] However, a definite split emerged between those who wished Swapo to accept as well (believing they could do business with a Swapo government if it won the election and seeing no international approval or domestic stability without an election contested by Swapo), and those who hoped Swapo would reject the proposals and thus precipitate an 'internal solution'.[22] The slightly earlier buying out of the two major newspapers and the firing of their editors was clearly an attempt to bolster an internal settlement by reversing the previous editorial drift toward support for 'internal' Swapo and turning them instead into Turnhalle Democratic Alliance sounding-boards.[23]

The high rate of inflation imported from SA, which provides c. 75% of Namibian imports, and the continuing decline in the copper price, which forced the closure of the Otjihase mine after only one year's operation, meant there was little overall growth in the economy. Future prospects were further affected by the catastrophic decline in the pilchard catch, while uncertainty over the future status of Walvis Bay clouded the outlook for the fishing industry. However during 1977, Rossing overcame its initial teething problems, increasing uranium oxide output to 3,042 short tons, while De Beers raised output at Oranjemund to a record 2m carats.

Namibia's economic potential was extensively surveyed in studies by the German Development Institute and the Commonwealth Secretariat.[24] The former analysed the Namibian economy in terms of the economic potential of its natural resources and the measures necessary to overcome the existing structural dependency on SA. It argued that even within the parameters of a free market economy, it would be possible for an independent Namibia to reverse this dependency and reduce its close ties with SA. The Commonwealth report focused on the Namibian mineral industry, and the economic, fiscal and legal implications of independence for the mining corporations presently active in the territory.

ECONOMIC PERFORMANCE IN 1977
1977 was a bad year for the commercial economy, both in terms of earnings and employment. The cost of living rose by 15% (following 13% in 1976 and 12% in 1975), as did prices for many essential imports from SA used in the ranching, fishing and mining sectors; but wages, salaries and export prices failed to keep pace. The continued recession in SA influenced Namibia's main market, while the heritage of over-fishing combined with SA's reluctance to extend the territorial fishing limit led to a drastic fall in catch. The slump in copper prices sent the second largest mine—Otjihase—reeling to closure. While moving more smoothly by late in the year, the start-up of Rossing had been beset by technical, managerial and industrial relations' snags. Only diamonds, where the CDM subsidiary of De Beers increased output at Oranjemund for the second year running and where prices continued to rise on world markets, enjoyed an untroubled year. Real GDP probably grew by up to 6% but that reflected the new output of Rossing and a moderate increase in diamond output, whereas the rest of the economy suffered stagnation or worse.

FISHING INDUSTRY
The 1977 fish catch fell 27% to 460,000 tonnes, of which only 195,000 tonnes were the key pilchard catch. In a belated attempt to remedy the damage, factory owners at Luderitz and Walvis Bay were to be limited to a total of 125,000 tonnes of pilchards in the 1978 season.[25] The industry—both on the fishing vessel and processing plant sides—is in a state of demoralization.[26] The 'return' of Walvis Bay to Cape Province does nothing to help this as it implies a potential barring of

Namibian waters to vessels based in the enclave. The demands for extension of territorial waters to 320 km (as is the case for SA)[27] has been viewed by Pretoria as impracticable. Heavy over-fishing in the 30 to 320 km zone—dominantly by Soviet, Spanish, Cuban and Bulgarian vessels—is a fact. At a meeting of the 15-nation International Commission for South Atlantic Fisheries (ICSAF) in early 1978, SA managed to secure an agreement that foreign trawlers would not fish more than 11,000 tonnes of pilchards and observe the closed season from August to March. With effect from 30 November 1977, SA extended its own territorial waters from 9.6 to 19.3 km and its fishery waters from 19.3 to 320 km; the extension included the coastline of Walvis Bay and the waters surrounding the Penguin Islands.

FARMING
Cattle offtake for commercial slaughter, which stood at 400,000 in 1976, fell in 1977 as a result of a reduced South African quota; 260,000 cattle had been railed live to the Republic in 1976, but the 1977 estimate was apparently 200,000.[28] While the 128,000 handled in the main Namibian processing plants in 1976 may have risen in 1977, this is unlikely to have offset the decline in sales to SA. New marketing arrangements, complaints of rising costs and static prices, and the first steps toward limited government subsidies dominated cattle ranchers' discussions in late 1977 and early 1978.[29]

MINING
The $55m Otjihase copper mine was closed as a producing unit in December 1977. It apparently required a £900 London price for copper to break even, whereas prevailing levels were nearer £700. Losses for 1976–77 approached $15m.[30] Besides costing 1,000 jobs, the closure also raised problems for the Tsumeb mining and smelting complex (alreading operating at a loss), which had been expanded to deal with the projected, but never fully reached, Otjihase output of 360,000 tonnes of concentrate a year. It also affected Rossing since pyrite from Otjihase was used as an input in the uranium oxide extraction process. Efforts by the dominant shareholder, Johannesburg Consolidated, to have Tsumeb take over Otjihase broke down. This was apparently because the major US shareholders in Tsumeb (AMAX and Newmont) realized that as Otjihase had only opened in 1975, it was subject to the World Court decision to the effect that after the 1966 revocation of the Mandate, SA had no right to be in Namibia and that economic 'contracts' with it in respect of Namibian resources were invalid. Tsumeb's own mines pre-date the revocation.

Rossing Uranium had a troubled year. Start-up in October 1976 was slow, and during 1977 technical problems were encountered with the ore; managerial weakness led to the replacement by RTZ of some top executives; and the cost of the underground mine needed to raise output to full capacity of 5,000 tonnes led to its deferral until 1979. It also proved nearly impossible to recruit workers from the immediate area; 'temporary' Ovambo employees were housed in quarters so bad as to lead to a strike. However, production in the 1977 financial year amounted to 3,042 short tons of uranium oxide (cf 771 short tons in 1976), and a programme to increase milling capacity to 40,000 tonnes of ore per day and raise recovery to 85% was due to be completed before the end of 1978. RTZ, which owns 46.5% of the Rossing equity, reported that a substantial rescheduling of deliveries had been necessary, while new capital and loan funds of $100m ($49m supplied by RTZ) had been arranged to finance major plant modifications.

Meanwhile, uranium prospecting moved ahead rapidly, and there was every reason to believe that Namibia could develop annual outputs of up to 20,000 tonnes of yellowcake a year from several mines. In the southern area, General Mining (ultimately part of the Anton Rupert group based on Rothmans) seemed almost ready to begin development following pilot plant operations. Goldfields of SA moved from exploration to deposit-proving drilling in the northern part of the 'uranium belt'. Anglo-American expanded its exploration programme jointly with Union Corporation and the French national petroleum companies, Aquitaine and CFP, while at least three other major companies including Johannesburg Consolidated Investments and Union Carbide (US) continued active prospecting programmes.[31]

Diamond production at Oranjemund by Consolidated Diamond Mines of SWA increased in 1977 by 307,223 carats to 2,001,217 carats, the highest for over ten years. This record output was officially attributed to the commissioning of a third conglomerate plant, but the figure confirmed some mining correspondents' conclusions, vigorously denied by De Beers, that the rate of mining was being deliberately stepped up. In August 1977, the CDM head office was symbolically moved from Kimberley to Windhoek. De Beers chairman, H. F. Oppenheimer, announced that CDM would conduct a five-year mineral survey of Namibia, the results of which would be placed on open file, while a new subsidiary to investigate investment in non-mining fields was to be established.

Diamond exports in 1977 probably exceeded $250m and may have approached $300m, accounting for between one-third and two-fifths of foreign exchange earnings (including exports to SA).[32]

GOVERNMENT INVESTMENT
Government investment rose in some fields. For instance, over $55m was committed to reconstructing three quays at Walvis Bay, expanding the Windhoek marshalling yard, relaying the Walvis Bay-Swakopmund line, and reconstructing the Gibeon-Kalkrand line on a new alignment. However, these transport improvements seemed prompted more by military considerations than general economic stimulation. Similarly, a projected $8m alternative water scheme for the North in part replaced supplies lost when the Calueque dam in Angola moved outside South African control. Moreover, the projected mid-1978 completion of Ruacana Falls dam and its linking to the national power grid is of dubious value given the loss of reservoir control along with Calueque.[33] In April 1977, $75m of previously approved capital projects, including almost $50m in the health sector, were frozen.[34]

STRUCTURAL DATA
For 1976 there are four different GDP estimates. The official one is R742.6m,[35] but two independent German research study estimates are R755 and R842.6m.[36] Analysis by the UN Institute for Namibia (UNIN) showed a 1977 GDP of R1,135m, an implicit 1976 estimate of R950m, and 6–7% real growth of output in 1977.[37] However, this is made up of major growth in uranium oxide and moderate growth in diamonds. Agricultural value added is estimated at R157.5m, including R20m subsistence; fishing at R40m and mining at R375m for a primary sector total of R575m accounting for 51% of GDP. Manufacturing is estimated at R85m, 60% of which is food processing. Construction stood at R60m in a secondary sector totalling R160m or about a seventh of GDP. The tertiary sector at R400m was estimated at 35% of GDP.

The population estimate for 1977 is 1.25m and the economically active population estimate 518,000 (including 240,000 in subsistence agriculture). This gives an overall GDP per capita of the order of R900 ($1,000 odd). However, value added per employee by sector is very unequal, ranging from under R100 in subsistence agriculture and c. R200 in domestic service (sectors which together account for over half the economically active population), to over R20,000 per employee in mining. The distribution of personal income is even more radically unequal between the settler-expatriate community and Black and Coloured Namibians. For the White group, average per capita income appears to be of the order of R3,000 and average salary (including fringe benefits) of the order of R7,000. White employees and individual proprietors have incomes of perhaps R300–315m. 'Non-European' incomes of all kinds total perhaps R150m, or R125 per capita. Corporate enterprise surpluses appear to be c. R500m.

The very large discrepancy between Domestic Product (territorial) and National Product (accruing to permanent residents) shows up in all the recent re-estimates. In the case of the 1977 estimates, GNP is given as R710m or 64% of GDP. Of the R425m difference, c. R300m is calculated as resulting from corporate profits, R85m from individual White remittances, and R40m from South African government and corporation surplus on recurrent revenue over recurrent expenditure in Namibia.

PUBLIC FINANCE

Namibian budgetary accounts are difficult to assess because even taking the Republic's 'SWA' Account and the 'SWA' Territorial Account together, the picture of expenditure remains incomplete. For 1974–75, these two accounts showed total revenues of R155.5m. Revised 1976–77 estimates of revenue total R186.8m, and 1977–78 estimates R206m. The largest single element consists of taxes on diamond production and profits (57.1, 51.5 and 73.1 million Rand respectively).[38] The general rates of taxation are low—distinctly below those for SA itself in respect of income and profit taxes.

Expenditure on recurrent account from the two main sets of estimates for 1976–77 was c. R140m, leaving a recurrent surplus of c. R47m. Capital account estimates of R115m exceeded the recurrent surplus, resulting in a cash flow deficit on recurrent and capital account taken together. However, the same is true of almost all national budgets including that of SA and is not convincing evidence of lack of financial viability nor of South African subsidization in the normal meaning of that term. Including a series of special expenditures and sub-territorial units, total recurrent revenue estimates for 1976–77 stood at R322m, recurrent expenditure at R180m and capital expenditure (including R48m for electric plant, equipment and dam construction) at R173m. Railways and Harbours and Posts and Telecommunication in 1976–77 generated c. R45m of revenue and spent R68m on recurrent account for an operating deficit of R23m, in part related to transport routes and patterns (e.g. live cattle shipments to SA) designed to serve Republic export and manufacturing interests. Their capital expenditure of R18m for 1976–77 further increased their total negative cash flow balance.

On the basis of the above data, very different analyses of Namibia's financial viability have been made. One financial journalist cited the very high profits outflow as evidence that higher taxes would have been possible. He suggested that the very high infrastructural capital spending (which had caused the budgetary deficit) related to South African efforts to justify its presence and not necessarily to promote real development.[39] One independent analysis concluded that Namibia's economy was potentially fiscally viable, able to borrow for capital works but having expenditure levels artificially inflated by South African apartheid policies both in hiring and providing services.[40] Another analysis, prepared by a former adviser to the Coloured delegation to Turnhalle, painted a much more ambiguous picture.[41] In its view, South African budget subsidies (and policies designed to attract them) as well as capital market loans were vital. The more optimistic assessments seem sounder, assuming that the independent Namibian economy—and especially the mining sector—can be run at levels near those prevailing in 1977, that Rossing moves to capacity and that copper prices recover by 1980. In that event, recurrent revenue of R400m (using more normal African company tax, diamond tax and other mineral export rates) would be a distinct possibility. At that level, a substantially increased recurrent budget could be locally financed, while leaving a substantial contribution toward capital budget items. Given the potential profit and savings levels, domestic borrowing should also be possible. Beyond the immediate transition after independence, the structural data suggest that Namibia can be more fiscally viable and less dependent on external grants or loans for basic capital expenditure than a majority of African states.

EXTERNAL ACCOUNTS

Exports in 1977 were of the order of R650m or 58% of GDP. Of this total, karakul pelts, cattle and beef products, and fish products contributed c. 12%, 8% and 10% respectively; diamonds perhaps 40%, uranium probably somewhat over 10%; copper c. 10% and other metals almost all the balance.[42] Merchandise imports may have been c. R400m (excluding military imports) for a trade surplus of R250m. Service account imports (including foreign remittances) were presumably at least R500m and service account earnings (including tourism) perhaps R25m, leaving a hypothetical current account deficit of R225m. Of this, R175m can be accounted for by South African state capital investment and several million by continued rundown of the territorial reserves held in SA.

These figures demonstrate quite clearly that SA and its corporate partners have profited from the exploitation of Namibian resources and manpower. For SA, the credit side included R400m of remittances; employment for a significant number of South African expatriates; a substantial trade surplus with the outside world (most exports are not to SA but through it, while most imports are from SA, so that the surplus on trade with non-South African economies is probably at least R400m); and certain useful or critical inputs into the South African economy (subsidized fishmeal, a balancing flow of meat, and in the future uranium oxide, etc). SA's actual investment of R175m should be seen less as a loss than as pump-priming for future surplus flows. Namibia, it seems, subsidizes SA, not the reverse.

However in one respect, Namibia has become an economic burden for SA, as in the past few years new costs have been incurred. These derive from waging a war against Swapo and from creating a military support infrastructure (at least two major airbases, four or more main base camps, a coastal radar network, a Marconi radio communications system and several hundred kilometres of surfaced highways). These are estimated to cost between R250m and R400m a year. At the lower level, Namibia might, in purely economic terms, be just 'breaking even' for SA; at the higher levels it would be a financial burden. The trend is very clearly toward escalating deficits and toward conditions in which economic expansion to offset the rising costs of occupation is not feasible.

1978-79 BUDGET

At R320m, the Budget for 1978-79 showed a 31.8% rise over last year's figures. The largest allocations were for miscellaneous services with R106m, African Affairs with R78m, followed by the Water Department and Coloured Affairs. Defence does not figure, being a direct South African responsibility until independence.

The Administrator-General said that the noticeable increase in the Budget had been made possible by a rise of R63m in taxes paid by the diamond mines, and of

R32m by other companies operating in the territory whose payments had previously gone to SA.

FOREIGN TRADE* (million Rand)

	1970	1974	1977
Exports	235	368	650
Imports	180	288	400
Balance	**+ 55**	**+ 80**	**+ 250**

MAJOR EXPORTS* (million Rand)

	1970	1974	1977
Diamonds	70	100	260
Base minerals	60	90	195
Fish/Fish Products	56	80	65
Karakul Pelts	25	50	71.5
Beef/Livestock	24	48	58.5

(*All figures authoritative estimates)

MINERAL PRODUCTION (thousand tonnes)

	1973	1974	1975	1976	1977
Gem diamonds[1]	1,599.6	1,569.9	1,747.7	1,693.9	2,001.2
Silver[2]	1,563.0	1,556.0	1,500.0	1,500.0	n.a.
Copper					
concentrates	56.0	50.0	55.0	42.4	n.a.
blister	35.4	45.8	35.7	28.2	n.a.
Lead					
concentrates	59.0	64.6	48.3	42.2	n.a.
refined	20.0	26.0	44.3	39.6	n.a.
Zinc concentrates	33.9	44.9	45.6	48.0	n.a.
Uranium oxide	—	—	—	0.7	3.0

[1] carats   [2] ounces

PELAGIC FISH CATCH (thousand tonnes)

	1973	1974	1975	1976
Pilchard	396.0	556.8	545.4	447.3
Anchovy	301.7	254.6	194.4	94.1
Others	9.2	26.1	19.4	31.1
Total	**707.0**	**837.5**	**759.2**	**572.5**

FISH PRODUCTS (thousand tonnes)

	1973	1974	1975	1976
Canned Pilchard	135.0	186.6	194.0	172.8
Fishmeal	143.1	161.2	146.6	106.1
Fish body oil	46.8	28.5	28.3	19.1

BUDGET (million Rand)

	1974–75	1975–76	1976–77
Revenue:	246.9	233.6	242.2
SWA Account of SA Consolidated Revenue Fund	146.8	133.7	136.4
SWA Territory Revenue Fund	102.1	99.9	105.8

	1974–75	*1975–76*	*1976–77*
Expenditure:	241.0	275.4	309.9
SWA Account	145.5	170.9	190.3
SWA Territory Revenue Fund	95.5	104.5	119.6
Balance	**+5.9**	**−41.8**	**−67.7**

Sources (for six preceding tables): De Beers Consolidated Mines Ltd *Annual Reports*; Economist Intelligence Unit, *Quarterly Economic Review of Southern Africa 1976–1977*; Rio Tinto Zinc Ltd *Annual Report*; World Bureau of Metal Statistics; World Mining; *The Mineral Industry of Namibia, Perspectives for Independence*, Commonwealth Secretariat, 1978.

NOTES

(Unless otherwise indicated, all references are to newspapers in SA and Namibia)

1. For background, see all previous editions of *African Contemporary Record (ACR)*, 1968–69 to 1976–77.
2. See *ACR* 1975–76, pp. B556–58; 1976–77, pp. B769–70.
3. See *ACR* 1976–77, pp. B780–81.
4. Also see Documents section, pp. C78–79.
5. See *ACR* 1976–77, pp. B768–69.
6. See chapter on SA under Foreign Affairs.
7. See *ACR* 1976–77, p. B774.
8. *Ibid*, p. B771.
9. The *Star*, 8 October 1977.
10. *Rand Daily Mail (RDM)*, 29 November 1977.
11. The DTA Constitution (Windhoek, 1977), 35pp.
12. *NNF Policy Manifesto and Alternatives* (Windhoek, 1977), 16pp.
13. *To the Point*, Brussels; 26 December 1977 and 6 February 1978.
14. The *Star*, 4 March 1978.
15. *The Times*, London; 23 June 1978.
16. Swapo, Lusaka, 1976.
17. See *ACR* 1976–77, p. B776.
18. *Johannesburg Star*, 4 February 1978.
19. *Toward Manpower Development for Namibia* (United Nations Institute for Namibia, 1978).
20. See Documents section, pp. C31–42.
21. *International Herald Tribune (IHT)*, Paris; 26 April 1978; *The Guardian*, Manchester; 27 April 1978.
22. *Financial Times (FT)*, London; 27 April 1978.
23. *The Guardian*, 26 April 1978.
24. *Toward Manpower Development for Namibia*. W. S. Barthold, *Namibia's Economic Potential and Existing Economic Ties with the Republic of South Africa* (German Development Institute, 1977). W. Thomas, *Towards Acceptable Development Strategies for Independent Namibia* (London: Commonwealth Secretariat, 1977).
25. *Financial Gazette*, 30 September 1977.
26. *RDM*, 7 September 1977: 'The R90m fish fiasco'.
27. *Ibid*: 'The great SWA fish disaster'.
28. *Windhoek Advertiser*, 24 May 1977. Dirk Mudge's report to Territorial Assembly.
29. *Ibid*, 10–12 August 1977, 3 February 1978, 22–24 February 1978.
30. *FT*, 22 December 1977.
31. *New African*, London; July 1977.
32. *Toward Manpower Development for Namibia, op. cit.*
33. *Financial Mail*, 7 October 1977; *Windhoek Advertiser*, 23 February 1978.
34. *Windhoek Advertiser*, 15 April 1977.
35. *Ibid*, 24 May 1977.
36. Thomas, *op. cit.* and Barthold, *op. cit.*
37. *Toward Manpower Development for Namibia, op. cit.*
38. Official estimates and Auditor-General's reports as presented in Thomas, *op. cit.*
39. *Sunday Times*, 24 July 1977.
40. Barthold, *op. cit.*
41. Thomas, *op. cit.*
42. *Toward Manpower Development for Namibia, op. cit.*

PART IV:

Rhodesia

Rhodesia

Efforts to produce a solution to the 12-year old Rhodesian conflict reached a dramatic climax early in March 1978 when Ian Smith, the leader of the Rhodesian Front, and three African leaders agreed that the country should become independent under a Black government at the end of the year. The three Black leaders were Bishop Abel Muzorewa of the United African National Council (UANC), the Rev Ndabaningi Sithole of the Zimbabwe African National Union (Zanu—Sithole wing), and Chief Jeremiah Chirau of the Zimbabwe United People's Organization (Zupo). Their prolonged negotiations for an 'internal settlement' were paralleled by talks, mostly outside the country, between British and American emissaries; the leaders of the Patriotic Front (PF), Joshua Nkomo and Robert Mugabe; and the Front-line Presidents (FLPs) of Tanzania, Zambia, Mozambique, Botswana and Angola.

Although the Salisbury 'internal settlement' was clearly an advance from a situation of endemic Black-White conflict and almost total White minority rule, it received only a cautious welcome from experienced observers because it left open three crucial questions by which the effectiveness and acceptability of any settlement would have to be judged. First, would it command sufficient authority to bring the fighting to an end? Second, could it command sufficient international support to end economic sanctions? Third, could it produce conditions inside the country that would allow for the preparation and holding of elections to choose a government before independence? As at April 1978, the 'internal settlement' had not yet proved itself able to meet any of these basic requirements. However, one measure of the extent of the apparent change in Smith's own formerly obdurate position was the fact that he envisaged the possibility—though not necessarily the likelihood—of the inclusion of the PF in a future government.[1] Earlier, in April 1977, Smith had faced rebellion in his own Rhodesia Front (RF); after the regime had agreed to repeal some of the country's discriminatory legislation, a dozen members left to form a new group further to the Right. At the end of August 1977, Smith went to the country in a general election and won all 50 White seats. With that mandate, having become more and more hostile to the Anglo-American settlement proposals, he began his own 'internal' talks.

The pressures on the Smith regime to reach a settlement were great: the country's economic problems had become much more acute; the cost of the war in men and money grew ever more serious; and the security position continued to worsen. The likelihood that fighting would spread through southern Africa as a whole caused the South African Government to continue its efforts to persuade Smith to reach an agreement with the Africans. Emigration reached record levels, with a net loss of Whites, Coloureds and Asians of 10,908 in 1977.[2]

POLITICAL AFFAIRS
SETTLEMENT MOVES (FEBRUARY 1977–FEBRUARY 1978)
The high hopes for the achievement of majority rule raised in 1976 by the Pretoria Agreement between Kissinger and Smith had evaporated by early 1977.[3] The Salisbury regime began backtracking on the agreement by explaining in secret documents to its supporters that the commitment to majority rule was only tactical.[4] It also insisted that the two-year transition period to independence would

only begin from the date that an interim government was actually formed. The new Carter Administration for its part quickly demonstrated that it intended to give a much higher priority to the problems of southern Africa.[5] The US Secretary of State, Cyrus Vance, told the Senate Foreign Affairs sub-committee on Africa on 10 February 1977 that the Rhodesian situation was of 'the greatest urgency'. Pressing for the repeal of the Byrd Amendment (which allowed the US to continue to import chrome despite UN sanctions), he said this step would be important in persuading Smith to act. 'The key to peace,' he added, 'lies in Mr Ian Smith's hands.' Vance also declared that 'the Rhodesian authorities should understand that under no circumstances can they count on any form of American assistance in their effort to prevent majority rule or to enter into negotiations which exclude leaders of the nationalist movements.'

On 27 March 1977, Bishop Muzorewa outlined the UANC's five-point plan for a settlement.[6] It called on Smith 'categorically and unequivocally to surrender political power and authority to the Black majority immediately' and to release all political prisoners; it urged Britain, through the UN or Commonwealth, to ensure free political activity and to supervise a national referendum to elect a national leader; it called for armed guerrillas to be allowed to participate in the referendum and for a constitutional conference to be convened.

Britain's new Foreign Secretary, Dr David Owen, decided that, unlike his predecessors, he would take personal charge of the negotiations.[7] On 10 April 1977, he began a visit to the capitals of the Front-line States and Pretoria, where he saw Ian Smith as well as Vorster. He also met with the PF leaders. Owen outlined two prerequisites for the new negotiations to succeed: the need for close US involvement, and for a constitutional conference to be representative of all shades of Black and White Rhodesian opinion. He apparently succeeded in persuading Presidents Nyerere, Kaunda, Machel and Seretse Khama to this view.[8]

On his arrival in Salisbury on 15 April, Dr Owen at once made it clear that the issue was the handing over of power to a Black majority government by the end of 1978. Asked in a radio and television broadcast in Rhodesia about Smith's commitment to majority rule, he said Smith would be judged by actions over a period of time, adding: 'If I have to look at actions, all the things that I have asked for in my visit to Rhodesia have been met. Mr Smith knows that the conference I am proposing is going to take as its objective the achievement of majority rule in 1978. He has said some things in Press comments which indicate that it might not be in the interest of Rhodesia to hang on until the end. A lot of what he is saying is not the language of someone who intends to go back on his word. He will obviously want to get the maximum protection he can for White Rhodesians. That is not an ignoble objective. There is no question that the economy and stability of this country will be greatly eased if a large number of White Rhodesians stay on in an independent country.'

Reaction among White Rhodesians to the prospect of renewed negotiations was mixed. An emergency congress of the Rhodesian Front was convened because of a rebellion by 12 RF Members of Parliament (see below). The debate was emotional, but in the end the congress voted by a large majority to give Smith a mandate to 'strive to reach an agreement within the party's principles and policies'. It accepted the need for a settlement and urged the Government to ensure that 'the rights of all communities are meaningfully guaranteed'.[9]

On his return, Dr Owen described to the House of Commons the kind of conference which the UK and US Governments hoped to convene. Its first task, he said, would be to draw up a constitution protecting 'basic human rights'; secondly, it would have to define an 'acceptable democratic process' for the transfer of authority to an independent nation. It would also discuss the role of an international development fund for the purpose of promoting economic stability in an independent Zimbabwe and encouraging the White population to stay and contribute to the country's future. If agreement were reached, Owen would bring the Constitutional Bill to the Commons for approval; Smith would resign; a caretaker government would supervise elections for an independent government (in which all participants forswore violence); sanctions would be lifted. Owen said he was convinced that many Africans engaged in the armed struggle were 'essentially men of peace'. He added: 'It is not difficult to understand the motives of those who feel they have no recourse but to arms. Much as we all wish violence to stop, we cannot immediately expect it to stop while the wall of scepticism and disbelief—which I met all over Africa—remains about the intentions of the Smith Administration.' John Davies, the Shadow Foreign Secretary, offered Dr Owen his congratulations on the success of his 'exacting and rigorous mission'. [10]

However, the hopes of convening a constitutional conference were at once frustrated. At a press conference in Lusaka on 20 April, the Patriotic Front leaders, Nkomo and Mugabe, laid down three conditions to be met before they could agree to the Anglo-American plans: (1) there should be no American participation in the conference; (2) the Patriotic Front must be the sole representative of the Africans in Rhodesia; and (3) the negotiations must be between Britain and the Patriotic Front. Smith should not be represented separately, but could be an extension of the British delegation. There was thus hardly any change in the stand taken by the PF since the end of 1976 at the abortive Geneva conference. [11]

In the face of this setback, Owen moved to formalize the Anglo-American initiative by establishing a joint committee of senior officials, headed by John Graham, Deputy Under-Secretary at the Foreign and Commonwealth Office, and Steven Low, the US ambassador in Lusaka. They kept up the momentum for negotiations by consulting with Black Rhodesian leaders in London, Lusaka and Dar es Salaam before going on to Salisbury on 26 May 1977. Meanwhile, on 6 May, Owen and Vance met in London to co-ordinate the Anglo-American strategy, at the same time as Callaghan discussed the initiative with President Carter. A month later, at the official opening of the Rhodesian Parliament on 21 June 1977, the 'President', John Wrathall, said that the regime was 'co-operating fully with the American and British Governments in their latest initiative'.

The settlement moves were thrown into confusion, however, by the growing split in the Rhodesian Front. Moreover, with the detention order against him revoked, Sithole returned to Rhodesia early in July 1977, a development which increased speculation that Smith might make a further attempt to reach an 'internal' settlement. The Anglo-American team of officials returned to Salisbury with suggestions for a conference including the internal and external Black leaders. Commenting on the team's departure on 10 July was a perceptive editorial in the London *Financial Times* headed 'Failure in Rhodesia': 'In strict logic, the pressures on Rhodesia ought to make the White regime anxious to settle for the best deal it can get. Unfortunately, the split in the Rhodesian Front is likely to make it more difficult than ever for Mr Smith to identify himself with the principle of a rapid transfer of power to the Blacks. Yet even if he were able to bring himself to look seriously for a settlement, his task has been made doubly difficult by the hardening position of the Black nationalists. The OAU has come out unequivocally in support of the Patriotic Front led by Joshua Nkomo and Robert Mugabe, and of the prosecution of the guerrilla war. President Kenneth Kaunda of Zambia has long hoped for a negotiated settlement, but he can hardly have improved the chances of negotiation by his announcement on Friday that he had reached a contingent agreement on military aid from Cuba and Somalia in the event of serious attacks from Rhodesia.'[12]

By the middle of July 1977, it was clear that Smith had rejected the latest Anglo-American proposals; in an 'Address to the Nation' on 18 July, he announced that he would hold an election on 31 August to seek a mandate for 'an internal settlement between internal Rhodesians'. As part of his plan, he proposed the creation of a broad-based government 'incorporating those Black Rhodesians who are prepared to work peacefully and constitutionally with Government, in order to establish a base from which we will be able to draw up our future constitution'. He also said that he would work towards the removal of 'any remaining discrimination which is considered unnecessary and undesirable'.[13]

Smith's announcement was greeted with regret in London and Washington. In a speech to the Commons on 25 July, Owen was strongly critical of Smith and expressed doubts about his commitment to Black majority rule: 'If it had been in my power, I would have removed Mr Smith the day I took office'. Nevertheless, he felt Smith had a contribution to make and so had to be involved in the negotiations.

Pessimism and a warning of violence came from the South African Foreign Minister, Pik Botha, who said it must be accepted that there could no longer be a completely peaceful solution to the Rhodesian problem.[14] In any settlement, he said, there will be losers who 'will keep on fighting for a while'. Making it clear that he thought the 'losers' would be the Patriotic Front, he criticized the British Government for 'trying to lean over backwards to please the men with the guns'. At the same time, Black and White opinion was hardening all around, especially with the beginning of the election campaign in Rhodesia where the new opposition Rhodesian Action Party (see below), began its campaign with a strong attack on Smith 'and his clear plans to introduce a Black puppet government' in Rhodesia.[15] On the eve of the election, Smith visited Pretoria for talks in which he and Vorster examined 'in a realistic and pragmatic manner . . . the grave problems which confront our two countries'.[16] Smith added that he had told Owen in the previous month that some features of the Anglo-American proposals were quite unacceptable.

It became evident at this time that a substantial difficulty in the negotiations was over the role of the Rhodesian Army during the transition to independence. Led by Nyerere, the Front-line Presidents insisted that a *sine qua non* was the complete removal of Smith's forces and the assumption of military control inside Rhodesia by the British or some other independent agency. The Anglo-American proposal therefore recommended a UN Peacekeeping Force. But when Nkomo arrived in London for talks with Owen on 26 July, he firmly ruled out any idea of such a force. In fact the Patriotic Front became more insistent that military control during the transition period be exclusively in the hands of the guerrilla forces. Mugabe emphasized that the question was 'who will hold power in the transition and at independence. The real issue is the Army: whose Army will be in control, the Rhodesian forces or ours?'[17] Nor would he agree to integrate the Blacks fighting in the Rhodesian Army whom he dismissed as 'mercenaries'. He was prepared only to accept the formula of the guerrilla forces being phased in while the Rhodesians were phased out. Mugabe was also uneasy about Britain's role. 'We don't trust the British, because the British are reluctant to see the Patriotic Front in control,' he said. He refused to consider the possibility of an external 'police' force from the Commonwealth, UN or OAU to maintain law and order during the transition. 'We cannot have other people looking after our security. We have said we are our own liberators and we are our own peacekeepers. . . . The forces that are fighting are the people's forces. We are not fighting against the people. We are fighting with the people.' Any constitutional conference should only be between Britain and the Patriotic Front; Mugabe would agree to others being present only if it had first been accepted that the guerrillas should become the country's security force.

Any hope that the Anglo-American initiative could get all the parties to the conflict to a constitutional conference began to fade fast in August. Smith said in an interview on 3 August that while he had not yet finally given up all hope, he expected little from the West who 'did not confront the Russians over Angola, and I see no signs that they will over Rhodesia'.[18] The Western powers had failed to produce any guarantees that Rhodesia would not be 'reduced to the level of Angola and Mozambique in a chaotic Marxist state'. At the same time, he announced that he was about to embark on his own internal negotiations after satisfactory talks with Muzorewa. The Bishop's aides confirmed on 8 August that the two sides were 'very close to accord'.[19]

Nkomo met Andy Young for the first time on 2 August when both happened to be in Guyana. Young said he was impressed by the conciliatory attitude adopted by Nkomo. However, when he went to Washington for talks with Vance on 5 August, Nkomo said that the Rhodesian problem was not a joint Anglo-American affair. Mugabe met Young for the first time in Lagos on 25 August during the international conference on sanctions against SA. He was reported to have said that, provided the settlement terms being worked out by London and Washington were implemented immediately, they might prove acceptable.[20] But a few days later, he was reported to have told 100 of his supporters at a secret meeting in Maputo that it was 'Britain's idea to remove Smith and maintain the *status quo*—the Air Force and Army. And they want us to accept it because Britain would be in charge of the situation.'[21] He added: 'The removal of Smith, the figurehead of British imperialism, does not change things because Smith represents Britain'. He repeated that the issue was the dismantling of the Rhodesian forces and their replacement by guerrillas. This demand was predictably rejected out of hand by Rhodesia's Minister of Combined Operations, Roger Hawkins, who said that not only would they never agree to dismantling the Rhodesian forces, but 'our security forces will never be defeated by the terrorists'.[22]

During a visit to Washington in August, Nyerere insisted that there could be no prospect of a settlement until agreement was reached on dismantling Smith's forces. He repeated this view when he stopped over in London on his return home. Back in Dar es Salaam, he said that he had received assurances from the British and American governments that they accepted the principle that the guerrilla forces would form the basis of the Zimbabwe army and that the Rhodesian Army would be completely disbanded as soon as the transition period to independence began.[23]

However, the statements attributed to Nyerere did not accurately reflect Anglo-American thinking on this issue. What was envisaged at the time was that, after terms for a settlement had been agreed, a Zimbabwe army would be built up by recruiting from the guerrillas, while phasing out the most objectionable of the Rhodesian forces—such as the Selous Scouts and the First Rhodesian Regiment; the remnants of the existing Army and Air Force would be integrated into the new force (for details, see below).

On 25 August 1977, Callaghan warned that the new Anglo-American plan about to be unveiled could prove to be the very last chance for a negotiated transition to independence. Britain, he said, would accept 'certain limited responsibilities for a short period' during the transition.[24] On the following day, the Security Council again discussed the problem of Rhodesia and adopted a strong resolution demanding an immediate end to the Smith regime. The Anglo-American plan, announced on 1 September, called for the resignation of the Smith regime to allow the country to return to legality.[25] It made provision for direct British rule for a limited period; for the appointment of a British Resident-Commissioner (later named as Field Marshall Lord Carver) with full executive and legislative powers who would hold ultimate control over the armed forces and police; for a UN Peacekeeping force and a special UN representative to work with the British authority; for sanctions to be lifted when the Smith regime handed over to an interim British administration; for independence to follow after general elections; for new Constitution which would provide for a Bill of Rights; for the minority communities to be entitled to one-fifth of the members of the new parliament; and for a Zimbabwe Development Fund of between $1-1.5 bn, of which the UK would contribute 15% and the US 45%.

Details about the security forces to be created to supervise the transition did not form part of the White Paper, but were outlined separately in a statement made by Dr Owen during a visit to Salisbury. Though open to all citizens, the new army would 'be based on the liberation forces'. It specifically proposed to disband units of the present Rhodesian forces—the Selous Scouts were named. But disbandment of both the Rhodesia and the liberation armies was an implied, if not specific, condition for the creation of a new army. The Anglo-American objectives were to organize the maintenance of law and order during the transitional period and to create 'the single army of Zimbabwe'. While primary responsibility for law and order during the transition would lie with the police (who would have a new Commissioner and some members appointed by the UN special representative), a UN force would supervise the ceasefire.

Initial reactions to the Anglo-American proposals were lukewarm rather than wholly condemnatory. Having just seen the Rhodesian Front win all the 50 White seats, Smith spoke in highly critical fashion of the Anglo-American proposals, but he was careful not to reject them outright. He described the plan as 'a very cunning scheme' to get the PF of Nkomo and Mugabe into power, and dismissed as a 'crazy suggestion' the idea that the guerrillas should form the basis of the future security forces. On the presence of a UN Peacekeeping force, Smith said: 'If they should agree to come in and assist us under the control of our command, this is something we would consider. But if it is a question of surrendering our power to some such organization, that would be chaotic. It seems to be an almost insane suggestion.' Besides taking strong exception to the proposal that he should surrender power to a British Resident-Commissioner during an interim administration, Smith also turned personally on Owen, as he has done on every British Minister with whom he has dealt. Of his last talks with the British Foreign Secretary, he said: 'I detected more than I have ever detected before on the part of Dr Owen an attempt to exact retribution on Rhodesians for what took place in 1965 [the date of UDI]. It seems to me they are seeking revenge, and if that is so I think it bodes ill for trying to come to a reasonable settlement of our constitutional problem.'[26]

The Patriotic Front also rejected aspects of the Anglo-American proposals, though indicating that the White Paper could form the basis for further negotiations. In a joint statement, Nkomo and Mugabe said the 'mechanics' for the transfer of power to the Black majority would not lead to a genuinely independent Zimbabwe, adding that the guerrilla war would continue until genuine independence was attained. They listed three main objections to the proposals. The first was that the Resident-Commissioner could not be seen as a neutral or impartial officer in view of the powers at his disposal—'absolute colonial powers'. Second, they rejected proposals that the police force and elements of the army should remain intact during the transition. Third, they were opposed to the creation of a UN Peacekeeping force, arguing that it would be used to frustrate and not advance the liberation struggle.[27] Thus, even though the PF leaders did not reject the Anglo-American plan outright, their objections to it were in fact fundamental.

Both Muzorewa and Sithole welcomed the broad details of the plan, but reserved their positions pending further clarification. At that time Muzorewa was still saying: 'It is dangerous to talk to Smith. . . . Anything that is led by Ian Smith is completely out.'[28]

Dr Owen and Andy Young set off at the beginning of September to discuss their proposals with African leaders including Vorster, and to open discussions with the Smith regime. Their immediate aim was to negotiate for an immediate ceasefire to enable talks about a constitutional conference to begin. SA privately gave a cautious welcome to the proposals, but made no public comment. However, it was made clear that the Vorster regime would under no circumstances agree to the guerrillas being moved in to take over from the Rhodesian Army. On 28 September, Smith invited Carver to Salisbury for talks to explore the idea of a ceasefire. On the same day, the UK formally proposed that the Security Council endorse the proposal to appoint a UN representative to participate in the negotiations (see p. C72). The proposal was accepted and Lt-Gen Prem Chand (India) was designated as the head of any UN Peacekeeping force that might be established.

During October, it became increasingly clear that insuperable obstacles stood in the way of obtaining a ceasefire and proceeding towards constitutional talks. Smith, for one, continued to pursue his independent initiative. Early in October he flew to Lusaka for a secret meeting (arranged by Tiny Rowland, the managing director of Lonrho) to explore with President Kaunda the possibility of inducing Joshua Nkomo to participate in a broad-based government to discuss the new constitution. The talks yielded no result; but they did upset Nkomo's partners in the PF (see below). On 27 October, Nkomo indicated a toughening stand towards the proposals by calling for a drastic reduction in the powers to be conferred on the Resident-Commissioner. Kaunda, too, broke ranks with his Front-line colleagues by describing the Anglo-American proposal for elections before independence as an invitation to civil war. This led to a period of tension between him and the other FLPs who supported Nyerere's strong stand on NIMBAR (No Independence before Majority Rule).

Although Lord Carver had upset White Rhodesians over remarks he had made to the effect that he had 'no sympathy' with Smith's political position, he nevertheless went to Salisbury on 2 November, accompanied by Prem Chand, stopping first in Dar es Salaam for talks with Nyerere, Nkomo and Mugabe. Although press reports spoke of the PF leaders snubbing the military emissaries, Carver emphatically denied this and should be believed. Even before his arrival in Salisbury, Smith described Carver's task as 'well-nigh an impossibility'. He said he held out little hope of the Anglo-American plan succeeding, and admitted that he was keeping open his 'internal settlement' option. In his view, Muzorewa, Sithole and Chirau among them could count on 'at least' 85% of Black Rhodesian support, with Nkomo enjoying 15%, and Mugabe none.[29] The rebel Foreign Minister, P. K van der Byl, was much more scathing in his attitude to the Anglo-American plan, which he described as 'an Anglo-American-Russian plan set-up'; the proposals were 'totally outrageous; based on the 'imposition of unconditional surrender on an undefeated people who are not enemies'.[30]

Lord Carver's visit to Salisbury lasted from 2–9 November, but was a complete failure. According to Smith, Carver had proposed that virtually every White unit of the Rhodesian forces be disbanded (with the exception of the Air Force but including the territorial forces) and that the Rhodesian African Rifles be confined to barracks. Smith said he told the British envoy in no uncertain terms that this was 'just not on'.[31] He agreed with his military leaders who said such an act would amount to total surrender. Smith repeated that any attempt to achieve a ceasefire before a political solution in Rhodesia was putting the cart before the horse and was therefore quite impracticable.

Nkomo was upset by Carver and Prem Chand having talks while in Salisbury with Muzorewa and Sithole, whom he described as 'totally irrelevant' since they were not waging the war. He warned Britain that the PF would break off all negotiations if it was not accepted as the only party to speak for Zimbabweans. On 14 November, Nkomo dismissed the Anglo-American initiative as 'a total failure'. Undeterred by this, Owen told the House of Commons on 11 November—when sanctions against Rhodesia were renewed for another year—that he still believed an independent Zimbabwe was possible by the end of 1978. With the initiative temporarily stalemated, the Anglo-American team again met in London in mid-November to discuss how to sustain the momentum towards convening an all-party conference to discuss the new constitution. But before they could re-launch the initiative, Smith pre-empted them. On 24 November, he proceeded with his 'internal settlement' option.

In a statement issued on 24 November, Smith explained that 'in view of the failure of the latest Anglo-American initiative', he had invited the leaders of the Black political parties to enter into constitutional negotiations with the regime 'with a view to reaching a constitutional settlement in Rhodesia, and thus to bring peace to the country'. The statement added: 'The Black leaders, without exception, impressed upon the Prime Minister that the only way of successfully launching the negotiations would be for the Government to make a firm commitment to the principle of majority rule based on adult suffrage. The Prime Minister pointed out that his Government's interest in a qualified franchise was as a means of ensuring the maintenance not only of standards, but also of the confidence of the White Rhodesians. Constitutional and other evidence now available indicated that there were other and possibly better ways of maintaining standards and retaining this confidence than by means of a qualified franchise. Accordingly, Government would reserve the right to pursue these aspects in any constitutional negotiations. The Black political leaders fully endorsed the desirability of retaining White confidence, and accepted Government's right to follow this course at the conference table. In view of this undertaking, Government is prepared to enter the negotiations on the understanding that if their requirements in this regard are met, they will accept the principle of majority rule, based on adult suffrage.'[32]

Senator Chief Chirau, Zupo's President, welcomed the plan. Sithole said if Smith were prepared to surrender power to the majority, the people would not hesitate to receive it. Muzorewa stated that by calling the conference, Smith had capitulated to demands for the transfer of power to the Black majority.[33] The *Rhodesia Herald* commented: 'The announcement by the Prime Minister that the Government is prepared to accept the principle of majority rule based on adult suffrage in return for other safeguards marks a dramatic start to a new attempt to bring peace to Rhodesia. Mr Smith has shown courage in committing the Government to this course, for he will undoubtedly be the target for criticism from those who will see the move as appeasement. 'But we believe the Prime Minister is being realistic in accepting the argument of the leaders of Black political parties in the country that without the commitment to one-man one-vote, the negotiations would be doomed. Once the principle of majority rule had been accepted, it was inevitable that eventually adult suffrage would follow.'[34] Predictably, the Patriotic Front denounced Smith's plan.

The talks for an internal settlement made an abortive start at the beginning of

December 1977 when neither Muzorewa nor Sithole was in the country; but they began in earnest on 9 December, with all leaders present. Smith was assisted by P. K. van der Byl, the regime's Foreign Minister; Hilary Squires, Minister of Law and Order; David Smith, Minister of Finance; and Jack Gaylard, the Cabinet Secretary. A short communiqué stated that progress had been achieved on the question of adult suffrage and constitutional safeguards, and that further meetings would be held 'frequently . . . to ensure as rapid progress as possible'.[35]

Once the talks got under way, several more exiles returned, the most prominent being George Nyandoro, external affairs secretary of the UANC and an inseparable ally of Chikerema's; Prof Stanlake Samkange, author of *Origins of Rhodesia* (1968); Lawrence Vambe, a former Rhodesian editor who was appointed Muzorewa's public relations officer; and Enoch Dumbutshwenya, a barrister and veteran nationalist.

From this point on, the internal talks proceeded in parallel with a more vigorous Anglo-American initiative. Early in December, for instance, Mugabe said in Maputo that the PF would not accept an invitation from Dr Owen to attend talks in London; two days later Nkomo, who had earlier accepted the invitation, also rejected it. The Front leaders refused further discussions until Owen recommitted himself to the removal of Smith and the dismantling of the Rhodesian Army.[36] Meanwhile, on 12 December 1977, Sithole stated that agreement had been reached on the definition of the term 'universal adult suffrage'. The session on that day had been chaired by Sithole; as Nicholas Ashford commented in *The Times*: 'The fact that Mr Smith was prepared, for the first time since his unilateral declaration of independence 12 years ago, to take part in formal negotiations under the chairmanship of a Black nationalist symbolizes the apparent desire by all parties involved to ensure that this round of talks ends in success.'[37]

Although Smith forecast a major settlement breakthrough within two months, by the time the talks adjourned at Christmas, this had not come, and when they resumed after the holiday there was deadlock over the question of the proportion of White representation in a Parliament under majority rule. Smith's demand was for one-third of the seats for Whites in a future Parliament—a proportion that would enable them to veto constitutional change under an entrenched blocking mechanism written into the constitution. The African nationalists refused to concede that such seats should be chosen by a separate White electorate.[38]

While the Salisbury talks continued, fresh moves were made to revive the Anglo-American proposals when Lord Carver and Lt-Gen Prem Chand visited Mozambique early in January 1978. After talks with President Samora Machel, a communiqué referred to 'a unanimous willingness to put an end as soon as possible to the illegal minority racist regime and install mechanisms of transition conducive to the total and complete independence of Zimbabwe, and the need for holding talks as soon as possible between the British Government and the Patriotic Front on the basis of the so-called Anglo-American proposals.[39]

In Salisbury, the argument continued over the 'blocking mechanism'; but behind the arguments were clear signs of a wish, by both White and Black leaders, to achieve a settlement. Bridget Bloom discussed the position in the *Financial Times* (9 January 1978): 'But many people here believe that these talks are different from any of the others which have taken place so far. This is not just because of the obvious fact that those who are waging the guerrilla war under the banner of the Patriotic Front are not taking part, though this alone could negate any agreement that might finally be signed. The main difference is that for Smith the talks probably represent the very last chance that he will have of negotiating any special position for White Rhodesians in a Black-ruled Zimbabwe, and for the Black leaders—Bishop Abel

Muzorewa, the Rev Ndabaningi Sithole and Chief Chirau—they are probably also a last chance, for any other solution would probably see them swept away by the guerrilla military forces which they do not control.' She went on: 'White representation apart, the Achilles heel of the current negotiations will be international recognition . . . .'

On 20 January 1978, the 'internal settlement' negotiators agreed in principle on the size of the blocking group of seats. On the same day, Nkomo and Mugabe, reversing their previous position, accepted an invitation from Owen to attend talks in Malta. Smith condemned the British Foreign Secretary for joining in an 'unholy alliance' with the Patriotic Front to discredit the internal Black leaders and any internal settlement that might be reached.[40] Just before the Malta talks began, Muzorewa walked out of the Salisbury negotiations, claiming that he had been insulted by members of Smith's team. For several days the talks hung in the balance, but the Bishop returned to the conference room on 1 February 1978. No public apology was forthcoming. There were accusations from the Smith side that Muzorewa was being subverted by the Anglo-Americans.

The Malta talks, which were attended by Andrew Young as well as Dr Owen and the Patriotic Front leaders, ended without agreement on 2 February. However, the gap between the parties narrowed and there was a prospect of further discussions, probably in Africa.

Reporting on the Malta talks to Parliament on 2 February, Owen admitted that in certain circumstances the British Government would have to consider recognizing a government in Rhodesia resulting from the internal settlement talks. He said: 'Although we should pursue peace up to the last moment, I envisage a situation in which we must consider recognizing a government which had assumed power while there was still a conflict. That is the reality. We have to assess that decision on the basis of how many people voted in the election and whether the government was reasonably representative.'[41]

In an article on the private discussions which had taken place in Malta, Colin Legum reported that the PF insisted that Smith had agreed to the internal settlement talks on the basis of majority rule solely because of the impact of the armed struggle, which it alone had been waging. The PF felt it was getting the upper hand and was not about to stop fighting unless its dominant position was recognized and entrenched. 'The over-riding consideration of the Anglo-American side is that any political agreement should ensure three fundamental results: that the fighting will be stopped permanently; that it should be internationally acceptable, otherwise there will be no way of ending economic sanctions; and that free elections will be held in which both the internal and external forces will be allowed to participate freely and equally. Unless these results can be guaranteed, no agreement will be worth the paper it is written on. The war will continue and indeed probably escalate through greater international involvement; the country's economy will continue to bleed to death. Independence would then come through violence and, instead of an orderly transfer, there would be chaos. What the Conservatives who criticized Dr Owen in Parliament have still failed to grasp is that the PF is in fact indispensable to any agreement that would avoid these dangers.'[42]

Meanwhile, back in Salisbury, agreement was reached on 15 February 1978 on the composition of a 100-seat Parliament based on a compromise proposal put forward by the Sithole delegation. There would be 20 White MPs elected on a preferential voting system by White voters enrolled on the common role, and another eight White MPs elected by Black and White voters enrolled on the common roll, from a minimum of 16 candidates nominated by an electoral college. 'For the first election, this electoral college will comprise the 50 White members of the present Parliament. For the second and subsequent elections within the first ten years, the electoral college will comprise 28 White members of the Parliament, which will be dissolved immediately prior to such election.' Other points of agreement included provision for a Bill of Rights, independence of the Judiciary entrenched in the Constitution, and the establishment of a transitional government to oversee a ceasefire and related matters, and arrange a general election as early as possible.[43] The Salisbury negotiators next turned their attention to the composition of the armed forces of a future Zimbabwe. Smith was reported to have agreed in principle that guerrillas wishing to return and join the armed forces might do so on certain conditions.

THE INTERNAL SETTLEMENT, MARCH TO JUNE 1978

The agreement for the 'internal settlement' was finally signed on 3 March 1978 (for complete document, see pp. C73–76). Joshua Nkomo described it as 'the greatest sell-out in the history of Africa'. Even allowing for hyperbole, Nicholas Ashford wrote: 'In a sense, Mr Nkomo's "sell out" charge is not altogether unjustified. Mr Smith has had his way on practically every point. Even after majority rule has been achieved, the White minority, and in particular the RF, will still wield political influence which is proportionately far greater than the number of Whites in the country. But does that really matter? The agreement reached between Mr Smith and the three Black leaders means that the new government of an independent Zimbabwe will be entirely Black and there will be a majority of Blacks in parliament voted on the basis of universal adult suffrage. And Mr Smith will probably have retired to his farm in Selukwe. These are very considerable achievements and certainly go far beyond what Mr Nkomo hoped to be able to extract from Mr Smith when he was holding settlement talks in Salisbury two years ago.'[44]

Official British and American reactions were cautious. Andrew Young said the agreement failed to resolve the issues that had led to armed struggle because it ignored the PF.[45] Dr Owen described the settlement as 'a significant move towards majority rule' which should be welcomed, but added that there were still crucial issues to be resolved.[46] The problem for the British and Americans was how to avoid totally condemning the internal settlement while upholding the claims of the PF to speak for Black Rhodesians.

South Africa's Prime Minister gave the agreement a qualified welcome: 'How successful it will be in practice will depend on the one hand on the goodwill with which the parties abide by it and implement it, and on the other hand whether they will be allowed to organize and determine their own affairs by so-called public opinion, as well as by the African and world organizations and by neighbouring and distant countries. Only time can give an answer to this.'

Other African reactions were almost uniformly hostile. The Nigerian government said it had been prepared to support the Anglo-American proposals because it recognized that the PF would form the basis of the Zimbabwe army and that Smith would have to go; but the proposed settlement was 'a sell-out'. The *Times of Zambia* (4 March 1978) said that the new agreement allowed the Whites to remain virtually in control of affairs for another ten years. The Front-line Presidents, who met in Dar es Salaam from 25–26 March, issued a joint communiqué describing their role in the Anglo-American initiative and challenging London and Washington to state categorically whether they still stood by their proposals.[47] The last three paragraphs of the communiqué stated:

> 7. The PF and the Front-line States have, however, noted with grave concern that rather than condemn these Smith manoeuvres which aim at defeating their own proposals and the current negotiations, the UK and US Governments have

WHITE POLITICS

At the end of April 1977, 12 RF rebel MPs, together with the ruling party's deputy chairman, Harold Coleman, were expelled from the party. By the end of June, the expelled MPs (including Ted Sutton-Pryce, the former Deputy Minister in Ian Smith's own department, and Reg Cowper, the former Defence Minister) were set to form a new Right-wing party. At the beginning of July, the RF chairman, Des Frost, himself resigned in protest against Smith's policies. The new party, the Rhodesian Action Party (RAP), came into being with Ian Sandeman, a RF MP for the past seven years, as its interim chairman.

At the opposite end of the White political spectrum, an amalgam of liberal-minded opponents of Smith formed the National Unifying Force (NUF) under Allan Savory's leadership. The NUF did not see itself as an alternative government, but rather as a pressure group to try to unite Blacks and Whites in preparation for eventual Black rule.

The revolt in the RF on the question of ending racial discrimination underlined traditional White Rhodesian racial attitudes.[50] On the other hand, the RF victory and the complete rout of the Right-wing defectors grouped in RAP in the August elections indicated not a change in traditional attitudes, perhaps, but a growing sense of realism. The political battle-cries, too, had changed. There were no longer comforting references to 'high standards' being maintained in 'civilized hands'; instead, Smith told his audiences that a 'broad-based government' would rule responsibly and incidentally do away with discrimination that 'infringes upon human dignity'.[51] A more forthright version of the same message came from the NUF during the election campaign. Allan Savory argued for Black majority rule now—a policy denounced by RAP as surrender terms and tantamount to national suicide. No NUF members were elected, but in most of the 18 seats the party contested, RAP candidates were beaten into third place. This was one of the more significant pointers to a discernible shift in White Rhodesian thinking, a widespread acceptance that majority rule is not only inevitable but imminent.[52]

The need to accept change in attitudes was put frequently to White Rhodesians during 1977. In March, for instance, Rowan Cronje, Rhodesia's Minister of Health, Manpower and Welfare, spoke in SA of the need to accept changes 'even if they leave a bitter taste in the mouth'. He added: 'Yesterday's solutions are not good enough for today. . . . As Afrikaners and Rhodesians, we must look the problems square in the face. . . . Since last September, we have conceded the un-thinkable. Principles which only months ago were holy to us now seem like trivialities.'[53]

Reaction to the repeal of some of the discriminatory legislation affecting Africans' rights to use hotels and attend multiracial gatherings was reported to be mixed: 'By and large, White Rhodesians appear to be adjusting with comparative ease to sharing their amenities with the few middle-class Blacks equipped to meet them on the same social level'.[54] More than 400 businessmen belonging to the Bulawayo Chamber of Commerce and the Chamber of Industries overwhelmingly agreed to study ways of assisting the efficient transition to Black majority rule. Their proposals, made in July 1977, included positive assistance to member companies to eliminate racial structures in employment.[55]

At the time of the twelfth anniversary of UDI, Nicholas Ashford wrote that the majority of Whites 'now seem to be prepared to live under a moderate Black Government so long as there was a reasonable chance that law and order and general standards were maintained. . . . This change in attitude is the result of a growing sense of war-weariness.'[56]

GOVERNMENT CHANGES

There were two changes in the Cabinet early in 1977, followed by a radical trans-formation in April 1978 after the 'internal settlement'. Reginald Cowper resigned as Minister of Defence in February 1977, and Rowan Cronje was appointed to take charge of military manpower requirements. Roger Hawkins became Minister of Combined Operations in March 1977. In July, three Ministers announced that they would not stand in the general election: Elly Broomberg (Information, Immigration and Tourism); Philip Smith (Lands); and Ian Dillon (Mines). The Defence and Combined Operations portfolios were combined in September 1977 under Hawkins. Mark Partridge moved from Defence to Agriculture, and Rollo Hayman, former Agriculture Minister, took on Internal Affairs. P. K. van der Byl added Information, Immigration and Tourism to his Foreign Affairs portfolio. Andre Holland was appointed Deputy Minister for Information, Immigration, Tourism and Public Services; Alexander Moseley was appointed Deputy Minister of Internal Affairs.

Smith dropped three of his Ministers in the April 1978 changes: the 68-year old hard-liner, Senator Desmond Lardner-Burke (a Minister for 14 years); Air Marshall Archibald Wilson; and Denis Walker, who had been criticized for his handling of the Education Ministry to which he had only recently been appointed.

INTERNAL SETTLEMENT GOVERNMENT (as at 12 April 1978)

'Prime Minister'	Ian Douglas Smith	
'Co-Ministers':		
Finance, Commerce and Industry	David Smith	Ernest Bulle (UANC)
Transport and Power Mines, Roads and Traffic and Posts	William Irvine	James Chikerema (UANC)
Internal Affairs, Local Government, Housing and Works	Rollo Hayman	Chief Kayisa Ndiweni (Zupo)
Education, Health, Man-power and Social Affairs	Rowan Cronje	Gibson Magaramombe (Zupo)
Defence and Combined Operations	Roger Hawkins	John Kadzwiti (ANC-S)
Agriculture	Mark Partridge	Joel Mandaza (ANC-S)
Justice and Law and Order	Hilary Squires	Byron Hove* (UANC)
Foreign Affairs, Information, Immigration and Tourism	P. K. van der Byl	Dr Elliot Gabellah (ANC-S)
Lands, Water Development, Natural Resources and Rural Development	Jack Mussett	Aaron Mgutshini (Zupo)

*Dismissed on 28 April 1978.

THE DIVIDED NATIONALISTS

By 1977 only one obstacle stood in the way to achieving a Black-ruled Zimbabwe: the divisions in the nationalists' own ranks. This point was made strongly in an editorial in the *Zambia Daily Mail* on 20 October 1977, which declared that if the PF had 'adopted a positive attitude towards its own problem of unity, the Rhodesian problem would soon be a thing of the past and the nationalists would be within real smelling distance of Black majority rule. If the PF delays its unity and allows Smith to confuse the situation by getting stooges on his side, the PF must not equivocated with a view to abandoning their previous commitment to the PF, the Front-line States and the Security Council on the Anglo-American proposals.

8. The Front-line States and the PF call upon the British and American governments to make known their position *vis-à-vis* their own proposals. If they still support these proposals, they should then move ahead and convene, in the shortest time possible, a meeting to follow up what was agreed in Malta. If on the other hand, they have decided to abandon their commitment to their own proposals for which they had requested and obtained the support of the PF, the Front-line States, and the international community, they should so declare unequivocally without any further delay. In particular, they should go back to the Security Council and move a revocation of the mandate given to the Secretary-General to appoint a Special Representative.

9. The present circumstances demand an intensification of the just armed struggle for the liberation of Zimbabwe. The Front-line States therefore reaffirm their total and unwavering support to the armed struggle being waged by the people of Zimbabwe under the leadership of the PF for the attainment of complete independence and the establishment of a genuine democratic government.

Owen invited Nkomo and Mugabe to London for talks to discuss future plans. He suggested that it was still desirable to try to arrange a conference between the PF and the signatories to the internal settlement, but Nkomo and Mugabe ruled out any such idea. Nkomo's view was that the internal settlement had changed nothing in Rhodesia since 'the seat of power, the Army, the police, the judiciary and the civil service, are firmly in the hands of Mr Smith and his minority'.

In mid-April 1978, Cyrus Vance, Carver and Prem Chand joined David Owen in a visit to Africa to try to regain the initiative. Although Nkomo and Mugabe agreed in Dar es Salaam that a new conference could be held involving all the parties to the Rhodesian conflict, Owen summed up the talks as 'not totally negative, but not totally positive either'. In fact, the PF put forward detailed proposals for changes in the Resident-Commissioner's role which would have 'fundamentally' affected the Anglo-American plan. On the other hand, the PF now accepted the idea of a UN force but, as Mugabe explained, only for three purposes: 'to ensure that a ceasefire was adhered to; to disarm and dismantle the existing Rhodesian security forces; and to defend the country against outside enemies who may want to interfere with the independence process'. The Resident-Commissioner would be allowed executive authority over the security forces, provided the PF was the dominant force in the governing council of which Carver would be a member. The PF's proposal was for a governing council of 12: Carver, three from the internal front (possibly Smith, Muzorewa and Sithole), and eight from the PF. Nyerere was upset by the largely negative reaction of Owen and Vance to the PF's proposals since, in his view, the Front had moved forward considerably from its stand even at Malta.

Owen and Vance went on to SA and Rhodesia. While none of the internal front leaders objected to the idea of an all-party conference, Smith said that he believed it a waste of time. He was willing to consider the Anglo-American proposals, but made attendance at such a conference conditional on not going back on the 'internal settlement'. In a formal reply to Owen and Vance on 25 April, the Rhodesian interim government stated that while it appreciated their desire to achieve a peaceful transition through the democratic process of free and fair elections, it did not believe an all-party conference would stand any more chance of success than that of Geneva in 1976. It therefore urged the Anglo-Americans 'to re-examine their policies in the light of the radically changed circumstances in Rhodesia'.

The Owen-Vance mission thus failed in its immediate purpose of regaining the momentum in favour of all-party negotiations which could have prevented a deepening of the divisions between the internal and external Black leaders. But for the time being, both sides were left to confront each other: the PF to intensify its armed struggle, and the internal front to try to make its settlement work. If neither side succeeded in its aim (which the Anglo-Americans believed would be the case), there might still be an opportunity to bring the two sides together for yet another 'final' attempt to avoid total violence and economic disaster.

The new Transitional Executive Council, formed on 21 March 1978, comprised Ian Smith, Bishop Muzorewa, the Rev John Sithole and Chief Chirau. The Black leaders, who were sworn in under the pre-UDI Constitution of 1969, chose to have the oath administered by the Anglican Suffragen Bishop of Mashonaland rather than by the 'President'. The ceremony was conducted in private; not even the Press was admitted. 'There is a time,' the Bishop said in answer to a question as to whether he minded swearing an oath to the existing State, 'when you have to swallow your pride for the greatest good'. The chairmanship of the Council was to rotate on a monthly basis; Smith won the first draw for the post.

It took a fortnight of bargaining among the African parties to arrange the distribution of the 26 Cabinet portfolios allocated to them. UANC and Zupo finally got ten each, and Sithole's group only six. The Ministerial Council comprises nine Black and nine White Ministers (see Government List, below). The Executive Council also set up a Constitutional Committee to prepare a draft to implement the principles agreed upon in the settlement talks.

Four days after taking office, Byron Hove (UANC) was dismissed by the Executive Council as Co-Minister of Justice, Law and Order after criticizing police brutality and the structure of the Judiciary. He was publicly repudiated by his White Co-Minister, Hilary Squires, and by Gen Walls, the Commander of Combined Operations. On 5 April, a start was made in releasing political detainees; by 26 April, 561 had been freed. All hangings of people convicted of political crimes were also stopped. At the same time, the UANC vice-president, James Chikerema, warned that guerrillas who continued to harass the government would be severely dealt with. Three months' prison sentences were handed out to 78 Black students who had demonstrated against the internal settlement on 25 April. The secretary of ANC-S described them as a 'bunch of intellectuals' demonstrating on full stomachs. But a *Zimbabwe Times* editorial insisted that the right of free speech, free assembly and demonstration were among the important elements of democracy.

After almost four months of the interim government, there was still no sign of any willingness by the guerrillas to lay down their arms, or any prospect of ending sanctions and so preventing further deterioration in the economy. Nor was there any serious hope of holding free elections in the foreseeable future. A debate in the Rhodesian Assembly on 22 June 1978 showed just how disillusioning an experience the settlement had so far been. A leading RF MP, Wing Commander Robert Gaunt, called on the four members of the Executive Council to 'bury the hatchets—and not in each other's heads'. He disclosed that turnouts at public meetings over the past three months had been 'pathetic'—no more than 500 to 1,000 'unless we lay on a train, buses, beer and bribes'. A Black MP, Thomas Zawaira, endorsed the views expressed by Gaunt and other RF members: 'We are heading for another Angola,' he declared. The atmosphere in the Senate was no better. Looking around the chamber at what he called 'the passing order', Senator Dr Peter Barnard Rose lamented: 'Those who are about to die salute you'.[48] Muzorewa admitted that there was justifiable concern about the lack of progress towards a ceasefire, but denied that the transitional government had failed.[49]

be surprised if it later loses the support of the Zambians, Mozambicans, Tanzanians and the people of Botswana.'

However, the problem was not just disunity in the PF nor even rivalry between the external and internal forces. The latter camp was also divided, with the Rev Ndabaningi Sithole's African National Council (known as ANC-S) coming out in open rivalry to Bishop Abel Muzorewa's United African National Council (UANC)—now more frequently described as ANC-Z. Chief Jeremiah Chirau's Zimbabwe United People's Organization (Zupo) floated between the two. Inside the UANC, internal divisions produced a breakaway group, leaving uneasy tensions between the Bishop and one of his main lieutenants, James Robert Chikerema. Externally, PF unity between Joshua Nkomo's Zimbabwe African People's Union (Zapu) and Robert Mugabe's Zimbabwe African National Union (Zanu) was still only an aspiration. While Zapu remained firmly under Nkomo's command, Zanu could be controlled only by a coalition led by Robert Mugabe and Josiah Tongogara, the guerrillas' commander.

These divisions are usually explained as being entirely due to 'tribalism' between the Shona and the Ndebele—an oversimplification to the point of distortion. While tribalism or regionalism is an important element in African politics, it is by no means the main reason for the bitter power struggles in Zimbabwe. The equation of Zapu = Ndebele and Zanu = Shona is plainly erroneous, as Muzorewa and Mugabe both draw their main support from the Shonas. This would suggest an inter-Shona rather than a Shona-Ndebele conflict. While there is inter-Shona conflict involving a number of clans—especially the Karanga—this is not a complete explanation either since different Shona clans are represented in each of the major parties, including 'Ndebele' Zapu. Nor are all the Karanga even in the same group. Moreover, if one looks closely at the composition of Zapu, its leadership will be found to have few pure Ndebele representatives: it is mainly dominated by the minority Kalanga group in the 'Ndebele' south. The Kalanga derive from the Shoan Karanga tribe. Nkomo himself is Kalanga, though he has some Ndebele connections.[57]

Nor is there a simple ideological explanation for the nationalists' disunity. While ideology has begun to take root (especially in Zanu), its impact is still relatively unimportant. An adequate explanation for the power struggle would certainly have to take account of ideology as well as tribal and especially clan conflicts as occurred in the Scottish Highlands in the 18th and 19th centuries. But a main reason for the cleavage is to be found in the experience of the Zimbabwe nationalist struggle over the last 20 years, during which time quarrels over tactics and personalities have produced rival parties owing allegiance to particular leaders. Developments in the 1950s and 1960s have thus helped to shape the present form of the power struggle. But, here again, it would be misleading to see the clash between Muzorewa, Sithole, Mugabe, Nkomo and Chikerema simply in terms of personal rivalries. The phenomenon of bitter rivalries dividing nationalist movements is universal to all liberation struggles—not just to those of Zimbabwe or of Africa.

THE PATRIOTIC FRONT[58]

The PF was formed in October 1976 as a marriage of convenience between Zapu and Zanu to confront the forces of Muzorewa's UANC and Sithole's ANC, and to serve as a common front in the negotiations with Britain. The PF owed its formation mainly to the pressures of the Front-line African Presidents (FLPs) in their desire for a single instrument to challenge the Smith regime.[59] Instead, it deepened the cleavage between those forces supported or rejected by the FLPs. The bitterness of feeling is shown by this statement typical of many made by Muzorewa and his supporters: 'Nkomo is being aided and abetted by Dr Kaunda in building up an army not to fight Smith, but to fight the people of Zimbabwe when Zimbabwe is free without his leadership. I find it crude that he has no sense of shame about announcing his evil intentions to the whole wide world.'[60] On its side, PF spokesmen threatened that those 'conniving with the enemy'—like Muzorewa, Sithole and Chikerema—would 'one day be tried by court martial'.[61] When Kaunda succeeded in persuading the OAU at its summit meeting in Libreville to give exclusive recognition to the PF,[62] the PLFs in effect left Muzorewa and Sithole with little alternative but to form their internal Rhodesian camp and to seek to win the power struggle by making a deal with the Smith regime. Thus the 'internal settlement' was at least indirectly the result of the FLPs' tactics.

Repeated attempts were made in 1977 to unify the two wings of the PF, and especially of their armies—Zapu's Zimbabwe Revolutionary Army (Zipra) and Zanu's Zimbabwe's African National Liberation Army (Zanla). Although some progress was made towards getting closer political co-operation, the efforts at military unification failed. In fact, efforts proceeded to build up two much stronger rival armies, each dependent for training on rival communist powers. Zanla, based in Mozambique and Tanzania, depended almost entirely on Chinese military advisers, while Zipra, based largely in Zambia and Angola, was trained and equipped by Russians and Cubans. In this way, the Sino-Soviet rivalry became a factor in the internal PF conflict. This was reflected in Mugabe's adoption of Maoism (see below), and in Nkomo's more frequent visits to Moscow and Havana and in acquiring their political rhetoric.

The rivalry for power between Zapu and Zanu was also sharpened by the tendency of some African countries to take sides. Thus, President Kaunda of Zambia and President Neto of Angola strongly supported Nkomo, while President Machel of Mozambique backed Zanla, but not necessarily Mugabe. Tanzania's President Nyerere—while not on good personal terms with Mugabe—did not favour one party over the other. The British and Americans, too, showed a greater preference for Nkomo (despite his Moscow-Havana connections) than for Mugabe.

The two PF wings met in Dar es Salaam in May 1977 to discuss ways of merging their armies. At that point Zanla was still the stronger, having between 15,000–20,000 in training camps and c. 3,000 in actual combat, while Zipra had perhaps 8,500 cadres, mainly recent recruits not yet properly trained. Memories of the fighting between Zapu and Zanu cadres in Mgagao and Morogoro camps in Tanzania after the 1976 attempts to unify the two forces under a single command still rankled.[63] At the end of a special meeting of the FLPs in Dar es Salaam in July held to try to overcome the obstacles to military unification, President Nyerere said: 'We are agreed that in Zimbabwe we need one army, both for waging the struggle for independence and for safeguarding the national integrity and security of an independent Zimbabwe. A multi-army system is not a system which anyone should advocate. But we have had problems over the unification and strengthening of the armed struggle and the Patriotic Front.'[64]

Hopes of progress towards effective unification again received a setback in September 1977 when it became known that President Kaunda had met with Ian Smith at Lusaka airport to discuss the possibility of Nkomo returning to participate in negotiations for an 'internal settlement' (see above). Mugabe strongly criticized Kaunda on 19 October for 'creating mistrust in the ranks of the PF'. He said the meeting with Smith should never have been allowed to take place. 'Everyone else knew about the meeting. I was the only one who wasn't told.' This criticism evoked a strong attack from the *Times of Zambia* on 20 October. 'Who does guerrilla Mr Mugabe speak for?' it asked. 'Is it the people of Zimbabwe? Is it for himself?

Whose mouthpiece is he? We are not sure. He seems to be very good at talking. What a pity, then, that he does not get down to talking about the unity between the Zapu and Zanu wings of the PF. That sort of talking is more likely to bring freedom to Zimbabwe than the atrocious insults that he dares to hurl at President Kaunda. . . . Our stand on the right of Zimbabwe to be free is based on human dignity, not on the perverted interposition of a foreign ideology. It is a so-called freedom fighter hopping from capital to capital in luxury jets who is diverging from the purpose of the struggle.'

Despite these disagreements within the PF, its leadership nevertheless succeeded in maintaining a collective front against the 'internal settlement', and in pursuing their negotiations with the Anglo-Americans. Robert Mugabe frankly summed up the position as follows: 'It's no use pretending we've got unity. We are agreed on the structures: the merging of Zanu and Zapu branches, and all the way up the line to Provincial Committees and the Central Committee. But our branches inside Rhodesia are still clandestine and there is no way of implementing this agreement so far as they are concerned. The first step must be to unify our two armies—but although we are agreed about this, it still hasn't happened.'[65]

Another attempt to achieve unity was made at a meeting in Lusaka on 14 February 1978 when detailed plans were agreed to establish a single political party, to prepare a detailed constitution for it, and to have a joint high command. A code of discipline was drawn up for a joint force and a single system for guerrilla training. It was further agreed that a national leader would be elected at a special Zanu-Zapu congress when conditions allowed for this to be held inside Rhodesia. But one basic division still remained: Zapu insisted that political unity must precede military unity, whereas Zanu believed that the fact that the armed struggle was currently under way required the two armies to be unified first.[66]

Zimbabwe African People's Union

Unlike Zanu, Joshua Nkomo's Zapu was able to maintain both external and internal wings, with a number of old-time nationalist leaders like Josiah and Rose Chinamano and Willie Masurawa (all three of them Shonas) holding the fort in Salisbury and Bulawayo. Nkomo's influence grew for a number of reasons, first and foremost because of the much greater strength of his guerrilla battalions which increased from c. 700 in 1974 to between 8,000–15,000 in 1977. He was thus no longer the junior military partner to Zanu. Zambia not only gave him strong political support, but also co-operated in bringing in his floods of new recruits (via Botswana) and in establishing them in camps on its territory. Angola, too, proved a strong Nkomo ally, permitting Zipra forces to be brought from Zambia for training and to be equipped by the Russians and Cubans. Zipra was also more tightly disciplined that Zanla; unlike Mugabe, Nkomo was the single dominant figure in his movement. Although there was some trouble between Kalanga and Ndebele elements in Zipra camps (which resulted in the wounding of its military commander, Alfred 'Nikita' Mangena, in Lusaka), Nkomo's forces suffered much less from internal divisions than Mugabe's. (Mangena was later killed in an accident.)

Apart from his strong African backing, Nkomo also succeeded in keeping the support of the Soviet bloc and Cuba, as well as of the Western nations. Between his increasingly frequent trips to the communist capitals in Eastern Europe and Havana, he kept up his close contacts in London and Washington. Straight from denouncing Western imperialism in Moscow, he invariably stopped in London to talk to the Foreign Office and to see friends like Tiny Rowland, chairman of Lonrho. Nkomo's skill in walking the tight-rope between East and West enabled him to outmanoeuvre Zanu in their competition for foreign backing. But if

Nkomo's diplomacy was subtle, his political stand was uncompromisingly tough: his demand was for total capitulation by the Smith regime to the PF's demands.

Zimbabwe African National Union

While Zapu was rapidly building up and consolidating Zipra, the bulk of the fighting in Rhodesia was carried on throughout 1977 and early 1978 by Zanu's forces. In fact, Zanu became suspicious about why Nkomo was not committing his forces in greater numbers. But while holding the military initiative, Zanu continued to be troubled by bitter internal dissension. It elected a new Central Committee in April 1977 and then enlarged it in September when Robert Mugabe became President, with Zanla's military commander, Josiah M. Tongogara, as Secretary for Defence (see list below). The new executive represented a merger of the political and military leadership, with the latter predominating. The party organ explained that 'this was necessary because it brings about the integration of the fighters and leadership, which in turn helps to consolidate the ideological unity of the party'.[67]

From various Central Committee declarations, the direction of the new executive was shown to be Maoist. For instance, Mao was quoted in support of the Zanu directive that 'the only way to settle questions of an ideological nature or con- troversial issues among the people is by the democratic method, the method of discussing or criticism, of persuasion and education, not by the method of coercion or repression'.[68] The Central Committee also referred to Herbert Chitepo as the 'martyr hero' of the Zimbabwe struggle. (Ironically, a number of its members had been put on trial in Zambia in 1976 on charges of killing Chitepo and his sup- porters.) Zanu committed itself fully to Maoism at the Central Committee meeting held in Chimoio (Mozambique) from 31 August to 8 September 1977. There, Mugabe declared that the movement has 'become even more firmly committed to Marxism-Leninism-Mao Tse-tung Thought, taking full account of the objective and subjective political, economic and social realities of the Zimbabwe national milieu'.[69] He added that the new stage of development—Zanu's acceptance of the principles of scientific socialism—'brought a socialist revolutionary dimension to the struggle that demands of us that the enemy's political structure be dismantled to create room for a new political socio-economic order'. That, he said, was Zanu's long-term objective; it was now committed to a 'military-revolutionary struggle', as embodied in the Shona word *Chimurenga*.

When in Peking in June-July 1977, Mugabe reportedly said at a banquet that 'social-imperialist aid' had ulterior motives, aimed at dividing spheres of influence and scrambling for hegemony and fostering proxies. . . . The people of Zimbabwe are facing a menace from both Western imperialism and social imperialism, and the menace from social imperialism in particular is more insidious and dangerous.'[70] However, Moscow accused the New China News Agency of falsifying what Mugabe had said: 'The true position quickly came to light. Joshua Nkomo, the other co- leader of the PF, speaking at a Press conference in Libreville (Gabon) where the OAU was meeting, at once questioned the veracity of these reports. He said that Robert Mugabe's words were being deliberately distorted in order to split the PF. The Soviet Union, he said, had rendered all-round assistance to the people of Zimbabwe from the very beginning of their struggle. A few days later, Robert Mugabe himself arrived in Libreville and gave a Press conference at which he firmly denied that he had made the anti-Soviet statements attributed to him. He added that these fabrications were aimed at undermining the PF. It was absurd, he continued, to come out against the Soviet Union which was making a considerable contribution to the cause of the liberation of Southern Africa from the yoke of racialism. ''We highly appreciate the USSR's effective and unselfish assistance and we always say

ZANU CENTRAL COMMITTEE* (as at 4 September 1977)

	Heads of Departments	Deputy Heads of Departments
President	Robert G. Mugabe (1)	
Vice-President	Simon V. Muzenda (2)	
Secretary General	Edgar Z. Tekere (3)	Don Muvuti (16)
Other Secretaries		
External Affairs	Mukudzei Mudzi (4)	Webster Gwauya (17)
Defence	Josiah M. Tongogara (5)	Rex Nhongo (18)
Chief Political Commissar	Meya Hurimbo (6)	Josiah Tungamirai (19)
Information and Publicity	Rugare Gumbo (7)	Eddison J. M. Zvobgo (20)
Finance	Ernest R. Kadungure (8)	Didymus N. E. Mutasa (21)
Manpower, Planning and Labour	Matuku Hamadziripi (9)	Robson Manyika (22)
Welfare and Transport	Kumbirai Kangai (10)	Justin Chauke (23)
Health	Herbert S. M. Ushewokunze (11)	Sidney Sekeramayi (24)
Education and Culture	Dzingai Mutumbuka (12)	Sheba Tavarwisa (25)
Production, Construction and Development	Crispen P. Mandizvidza (13)	Peter Baya (26)
Women's Affairs	Teurai Ropa (14)	
Special Assistant in the Office of the President	Emerson Munangarwa (15)	

Others without special Central Committee functions include Sheba Gava, Charles Dauramanzi, Joshua Misihairambwi, Henry H. Makoni, Ray Musikavanhu, Sarudzai Chinamaropa (28 to 33 respectively).

*Numbers represent Order of Command.

so. Due to the Soviet Union, the PF of Zimbabwe has been able to score impressive victories in the struggle against Smith's racialist regime.''' [71]

Zanu's internal troubles continued in 1977. At the beginning of the year, the following were reported to have been arrested: Dzinashe Machingura, Chief Political Commissar; Elias Hondo, Director of Operations; James Nyikadizinashe, Director for Training and Supplies; Dr Augustus Mudzingwi, Head of the Medical Corps; and Sam Geza, Publicity Secretary who is also Mugabe's brother-in-law. As none of these names appears in the new Central Committee list, it must be assumed that they have either been liquidated or are still in detention. Their downfall is believed to have been connected with the internal power struggle that preceded Mugabe's election as President in April 1977 and the creation of a new Central Committee. Another serious rift occurred after the August-September Central Committee meeting when there was a reported attempt to poison Mugabe. Two of the members on the new Central Committee were arrested and said to be facing court martial: Henry Matuku Hamadziripi, the Secretary for Manpower, Planning and Labour, the ninth ranking member; and Rugare Gumbo, the Secretary for Information and Publicity and seventh ranking member. According to their critics, they formed part of a hardcore group who sought to promote Karanga hegemony.

THE 'INTERNAL SETTLEMENT' FRONT

The three groups forming this front have little in common other than their hostility to the PF. While Muzorewa's UANC and Sithole's ANC have a longstanding commitment to majority rule and of opposition to the Smith regime, Chief Chirau was until 1976 a minister in that regime. Sithole took the main initiative in starting the 'internal settlement' negotiations and retained it during much of the discussions, making no effort to disguise his interest in establishing supremacy over the Bishop.

Muzorewa simply brushed aside Sithole, claiming that he had the support of 90% of all the guerrillas (allowing the PF the remaining 10%, with none at all for Sithole).[72] Speaking later in August, Sithole in turn predicted that before long he would be the sole leader of the Black nationalists inside Rhodesia, saying that he was draining away all of Muzorewa's supporters—a claim hardly borne out by events in the subsequent six months.[73] In February 1978, the Bishop sued Sithole for £5m damages, alleging libel in pamphlets reprinted in the *Zimbabwe Times*.

The United African National Council (ANC-Z)[74]

The Bishop's failure to develop as a strong political leader upset his closest supporters, although his very ineptitude has been interpreted positively: 'The Bishop is credited with a power to unify Rhodesia's divided nationalists simply because many Africans probably rightly believe that he is ambitious for his country rather than himself. The Bishop's bumbling, fumbling political style tends to reinforce this viewpoint. Lacking the manipulative skills of his nationalist rivals, Abel Muzorewa appears to many Africans as a man who has the honesty to identify with their interests rather than his own. The irony is that he may well find himself a nationalist leader with a large following and a very small organization.'[75]

The Bishop faced a setback in August 1977 when six of his top lieutenants resigned. Among them was Dr Elliott Gabellah, the UANC Vice-President, who said the Bishop had failed to unite the people or give them the necessary sense of direction. Implicit in his complaints was the influence over the Bishop of James Richard Chikerema (see below). Gabellah joined forces with Sithole. The Bishop's response to these defections was to dismiss the entire Central Committee and National Executive of the UANC and to appoint a nine-man interim committee. This move led to the resignation of another key figure, Dr Gordon Chavunduka, who accused the Bishop of behaving 'dictatorially and stupidly'. He proposed leaving politics altogether.

These withdrawals left the Bishop depending more than ever on James Chikerema (52) and his loyal supporter, George Nyandoro. 'Chik'—as he is widely known—ended his 13-year exile in Zambia in September 1977, as did Nyandoro shortly afterwards. These two men had flanked Nkomo when he launched the modern nationalist party in Rhodesia in 1957; energetic, militant and splendid orators, they contributed enormously to building up the ANC. When UDI was declared, both left for Zambia where they organized Zapu's first guerrilla group in 1967. But they quarrelled with Nkomo in 1974–75. On his return to Salisbury, Chikerema accused the British of being 'treacherous, gutless, spineless, speechless'—a fair flavour of his oratory. In the 'internal settlement' negotiations, he proved more accommodating to White Rhodesian wishes than most other UANC leaders.

Muzorewa faced a difficult decision when Byron Hove was dismissed as co-Minister of Law and Justice soon after his appointment (see 'Internal Settlement', above). If he were to withdraw all his Ministers from the interim government, he would leave the field open to Sithole and be forced back into the political wilderness, either to struggle alone or to build bridges to the PF. (Up to the time of the 'internal settlement', the Bishop had stayed in touch with Robert Mugabe, but would have nothing at all to do with Nkomo.) On the other hand, if he stayed in the government (as he did), he would lay himself open to criticism that he did not have the power or the courage to back up his own Minister on the vital issue of reforms in the police and the Judiciary.

The African National Congress (Zanu-S)

With fewer forces at his disposal than any of the other nationalist leaders, the Rev Ndabaningi Sithole showed considerable skill in projecting himself as a serious challenger to power.[76] Not only did he take the initiative in making the 'internal settlement' possible, but at every critical point in the negotiations played a key role in overcoming obstacles.

Supremely confident, toughened by prison, exile and his long political experience, the rotund cleric returned to Rhodesia in 1977 apparently with considerable financial backing—its source remains a mystery—which enabled him to dispense cars and other rewards and patronage in building up his organization. His two daughters bought a house in an expensive suburb of Salisbury reserved exclusively for Whites: an attempt to oust them was stopped by the regime. Once jailed for six years after being convicted of planning the murder of Ian Smith, Sithole now accompanied the White Rhodesian leader around the country and succeeded in winning the confidence of many Whites, promising that under his rule Zimbabwe would become a non-racial society with a mixed economy. Sithole dismissed Mugabe (who had ousted him from Zanu's leadership while the two were still in jail) as 'just a rebel'. But Sithole's political credibility came under a cloud in April 1978 when he failed to fulfil a promise that on his instructions and with a promise of amnesty, the guerrillas would lay down their arms. The first batch of men who gave up their weapons were shown—by the UANC—not to have been guerrillas at all.

Zimbabwe United People's Organization

Chief Chirau's Zupo described itself as 'an independent, multiracial Rhodesian national party, supporting majority rule by peaceful negotiations. A pro-West free enterprise group, it claims the support of the majority of Africans in Rhodesia.'[77] It also established an office in London with a sophisticated public relations organization headed by Nicodemus Mutuma.

Zupo held its first congress in Salisbury in October 1977 at which it was stated that the organization was formed after 'all tribal leaders in the country had been consulted and agreed to support the initiative'.[78] Chirau explained that he thought the time had come for 'traditional leaders to become involved in politics'. (Of course, most of them had been previously involved, willy nilly, in the politics of the Smith regime which had always insisted that the chiefs were the true representatives of Black Rhodesians.) Chirau himself had been a Senator and a Minister in the Smith regime from 1976 until he resigned in January 1977.

DEFENCE AND SECURITY

THE COURSE OF THE WAR

Virtually the whole of Rhodesia was officially designated a war zone in 1976, divided into four operational areas:

> *Operation Hurricane*, the first operational area to be declared in response to guerrilla incursions in December 1972; covers the north-east of the country.
> *Operation Thrasher*, opened in February 1976 along the eastern border with Mozambique and centred on Umtali.
> *Operation Repulse*, covers the southern part of the country including all the key road and rail links with SA; opened in May 1976.
> *Operation Tangent*, officially announced in December 1976 in the north-west and west, covering the border with Botswana; based on Bulawayo.

Security force initiatives at the regional level are co-ordinated through a system of Joint Operations Command (JOC), comprising senior representatives of the main military divisions—army, air force, police and internal affairs—with the army taking precedence. Smith exercises a close and personal influence over the conduct of the war through his chairmanship of a War Council consisting of senior ministers and security force commanders. A Minister of Combined Operations was appointed in March 1977 with overall·responsibility for co-ordinating the civilian war effort with that of the military.

Guerrilla activity· increased throughout 1977 and even more in the first half of 1978. Avoiding open confrontation with the Rhodesian armed forces, the guerrillas' first aim was to infiltrate into the rural areas—the so-called Tribal Trust Lands (TTLs)—where they were given cover and protection by the peasants, achieving the Maoist strategy of 'swimming like fish in the sea'. The cells of guerrillas spread like a cancer throughout the countryside. The people in the TTLs found themselves trapped between the demands of the guerrillas and the coercion of the security forces. By mid-1977, virtually no males between the ages of 14–50 remained in the more disaffected TTLs: many had fled into exile to join the guerrillas or to find refuge; others were removed into 'protected villages' (see below).

In April 1977, the official estimate of the number of guerrillas operating inside the country was 2,500. By September 1977, the estimate had risen to c. 3,600, according to a security forces spokesman, who added that there were also c. 5,000 deployable Zanu insurgents in Mozambique and c. 3,000 Zapu guerrillas in Zambia.[79]

By early 1978, guerrilla activity increased in the heart of Rhodesia, as shown by an attack on two township beerhalls 25 miles from Salisbury. The attackers, believed to belong to Zanla, Zanu's military wing, were reported to be moving closer to the capital.[80] On 7 January 1978, the Smith regime imposed restrictions which prevented any reporting of military activity unless it was cleared by the authorities. This was used to stop publication of news or comment in Rhodesia on the amnesty—the 'safe return' policy—offered by the Smith regime to guerrillas. In mid-January 1978, leaflets were dropped by Rhodesian aircraft advising guerrillas to surrender and saying: 'If you return in peace, your life will not be in danger'.

By early 1978, too, there were reports of a rapid build-up in the military strength of Nkomo's Zapu wing, which was said possibly to outnumber the regular Rhodesian forces. The Zapu army, known as Zipra (Zimbabwe Revolutionary Army) was said to be at least 8,000 strong. Some 15,000 men may have fled Rhodesia in recent years, many to join Zipra which has training camps in Zambia and Angola. Writing in the *Financial Times* about Nkomo's army, Bridget Bloom referred to the use of Cuban forces based in Angola to train Zipra: 'Although Zambia does not permit Cuban forces to be based in the country, in a distinct change of policy President Kaunda now allows Cuban units to "escort" Zipra forces to their camps inside Zambia'.[81]

There were reports in April 1977 of a shipment of Soviet weapons to Mozambique, which for the first time could neutralize Rhodesian air power.[82]

In May 1977, 35 African civilians, including women and children, were killed in crossfire during a search-and-destroy operation mounted by the security forces in south-east Rhodesia. This was the worst reported incident involving civilian deaths since September 1976. Commenting on the incident, Supt Jim Carse said he did not think security forces would be blamed; the tribesmen knew they had done wrong by allowing terrorists into the area to hold a meeting.[83] But others felt the incident would be a setback to the regime's campaign to 'win the hearts and minds of African tribespeople in operational areas'.[84] At the end of May 1977, Rhodesian forces carried out another raid into Mozambique—an action strongly criticized by the British and US Governments.

In July 1977, the OAU summit in Libreville gave exclusive recognition to the PF at the urging of President Kaunda of Zambia, who endorsed a military solution for the Rhodesian problem.[85] By mid-1977, all Whites under the age of 38 were expected to serve at least 190 days a year in uniform, and those aged between 38 and 50 at least 70 days. Military leaders spoke less about winning the guerrilla war and more about holding the position until a political settlement was achieved. The generals strongly emphasized the political neutrality of the armed forces and their readiness to serve whatever government came to power.[86]

In August 1977, bomb blasts were reported in Salisbury for the first time for more than a year. On 6 August an explosion in a Woolworth's store killed 11 people and wounded 76. The next day a blast damaged the Sinoia rail line and a bridge near the Black township of Kambazuma on the city's outskirts. On 13 August, another bomb exploded in an office block. On 9 August, two women missionaries, a German doctor and a nun were murdered in an attack on a mission in the south-west of the country. The doctor, Johannah Decker, had been in Rhodesia for nearly 30 years; the nun, Sister Ferdinanda, had recently volunteered for missionary duty. Early in October 1977, guerrillas bayoneted a six-month old White child, dragging her from her nanny's arms, in the Melsetter district.

In November 1977, there were more raids on Mozambique, this time on a large scale. Salisbury announced that Rhodesian forces had killed more than 1,200 armed men and wounded hundreds more in two attacks on guerrilla camps. The first was on the main Zanla operational headquarters and a large refugee village near Chimoio, on the road between Umtali and the Mozambique port of Beira. A day later there was a second attack on Tembue, a guerrilla holding camp north of the Zambesi River which had a preponderance of civilians. Rhodesian troops flew nearly 140 miles into Mozambique to make their attacks which Bishop Muzorewa described as massacres. Over 160 people were killed—the majority (as documented in films) women and children. Rhodesian military sources acknowledged that women and children may have been among those killed, but blamed the guerrillas for allowing them into the camps. The Smith regime said the targets were well-known 'terrorist bases'. Later, Lt-Gen Walls said the raid eliminated a part of the Zanla leadership, although the two main commanders of the guerrillas, Josiah Tongogara and Rex Nhongo, were away when the raid occurred.[87]

Early in December 1977, a White farmer, Johannes van Maarseveen, was killed by guerrillas in the Cashel district of eastern Rhodesia, the 115th White civilian to die during the five-year civil war. During the same period, more than 1,200 Black civilians lost their lives. Early in January 1978, a White farmer's wife, Sheila Cumming, and her 15-year old daughter were killed in an attack on a farm less than 30 miles west of Salisbury.

ARMY CHANGES AND SECURITY MEASURES

Major changes were announced in the Rhodesian military command in early 1977. Lt-Gen Peter Walls was promoted from Commander of the Army to Commander of Combined Operations. Lt-Gen John Hickman became Commander of the Army, with Maj-Gen A. L. C. Maclean as Chief of Staff (Operations) and Maj-Gen A. N. O. Macintyre as Chief of Staff (Administration). Gen Walls gained early experience in counter-insurgency warfare in Malaya.

These changes were made against a background of greatly increased guerrilla activity in Rhodesia leading, for example, to warnings to holidaymakers at Easter 1977 to travel in convoys and observe curfews.[88] At the same time, the policy of 'resettling' Africans in protected villages was being stepped up to the point where, according to Rhodesian military spokesmen, they would hold c. 250,000 people.[89] In June 1977, the Minister of Internal Affairs revealed that 145 protected and 40 consolidated villages had been completed; another 32 protected villages would be in operation by the end of 1977. Other sources, notably the Catholic Commission for

Justice and Peace, put the figure much higher. [90] Backed up by detailed information from Mashonaland, Manicaland and Victoria Provinces, it reported a total of 203 protected villages accommodating 580,832 people in August 1977. [91]

ARMED FORCES
Defence expenditure for 1977–78 was R$98.4m, plus R$47.5m in the police vote. In February 1977, conscription was extended to White, Asian and Coloured males between 38 and 50. In September 1977, deferment of national service for university students was abolished; a bonus scheme was introduced to encourage conscripts deployed in an operational combat role (and others who have been discharged) to serve longer than the statutory 18 months; and men of all ages who have been granted continuous exemption from call-up were to be inducted on a part-time basis into either the Police Reserve or the Urban Special Constabulary. [92] Under regulations published in August 1977, African doctors were made liable for military service, the first category of Africans to be affected by the National Services Act of 1976.

The potential strength of the Rhodesian armed forces is 111,550 men and women, made up as follows: Army regulars 5,000; full-time National Servicemen 3,250; Territorial Force (of which c. 15,000 are called up at any time) 55,000; Reserve Holding Unit (men over 38) 3,000. Air Force 1,300; British South Africa Police regulars 8,000; Reservists 35,000; Guard Force (responsible for defence of protected villages) 1,000. [93]

The regular army has five main fighting units: 1) Rhodesian Light Infantry, with one all-White battalion of c. 1,000 men believed to contain many overseas mercenaries and trained for counter-insurgency bush warfare; also two Black battalions with a third Black forming; 2) Rhodesian African Rifles composed of Africans largely under White officers; 3) three Special Air Service squadrons—all White élite troops; 4) Selous Scouts, believed to number c. 1,000 men; mainly Africans, whose main function is to seek out and destroy guerrilla units and who have a reputation for ruthlessness and brutality; and 5) Grey's Scouts, mounted infantry, both Black and White, with a total strength of c. 250. There is also one engineer squadron. Equipment consists of 60 AML-90 Eland armoured cars; Ferret scout cars; UR-416 light armoured personnel carriers; 25-pounder, 105mm pack and 5.5-in howitzers, and 105mm recoilless rifles.

The Air Force, with 48 combat aircraft, has one light bomber squadron with five Canberra B2 and two T4; two ground-attack fighter squadrons, one with 10 Hunter FGA9 and one with 12 Vampire FB9; one training/reconnaissance squadron with eight Provost T-52 and 11 Vampire T55; one transport squadron with nine C-47, one Baron 55 and six Islander; one light transport squadron with 12 A1-60C4 and 18 Cessna 337, and two helicopter squadrons with 55 Alouette II/III. [94]

The BSA Police contains a mounted unit, similar to the Grey's Scouts, set up in early 1977. Other units include: Police Support Unit, operating in a similar way to the Selous Scouts; Special Unit, to counter urban guerrilla warfare, consisting of c. 30 men in the Salisbury area; and a Criminal Investigation Department, heavily involved in counter-insurgency operations.

DEFENCE SPENDING AND RECRUITING
The cost of defence continued to rise, with a 44% increase to £132m, according to the public expenditure estimates tabled at the end of June 1977. In addition, at least £60m more was to be provided under various other headings. [95] In September 1977, an additional £15m was allocated to defence spending. This was further supplemented by $R10m on 14 February 1978, plus another $R7.34m for the Army and

Air Force, bringing the Defence vote to c. $R150m (cf $R20m in June 1972 when guerrilla operations first began to be taken seriously).

Shortages of White manpower led the regime to increase African recruitment to the forces. Two African battalions in training in August 1977 were due to be operational by November, thus increasing the preponderance of Blacks in the Rhodesian army. Africans continued to come forward in large numbers, partly because of high unemployment.[96]

The number of foreign mercenaries active in 1976 exceeded the earlier estimate of 1–2,000.[97] Diplomatic sources reported that 100 former French Legionnaires under two majors enlisted at the end of 1977.[98] Nkomo claimed on 6 February 1978 that there were c. 11,200 foreign mercenaries 'concentrated' on the Zambia border—a claim rejected by diplomatic sources. Reuter quoted Nkomo as saying the mercenaries included 600 Israeli commandos; 4,500 South Africans; 2,000 British; 2,300 Americans; 1,000 French and an unspecified number of Portuguese and West Germans. However, Western intelligence sources in Lusaka said the number of foreign troops in the Rhodesian Army was c. 1,400.

TERROR AND COUNTER-TERROR

The Catholic Commission for Justice and Peace produced a report entitled *Rhodesia: The Propaganda War*, giving well-documented details of harassment and torture of Black civilians by the Rhodesian military forces. The report was banned in Rhodesia, and four members of the Commission arrested at the end of August 1977 (see below). Published in London by the Catholic Institute for International Relations, the report described 'a policy of systematic torture' pursued by the Rhodesian Army and commented: 'Reports of torture at the hands of government security forces continue to be the rule rather than the exception. Furthermore, under the provisions of the Indemnity and Compensation Act, a soldier or other government official can torture or kill a prisoner and the matter cannot be brought to court if the Minister certifies that the action was committed in good faith to suppress terrorism or to maintain public order.' The report continued: 'It is certain that civilians bear the brunt of the war. Since December 1972, a total of 1,552 African and 82 European civilians have died, victims of both sides in the conflict. This is five times the number of security forces killed during the war (329), and more than half the number of guerrillas killed (2,567). Among these deaths were 222 curfew breakers and 227 listed as 'running with or assisting terrorists. . . . One can easily understand the confusion of villagers when so many of them meet their death at the hands of the security forces who purport to be their protectors. One can excuse them for asking whether they have more to fear from the army than from the guerrillas.'[99]

James Chikerema, vice-president of the UANC, alleged in October 1977 that Rhodesian troops had shot and bayoneted Black babies while fighting the guerrilla war—an allegation 'vehemently and categorically denied' by Roger Hawkins, the Combined Operations Minister.[100] (Chikerema later became Minister of Transport under the 'internal settlement' government.) The Combined Operations Ministry admitted for the first time in November 1977 that it was officially investigating allegations of atrocities by Rhodesian troops: a board of inquiry had reportedly begun work on 26 September 1977.[101]

In December 1977, wide publicity was given to an account of actions by Rhodesian troops witnessed by Ross Baughman, a photographer with the Associated Press agency. He said that in September 1977, he had seen members of a 25-man Rhodesian army cavalry unit from the Grey's Scouts loot and burn huts, beat a local Black politician and torture his wife and daughter. His presence had been arranged with the help of a Rhodesian army major, an American, with government approval. However, when more senior Rhodesian authorities found out who Baughman was, he was ordered to return to Salisbury where some of his film was confiscated or spoilt. He said the incidents took place in the area of Lupani, 80 miles from the border with Botswana. [102]

LAW AND TRIALS

The Law and Order (Maintenance) Act, (under which the death sentence is mandatory for murder, commission of acts of terrorism and sabotage and unlawful possession of arms of war) continued to be used widely against captured guerrillas. Over 130 people have been executed since 1968, most of them hanged in secret. Numbers executed rose dramatically after 1975; between April 1975 and September 1977, at least 136 people were known to have been sentenced to death, 109 on charges under the Law and Order (Maintenance) Act. [103]

The International Defence and Aid Fund reported in September 1977 that at least 11 executions were believed to have been carried out by the Smith regime since the beginning of July 1977; these included Robert Bhebe and Painos Zehama, two leading officials of the ANC/Zimbabwe. Attempts to save the life of Bhebe (who had been released from detention in 1974 to take part in talks in Lusaka) included an appeal by Shridath Ramphal, the Commonwealth Secretary-General, to the International Committee of the Red Cross. However, when Bhebe's relatives arrived at Salisbury prison to visit him on 13 July 1977, they were told he had already been hanged.

Four members of the Catholic Commission for Justice and Peace were also charged under the Law and Order (Maintenance) Act in September and October 1977. John Deary, chairman of the Commission; Father Dieter Scholz, deputy chairman; Brother Arthur Dupuis, the organizing secretary; and Sister Janice McLaughlin, Press secretary, were arrested by the Rhodesian Special Branch on 31 August 1977. The first three appeared before a Salisbury magistrate, but with no charges preferred were given bail. Sister Janice was held in prison under a detention order, having previously collected documentary evidence of the use of torture and atrocities by Rhodesian troops. She finally appeared in court on 13 September 1977 charged under the Act with spreading 'fear, alarm or despondency' among the Rhodesian public, and with obtaining classified military and government information relating to the war. Nine days later, she was declared a prohibited immigrant and deported. The other three were quietly released after the 'internal settlement'.

Other Whites declared prohibited immigrants included Father Laurence Lynch, an Irish Catholic priest, who had been given a suspended prison sentence in April 1977 for assisting and failing to report guerrillas; and Michael Pocock, the Anglican headmaster of St Mary Magdalene School (Inyanga) who was tried and sentenced with Father Lynch. Those deported included Charles Robert, a lecturer in sociology at the University of Rhodesia, in August 1977; Sister Teresa Corby, the only doctor for the Buhera and Charter areas around Mount St Mary's Mission in Wedza Tribal Trust Land, in September 1977; and Father Pascal Slevin, the superintendent of Mount St Mary's Mission, who made available evidence on atrocities committed by the Rhodesian forces, in October 1977. Roger Riddell, a British-born Jesuit missionary, was banned from re-entering the country in October 1977. [104] Dr Iden Wetherell, a lecturer in political history at the University of Rhodesia, was declared a prohibited immigrant in February 1977. [105]

SOCIAL AFFAIRS

EDUCATION

From April 1977, private schools were permitted to admit children of different races if that was the wish of parents and governors; State schools remained segregated. Education remained compulsory for White children but not for Black. The regime spent over ten times as much on the education of a White child as on a Black child (R$557 and R$46 respectively). [106]

The number of new White entrants to the University of Rhodesia dropped by 47 in 1978, while the number of African entrants rose by 155. Figures released by the University also show that the total enrolment for 1978, including part-time students and those registered for higher degrees, rose from 2,057 to 2,186. [107]

PRESS

A new weekly newspaper, the *National Observer*, was launched in mid-March 1978 by a Salisbury company, Independent Newspapers, a subsidiary of the Rhodesian Printing and Publishing Co. In its initial editorial, it attacked the British and American governments for their rejection of the Salisbury accord. Initial circulation figures of 20,000 were quoted.

EMPLOYMENT

The gap in wages between Black and White workers continued to widen. According to the Central Statistical Office, more than 122,000 Africans earned less than R$10 a month in 1977. Most Blacks employed in private domestic service earned between R$10 and R$20 a month; most of those in mining and quarrying between R$20 and R$30. [108] The table below shows earnings and employment by race for 1976: [109]

Industrial sectors		Total employed	Average annual earning (R$)
Agriculture and forestry:	Africans	356,100	201
	Non-Africans*	5,900	4,915
Mining and quarrying:	Africans	61,400	567
	Non-Africans	3,900	7,590
Manufacturing:	Africans	131,000	805
	Non-Africans	21,900	6,347
Private domestic service:	Africans	126,000	392
All sectors	Africans	926,000	517
	Non-Africans	120,000	5,583

*Non-Africans include White, Asians and Coloureds.

For the first six months of 1977, African employment fell by 1.7%. [110]

EMIGRATION

In the first ten months of 1977, a total of 9,300 Whites emigrated, the largest net outflow in the country's history. By the end of the year, the figure had risen to 10,908 Whites, Coloureds and Asians. Set against the natural rate of increase in the White population (around 2,000 a year), this means that by the end of 1977, the number of Whites would have decreased by c. 10,000. [111] In December 1977, the regime launched an advertising campaign to persuade people to remain in the country with such slogans as 'Once you're a Rhodesian, no other land will do'.

POPULATION

At the end of June 1977, the estimated breakdown in population was 6,440,000 Blacks; 268,000 Whites; 22,000 Coloureds; 10,300 Asians.

ECONOMIC AFFAIRS (1.28 Rhodesian dollars = £1 sterling)

During 1977, Rhodesia's economic situation worsened steadily. As Smith confessed in early 1978, this was a major reason for the regime's wish to try to achieve a political settlement. Smith pointed to the fact that 100 Black Rhodesians were leaving their jobs every day as a result of the economic impact of war and sanctions. A number of adverse factors combined to damage the economy and were listed by one commentator as follows: the mounting pressure on White manpower through call-ups and emigration; rising unemployment among Blacks; tightening sanctions and world recession; a grave shortage of foreign exchange and lack of foreign investment; the shrinking number of foreign tourists; rising defence expenditure, and the growing vulnerability of external transport links.[112]

The repeal of the Byrd Amendment by the US Senate made exports of ferrochrome difficult, and several mines closed as a result. This hit particularly hard, as in 1976 mineral production reached record levels. Nevertheless, mineral output rose in value by 3.7% to R$156.8m in the first eight months of 1977, compared with the same period in 1976.[113] Industrial production fell for the third successive year in 1977, according to official figures released on 26 February 1978. The volume of manufacturing production fell 6% in 1977 following a 6.6% fall in 1976 and a marginal 1.3% decline in 1975. Output in 1977 was running at its lowest level since 1971. Due to higher prices, mining revenue increased 3%, though the volume of production fell 5.5%. The value of farm produce also rose nearly 4% in 1977, in spite of significantly lower cash sales by Black producers.

A frank picture of the state of the economy was painted in the *Economic Bulletin* (February 1978) of the Rhodesian Banking Corporation (Rhobank). Its predictions for the future were gloomy in virtually every economic sphere. 'The declining trend in manufacturing production has now been in force for two-and-a-half years and still there is little to suggest that the fall in output will be reversed or even arrested in the foreseeable future.' The volume index of the manufacturing sector fell by 5.9% from October 1976 to October 1977, one of the prime reasons being the shortage of foreign exchange. Exports to SA were also hard hit by the South African import surcharge. The mining sector produced 5% less, in terms of volume, between January and October 1977 than during the corresponding period of 1976. 'As of now there is very little likelihood of a recovery in mining output materializing in 1978.' In the building sector, the value of plans approved for all types of buildings during the first ten months of 1977 was 18.2% below the level in 1976 and 56.7% below the figure for 1973. The heaviest decline was in industrial buildings. The retail trade index slumped by 8.8% during the first nine months of 1977.

'Real incomes are still falling under the impact of the wage freeze and inflation, and with the prospect of further increases in taxation and renewed inflationary pressure, this trend is unlikely to change. Inflation fell during the second half of 1977 from a high of 11.5% during May to an average of 9.6% for the year, an increase over 1976 when inflation measured 9%. 'Regardless of political developments in 1978, inflation seems destined to accelerate once again—a stark reminder of the heavy strains being imposed on the country's financial and other resources by the intensifying economic and shooting wars.'

The Rhobank review noted that 1977 turned out to be the worst year on record so far as White emigration was concerned. While the net rate of emigration slowed towards the end of the year, 'this does little to disguise the seriousness of the drain on White skills. Until such time as a universally acceptable solution is found to the political impasse, the outflow of Whites is likely to continue and so, too, the depletion of the country's skilled manpower resources.' Tourism was also dealt a heavy blow. During the first 11 months of 1977, there were 13.3% fewer foreign tourists to Rhodesia than during the corresponding period of 1976, and 58.9% fewer than in 1975. However, 1,200 South Africans arrived in Rhodesia during December 1977, 86% more than in December 1976.

The Standard Bank took a view as bleak as Rhobank's in its *Economic Bulletin* for March 1978. 'Time,' it said, 'is running out for the Rhodesian economy.' It estimated that the fighting and sanctions between them were costing R$1m (£800,000) a day. It predicted that the next fiscal year could see this bill rising a further 20–25%. Looking to the longer term position, the Standard Bank drew attention to the fact that by the end of 1978, per capita income (in real terms) will have fallen c. 27% from its 1974 peak. It warned that even assuming a return to positive growth in 1979—which is by no means assured—it will take until 1984, even on favourable assumptions, to regain the living standards of 1974. It also said that in the past four years, a backlog of at least 250,000 unemployed Black workers had built up.

In October 1977, the Rhodesian dollar was devalued by 6% against world currencies and 3% against the South African rand. Announcing the devaluation, the Finance Minister said it was necessary because Rhodesia was experiencing its most unfavourable terms of trade since 1965. Because of the prolonged international recession and general decline in commodity prices, Rhodesia was suffering major balance of payments strains. Reaction from the Rhodesian business community to devaluation was muted.

Rhodesia Railways suffered a 25% reduction in first-class passengers and a 15% reduction in the number of other passengers during the financial year ending 30 June 1977. The RR annual report commented on the problems experienced in nearby countries which 'made goods' traffic irregular and affected the availability of wagons'.

The price of petrol was increased by two cents a litre early in 1978, and diesel oil and paraffin by 2.7 cents a litre. This was necessitated by increased procurement and transport costs. [114]

Property sales in towns rose 2.8% in number in the first eight months of 1977, but fell 11.3% in total value, reflecting a fall in the average price paid of 13.8%.

BUDGET

The main feature of the Budget, introduced in July 1977, was the big increase for defence (see above), which accounts for c. 25% of total expenditure. There are also heavy costs in the economic war, with subsidies supporting the tobacco, beef, milk and soyabean industries, iron and steel and railways. [115]

The Minister of Finance forecast a deficit of R$81m (R105m) which had to be covered by borrowing. In addition, there were loan repayments in the fiscal year to 30 June 1977 of more than R$68m (R88m). A further burden was the provision of long-term loans to statutory boards and local authorities which cost another R$26m (R34m). The net effect was a public sector borrowing requirement in 1977 of R$72m (R94m). By January 1978, the Minister had raised almost half his requirement of R$88m (R104m). In that month, he launched a new loan of R$50m, repayable at par in January 2003 or between January 1998 and January 2003.

SANCTIONS

The UN Security Council passed a resolution in May 1977 to expand mandatory sanctions against Rhodesia by barring the outflow of funds by the Smith regime for any office or agency established in any other country, except those set up exclusively for pension purposes.

Early in 1977, Shell and BP were accused by the Anti-Apartheid Movement of being indirectly involved in sanctions-breaking by selling oil to a South African intermediary which in turn apparently exported it to Rhodesia. The British Foreign Secretary appointed an official inquiry into the allegations. Early in 1978, Tiny Rowland, chairman of the Lonrho group, brought an action against 29 major oil companies for sanctions-breaking activities. Shell and BP were among those accused, but were upheld by the High Court in their plea that the dispute should go to arbitration rather than be tried in public. [116]

CENTRAL GOVERNMENT BUDGET ACCOUNT* (thousand Rhodesian dollars)

	1975–76	1976–77	July–Sept. 1977	Estimate for year 1977–78
Revenue				
Taxes on income and profits	269,611	280,065	62,079	312,800
Taxes on goods and services	108,342	165,075	46,044	224,500
Miscellaneous taxes	5,456	4,936	932	5,420
Revenue from investments and property	37,429	41,313	3,493	44,300
Fees: departmental facilities and services	11,876	12,395	3,122	12,900
Sale of State property	2,336	2,525	609	2,500
Recoveries of development expenditure	7,513	5,640	1,626	4,000
Others	19,720	18,921	12,141	39,700
Total Revenue	**462,283**	**530,870**	**130,046**	**646,120**
Expenditure				
Goods and services	242,143	311,194	88,284	368,462
Transfers	158,027	211,773	128,831	294,295
Capital expenditure	56,078	67,670	12,881	64,689
Total Expenditure	**456,248**	**590,637**	**229,996**	**727,446**
Budget Account Deficit (–) Surplus	6,035	–59,767	–99,950	–81,326

*Year ending 30 June.

Source: Central Statistical Office, *Supplement to the Monthly Digest of Statistics.*

BALANCE OF PAYMENTS: CURRENT AND CAPITAL TRANSACTIONS† (million Rhodesian dollars)

Year	Merchandise, net	Invisible Transactions, net			Net balance on Current Account	Capital Transactions, net	Net Inflow on Current and Capital Accounts
		Services	Investment Income	Transfers			
1966	29.7	–10.2	–19.2	–4.1	–3.8	–4.6	–8.4
1967	10.8	–13.5	–13.4	–0.1	–16.2	23.7	7.5
1968	–22.0	–11.2	–14.9	–1.0	–49.1	39.5	–9.5
1969	32.0	–5.3	–17.8	–4.3	4.6	9.9	14.4
1970	27.9	–16.8	–21.0	–2.6	–12.5	26.3	13.8
1971	3.1	–24.8	–30.4	–3.3	–55.4	30.5	–24.9
1972	62.5	–21.8	–35.1	–2.8	2.7	–2.3	0.4
1973	89.6	–58.5	–38.5	–6.9	–14.4	51.6	37.2
1974	60.7	–81.9	–39.8	–18.8	–79.2	62.6	16.6
1975	39.5	–90.1	–39.0	–26.5	–116.1	101.7	–14.4
1976*	170.1	–79.4	–50.3	–23.2	17.3	25.7	43.0

*Provisional.

†Figures for all years have been amended following the reclassification of certain items and minor improvements in coverage.

EXPENDITURE ON THE GNP (million Rhodesian dollars)

Item	1967	1968	1969	1970	1971	1972	1973	1974	1975	1976
Private consumption	482.2	516.3	599.7	649.6	737.2	807.7	904.4	1,039.6	1,150.9	1,222.0
Private non-profit-making bodies	16.7	19.0	20.2	23.2	23.3	24.9	26.6	27.8	28.5	28.7
African rural household consumption of own production	54.2	37.4	52.3	40.3	58.5	64.2	41.0	77.5	68.3	79.3
Net government current expenditure	94.9	103.6	113.6	121.7	140.2	152.6	174.8	211.6	252.5	323.8
Gross fixed capital formation	103.8	150.5	149.1	177.3	224.1	258.3	322.8	416.1	461.7	375.2
Increase in stocks	51.1	51.2	37.4	52.0	76.2	54.7	45.4	97.2	95.4	1.6*
Domestic expenditure (market prices)	802.9	878.0	972.3	1,064.2	1,259.6	1,362.4	1,515.0	1,869.8	2,057.3	2,030.6
Net exports of goods and services	-3.2	-34.2	25.7	9.6	-23.7	38.7	28.1	-24.1	-52.5	91.9
GDP (market prices)	799.7	843.8	998.0	1,073.8	1,235.9	1,401.1	1,543.1	1,845.7	2,004.8	2,122.5
Less net income paid abroad	-13.4	-14.9	-17.8	-21.0	-30.4	-35.1	-38.5	-39.8	-36.7	-45.1
GNP (market prices)	786.3	828.9	980.2	1,052.8	1,205.5	1,366.0	1,504.6	1,805.9	1,968.1	2,077.4

*Includes errors and omissions.

GDP AT FACTOR COST BY INDUSTRY OF ORIGIN (million Rhodesian dollars)

Item	1967	1968	1969	1970	1971	1972	1973	1974	1975	1976
Agriculture and forestry:										
European, Asian and Coloured	85.3	78.9	103.5	98.3	125.4	146.7	151.3	202.5	227.0	231.2
African	70.2	45.6	66.2	55.1	74.9	86.9	63.7	113.4	95.1	108.2
Mining and quarrying	47.1	48.1	63.7	68.3	70.9	72.0	97.3	127.3	123.5	161.6
Manufacturing	133.4	152.4	177.2	212.2	252.4	298.3	343.6	425.2	454.2	441.2
Electricity and water	26.1	26.9	30.0	31.6	33.8	37.7	41.1	41.5	50.0	54.5
Construction	33.1	43.9	52.0	54.3	57.4	73.4	81.0	81.0	94.5	76.0
Finance and insurance	26.9	29.5	33.4	37.6	41.3	54.7	62.1	76.0	88.9	93.6
Real estate	19.3	22.5	27.7	31.8	34.9	38.6	42.7	45.6	44.9	41.7
Distribution, hotels and restaurants	98.7	108.9	122.7	135.6	151.7	171.3	197.2	235.3	252.4	254.0
Transport and communications	66.2	74.1	88.0	85.5	95.8	105.4	105.2	113.3	128.3	137.3
Public administration	47.8	51.2	57.3	61.9	69.9	78.0	91.2	106.7	126.6	160.1
Education services	26.8	29.2	31.9	34.1	39.5	43.0	48.0	55.0	64.9	72.7
Health services	13.0	14.2	15.3	16.4	18.9	20.8	22.4	25.9	31.0	34.6
Private domestic services	24.6	26.6	27.7	30.2	32.9	35.2	37.0	39.9	45.0	49.4
Other services, n.e.s.	40.0	45.8	51.1	57.2	61.1	67.1	79.0	89.8	103.0	107.4
Less imputed banking service charges	-14.0	-16.0	-17.9	-20.8	-22.9	-29.5	-32.5	-42.2	-52.3	-54.0
Total	744.5	782.1	929.9	989.5	1,138.0	1,299.5	1,430.3	1,736.1	1,877.0	1,969.5

GROSS OUTPUT OF THE MANUFACTURING SECTOR BY INDUSTRIAL GROUPS (million Rhodesian dollars)

Period*	Food-stuffs	Drink and Tobacco	Textiles including Cotton Ginning	Clothing and Footwear	Wood and Furniture	Paper and Printing and Publishing	Chemical and Petroleum Products	Non-Metallic Mineral Products	Metals and Metal Products	Transport Equip-ment	Other Manu-facturing Groups	All Manu-facturing Groups
1964	92.5	37.2	25.2	27.0	13.0	20.4	49.4	8.6	59.1	31.4	4.8	368.5
1965	103.2	38.8	29.8	28.3	13.7	21.9	55.8	9.8	66.1	33.4	3.0	404.0
1966	103.0	36.9	29.5	29.9	13.8	22.0	52.0	11.3	62.9	20.5	3.1	385.0
1967	102.0	37.9	36.1	34.3	15.2	23.4	53.8	12.6	75.6	14.1	4.1	409.3
1968	114.9	38.9	42.7	35.9	16.0	25.4	61.7	17.0	81.7	15.0	4.9	454.1
1969	119.6	44.5	58.0	39.6	18.2	29.2	71.8	19.6	103.8	22.1	5.8	532.1
1970	141.2	48.8	57.6	46.2	22.3	34.1	82.6	24.0	139.9	23.5	6.6	626.8
1971	157.1	54.8	71.9	53.4	25.3	37.7	98.5	28.3	167.2	31.7	7.8	733.7
1972	177.9	63.1	88.5	60.6	28.2	43.1	112.7	33.9	186.3	36.7	9.3	840.3
1973	218.9	69.1	104.0	69.7	32.2	51.5	119.6	39.2	221.9	43.4	10.9	980.4
1974	237.2	79.1	140.6	84.1	38.6	65.5	164.3	45.1	296.0	48.4	13.7	1,212.6
1975†	264.8	90.2	136.9	88.1	36.5	69.7	183.4	48.7	330.7	55.9	13.5	1,318.4
1976†	310.6	104.0	162.1	89.7	37.2	70.0	175.0	42.3	325.3	59.4	13.9	1,389.5

EXTERNAL TRADE: TERMS OF TRADE (Excluding net gold sales)

Year	Unit Value Indices		Terms of Trade*
	Imports	*Exports*	
1964	100.0	100.0	100.0
1965	103.5	104.3	100.8
1966	114.0	93.8	82.3
1967	113.8	90.8	79.8
1968	112.0	92.7	82.8
1969	114.1	98.2	86.1
1970	119.2	102.0	85.6
1971	127.1	103.2	81.2
1972	124.4	102.5	82.4
1973	129.6	110.3	85.1
1974	176.6	144.6	81.9
1975	195.1	155.9	79.9
1976	221.1	164.2	74.3

*The terms of trade are defined as the unit value of exports divided by the unit value of imports. A fall in the terms of trade indicates a rise in import prices relative to export prices.

NOTES

1. *The Times*, London; 2 March 1978.
2. Radio Salisbury, 26 January 1978.
3. See *Africa Contemporary Record (ACR)* 1976–77, pp. A34–36.
4. See Documents section, pp. C56–59.
5. See essay, 'US Year in Africa'.
6. For full text see *Zimbabwe Report* (official organ of UANC), London; May 1977.
7. See essay, 'Britain's Year in Africa'.
8. See David Martin, *The Observer*, London; 17 April 1977.
9. *The Times*, 18 April 1977. Also see *ACR* 1976–77, p. B907.
10. *Ibid*, 20 April 1977.
11. See *ACR* 1976–77, pp. A41ff.
12. *Financial Times (FT)*, London; 11 July 1977.
13. *For the Record*, No 42 (Salisbury: Government Printer).
14. *The Times*, 28 July 1977.
15. *Daily Telegraph*, London; 30 July 1977.
16. Radio Salisbury, 30 August 1977.
17. *The Observer*, 31 July 1977.
18. *Daily Telegraph*, 4 August 1977.
19. *Ibid*, 9 August 1977.
20. *The Guardian*, Manchester; 26 August 1977.
21. Observer Foreign News Service, 30 August 1977.
22. *Daily Telegraph*, 23 August 1977.
23. *The Guardian,* 26 August 1977.
24. *Ibid*.
25. See Documents section, pp. C68–72.
26. *The Times*, 3 September 1977.
27. *The Guardian*, 15 September 1977.
28. *Ibid*, 7 September 1977.
29. *Daily Telegraph*, 24 October 1977.
30. *The Times*, 11 November 1977.
31. *Ibid*, 14 November 1977.
32. *For the Record*, No 43.
33. *The Times*, 28 November 1977.
34. *Rhodesia Herald (RH)*, Salisbury; 25 November 1977.
35. *The Times*, 10 December 1977.
36. *Ibid*, 9 December 1977.
37. *Ibid*, 13 December 1977.
38. *The Observer*, 1 January 1978.

39. Radio Maputo, 9 January 1978.
40. *The Times*, 26 January 1978.
41. *Ibid*, 3 February 1978.
42. *The Observer*, 5 February 1978.
43. *The Times*, 16 February 1978.
44. *Ibid*, 4 March 1978.
45. *Ibid*, 16 February 1978.
46. *Ibid*, 17 February 1978.
47. *Africa Research Bulleting (ARB)*, Exeter; 1–31 March 1978.
48. *Daily Telegraph*, 23 June 1978.
49. *FT*, 23 June 1978.
50. See *ACR* 1976–77, p. B907.
51. *The Guardian*, 29 August 1977.
52. *Daily Telegraph*, 12 September 1977.
53. *The Star*, Johannesburg; 19 March 1977.
54. Michael Knipe in *The Times*, 29 April 1977.
55. *The Star*, 2 July 1977.
56. *The Times*, 10 November 1977.
57. For a more detailed analysis of the tribal factor, see *ACR* 1976–77, pp. A14–22.
58. *Ibid*, pp. A19–20.
59. *Ibid*, pp. A10–13.
60. *Zimbabwe Report*, May 1977.
61. Radio Salisbury, 11 October 1977.
62. See essay, 'The Disunited OAU'.
63. See 'Stresses and Strains in the Front' in *Africa*, London; November 1977.
64. *The Guardian*, 26 July 1977.
65. Interview with Colin Legum in Malta, 2 February 1978.
66. *The Times*, 15 February 1978.
67. *Zimbabwe News*, Maputo; Vol 9, No 3 (March-April 1977).
68. *Ibid*.
69. *Ibid*, Vol 9, Nos 5 and 6 (July-December 1977).
70. *Peking Review*, 1 July 1977.
71. *Soviet News*, 12 July 1977.
72. *The Guardian*, 16 August 1977.
73. *The Times*, 23 August 1977.
74. See *ACR* 1976–77, pp. A14–15.
75. James McManus in *The Guardian*, 23 August 1977.
76. See *ACR* 1976–77, pp. A15–16. Also see Sithole, *In Defence of the Rhodesian Constitutional Agreement* (Salisbury: Graham Publishing, 1978).
77. Zupo Press Kit, 28 Charing Cross Road, London WC2.
78. *Voice of Zimbabwe*, Salisbury; No 1, 4 October 1977.
79. Radio Johannesburg, 16 September 1977.
80. *The Guardian*, 6 January 1978.
81. *FT*, 4 February 1978.
82. *The Guardian*, 25 April 1977.
83. *RH*, 10 May 1977.
84. *Daily Telegraph*, 11 May 1977.
85. See essay, 'The Disunited OAU'.
86. *Daily Telegraph*, 6 July 1977.
87. *The Times*, 17 December 1977.
88. *RH*, 7 April 1977.
89. *The Times*, 7 April 1977.
90. See *ACR* 1976–77, p. B914; and *Zimbabwe: The Facts about Rhodesia*, (London, November 1977).
91. *Rhodesia: The Propaganda War* (London: Catholic Institute for International Relations, September 1977).
92. *Focus on Political Repression in Southern Africa*, No 13, London.
93. *The Military Balance 1977–78* (London: International Institute for Strategic Studies).
94. *Ibid*.
95. *FT*, 1 July 1977.
96. *The Guardian*, 20 August 1977; and *Daily Telegraph*, 29 September 1977.
97. See *ACR* 1976–77, p. A50.
98. *The Guardian*, 1 February 1978.
99. *Rhodesia: The Propaganda War, op cit*.

100. *The Guardian,* 15 October 1977.
101. *Ibid*, 24 November 1977.
102. *The Times*, 3 December 1977.
103. *Zimbabwe: The Facts about Rhodesia, op cit.*
104. *Focus,* no 13.
105. Personal letter to author.
106. *Financial Mail (FM)*, Johannesburg; 25 February 1977.
107. Salisbury Radio, 16 March 1978.
108. *RH*, 10 March 1977.
109. *Monthly Digest of Statistics, Supplement* (Salisbury, April 1977).
110. *RH*, 3 November 1977.
111. *FM*, 9 December 1977.
112. Dr Erich Leistner, Deputy Director of the African Institute in the *Star*, 13 August 1977.
113. *RH*, 3 November 1977.
114. Radio Salisbury, 6 January 1978.
115. *FM*, 1 July 1977.
116. *Daily Telegraph*, 1 February 1978.

PART V:

Documents

The USSR and Africa

Treaty of Friendship and Co-operation between USSR and Mozambique

Text of the Treaty of Friendship and Co-operation between
the USSR and the People's Republic of Mozambique signed in Maputo on
31 March 1977 by President Nikolai Podgorny and
President Samora Machel

The Union of Soviet Socialist Republics and the People's Republic of Mozambique: considering that the relations of friendship and co-operation which took shape between the Soviet and Mozambique peoples in the difficult years of the people's war for the liberation of Mozambique and which have grown stronger since the formation of the People's Republic of Mozambique are in keeping with the vital interests of both sides and serve the cause of world peace; being determined to support each other in the creation of more favourable conditions for the consolidation of the revolutionary social and economic gains of both peoples; inspired by the ideals of the struggle against imperialism, colonialism and racialism; prompted by the desire to render support to the struggle for world peace and security in the interests of the peoples of all countries; declaring themselves in favour of the unity and co-operation of all progressive forces in the struggle for independence, freedom, peace and social progress; reaffirming their loyalty to the aims and principles of the UN Charter; and striving to strengthen the existing relations of friendship and mutually-beneficial co-operation between their two states and peoples, which are natural allies; have decided to conclude this Treaty of Friendship and Co-operation and have agreed on the following:

I. The High Contracting Parties proclaim their resolve to strengthen and deepen the unbreakable friendship between the two countries and peoples and to develop all-round co-operation. On the basis of respect for sovereignty, territorial integrity, non-interference in each other's internal affairs and equality, the two parties will co-operate in every possible way in creating ever more favourable conditions for preserving and deepening the social and economic gains of the peoples of the Union of Soviet Socialist Republics and the People's Republic of Mozambique.

II. The High Contracting Parties attach great importance to all-round co-operation between them and to the exchange of experience in the economic, technical and scientific spheres. For these purposes, they will expand and deepen co-operation in industry, transport and communications, agriculture, fisheries, the development of natural resources, the development of [energy] and other spheres of the economy, and also in the training of national personnel.

Both sides will expand trade and shipping on the basis of the principles of equality, mutual benefit and most-favoured nation treatment.

III. The High Contracting Parties will promote the development of co-operation, mutual assistance and the exchange of experience in science, culture, art, literature, education, the health services, the press, radio, the cinema, tourism, sports and other spheres.

The two sides will promote the broadening of co-operation and direct links between political and public organizations, enterprises and cultural and scientific institutions in order to deepen mutual knowledge of the life, work, experience and achievements of the peoples of both countries.

IV. In the interests of reinforcing the defence potentials of the High Contracting Parties, they will continue developing co-operation in the military sphere on the basis of appropriate agreements.

V. The Union of Soviet Socialist Republics respects the policy of non-alignment pursued by the People's Republic of Mozambique—a policy that is an important factor in maintaining world peace and security.

The People's Republic of Mozambique respects the policy of peace aimed at strengthening friendship and co-operation with all peoples that is being pursued by the Union of Soviet Socialist Republics.

VI. The High Contracting Parties will continue the struggle for world peace and will go on making every effort to deepen the relaxation of international tensions. They will support its implementation in specific forms of mutually-beneficial co-operation between states. Both sides will make every effort to achieve general and complete disarmament, including nuclear disarmament, under effective international control, to settle international disputes by peaceful means and to conclude an international treaty on the renunciation of the use of force in international relations.

VII. The High Contracting Parties will continue the consistent struggle against the forces of imperialism and for the final abolition of colonialism, neo-colonialism, racialism and apartheid. They support the complete implementation of the UN Declaration on the Granting of Independence to Colonial Countries and Peoples.

The two sides will co-operate with each other and with other peaceful states in supporting the just struggle of the peoples for freedom, independence and social progress.

VIII. The High Contracting Parties, expressing profound interest in ensuring peace and international security and attaching great importance to their co-operation in the international field for the purpose of achieving these goals, will regularly exchange views on important international questions in the spirit of mutual understanding. Such consultations and exchanges of opinion will also include questions of a political, economic and cultural nature and other questions concerning bilateral relations.

Consultations and exchanges of opinion will be held at various levels, and specifically through meetings between leading statesmen of both countries, during visits of official delegations and special representatives and through diplomatic channels.

IX. If situations arise that threaten peace or lead to an outbreak of war, the High Contracting Parties will immediately get into touch with each other in order to co-ordinate their positions in the interests of eliminating the threat that has arisen or restoring peace.

X. Each of the High Contracting Parties declares that it will not enter into any military or other alliance, or take part in any groupings of states, or in actions or measures directed against the other High Contracting Party.

XI. The High Contracting Parties declare that their commitments under existing international treaties are not at variance with the provisions of this treaty, and pledge themselves not to conclude any international agreements incompatible with it.

XII. Questions that may arise between the High Contracting Parties concerning the interpretation or the application of any provision of this treaty will be settled in a bilateral way, in the spirit of friendship, mutual understanding and mutual respect.

XIII. The present treaty will operate for 20 years from the day it comes into force.

If neither of the High Contracting Parties expresses its wish to terminate the treaty one year before the expiration of the aforementioned term, the treaty will remain in force for the next five years, and so on, until one of the High Contracting Parties makes a written statement, one year before the expiration of the current five-year period, signifying its intention to terminate the treaty.

XIV. The present treaty is subject to ratification and will come into force on the day of the exchange of the instruments of ratification, which is to take place in Moscow.

(For statistics on Communist economic credits to Africa, Communist military and economic technicians in Africa, African students and military personnel being trained in Communist countries, see Tables following section on *Economic Developments,* below. For Soviet-Somali relations, see subsection *Horn of Africa,* below.)

Source: Soviet News, 19 April 1977.

British Policy in Africa

Statement by Dr David Owen, Foreign Secretary, to the Young Fabians

Brighton, October 1977

There were always contradictions and inconsistencies in British colonial policy towards Africa.

The central contradiction sprang from applying to Africa policies of self-government that derived from our experience in Canada and Australia, where the bulk of the population had been settlers from Europe. But in the African colonies the aspirations of the majority were not compatible with white self-government.

A similar ambiguity persists today in British policy towards Africa in the post-colonial era. There are sectors of British public opinion who seem oblivious of the feelings of the black majority and their wish for freedom and who identify exclusively with the white minority regimes in southern Africa.

This identification readily finds political expression in this country. It has meant that our opposition as a nation to apartheid, and our determination to bring democratic majority rule to Rhodesia, has at times been seen to be at best equivocal. As a result, our generally good colonial record in Africa has become tarnished and our motives suspect.

The challenge for a Labour Government which, as a matter of conviction and policy, is implacably opposed to racialism in all its forms, is to point the way unswervingly to where the future of Africa must lie. This is not only a moral obligation: it is the assertion of our long-term national interest.

Last year, trade in each direction with SA was worth more than £600m. Black Africa took more than £1.3bn of British exports, twice as much as SA. Nigeria has now replaced SA as our single largest trading partner on that continent.

A universal ban on trade with SA would cause major problems and higher unemployment in British exporting industries. It would also disrupt industries at present dependent on imports of South African raw materials—principally chrome, manganese, platinum and other minerals.

We are living in a real world and this is a harsh fact that we, more than any other Western European country, have to take into account. Yet with the passage of time the overall balance of advantage must lie with black Africa.

To evolve a consistent policy with a firm moral base is more easily said than done, but one thing is clear. We must stay true to the basic human values we proclaim.

In SA, as in Rhodesia and Namibia, the promotion of human rights means the right of all people, regardless of colour, to live and work in peace, equality and mutual respect.

Violence is the last resort. To use violence where peaceful means are available runs counter to the whole system of values which we are pledged to sustain. But as long as repressive systems of white minority rule, impervious to peaceful political pressures, remain in existence, they will inevitably generate frustration and a sense of humiliation on such a scale that the black African populations will understandably be driven in increasing numbers to violence and the armed struggle. We cannot brand them as enemies of democracy and disciples of Moscow because they are fighting for their rights: had it not been for the defeat of Portuguese colonialism by the freedom fighters and the military pressures which have been brought to bear on the Rhodesian regime, Mr Smith would not now be near to genuinely accepting, as I think he is, majority rule.

Our present initiative is inspired by the belief that a settlement is possible and that it can bring independence and majority rule before the end of 1978. Our proposals differ fundamentally from earlier attempts at a settlement in facing up to the fact that on her own Britain cannot bring peace to Rhodesia and that without the weight of American support a political settlement is impossible.

The decision of the Security Council to associate the UN with the Anglo-American proposals on Rhodesia shows that the international community, influenced strongly by black African opinion, not least the Front-Line Presidents and the black nationalists, think that our proposals form the basis for a negotiated settlement. No one has committed himself yet to the package as a whole; it is premature to do that.

On one thing we must be absolutely clear. I shall not go back to the UN Security Council—nor shall I ask the House of Commons to agree to our assuming responsibility in Rhodesia—unless I am as confident as I can be that during the transition period law and order will be maintained and free and fair elections can be held giving all Zimbabwe politicians an equal chance of success.

In SA our task is to consider how best we can encourage a peaceful evolution of society based on internal reforms.

Hitherto the instruments of moral and political persuasion used by the international community—public condemnation, SA isolation at the UN, the discouragement of sporting contacts, the voluntary arms embargo—have not worked well enough.

Any change for the better is welcome. But the minor changes so far registered are totally inadequate to the scale of reforms needed. The tough code of conduct recently adopted by the European Community for its companies operating in SA is a major step forward.

We and the other Western democracies can justify our economic stake in SA only if it can be used, and be seen to be used, as an effective instrument for promoting change: abolition of the Immorality Act and the Pass Laws, the abolition of the most deeply offensive overt signs of apartheid and of detention and restrictions without trial.

These changes must come quickly if hope is to be kept alive. Without hope there is only desperation, and desperation is the crucible of violence: urban violence, guerrilla violence and the shadow of nuclear tests—all of this could come to SA. The new thrust of the US Administration's policy towards the African continent is the best hope for peaceful change.

If change does not come from within, the pressures to compel it from without will become irresistible, facing the international community with momentous and difficult decisions. In the UN the pressure for mandatory economic sanctions will inevitably grow.

Yet it is no good imposing sanctions only as a moral gesture or simply to punish recalcitrant behaviour. We must count the cost of our actions—to others as well as to ourselves—and adjust them to our goals. We obviously do not want to introduce measures that will make white South Africans so desperate that they would not only resist change in any form but would produce an even more repressive regime.

If that were to happen, it would be those whom we most want to help—the non-white majority—who would suffer most.

There is nothing glamorous in violence. The liberation struggle in SA if it were to depend only on violence, would be bloodier than anywhere in the world.

Sooner or later the conditions in southern Africa that today mock human dignity and stir up racial tension will be eliminated. The only question is whether the transition will come peacefully or through further violence. Our task is to ensure that it is the path of peace that leads to justice.

Source: The Observer, London, 9 October 1977.
(For the British Government White Paper 'New Proposals for a Settlement' in Rhodesia, see below, sub-section on *Rhodesia*.)

US Policy in Africa

Interview given by President Carter
to Raph Uwechue, Editor-in-Chief of *Africa*

December 1977

Part of our interest in Africa, of course, comes from the fact that it is a continent of enormous potential in resources and human talent. It is in our interest to have good relations with Africa in years to come. However, there are other good reasons beyond the traditional narrow definition of national self-interest for adopting a more committed and more active policy toward Africa. We believe, for example, that our attitude toward questions such as majority rule and racial justice has a direct bearing on the strength of American society, which will be reinforced if our policy abroad is consistent with our own standards on these questions here at home. We also believe that our overall conduct of foreign relations will be strengthened by the moral premise inherent in our stance on these questions.

The conflict in southern Africa has resulted in a tremendous cost in human lives and in its effect on economic development in the region. We believe that the US, Africa and the rest of the world share an interest in keeping the conflict from escalating further and bringing it to a halt as soon as possible. This is the reason for our efforts to help find a just solution. Our position also flows from our beliefs about human justice. We have made progress in this country toward fully accepting the proposition that all human beings were created equal and deserve the same benefits from their society. All Americans, black and white, share an allegiance to this view. We cannot afford to diminish it by an equivocal attitude toward racial equality abroad. Our interest in Africa is natural since more than 11% of our people trace their roots back to that continent, and have become increasingly conscious of their African heritage and of events in Africa.

'Super-power' rivalry in Africa is something we hope to avoid. One fundamental objective is to help Africans create a strong prosperous Africa at peace with itself and with the world, not to gain some advantage over the Soviets or Cubans or any other power. If we—or if the Soviet Union and its allies—yield to the temptation to make Africa a source of power confrontation, our chances of helping Africa develop in the peaceful direction its people choose will be greatly reduced.

Cuba's apparent inclination to revive aspects of colonial intervention that have been internationally discredited cannot help bring peace or prosperity to Africa. The presence of some 18,000 Cuban soldiers on African soil, actively engaged in combat against Africans, raises legitimate concerns of neo-colonialist intrusion and can aggravate tensions in other areas of the world.

We have made very clear that we oppose apartheid. We think that because the South African system is unjust it may well lead to increasing violence over the years; we hope this can be prevented by removing the injustices, and we hope there is still time in which this may be done. Because of the recent unfortunate events in SA, we have supported a UN embargo of all military equipment to SA and, in addition, prohibited sales of any kind, whatever the nature of the items, from the US to the South African police or military. We will continue to look for ways to influence SA to change unjust policies, and our commercial and financial relations with SA are now under review.

I ought to say, however, there is no clear agreement as to whether Western investment in SA is a good thing or a bad thing. Some, including many blacks in SA and many in the black community in America, believe that the economic benefits which Western investment brings to South African blacks are a factor for political change because they generate pressures for increased fairness and against apartheid. Others argue that foreign investment supports the apartheid system. Our position has been that we will neither encourage nor discourage private investment in SA.

We would be the first to acknowledge, with regret, that we have not completed the job of ensuring full equality for all of our citizens. But we are committed to this goal, and we are prepared to invest the resources we know this commitment will require. We realize that when we talk about human rights around the world, we must be ready to endure scrutiny of our actions at home. We believe that this country's experience demonstrates what can be done in the area of human rights. It also reflects the fact that this struggle requires continued attention, and that even then we will suffer setbacks from time to time. This is especially true in the employment field, although we are beginning to make progress on black unemployment in some cities.

Andy Young deserves a good deal of credit for the more frank and productive relations we now have with many African countries. I also believe that he has been a positive force for our improved relations in the UN more generally. There are other blacks working in my administration who have contributed to our work in Africa. In addition to our black ambassadors, blacks now contribute directly on African policy issues in the African Affairs Bureau and policy planning staff in the State Department and on the National Security Council in the White House.

The Congressional Black Caucus is also playing an important role. This is a start, and we would hope that over time blacks will be represented more heavily in the making of foreign policy. A number of blacks have a personal interest in work related to Africa, but we have no intention of limiting them to that area of foreign policy alone.

Source: Africa, London; No. 76, December 1977.

(For a description of US trade with Africa and accompanying tables, see below, section on *Economic Developments*. For US policy on the Ogaden war, see subsection *Horn of Africa* below.)

The CIA in Africa

*Letter sent to Admiral Stanfield Turner, the new
Director of the Central Intelligence Agency, by
John Stockwell, former Chief, Angola Task Force,
dated 31 March 1977*

We have not met and will not have the opportunity of working together, as you are coming into the Central Intelligence Agency (CIA) as I am leaving. Although I am disassociating myself from the Agency, I have read with considerable interest about your appointment and listened to some of your comments.

You have clearly committed yourself to defending the Agency from its detractors and to improving its image, and this has stirred a wave of hope among many of its career officers. However, others are disappointed that you have given no indication of intention, or even awareness of the need, for the internal housecleaning that is so conspicuously overdue in the Agency.

You invited Agency officers to write you their suggestions or grievances, and you promised personally to read all such letters. While I no longer have a career interest, having already submitted my resignation, numerous friends in the Deputy Directorate for Operations (DDO) have encouraged me to write you, hoping that it might lead to measures which would upgrade the clandestine service from its present mediocre standards to the élite organization it was once reputed to be.

While I sympathize with their complaints, I have agreed to write this letter more to document the circumstances and conditions which led to my own disillusionment with the CIA.

First, let me introduce myself. I was until yesterday a successful GS 14 with 12 years in the Agency, having served seven full tours of duty including Chief of Base, Lubumbashi; Chief of Station, Bujumbura; Officer in Charge of Tay Ninh Province in Vietnam, and Chief, Angola Task Force. My file documents what I was told occasionally, that I could realistically aspire to top managerial positions in the Agency.

I grew up in Zaire, a few miles from the Kapanga Methodist Mission Station, which was recently 'liberated' by Katangese invaders, and I speak fluent English and Tshiluba, 'High' French and smatterings of Swahili and other dialects.

My disillusionment was progressive throughout four periods of my career. First, during three successive assignments in Africa, from 1966 through 1977, I increasingly questioned the value and justification of the reporting and operations we worked so hard to generate.

In one post, Abidjan, there was no Eastern bloc or Communist presence, no subversion, limited US interests and a stable government. The three of us competed with State Department officers to report on President Houphouet-Boigny's health and local politics.

I attempted to rationalize that my responsibility was to contribute, and not to evaluate the importance of my contribution, which should be done by supergrades in Washington. However, this was increasingly difficult as I looked up through a chain of command which included, step-by-step: (a) the Branch Chief, who had never served in Africa and was conspicuously ignorant of black Africa; (b) the Chief of Operations, who was a senior officer although he had never served an operational overseas tour and was correspondingly naive about field operations; and (c) the Division Chief, who was a political dilettante who had never served an operational tour in Africa. . . . Their leadership continuously reflected their inexperience and ignorance.

Standards of operations were low in the field, with considerable energy devoted to the accumulation of perquisites and living a luxurious life at the taxpayer's expense. When I made Chief of Station, a supergrade took me out for drinks and, after welcoming me to the exclusive inner club of 'chiefs', proceeded to brief me on how to supplement my income by an additional $3,000 to $4,000 per year, tax free, by manipulating my representional and operational funds. This was quite within the regulations. For example, the Chief of Station Kinshasa last year legally collected over $9,000 from CIA for the operation of his household.

Most case officers handled 90% of their operations in their own living rooms, in full view of servants, guards and neighbours. And I expect few individuals would accept CIA recruitments if they knew how blithely their cases are discussed over the phone: 'Hello, John . . . when you meet your friend after the cocktail party tonight . . . you know, the one with the old Mercedes . . . be sure to get that receipt for $300 . . . and pick up the little Sony, so we can fix the signalling device.'

In Burundi, we won a round in the game of dirty tricks against the Soviets. Shortly after my arrival, we mounted an operation to exploit the Soviets' vulnerabilities of having a disproportionately large embassy staff and a fumbling, obnoxious old ambassador, and discredit them in the eyes of the Barundi. We were apparently successful, as the Barundi requested that the ambassador not return when he went on leave, and they ordered the Soviets to reduce their staff by 50%.

We were proud of the operation, but a few months later the Soviets assigned a competent career diplomat to the post, and he arrived to receive a cordial welcome from the Barundi, who were more than a little nervous at their brashness, and eager to make amends. For the rest of my tour, relations were remarkably better between the two countries than before our operation. The operation nevertheless won us some accolades. However, it left me with profound reservations about the real value of the operational games we play in the field.

Later, Africa Division policy shifted its emphasis from reporting on local politics to the attempted recruitment of the so-called 'hard targets', i.e. the accessible Eastern European diplomats who live exposed lives in little African posts. I have listened to the enthusiastic claims of success of this programme and its justification in terms of broader national interests, and I have been able to follow some of these operations wherein Agency officers have successfully befriended and allegedly recruited drunken Soviet, Czech, Hungarian and Polish diplomats by servicing their venal and sexual (homo and hetero) weaknesses.

Unfortunately, I observed, and colleagues in the Soviet Division confirmed to me, that none of these recruited individuals has had access to truly vital strategic information. Instead they have reported mostly on their colleagues' private lives in the little posts. Not one has returned to his own country, gained access to strategic information and reported satisfactorily.

Agency operations in Vietnam would have discouraged even the most callous, self-serving of adventurers. It was a veritable catch-22 of unprofessional conduct. 98% of the operations were commonly agreed to be fabrications, but were papered over and promoted by aware case officers because of the 'numbers game' requirements from Headquarters for voluminous reporting. . . . At the end, in April 1975, several senior CIA field officers were caught by surprise, fled in hasty panic and otherwise abandoned their responsibilities.

One senior officer left the country five days before the final evacuation, telling subordinates he was going to visit his family and would return. Later it became apparent he never intended to return and was abdicating all responsibility for the people who had worked for him and for the CIA in his area. Almost 90% of the Vietnamese employees from his area were abandoned in the evacuation. Numerous middle and lower-grade officers vigorously protested this conduct, but all of these senior officers, including the one who fled, have subsequently received responsible assignments with the promise of promotion.

After Vietnam, I received the assignment of Chief, Angola Task Force. This was despite the fact that I and many other officers in the CIA and State Department thought the intervention irresponsible and ill-conceived, both in terms of the advancement of US interests, and the moral question of contributing substantially to the escalation of an already bloody civil war, when there was no possibility that we would make a full commitment and ensure the victory of our allies.

From a chess player's point of view, the intervention was a blunder. In July 1975, the MPLA was clearly winning, already controlling 12 of the 15 provinces, and was thought by several responsible American officials and senators to be the best qualified to run Angola; nor was it hostile to the US. The CIA committed $31m to opposing the MPLA victory, but six months later the MPLA had nevertheless decisively won, and 15,000 Cuban regular army troops were entrenched in Angola with the full sympathy of much of the Third World, and the support of several influential African chiefs of state who previously had been critical of any extra-continental intervention in African affairs.

At the same time, the US was solidly discredited, having been exposed for covert military intervention in African affairs, having allied itself with SA and having lost.

This is not Monday-morning quarterbacking. Various people foresaw all this and also predicted that the covert intervention would ultimately be exposed and cur-tailed by the US Senate. I myself warned the Interagency Working Group in October 1975, that the Zairian invasion of northern Angola would be answered by the introduction of large numbers of Cuban troops—10,000 to 15,000 I said—and would invite an eventual retaliatory invasion of Zaire from Angola.

Is anyone surprised that a year later the Angolan government has permitted freshly armed Zairian exiles to invade the Shaba Province of Zaire? Is the CIA a good friend? Having encouraged Mobutu to tease the Angolan lion, will it help him repel its retaliatory charge? Can one not argue that our Angolan programme provoked the present invasion of Zaire, which may well lead to its loss of Shaba's rich copper mines?

Yes, I know you are attempting to generate token support to help Zaire meet its crisis; that you are seeking out the same French mercenaries the CIA sent into Angola in early 1976. These are the men who took the CIA money but fled the first time they encountered heavy shelling.

Some of us in the Angolan programme were continuously frustrated and disappointed with Headquarter's weak leadership of the field, especially its inability to control the Kinshasa station as it purchased ice plants and ships for local friends, and on one occasion tried to get the CIA to pay Mobutu $2m for an airplane which was worth only $600,000. All of this and much more, is documented in the cable traffic, if it hasn't been destroyed.

I came away from the Angolan programme in the spring of 1976 determined to reassess the CIA and my potential for remaining with it. I read several books with a more objective mind, and began to discuss the present state of the American in-telligence establishment from a less defensive position. I read (Morton) Halperin's book and (Joseph) Smith's and (David) Philips'. I was seriously troubled to discover the extent to which the CIA has in fact violated its charter and begun surveilling and mounting operations against American citizens. I attempted to count the hundreds, thousands of lives that have been taken in thoughtless little CIA adventures.

A major point was made to me when I was recruited in 1964 that the CIA was high-minded and scrupulously kept itself clean of truly dirty skulduggery such as killing and coups, etc. At that exact time the CIA was making preparations for the assassination of certain Latin American politicians and covering its involvement in the assassination of Patrice Lumumba.

Eventually we learned Lumumba was killed, not by our poisons, but beaten to death, apparently by men who were loyal to men who had Agency cryptonyms and received Agency salaries. In death he became an eternal martyr and by installing Mobutu in the Zairian presidency, we committed ourselves to the 'other side', the losing side in central and southern Africa.

We cast ourselves as the dull-witted Goliath, in a world of eager young Davids. I for one have applauded as Ambassador (Andrew) Young thrashed about trying to break us loose from this role and I keenly hope President Carter will continue to support him in some new thinking about Africa.

But, one asks, has the CIA learned its lesson and mended its ways since the revelations of Watergate and the subsequent investigations? Is it now, with the help of oversight committees, policed and self-policing?

While I was still serving as the Central Branch Chief in Africa Division last fall, a young officer in my branch was delegated away from my supervision to write a series of memos discussing with the Justice Department the possibilities for prosecution of an American mercenary named David Bufkin.

Bufkin had been involved in the Angola conflict, apparently receiving monies from Holden Roberto, quite possibly from funds he received from the CIA. In anticipation of the possibility that during a trial of Bufkin the defence might demand to see his CIA file under the Freedom of Information Act, it was carefully purged.

Certain documents containing information about him were placed in other files where they could easily be retrieved but would not be exposed if he demanded and gained access to his own file. I heard of this and remonstrated, but was told by the young officer that in his previous Agency assignment he had served on a staff which was responding to Senate investigations, and that such tactics were common—'We did it all the time'—as the Agency attempted to protect incriminating information from investigators.

None of this has addressed the conditions which my former colleagues have begged me to expose. They are more frustrated by the constipation that exists at the top and middle levels of the DDO, where an ingrown clique of senior officers has for a quarter of a century controlled and exploited their power and prestige under the security of clandestinity and safe from exposure, so that no matter how drunken, inept or corrupt their management of a station might be, they are protected, promoted and reassigned.

The organization currently belongs to the old, to the burned out. Young officers, and there are some very good ones, must wait until generations retire before they can move up. Mediocre performances are guaranteed by a promotion system wherein time in grade and being a 'good ole boy' are top criteria, i.e. there are no exceptional promotions and the outstanding individual gets his promotions the same as the 'only-good' and even some of the 'not-really-so-good' officers, and he must wait behind a line of tired old men for the truly challenging field assignments.

These young officers are generally supervised by unpromotable middle-grade officers who for many years have been unable to go overseas and participate personally in operational activity. These conditions are obviously discouraging to dynamic young people, demoralizingly so, and several have told me they are also seeking opportunities outside the Agency.

With each new Director they hope there will be a housecleaning and reform, but each Director comes and goes, seven in my time, preoccupied with broader matters of state, uttering meaningless and inaccurate platitudes about conditions and standards inside the DDO. The only exception was James Schlesinger, who initiated a housecleaning but was transferred to the Department of Defence before it had much effect.

You, Sir, have been so bold as to state your intention to abrogate American constitutional rights, those of freedom of speech, in order to defend and protect the American intelligence establishment. This strikes me as presumptuous of you, especially before you have even had a good look inside the CIA to see if it is worth sacrificing constitutional rights for.

If you get the criminal penalties you are seeking for the disclosure of classified information, or even the civil penalties which President Carter and Vice-President Mondale have said they favour, then Americans who work for the CIA could not, when they find themselves embroiled in criminal and immoral activity which is commonplace in the Agency, expose that activity without risking jail or poverty as punishment for speaking out. Cynical men, such as those who gravitate to the top of the CIA, could then by classifying a document or two protect and cover up illegal actions with relative impunity.

I predict that the American people will never surrender to you the right of any individual to stand in public and say whatever is in his heart and mind. That right is our last line of defence against the tyrannies and invasions of privacy which events of recent years have demonstrated are more than paranoic fantasies. I am enthusiastic about the nation's prospects under the new administration, and I am certain President Carter will reconsider his position on this issue.

And you, sir, may well decide to address yourself to the more appropriate task of setting the Agency straight from the inside out.

Policy Statement made by Vice-President Walter Mondale

After meeting with the Prime Minister of South Africa, John Vorster, in Vienna, 20 May 1977

'I have been meeting with South African Minister Vorster and his Government at the request of President Carter to convey the new policies of our administration regarding southern Africa, specifically Rhodesia, Namibia and SA itself. We had a day and a half of very frank and candid discussions. Both sides were aware before the meetings began of possible fundamental differences and yet we pursued these discussions in a constructive spirit in order to improve the possibility of mutual understanding and progress.

'Put most simply, the policy which the President wished me to convey was that there was need for progress on all three issues: majority rule for Rhodesia and Namibia and a progressive transformation of South African society to the same end.

'We believed it was particularly important to convey the depth of our convictions. There has been a transformation in American society of which we are very proud. It affects not only our domestic life, but our foreign policy as well. We cannot accept, let alone defend, the governments that reject the basic principle of full human rights, economic opportunity and political participation for all of its people regardless of race. This basic mission was accomplished during these talks. I believe our policy is clear, and I believe the South African Government now appreciates that it is deeply rooted in American experience and values.

'I do not know how or whether this will affect the decisions that confront SA, particularly in regard to its own system, but I made it clear that without evident progress that provides full political participation and an end to discrimination, the [pressure] of international events would require us to take actions based on our policy and to the detriment of the constructive relations we would prefer with SA.

'As for Rhodesia and Namibia, I believe we registered some useful progress, but the significance of this progress will depend on future developments. Prime Minister Vorster agreed to support British-American efforts to get the directly interested parties to agree to an independence constitution and the necessary transitional arrangements, including the holding of elections in which all can take part equally so that Zimbabwe can achieve independence during 1978, and peace.

'Likewise every effort will be made to bring about a de-escalation of violence, and it is believed that the negotiating process will be the best way to achieve this end. We believe this is an encouraging step in a positive direction. Hopefully we will work together to bring the interested parties to find a peaceful solution to the conflict in Rhodesia.

'The extent to which this pays off will, of course, remain to be seen as we pursue the British initiative. In this connection, I made clear our support for these efforts and the closest collaboration with them. In this connection, I explained that our concept of the Zimbabwe development fund is different from that of the previous American administration. Instead of being a fund aimed at buying out the white settlers in Rhodesia, we want to reorient that fund to a development fund, one which will help build a strong economy and one that will encourage the continued participation of the white population in an independent Zimbabwe.

'I emphasized that the US would support a constitution for Zimbabwe that would contain guarantees of individual rights such as freedom of speech, religion, assemblage, due process of law, and an independent judiciary, and that we believe these are essential to a democratic system of government.

'On Namibia, I made clear that we supported the efforts of the so-called "Contact Group", which consists of the US, West Germany, Britain, France and Canada, in their efforts to implement Security Council resolution 385.

'In some respects, the position of the South African Government as reflected in the earlier talks was encouraging. In those talks they agreed to free elections to be held on a nation-wide basis for a constituent assembly which would develop a national constitution for an independent Namibia. They agreed that all Namibians inside and outside the country could participate, including Swapo. They agreed that the UN could be involved in the electoral process to assure that it was fair and internationally acceptable.

'However, potentially important differences over the structure and character of the interim administrative authority that would run Namibia while this process takes place became much clearer in the process of our talks. SA wants an administrative arrangement that draws upon the structure developed at the Turnhalle Conference.

'This structure [and] the Conference that proposed it is based on ethnic and tribal lines and as it stands it is unacceptable to us. We emphasize that any interim administrative arrangement must be impartial as to the ultimate structure of the Namibian government. Moreover, it must be broadly representative in order to be acceptable to all Namibians and to the international community.

'For his part, Mr Vorster felt quite strongly that any such structure would be based on the work of the Turnhalle Conference. We agreed to propose that the five-nation Contact Group meet with the South African Government before the end of the month in Cape Town at a time to be determined, if the other members of that Group agree, to hear South Africa's views and the details of the proposed interim administrative authority, to see if an impartial, broadly-based and internationally acceptable structure can be found. We hope that it can be.

'It is my view that the South African position in Namibia is involved in a positive direction in certain important respects. But unless this last issue can be satisfactorily resolved by the South African Government, fair free elections will be difficult, if not impossible. I hope that the most serious effort will be made to find a solution that provides an impartial, broadly representative and internationally acceptable interim authority in Namibia.

'I also raised [the] question of political prisoners with regard to Namibia. I said that the US believes that all political prisoners should be released. Mr Vorster said he believes that what he called political detainees, some of which are held in other African countries, should be released. He said he would favourably consider our suggestion that all Namibian political prisoners be turned over to Namibia and that in the event of a difference in view of whether a particular prisoner was political or criminal, a body of international jurors review the case and make a determination. This suggestion will be pursued as well when the Contact Group meets in Cape Town.

'South African prospects are much less bright for progress toward the change of course which we believe is essential to provide justice, stability and peace in that country. We hope that SA will carefully review the implications of our policy and the changed circumstances which it creates. We hope that South Africans will not rely on any illusions that the US will in the end intervene to save SA from the policies it is pursuing, for we will not do so.

'I think the message is now clear to the South African Government. They know that we believe that perpetuating an unjust system is the surest incentive to increase Soviet influence and even racial war, but quite apart from that, is unjustified on its own grounds. They know that we will not defend such a system; in all honesty, however, I do not know what conclusions the South African Government will draw. It is my hope that it will lead to a reassessment, to a change of course which enables us to be helpful and supportive in the difficult times that change inevitably entails.

'But I cannot rule out the possibility that the South African Government will not change, that our paths will diverge and our policies come into conflict should the South African Government so decide. In that event, we would take steps true to our beliefs and values.

'We hope to be able to see progress in Rhodesia, Namibia and SA. But the alternative is real, much as we dislike it. For a failure to make progress will lead to a tragedy of human history. Thank you.'

Question: Mr Vice-President, I wonder if you would tell us if these talks which appear indeed to have been extremely tough, what the atmosphere was, whether it was acrimonious or whether you could tell us that it really wasn't as tough as it seemed to be.

Answer: 'We were very anxious, as I indicated earlier, to conduct these talks in a constructive environment, in a non-confrontational environment. We were anxious at the same time that this meeting be one in which we could very clearly define American policy, and further make clear the depth and the permanence of our commitment to human rights as a central element in our relations with the Government of SA and as a policy guiding our affairs in southern Africa.

'The talks were candid and they were frank, and I think they were non-confrontational. We think there may be some progress in Rhodesia. We think the statement indicated today indicates hope. We are hopeful that the talks surrounding the details which I mentioned in Namibia will produce results that are effective and will permit the independence of Namibia within the outline and framework of UN resolution 385, and that the upcoming talks in Cape Town will bring that result about.

'On the issue of South African policies, it is our position that separateness and apartheid are inherently discriminatory, and that that policy of apartheid cannot be acceptable to us. We also are of the opinion, strongly held, that full political participation by all the citizens of SA—equal participation in the election of its national government and its political affairs—is essential to a healthy, stable and secure SA. South Africans take the view that their apartheid policies are not discriminatory. There is a basic and fundamental disagreement. They take the position that they have different nations within SA, and that the full participation that we discussed is irrelevant.

'There is a fundamental and a profound disagreement, and what we had hoped to do in these talks was to make it clear to the South African leadership the profound commitment that my nation has to human rights, to the elimination of discrimination and to full political participation; and to explain to them how our nation went through essentially the same dispute and how the elimination of discrimination and the achievement of full political participation has contributed enormously to the health, vitality, the stability, the economic growth, the social health and the spiritual health of our country. We are convinced that those same policies will have the same effect in other societies. That was the nature of the discussion; it was very frank. It was very candid.'

Question: What steps would you take in SA if it doesn't go along with our policy?
Answer: 'The purpose of this meeting was not to provide a list of remedies that this nation, that is the US, might take by itself or in co-operation with the others through the UN or in other ways, to pursue its values as I have described them, of human rights. We did, however, make it very clear. First of all, we hope that there would be progress in these areas that would permit an improved relationship. In other words, our basic objective is not to have a confrontation, but to have an understanding that will lead to progress and that we hope for improved relations.

'We also said that these values that we hold, and these objectives for an independent Rhodesia, with an independent constitution, with a freely-elected government, and a Namibian government established under the general outlines of UN resolution 385 with a freely-elected government, and the social transformation of the South African Government as we described it, were important objectives, crucial objectives, affecting the relationship of our two countries. Any progress will be helpful, but we need progress in all three categories, and the failure to achieve it will lead to several elements, we think: increasing instability, increasing violence and bitterness, increasing opportunity for international caprice, and a worsening of US relations with the Government of SA and of relations between that Government and the international communities.

'We did not go into what those steps would be because it is our hope that we can have progress and that that will not be necessary; there will be other occasions on which that policy in the case of deteriorating relations will be described.'

Question: In regard to the transformation or progress that you speak of with SA itself, how is that to be measured, and specifically, did you suggest or outline any possible things that you would like to see done there on a step-by-step basis, or are you leaving this to the South Africans to ponder? And the second part of the question is, did they give any sign during these talks that they would possibly modify such elements that would permit the joint participation and unify SA politically?
Answer: 'Let me answer the last part of your question first: the answer was that they did not intend to do so. What I said was that we see two fundamental principles as essential: the elimination of discrimination—and we think apartheid is discriminatory—and full political participation by all its citizens on an equal basis where essential to the transformation that would be the prerequisite to a stable SA and to the best possible relations with this country. We also talked about steps, but not in detail, because we did not want to get into the position of prescribing what particular steps they should be taking. We said any progress would be helpful. For example, I said if the Pass Laws were repealed so that the citizens of SA could travel in and around SA as they chose, that would be helpful. We mentioned the retaining of political dissidents, Mrs Mandela, and the intimidation of political dissidents as an example.

'I did not get into a specific list of particular laws and schools, the set-aside of certain jobs (I forget the exact name) that can only be held by certain people of certain race. There is a long list that we could get into, but I did not want to do that because I wanted to get the emphasis on the principles, the long-term objectives that we see crucial to fundamental reform in SA.'

Question: You pointed out that apartheid and full participation were two separate matters. Now you said that the Prime Minister offered you no hope on full participation politically. You said he did not want to get into detail on questions of apartheid. But did he tell you that he plans any progress at all on certain race discrimination?
Answer: 'Mr Vorster went into some detail about the number of black Africans within SA now going to school. The income of South African minorities compared to the income elsewhere in Africa, the meetings that they have had with certain black leaders. One of the proposals I made in response . . . was that they should meet early with a broad range of the legitimate non-white leaders of SA to hear

from them as to the process and the approach and the steps to be taken. His answer to that was that they had already had such meetings. But it is our opinion that many of the legitimate leaders of the non-white community have not engaged in such a conference, and that such a conference would be very helpful. That was the nature of this discussion, but I would have to be very candid, that on the issue of apartheid and on the issue of full political participation in the sense we are talking, namely, voting for the National Government, they were very direct in its rejection.'

Question: If there is no progress on full participation, would that produce the deterioration in our relations that you had spoken of? Even if there had been some progress on apartheid or on Namibia and Rhodesia?

Answer: 'We see all three issues of basic importance. We don't think progress on one issue excuses no progress on another. But any progress of significance will be appreciated, will be able to create a healthy, independent Rhodesia based on majority rule. That's something that is very important. If we are able to achieve the objectives of an independent Namibia based on the principles of UN resolution 385, that's a very important objective. If the South African Government helps achieve those objectives, they should be commended for it. If there is progress within SA to remove laws such as the Pass Laws, discrimination laws, these job set-aside laws, laws to permit active political expression without intimidation, those things should be encouraged and appreciated. But I thought it was important, and I believe it to be fundamental, that the basis of the problems in SA stem from two fundamental principles: discrimination, and the absence of full political participation, rights available to all their citizens.'

Question: **Mr Vice-President, could you possibly go into slightly more detail on your concept of full participation as opposed to one man one vote? Do you see some kind of compromise?**

Answer: **'No, no. It's the same thing. Every citizen should have the right to vote and every vote should be equally weighted.'**

Namibia

Report of a Meeting between the Five Powers' Contact Group and the South West Africa People's Organization (Swapo)

Held in Lusaka (Zambia), April 1977

This document is a confidential aide memoire of a meeting between Swapo and the UK Ambassador, James Murray, member of the Contact Group of five Western nations (UK, US, West Germany, France and Canada) who conducted negotiations between SA and Swapo over a settlement in Namibia.

The representatives of the five powers had six meetings with the South African Government. During their discussions, they reiterated Security Council Resolution 385 and stressed the necessity for the Namibian people to decide their own future. In the second meeting, they felt that they covered new ground which could form the basis of international acceptance of the proposals put forward by them. Earlier, the SA Government had proposed to create a central administrative authority for Namibia, consisting of 17 members, 11 to be drawn from the ethnic groups represented in the Turnhalle; the remaining ones to be chosen from unspecified groups.

The five powers emphasized that these proposals were not acceptable to them, and that they were incompatible with UN principles. The SA Government then decided to abandon the idea, and finally agreed to the idea of the five powers of an Administrator-General for the territory. It was made quite clear that the idea of the Turnhalle has been abandoned by the SA Government, and that the idea of an Administrator-General was not suggested by the Turnhalle.

The SA Government has already tabled legislation in Parliament for the establishment of the new system. The SA State President is to be asked to invoke the proclamation which will create the new administrative system.

The new Administrator-General is expected to be appointed in August this year. It has been indicated to the five powers that the person chosen will be impartial, most likely a judge, and definitely a South African.

The SA Government has agreed to the presence of the UN in the form of a UN Special Representative. He may proceed to Namibia as soon as the Administrator-General has taken up his appointment. The UN Special Representative may be accompanied by an unspecified number of UN officials. The details of UN involvement will have to be worked out with the UN Secretary-General.

The five powers emphasized the necessity of the UN presence being established at an early stage, and involving a greater number of people than the South Africans originally suggested.

Suggestions for UN Administrative Presence

The tasks of the special Representative would be as follows:

1. The UN Special Representative will have to satisfy himself that the discriminatory laws and all undesirable regulations be abolished.

Moreover, the process of arriving at general elections must not be [impeded].

2. Political campaigns must be free and conducted peacefully, with strict observation of electoral rules and procedures established by the UN.

3. News media to be used in an impartial way to secure that a proper balance of views is maintained.

4. Voting ballot must be secret and free from intimidation.

The SA Government has not raised any objections to these suggestions. On the contrary, they are welcoming the suggestions.

The Contact Group feels that it has achieved a noteworthy result.

Detainees

The Namibian political detainees must be released; the SA Government agreed, provided that Swapo agreed to release its own detainees. The SA Government also indicated that it would be prepared to release the Namibian political detainees under the following procedure:

An international commission of jurists would have to be established. This would have to include two South African jurists. The Commission will have to look into cases of individual prisoners, to determine whether their offences were of a political or criminal nature.

Transference of Power

The transference of power to the people of Namibia will have to be done through the process of free elections. The UN Special Representative will have to keep in close touch with the UN Secretary-General, and to liaise with the SA-appointed Administrator-General.

A deadline for Namibia's independence must be determined by the progress of the administrative machinery. Elections must take place six months after the appointment of the Administrator-General. The five powers expressed their doubts as to the feasibility of having elections in 1977, as time is too short.

Points Agreed during Earlier Meetings

Previous agreements between the SA Government and the five powers were:
1. Elections under UN presence.
2. Establishment of a Constituent Assembly.
3. Voting by secret ballot.
4. All Namibians regardless of political affiliation are free to participate in the elections.

Returnees

All persons born in Namibia and those who have established *bona fide* status are free to return to Namibia.

(For the Declaration of the Maputo Conference on the Liberation of Namibia, see above, subsection on the *UN and Southern Africa*.)

For the **Proposal for the Settlement of the Namibian Situation** presented to the President of the Security Council on 10 April 1978 by Canada, France, the United Kingdom, the United States and West Germany, see pp. C211–15.

Proposal for a Settlement of the Namibian Situation

Letter dated 10 April 1978 from the Representatives of Canada, France, Federal Republic of Germany, the United Kingdom of Great Britain and Northern Ireland and United States of America addressed to the President of the Security Council

On instructions from our Governments, we have the honour to transmit to you a proposal for the settlement of the Namibian situation and to request that it be circulated as a document of the Security Council. The objective of our proposal is the independence of Namibia in accordance with resolution 385 (1976), adopted unanimously by the Security Council on 30 January 1976. We are continuing to work towards the implementation of the proposal. (*Signed*) William H. Barton, Permanent Representative of Canada to the UN; M. Jacques Leprette, Permanent Representative of France to the UN; Rüdiger von Wechmar, Permanent Representative of the Federal Republic of Germany to the UN; James Murray, Deputy Permanent Representative of the UK to the UN, Chargé d'Affaires, a.i.; Andrew Young, Permanent Representative of the US to the UN.

I. Introduction

1. Bearing in mind their responsibilities as members of the Security Council of the United Nations, the Governments of Canada, France, the Federal Republic of Germany, the United Kingdom and the United States have consulted with the various parties involved with the Namibian situation with a view to encouraging agreement on the transfer of authority in Namibia to an independent government in accordance with resolution 385 (1976), adopted unanimously by the Security Council on 30 January 1976.

2. To this end, our Governments have drawn up a proposal for the settlement of the Namibian question designed to bring about a transition to independence during 1978 within a framework acceptable to the people of Namibia and thus to the international community. While the proposal addresses itself to all elements of resolution 385 (1976), the key to an internationally acceptable transition to independence is free elections for the whole of Namibia as one political entity with an appropriate UN role in accordance with resolution 385 (1976). A resolution will be required in the Security Council requesting the Secretary-General to appoint a UN Special Representative whose central task will be to make sure that conditions are established which will allow free and fair elections and an impartial electoral process. The Special Representative will be assisted by a UN Transition Assistance Group.

3. The purpose of the electoral process is to elect representatives to a Namibian Constituent Assembly which will draw up and adopt the Constitution for an independent and sovereign Namibia. Authority would then be assumed during 1978 by the Government of Namibia.

4. A more detailed description of the proposal is contained below. Our Governments believe that this proposal provides an effective basis for implementing resolution 385 (1976) while taking adequate account of the interests of all parties involved. In carrying out his responsibilities, the Special Representative will work together with the official appointed by SA (the Administrator-General) to ensure the orderly transition to independence. This working arrangement shall in no way constitute recognition of the legality of the South African presence in and administration of Namibia.

II. The electoral process

5. In accordance with Security Council resolution 385 (1976), free elections will be held for the whole of Namibia as one political entity, to enable the people of Namibia to freely and fairly determine their own future. The elections will be under the supervision and control of the UN in that, as a condition to the conduct of the electoral process, the elections themselves, and the certification of their results, the UN Special Representative will have to satisfy himself at each stage as to the fairness and appropriateness of all measures affecting the political process at all levels of administration before such measures take effect. Moreover, the Special Representative may himself make proposals in regard to any aspect of the political process. He will have at his disposal a substantial civilian section of the UN Transition Assistance Group, sufficient to carry out his duties satisfactorily. He will report to the Secretary-General of the UN, keeping him informed and making such recommendations as he considers necessary with respect to the discharge of his responsibilities. The Secretary-General, in accordance with the mandate entrusted to him by the Security Council, will keep the Council informed.

6. Elections will be held to select a Constituent Assembly which will adopt a Constitution for an independent Namibia. The Constitution will determine the organization and powers of all levels of government. Every adult Namibian will be eligible, without discrimination or fear of intimidation from any source, to vote, campaign and stand for election to the Constituent Assembly. Voting will be by secret ballot, with provisions made for those who cannot read or write. The date for the beginning of the electoral campaign, the date of elections, the electoral system, the preparation of voters rolls and other aspects of electoral procedures will be promptly decided upon so as to give all political parties and interested persons, without regard to their political views, a full and fair opportunity to organize and participate in the electoral process. Full freedom of speech, assembly, movement and press shall be guaranteed. The official electoral campaign shall commence only after the UN Special Representative has satisfied himself as to the fairness and appropriateness of the electoral procedures. The implementation of the electoral process, including the proper registration of voters and the proper and timely tabulation and publication of voting results, will also have to be conducted to the satisfaction of the Special Representative.

7. The following requirements will be fulfilled to the satisfaction of the UN Special Representative in order to meet the objective of free and fair elections:

    a. Prior to the beginning of the electoral campaign, the Administrator-General will repeal all remaining discriminatory or restrictive laws, regulations or administrative measures which might abridge or inhibit that objective.

    b. The Administrator-General shall make arrangements for the release, prior to the beginning of the electoral campaign, of all Namibian political prisoners or political detainees held by the South African authorities so that they can participate fully and freely in that process, without risk of arrest, detention, intimidation or imprisonment. Any disputes concerning the release of political prisoners or political detainees shall be resolved to the satisfaction of the Special Representative acting on the independent advice of a jurist of international standing who shall be designated by the Secretary-General to be legal adviser to the Special Representative.

    c. All Namibian refugees or Namibians detained or otherwise outside the territory of Namibia will be permitted to return peacefully and participate fully and freely in the electoral process without risk of arrest, detention, intimidation or imprisonment. Suitable entry points will be designated for these purposes.

    d. The Special Representative with the assistance of the UN High Commissioner for Refugees and other appropriate international bodies will ensure that Namibians remaining outside of Namibia are given a free and voluntary choice whether to return. Provision will be made to attest to the voluntary nature of decisions made by Namibians who elect not to return to Namibia.

8. A comprehensive cessation of all hostile acts shall be observed by all parties in

order to ensure that the electoral process will be free from interference and intimidation. The annex describes provisions for the implementation of the cessation of all hostile acts, military arrangements concerning the UN Transition Assistance Group, the withdrawal of South African forces, and arrangements with respect to other organized forces in Namibia, and with respect to the forces of Swapo. These provisions call for:

a. A cessation of all hostile acts by all parties and the restriction of South African and Swapo armed forces to base.

b. Thereafter a phased withdrawal from Namibia of all but 1,500 South African troops within 12 weeks and prior to the official start of the political campaign. The remaining South African force would be restricted to Grootfontein or Oshivello or both and would be withdrawn after the certification of the election.

c. The demobilization of the citizen forces, commandos and ethnic forces, and the dismantling of their command structures.

d. Provision will be made for Swapo personnel outside of the territory to return peacefully to Namibia through designated entry points to participate freely in the political process.

e. A military section of the UN Transition Assistance Group to make sure that the provisions of the agreed solution will be observed by all parties. In establishing the military section of UNTAG, the Secretary-General will keep in mind functional and logistical requirements. The Five Governments, as members of the Security Council, will support the Secretary-General's judgement in his discharge of this responsibility. The Secretary-General will, in the normal manner, include in his consultations all those concerned with the implementation of the agreement. The Special Representative will be required to satisfy himself as to the implementation of all these arrangements and will keep the Secretary-General informed of developments in this regard.

9. Primary responsibility for maintaining law and order in Namibia during the transition period shall rest with the existing police forces. The Administrator-General, to the satisfaction of the UN Special Representative, shall ensure the good conduct of the police forces and shall take the necessary action to ensure their suitability for continued employment during the transition period. The Special Representative shall make arrangements when appropriate for UN personnel to accompany the police forces in the discharge of their duties. The police forces would be limited to the carrying of small arms in the normal performance of their duties.

10. The UN Special Representative will take steps to guarantee against the possibility of intimidation or interference with the electoral process from whatever quarter.

11. Immediately after the certification of election results, the Constituent Assembly will meet to draw up and adopt a Constitution for an independent Namibia. It will conclude its work as soon as possible so as to permit whatever additional steps may be necessary prior to the installation of an independent Government of Namibia during 1978.

12. Neighbouring countries shall be requested to ensure to the best of their abilities that the provisions of the transitional arrangements, and the outcome of the election, are respected. They shall also be requested to afford the necessary facilities to the UN Special Representative and all UN personnel to carry out their assigned functions and to facilitate such measures as may be desirable for ensuring tranquillity in the border areas.

(See also above, pp. C78–79)

ANNEX

Timing	SAG	SWAPO	UN	Other action
(1) At date unspecified:			UNSC passes resolution authorizing SYG to appoint UNSR and requesting him to submit plan for UN involvement. SYG appoints UNSR and dispatches UN contingency planning group to Namibia. SYG begins consultations with potential participants in UNTAG.	
(2) As soon as possible, preferably within one week of Security Council action:			SYG reports back to UNSC. UNSC passes further resolution adopting plan for UN involvement. Provision is made for financing.	
(3) Transitional period formally begins on date of UNSC passage of resolution adopting SYG's plan:	General cessation of hostile acts comes under UN supervision. Restriction to base of all South African forces including ethnic forces.	General cessation of hostile acts comes under UN supervision. Restriction to base.	As soon as possible: UNSR and staff (UNTAG) arrive in Namibia to assume duties. UN military personnel commence monitoring of cessation of hostile acts and commence monitoring of both South African and SWAPO troop restrictions. Begin infiltration prevention and border surveillance. Begin monitoring of police forces. Begin monitoring of citizen forces, ethnic forces and military personnel performing civilian functions. UNSR makes necessary arrangements for co-ordination with neighbouring countries concerning the provisions of the transitional arrangements.	Release of political prisoners/detainees wherever held begins and is to be completed as soon as possible.
(4) Within six weeks:	Restriction to base continues. Force levels reduced to 12,000 men.	Restriction to base continues.	Appropriate action by UN High Commissioner for Refugees outside Namibia to assist in return of exiles. All UN activity continues.	Establishment in Namibia of provisions to facilitate return of exiles. Establishment and publication of general rules for elections. Completion of repeal of discriminatory laws and restrictive legislation. Dismantlement of command structures of citizen forces, commandos and ethnic forces, including the withdrawal of all South African soldiers attached to these units. All arms, military

equipment and ammunition of citizen forces and commandos confined to drill halls under UN supervision. AG to ensure that none of these forces will drill or constitute an organized force during the transitional period except under order of the AG with the concurrence of UNSR. AG with concurrence of UNSR determines whether and under what circumstances those military personnel performing civilian functions will continue those functions.

(5) Within nine weeks:	Restriction to base continues. Force levels reduced to 8,000 men.	Restriction to base continues. Peaceful repatriation under UN supervision starts for return through designed entry points.	All UN activity continues.	Completion of release of political prisoners/detainees wherever held.
(6) Within twelve weeks	Force levels reduced to 1,500 men, restricted to Grootfontein or Oshivello or both. All military installations along northern border would by now either be deactivated or put under civilian control under UN supervision. Facilities which depend on them (e.g. hospitals, power stations) would be protected where necessary by the UN.	Restriction to base continues.	All UN activity continues. Military Section of UNTAG at maximum deployment.	
(7) Start of thirteenth week:				Official start of election campaign of about four months' duration.
(8) On date established by AG to satisfaction of UNSR:				Election to Constituent Assembly.
(9) One week after date of certification of election:	Completion of withdrawal.	Closure of all bases.		Convening of Constituent Assembly.
(10) At date unspecified:				Conclusion of Constituent Assembly and whatever additional steps may be necessary prior to installation of new government.
(11) By 31 December 1978 at latest:				Independence.

AG = Administrator General; *SAG* = South African Government; *SWAPO* = South West Africa People's Organization; *SYG* = Secretary-General of the United Nations; *UN* = United Nations; *UNSR* = United Nations Special Representative; *UNSC* = United Nations Security Council; *UNTAG* = UN Transition Assistance Group.